Crimes against Children

Studies in
Legal History

Published by the
University of North
Carolina Press in
association with the
American Society
for Legal History

Thomas A. Green,
Hendrik Hartog,
and Daniel Ernst,
editors

Crimes against Children

Sexual Violence
and Legal Culture
in New York City,
1880 – 1960

Stephen Robertson

The University of
North Carolina Press

Chapel Hill and London

Designed by April Leidig-Higgins
Set in Monotype Garamond by Copperline Book Services
Manufactured in the United States of America

The paper in this book meets the guidelines for permanence
and durability of the Committee on Production Guidelines
for Book Longevity of the Council on Library Resources.

Portions of this book previously appeared in somewhat
different form:
  "Making Right a Girl's Ruin: Working-Class Legal
Culture and Forced Marriage in New York City, 1890–1950,"
Journal of American Studies 36, 2 (2002): 199–230. Reprinted
with permission of Cambridge University Press.
  "Age of Consent Law and the Making of Modern Child-
hood in New York City, 1886–1921," *Journal of Social History*
35, 4 (Summer 2002): 781–98. Published at George Mason
University. Reprinted by permission.
  "Separating the Men from the Boys: Masculinity, Psycho-
Sexual Development, and Sex Crime in the United States,
1930s–1960s," *Journal of the History of Medicine and Allied
Sciences* 56, 1 (January 2001): 3–35. Reprinted by permission
of Oxford University Press.

Library of Congress Cataloging-in-Publication Data
Robertson, Stephen (Stephen Murray)
Crimes against children: sexual violence and legal culture
in New York City, 1880–1960 / Stephen Robertson.
p. cm.— (Studies in legal history)
Includes bibliographical references and index.
ISBN 0-8078-2932-3 (cloth: alk. paper)
ISBN 0-8078-5596-0 (pbk: alk. paper)
  1. Child sexual abuse—New York (State)—New York
—History—19th century.   2. Child sexual abuse—
New York (State)—New York—History—20th cen-
tury.   3. Children—Legal status, laws, etc.—New
York (State)—New York—History—19th century.
4. Children—Legal status, laws, etc.—New York
(State)—New York—History—20th century.
5. Prosecution—New York (State)—New York—
History—19th century.   6. Prosecution—New
York (State)—New York—History—20th century.
I. Title.   II. Series.
HV6570.3.N7R63 2005
345.747'0253—dc22   2004019073

cloth 09 08 07 06 05   5 4 3 2 1

paper 09 08 07 06 05   5 4 3 2 1

For my Muses, Delwyn and Cleo

contents

acknowledgments

In 1992 I began work on the seminar paper that begat the dissertation that became this book. That process is common to most first-time academic authors; the same cannot be said of its setting. This project was conceived in Dunedin, New Zealand, begun in New Jersey, written in Chicago, reconceived in Fairfax, Virginia, and rewritten in Sydney, Australia. Moving repeatedly, and internationally, during the time I worked on this project, shaped my perspective on American history. As I tell the American study-abroad students who enroll in my classes, mine is not simply an outsider's view of the history of the United States. Each of those moves also added to the list of teachers, colleagues, and friends whose support, advice, and inspiration made it possible for this book to be written.

According to the conventions that govern acknowledgments, my wife should be the last to receive thanks, but in my case that would be illogical. Delwyn's experiences of sexual abuse as a child helped inspire my interest in this topic; debates with her shaped the central ideas underlying this project; her generous support and the sacrifices that she made without complaint in becoming a "student spouse" allowed me to successfully turn those ideas into a Ph.D. thesis, and to adjust to life in the United States; her courage in taking our six-month-old daughter Cleo on a trans-Pacific plane flight enabled me to finish the thesis; and her impatience and lack of interest in reading any more of the same old stuff ensured that the thesis became a book. Delwyn is not responsible for any of this book — it is certainly not the book that she would have written — but it is her book as much as mine. It has shaped her life as well as mine. I thank her with all my heart for our book and for our life together.

In a different way, our daughter Cleo has a share in this book. She appeared just at the moment that I began to grapple with how ideas of childhood shaped the sex crime prosecutions I was studying, and made me vividly aware of why child victims had such a powerful effect on modern Americans. It is to Cleo's timing that I also owe the insights I gained from moving between critically analyzing the creation of norms of child development in my office and devouring child-rearing advice that relied on those same norms at home. More recently, Cleo's excitement about her father's writing a book has ensured that I enjoyed the end of a very long process.

I have been incredibly fortunate in having a series of inspirational, caring teachers. At the University of Otago, Barbara Brookes and Dorothy Page opened my eyes to women's history; Roberto Rabel introduced me to American history and constantly challenged me to justify my assumptions; and Erik Olssen inspired and guided my first attempts at original research, and provided me with an enduring model of what a scholar and a teacher should be.

Barbara, Rob, and Erik also guided my applications to American graduate schools. However, without access to the wealth of information now available on the Web, my decision to go to Rutgers University was largely a stab in the dark. I still cannot believe how lucky I was; the History Department, and the Women's History program in particular, proved to be the ideal environment for me. As if that weren't enough, I also had the good fortune to arrive soon after Alice Kessler-Harris did, and to convince her to take me on as a student. Alice was quite simply the model adviser. I have a vivid memory of our first meeting. I was in my second semester of graduate school, struggling to adjust to an unfamiliar academic environment, and still coming to terms with the experience of encountering historians whose work I had read. Alice was co-teaching a course in women's labor history. In the first class, when I forced myself to venture a comment, and her colleague quickly dismissed it, Alice gently intervened to offer a more positive reading of what I'd said. As brief as that exchange was, it was crucial in helping me find my feet as a graduate student. It was also emblematic of how Alice advised me, giving me confidence in my ability as a historian, finding the strengths of my early efforts, and, as my research and writing developed, pushing me to ask more probing questions, and enthusiastically promoting the merits of the work that I produced. Alice's guidance also helped me manage my enthusiasm for history, so that it became, rather than a weakness, one of my qualities as a scholar. Alice has continued to be a mentor, an inspiration, and a touchstone for me in the years since I completed my degree. I still proudly introduce myself as her student.

My ability to write a thesis that crossed fields I owe to the patience and generosity of the diverse group of scholars who served on my dissertation committee: from Norma Basch I learned about the law; from John Gillis, about childhood; from James Reed, about medicine; and from Christine Stansell, about sexuality. Paul Clemens, Suzanne Lebsock, Jim Livingston, and Tom Slaughter, along with Cora Kaplan in the English Department, also shaped how I thought about history.

I am also grateful for the remarkable colleagues with whom I have worked: at Otago, Rebecca McLennan and Claudia Gieringer; at Rutgers, Karen Balcolm, Michelle Brattain, Jenny Brier, Kim Brodkin, Robert Churchill, Barbara Cutter, Joy Dixon, Allen Douglas, Kim Gunning, Beatrix Hoffman, Jan Lambertz, Tamara Matheson, and Martin Summers; at the American Bar Foundation (where I learned most of what I know about the law), Ben Forest, Jennifer Mnookin, Susan Shapiro, Chris Tomlins, and Vicki Woeste; at George Mason, Roy Rosenzweig, Larry Levine, and Mike O'Malley; and at Sydney, the other Americanists — Frances Clarke, Clare Corbould, and Michael McDonnell — plus Alison Bashford, Nick Eckstein, Andrew Fitzmaurice, Stephen Garton, Dirk Moses, Maggie Mackellar, Penny Russell, and Richard Waterhouse. Shane White is missing from that final group because I owe him so much. Since the moment I arrived at Sydney he has been my mentor and guide; a source of American gossip and regular doses of caffeine; a research collaborator; and, above all, a friend. I hope this book provides some return on his investment in me. I also owe a debt of gratitude to colleagues outside my institutional homes who provided crucial advice and support: Michael Grossberg; Mary Odem; Carolyn Strange; the fellows of the first ASLH Legal History Summer Institute; and my brother Craig.

Outside the academy, numerous friends and family enriched my life and work during the years I worked on this book: the Maxwell family, and extended family; Belinda Davis, Peter, Noah, and Sophia; the International Women's Group at Rutgers University, and the "affiliated" "Boy's Club"; the Wilders; my brother Craig, a colleague, but also a fellow traveler in the United States; my brother Grant and his partner Alf, who hosted us in New York City, and cared for me when pneumonia prolonged my stay; my parents, Doug and Yvonne; my in-laws, Selma, Brian, Michelle, Roseanna, and Patricia; Libby, Dave, Mitchell, and Caitlin Moussa; and Frances Clarke and Charles Fairchild, who brought an American sensibility to my life in Sydney just when I desperately needed it.

Grants from several institutions made it possible to research and write this book: an Excellence Fellowship from Rutgers University; a Littleton-Griswold Research Grant from the American Historical Association; a research fellowship from the F. C. Wood Institute for the History of Medicine,

College of Physicians of Philadelphia; a doctoral dissertation fellowship and a postdoctoral fellowship from the American Bar Foundation; a J. N. G. Finley Postdoctoral Fellowship from George Mason University; and a Faculty of Arts Research Seed Grant and a Sesqui New Staff Grant from the University of Sydney. I gratefully acknowledge the support of those organizations.

Most of the research for this project was done at the Municipal Archives in New York City. It would not have been possible, or as pleasant, without the patience and good humor of Ken Cobb and his staff over several years of requests and visits. I also received valuable help from staff at the New York Public Library, the New York State Archives, and the interlibrary loan departments of Rutgers University, George Mason University, and the University of Sydney. Although the New York Society for the Prevention of Cruelty to Children ultimately denied me access to their case files, the Society's archivist, Joseph Gleeson, generously provided his insights.

That I succeeded in transforming the dissertation into a book owes much to Lewis Bateman, who solicited the manuscript for the University of North Carolina Press, and to Chuck Grench, who succeeded Lew and saw the project through to its completion. I was extremely fortunate to publish in a series edited by Dirk Hartog and Tom Green. Their suggestions were unfailingly insightful, positive, and productive, and the book has been vastly improved by their input. I am also grateful to Kathy Peiss, who read much of the manuscript during her time in Sydney as a Fulbright scholar, and provided suggestions that significantly improved the first chapter; and to Stephen Garton, who, at very short notice, found a day in his life as dean of the Faculty of Arts at the University of Sydney to spend reading the complete manuscript and finding places where it could be cut. Graham White had the greatest impact on the final style of this book. Since I have been at Sydney, he has generously and patiently wielded his editor's pencil in an effort to make my writing more dramatic and engaging. In 2003, as I wrote the final draft of the book manuscript, his labors finally paid off. I discovered a voice in which to write. For that, I will be forever grateful to Graham.

All those I have thanked have given me even more than the help, advice, support, and inspiration I have described. History is one of the great passions of my life. I have wanted to be a historian for as long as I can remember. With the publication of this book, I feel I have attained that goal. The book is dedicated to my other great passion, Delwyn and Cleo, the "gorgeous girls" who have made my life so extraordinary. As much as I love being a historian, I love them even more.

Crimes against Children

In 1905, shortly after retiring from his position as professor of legal medicine at Harvard University, Frank Winthrop Draper published *A Textbook of Legal Medicine*. For almost a century, American physicians had been seeking a more prominent role in the legal system, and during that time they had learned much about the realities of what went on in the courts. In part, Draper wrote his textbook to pass on that knowledge, to ensure that future medical students would be better prepared for what they would encounter in the legal system than their predecessors had been. To that end, he included in his book a passage from the work of the eminent French medical jurist Paul Brouardel, which he clearly felt captured the thinking of Americans just as it did that of Europeans. "People unfamiliar with medico-legal practice," declared Brouardel, "have an idea that a rape or an attempt at rape is a struggle in which a young man, in full vigor, amorous, excited, brutal, endeavors by violence to obtain the favors of an attractive young woman, who succumbs to him only after energetic resistance. All the details of this picture," Brouardel wrote, "are false or only exceptionally true." The "reality" was "much sadder." The typical victim of rape was in fact "a little girl, defenceless, generally a mere child with stunted intellect, bred in poverty; one upon whom it is easier to distinguish the disorders and effects resulting from repeated acts to which she has habitually consented, rather than the traces of a single brutal assault leaving evidence of the violence used."[1]

Draper likely felt the need to include Brouardel's statement because in the United States the predominance of children among the victims of rape was a recent phenomenon. Child victims had always featured in American courts; in New York City in the years 1790 to 1876, with the exception of a spike in the 1820s, between one-third and one-half of the females in rape cases were younger than nineteen years of age, proportions typical of those elsewhere in the nation.[2] In the 1880s, however, the proportion of child complainants in rape cases jumped dramatically.[3] The examination of a large sample of the New York County district attorney's files from 1886 to 1955 undertaken for this book found that more than eight in every ten cases involved a victim less than eighteen years of age.[4] The same predominance of child victims marked prosecutions for the other felonies with which men who committed sexual violence were charged: namely, sodomy, abduction, seduction, incest, and carnal abuse. Combining those offenses with rape reveals that 85 percent of cases of sexual violence prosecuted by the New York County DA involved a complainant who was younger than eighteen years of age.[5]

This book explores sex crimes against children from their rise to prominence in the 1880s until 1960, by which time legal officials, jurors, and witnesses no longer showed a particular concern with child victims. It is first and foremost a book about the prosecution of sex crime in New York City, providing the first large-scale longitudinal study of how a twentieth-century American criminal court, and American society in general, dealt with and understood cases of sexual violence. As many, if not more, sexual assaults than the ones I have researched were never reported, let alone prosecuted in the courts. This book, however, focuses on the reported cases around which American attitudes toward sexual violence took shape.

In explaining why children came to dominate American understandings of sexual violence, this book also tells the story of how the concept of psychosexual development led to an extended debate about who was a child, and ultimately transformed understandings of childhood and sexuality. According to conventional wisdom, I should not have found that story in criminal prosecutions; in the modern era, science is generally seen as having taken law's central role in shaping meanings of childhood and sexuality. This book shows that, to the contrary, the criminal courts were crucial sites for the production of social meaning. That role is obscured when the law is seen narrowly as a singular, closed system of formal rules and statutes. The significance of the legal system as a context becomes clear only if we recognize that the boundaries of formal law can be permeable, if we step back from formal law and allow our perspective to become "wide enough to glimpse the tugs and pulls between those who contributed to law's formal statements, those subjected to its enforcement and yet able at times to resist and/or reinterpret, and those who consciously reconstructed the law for their own purposes." What we then see is a legal culture made up of a "plurality of authorized behaviours and authorizing discourses," "a multitude of possibilities, arguments, strategies, positions, located in various institutions and in the imaginations of a complex and diverse citizenry," and the relationships between all these elements.[6] By focusing on legal culture, this book highlights the attitudes and actions of working-class Americans, but I do not write out of the story the middle-class reformers, medical experts, and legislators who dominate most histories of childhood and sexuality. Rather, I relocate them in the history of the diverse efforts of working-class New Yorkers of different races and ethnicities to shape the law and understandings of childhood and sexuality.

The multitude of voices and actions evident in criminal prosecutions enriches our understanding of how twentieth-century Americans responded to modern ideas and shaped a modern culture. Most accounts of that process have concentrated on tracing the emergence of new ideas and on the role that middle-class Americans played in shaping the nation's culture. Historian Philip Jenkins's recent characterization of twentieth-century reactions to sex crime as a moral panic falls into this category, describing a uniform response that neglects both the persistence of older ideas and the cultural assumptions of groups outside the middle class.[7] Since the late 1980s, cultural historians have shown an increasing interest in working-class Americans and in their place in the formation of modernity. However, evidence of workers' reactions to modern culture has proved elusive and fragmentary. As a result, working-class Americans have generally been presented as being outside the main currents of modern American culture, or cast as opponents of new ideas. Those conceptions capture part of what occurred in the twentieth century, but they ultimately fail to grapple with the confluence and continuing tensions evident in the press and the courts.

This book argues that modern ideas did not simply supersede older notions, pushing them from the minds of Americans; nor did they simply fall victim to existing beliefs, ignored once they were judged unpersuasive. Rather, in "a cumulative process of historical overlay and accretion," new ideas emerged alongside older understandings of sexual violence and childhood, resulting in "the unrationalized coexistence of different models."[8] Physicians, psychologists, and psychiatrists argued that children passed through several stages of physical and psychological development, including a series of sexualities, before reaching maturity. From that framework they derived an understanding of sexual violence as particularly harmful to children, in that it not only caused a child physical injury, but also disrupted his or her psychological growth toward normal heterosexuality. Social reformers, politicians, and commentators influenced by those concepts prompted a wave of public discussion and legislative action.

At the same time, particularly in working-class communities, a strong current of older beliefs existed beneath that upsurge of new ideas. Concepts of childhood innocence, the idea that puberty marked the end of childhood, and a view of sexuality as centered on vaginal intercourse, and as primarily physical, rather than psychological, in nature, continued to flow through American society. So too did the related notion of sexual assault as an act that caused physical injury. More expansive notions of sexuality, and the concept of development, were overlaid on those older ideas and did not displace them. As a result, by the end of the 1950s, the idea that an individual's age determined how sexual violence harmed him or her had become diluted and diffused, taking the form of a general understanding that the experiences of childhood carried forward into adulthood.

At the heart of this book, then, is a reconstruction of the cases of sexual violence described in New York City's courtrooms, and of the responses those stories elicited from the people involved in the legal system. The New Yorkers who appeared in the city's criminal courts were almost without exception of the working class.[9] They came from diverse backgrounds, encompassing all the major groups in the American population: southern and eastern European immigrants, particularly Italians and Russian Jews, Germans, Irish, African Americans, and Puerto Ricans.[10] Despite their diverse ethnicities and races, New York City's workers shared the same broad legal culture.[11] Criminal prosecutions reveal that, for working-class New Yorkers, charging someone with a crime was often the final stage in a process that began outside the courts, and the legal system could be a means to an end other than the punishment laid down in the law.

By the end of the nineteenth century, middle-class culture promoted a very different understanding of the criminal law. Middle-class Americans had sought to avoid the courts since the eighteenth century, concerned to protect their privacy and reputation. They had also attempted to make the law an effective means of controlling working-class populations. Beginning in the second half of the nineteenth century, a shift took place from particularistic and decentralized institutions toward the more centralized bureaucratic institutions that characterized the administrative state. In New York City, elected legal officials, along with the party loyalists who received their patronage, were replaced by salaried professionals. The city's police force was also subject to repeated efforts to make it more professional and was brought under the jurisdiction of civil service regulations, although neither approach did much to stem corruption and brutality within the force. Partly in response to the limited success of those reforms, middle-class Americans set up private organizations that cooperated with legal officials and even helped run the legal system. In New York City, the most powerful such organization was the New York Society for the Prevention of Cruelty to Children (NYSPCC), which employed agents who made arrests, took custody of complainants, filed complaints, investigated cases for the courts, and assisted DAs with prosecutions.[12]

In conjunction with their efforts to employ the law to control working people, middle-class Americans shaped criminal law to promote modern concepts of sexuality and childhood. In New York, social reformers and legislators cooperated to progressively import the notion of development into the state's statute book, creating new legal categories: statutory rape, which encompassed any act of sexual intercourse with a female younger than eighteen years, the new age of consent; sodomy, which covered both anal and oral acts; and carnal abuse, which treated handling a child's genitals as a sexual act.

Neither middle-class attitudes nor the actions of reformers and legislators succeeded in preventing working-class New Yorkers from using the law on their own terms. The NYSPCC's reputation for interfering in working-class families notwithstanding, the Society did not instigate most prosecutions for sex crimes against children; working-class New Yorkers did. The law was thus not simply a mechanism of social control. At the same time, working-class New Yorkers entering the legal system did encounter emerging modern notions of childhood and sexuality. In the person of NYSPCC agents, and in the legal definitions of the offenses of which men were accused, New Yorkers involved in prosecutions, and their friends and neighbors, confronted ideas that were at odds with their own relating to the sexual character of children, the difference between male and female sexuality, and the nature of a sexual act. The nature of the law, the need for a verifiable, nonsubjective definition of childhood, also brought working-class Americans face to face with an unfamiliar way of designating who was a child, one based solely on age.

These encounters reveal that legal categories and practices influenced understandings of childhood and sexuality, and altered the social relations of New Yorkers. At the same time, we will see that the law did not simply determine social meaning. Throughout the period of this study, jurors showed themselves willing to nullify laws, to make decisions based on their own sense of what constituted a crime or an appropriate punishment, rather than on an assessment of how far the evidence satisfied the legal requirements. Working-class New Yorkers—generally with the collusion of jurors, prosecutors, and judges—also used the law for purposes other than those intended by legislators or authorized by appellate courts. Moreover, those rejections and misuses did not leave the law unaffected. In response to jurors' unwillingness to enforce laws, assistant district attorneys (ADAS) adjusted the ways in which they prosecuted cases, and legislators amended statutes so that they better conformed to how jurors saw an offense and how prosecutors were applying the law in practice. At the same time, the state legislature responded to social reformers' call to change the law in order to limit the ability of working-class New Yorkers to use charges of sexual assault for their own ends.

It is these shifting relationships that the DA's records capture in rich detail, making possible an examination of the legal process. The DA's office created a file for a case at the point at which a defendant was held for the grand jury. Its files do not include cases in which magistrates found insufficient cause to hold a defendant, but they do include cases dismissed by the grand jury, cases that are not in court records.[13] The contents of the files themselves come from the entire span of the legal process through which a case passed, from investigation to disposition, and, assuming a conviction, to sentencing—at which point, probation files pick up many cases, sometimes following those involved for months, or even years.[14] Such sources reveal how the presentation of a case changed as it passed from those who reported or witnessed it to the NYSPCC officer who conducted the preliminary investigation, to the deputy assistant district attorney (DADA) or ADA who took it to the grand jury, and, if the latter voted an indictment, presented it to a judge and trial jury, and finally, to the judge who determined how a convicted man should be punished.

Whenever I opened a case file, and spread the various documents it contained out in front of me, I felt a powerful urge to solve the puzzle, to reconcile the contradictions and put together the pieces so that they formed a consistent and complete narrative. But ultimately that approach is neither true to the sources, nor effective in capturing how social meanings are made in the legal system. It is the inconsistencies and differing emphases of the various accounts that reveal the diverse understandings that New Yorkers brought to the courts; it is the transformations that a case went through, as much as its outcome, that highlight the influence exerted by particular ideas.

The concept of psychosexual development that working-class New Yorkers encountered in the city's criminal courts did not emerge fully formed; it took shape gradually and unevenly. To capture that process, this book is divided into four parts, each dealing with different, sometimes overlapping, phases in the elaboration of the concept of development. All four phases occurred in an era of unprecedented interest in children and concern about their well-being. From the 1870s onward, middle-class Americans invested children with sentimental meaning, making children emotionally priceless and economically worthless, and oriented their families toward providing for and securing the young, rather than having the young contribute to the family.[15] At the same time, Americans who sought to bring order to the new urban-industrial nation saw children's "innocence and freedom" as making them "singularly receptive to education in rational, humane behavior."[16] It was consideration of the needs of the child that united campaigns for health, education, and a richer city environment, that made legal and penal reform popular, and that loomed large in campaigns for industrial safety and workmen's compensation. But the broadly shared concern with children was not matched by a consensus on their nature. Throughout the twentieth century, Americans oscillated between a view of children as creatures of primitive vitality and imagination, who needed to be able to pursue their instincts free of adult interference, and an image of children as impressionable creatures, who, since they formed habits in response to their stimuli, needed to be controlled by their parents. The shifts that took place in the boundary of childhood, in concepts of who was a child—which provide the structure of this book—are related to those currents of thought, but follow a somewhat different chronology.

The debate about who was a child provoked by the concept of development took eighty years to reach a resolution of sorts. In encompassing such a long span of time, this book departs from the conventional periodization of twentieth-century American history. In particular, it downplays the significance of both the 1920s and the 1950s as watersheds, as moments of such change that they marked the beginning of new eras. The story told here could be fitted to those conventional divisions by emphasizing the shift in the 1930s from the attention to physiology that had emerged at the end of the nineteenth century to a concern with psychology. However, that approach slights the developmental framework that underpinned both the concern with physiology and the attention to psychology, and the extent to which the focus on the psychological development represented an outgrowth of the attention to physical growth. In other words, the conventional periodization creates two stories out of what a longer view reveals to be two chapters in the story of the elaboration of the concept of development.

In response to the uneven manner in which modern ideas took shape in the twentieth-century United States, I have undertaken to cover a long time period and have organized the book in sections that treat overlapping parts of that span of time. The late-nineteenth-century concept of the child as a combination of a developing body and an innocent character was applied to prepubescent children and adolescent boys until the 1930s. Teenage girls, however, displayed a psychology and consent to sexual activity that, as early as the 1890s, caused them to be treated as different from children. Part 2, "The Age of Consent," explores that understanding, encapsulated in the new concept of adolescence, and traces its rise to a degree of cultural prominence by the 1920s.

It was not until the 1930s that psychological development was considered an aspect of prepubescent childhood and male adolescence. Although that recognition meant that a key difference between adolescents and younger children — their psychology — disappeared, it did not bring ideas about the two groups back into line or re-create a single category of childhood. Instead, the new ideas about prepubescent childhood contributed to an era of heightened concern about young children — the "Age of the Child" explored in part 3 — during which teenagers were cast as even more different from younger children, and sometimes as too different to warrant the protection given to children. It took until the 1950s for the concept of development to be applied to men who committed sex crimes against children, a project that produced the figure of the sexual psychopath discussed in part 4. Although more than fifty years, and two traditional watersheds in twentieth-century history, separate the appearances of the sexual psychopath and the developing child, the two figures are both products of the concept of development and need to be seen as facets of the same transformation.

This book also examines a long span of time in order to better capture the nature of the changes that created a modern culture. Examining shorter periods, or stopping in 1920 or 1945, would give prominence to the initial rush of enthusiasm for modern ideas, to the moments when those ideas dominated discussion and the gap between their promoters' intentions and their impact was still to be fully plumbed. Such a periodization captures middle-class reactions more effectively than it does those of working-class Americans. It also encourages a vision of change as a series of smooth transitions. Elements of continuity and the reactions of those outside the middle class often took longer to emerge. They appeared only after new ideas had been deployed, and were manifested in the changes that reformers and legislators made to their approaches in the wake of the working-class responses they encountered. A longer view offers the opportunity to examine new ideas once the novelty that enabled them to overshadow older beliefs has worn off, to see the coexistence of old and new. In the case of concepts of childhood and sexuality, such a perspective reveals that change occurred very slowly, and in a process that caused modern ideas to become heavily imbricated with older ones. While

Americans in the second half of the twentieth century recognized children as going through a process of development, they clung to a concept of childhood innocence.

For all the ambivalence that many early-twentieth-century Americans consequently displayed toward the understanding of sexual violence and childhood derived from the concept of psychosexual development, they never wavered in their concern about children. Such sustained attention to childhood requires, as Michel Foucault long ago suggested, that we include the child among the key figures around whom modern sexuality took shape. No matter how resistant to the notion of the sexual child Americans proved to be, it is clear that one of most sexually charged questions of the first half of the twentieth century was, "What is your age?"

The Age of Innocence

To Rescue the Developing Child

On 17 December 1874, the *New York Times* carried a report of a meeting held the previous day at the city's Association Hall. "Invitations were extended to a large number of prominent citizens interested in the welfare of children," the correspondent revealed, "and many [had] promptly responded." They had come, Mr. Elbridge Gerry, the meeting's chairman, announced, "to organize a society for the prevention of cruelty to children."[1] Gerry, a member of a wealthy New York City family whose forebears included one of the signatories of the Declaration of Independence, was a graduate of Columbia College and a successful lawyer. Six years earlier, at age thirty-three, he had left his private practice to become counsel for the American Society for the Prevention of Cruelty to Animals (ASPCA). Those who responded to Gerry's call, and assumed leadership of the new society, had similar backgrounds. They were "white, male, Protestant, and well-to-do." Several had served on the board of the ASPCA; most were involved in other philanthropic activities. In the remaining decades of the nineteenth century, the organization they established, the New York Society for the Prevention of Cruelty to Children (NYSPCC), became an integral part of the city's legal system, and the model for child protection agencies throughout the English-speaking world.[2]

One result of the work of the NYSPCC was a dramatic increase in the number of men who appeared in the legal system charged with committing sexual acts with children. The Society pursued law enforcement as the most effective means of protecting children. Such a focus on criminal prosecutions and convictions was not unique to New York City. Private child protection agencies in other states had powers similar to those possessed by the NYSPCC, and also used them to pursue criminal prosecutions. Unlike the NYSPCC, most of those agencies altered their philosophies in the early twentieth century, repudiating law enforcement in favor of strengthening families using the approach of social work. Notwithstanding that new concept of child protection, the actual activities of many agencies did not change substantially until the second half of the twentieth century. The Massachusetts Society for the Prevention of Cruelty to Children (MSPCC) and its director, Carl C. Carstens, for example, played a leading role in shifting the focus of the child protection movement toward an emphasis on professional guidance provided for the family. Yet in its work the MSPCC employed few professional personnel—as late as 1946 there was only one qualified social worker on the staff—and showed no marked decline in its reliance on criminal prosecution until the end of the 1920s.[3]

The NYSPCC's law enforcement work was centered not on discovering crimes and apprehending offenders—although its agents did undertake both those tasks—but on ensuring that legal action was taken against those accused of crimes against children. While the Society's agents discovered some crimes, working-class families and the police brought many more to their attention. The unique contribution of the NYSPCC was to take responsibility for all cases that involved child victims, provide advice to magistrates and prosecutors, and put complaints into a legal form. That role is best characterized as easing an offender's path into and through the legal process. To perform it, the Society had to do more than respond to legal categories and structures. New York City's legal culture was populated by a variety of different ethnic and racial groups, drawn from the working and middle classes, all of whom articulated different understandings of the law, of what was criminal, and of how particular criminal acts should be punished. Although efforts to professionalize the courts occurred at the turn of the century, legal expertise and experience were still in short supply among those charged with administering the legal system. Legal officials and jurors both claimed the discretion to decide the outcome of cases for themselves, often with little regard to the law. To win convictions, NYSPCC agents had to address themselves not simply to the law but also to the attitudes and beliefs of the ordinary working-class and middle-class New Yorkers who served on juries.

Since judges and jurors understood sexual violence in a way that made little allowance for child victims, the NYSPCC's efforts were focused on winning recognition of the ways in which children were different from adults, and from adult women in particular. To this end, the Society progressively brought the state's law into line with its understanding of childhood. In explaining child protection as an expression of a new humanitarian sensitivity to violence and pain, and of a new middle-class view of workers and immigrants as sharply different and threatening, historians have portrayed the movement as seeking to extend the middle-class vision of childhood across American society. But the NYSPCC's vision of childhood was more than simply an echo of middle-class ideals.

In a departure from the practice of the previous generation of reformers, the Society relied on age to define childhood, settling on sixteen years as its upper limit. A new conception of childhood lay behind that approach, one that saw children not only as innocent in nature, but also as possessing a body different from that of an adult. Now childhood was tied more closely to bodily immaturity and, as physicians studied children's bodies and attached age norms to growth stages, to age. When deployed in the law, age proved an unstable basis on which to define childhood, being, on occasion, at odds with what an individual said or with the appearance of his or her body. In addition, many New Yorkers still understood childhood as defined by a distinctive, innocent character, rather than by physiological immaturity. Relying on that concept, jurors made determinations as to who was a child based on what they heard an individual say, and not on evidence of age. NYSPCC officers responded to that competing understanding of childhood by presenting individuals under the age of sixteen years of age in such a way that their appearance and language were in line with what jurors expected of a child. In that way, the Society aimed to secure the convictions that it saw as offering protection to children.

The first step in recovering what went on in New York City's courts is to understand the NYSPCC and the legal culture of which it formed a part. The Society was only one participant, albeit a relatively powerful one, in what took place in the legal process, but bringing the NYSPCC and its agents into focus will help in deciphering that complex interplay between reformers, legal officials, and working-class New Yorkers. It will also make it possible to see more clearly what it was that produced changes in the understanding and treatment of sexual violence.

When Elbridge Gerry appeared at the sixth annual meeting of the NYSPCC in 1880, to deliver only his second presidential address, he felt obliged to defend the Society's attempt to enforce the law restricting children's performances on stage. He, after all, had been instrumental in having that law enacted. On this issue, the NYSPCC's traditional allies in the press had turned against them, and joined attacks on the Society as "fanatical, arbitrary and unjust."[4] Even among the membership of the NYSPCC were those who saw children's appearance on stage not as labor but as something more akin to play, a source of enjoyment, income, and a "liberal education."[5] Others in the audience would have been concerned about the impact of the press attacks on the Society's ability to secure the donations and state funding that it required to operate, and on its ability to justify the powers granted to it by the State Legislature.[6]

Gerry began his defense by dismissing as "specious" his critics' claim that "exhibiting children for a few hours at night in a theatre did not amount to any legal cruelty, provided the child was allowed to sleep in the day and was properly fed." He offered instead "a darker picture" of the child performer's lot. The exhibition of children on stage warranted treatment as a form of abuse, he maintained, because of the "moral degradation" that it produced in them, the "result of subjecting children at this early age to every species of temptation." Standing before his audience, Gerry was reticent about providing details of the child performer's likely moral decline. He did claim, however, that "deprived of their opportunity for proper education," and "with their little minds constantly running on the prospective applause of the audience," and lacking "any fixed occupation when not actually employed in the theatrical business," "their future [was] painfully suggestive."[7] In print, however, he was more expansive. Writing for the *North American Review*, Gerry described how child performers were "constantly brought into contact with persons about whose morality or virtue the less said the better." For girls, those "bad associations" led them to "soon lose all modesty and become bold, forward and impudent." By the time they reached sixteen years of age, which the Society defined as the end of childhood, female performers had usually become prostitutes, who went on to the "low dance-houses, concert saloons, and the early grave which is the inevitable conclusion of a life of debauchery." Unfitted for "useful work" by their "idle life" in the theater, boys followed a parallel path that ended in their becoming "thieves or tramps."[8] This characterization of the child performer rested on an understanding of childhood as being distinct from adulthood, as being marked by a distinctive innocence. The concept of childhood innocence had emerged in the eighteenth century, and been adopted by evangelical Protestants in the revivals of the early nineteenth century, from whence it was incorporated into the domestic ideology of the emerging middle class.

Gerry also advanced another ground for treating child performers as abused children: they suffered physical injury as a result of their appearance on stage. Singing and dancing left the child's "entire body over-heated and frequently over-exhausted," Gerry warned, and children's "little nervous systems [were] over-stimulated by the applause." Even though it was "well known that a child requires more sleep than a grown person," stage children got little rest as a result of the late hour at which the shows in which they appeared finished. Repeated performances eventually caused a child's health to break down; the child grew "prematurely old, and finally end[ed] in a hospital and usually an early grave."[9] This concern with the body was a more recent addition to understandings of how children differed from adults. It was only after the Darwinian revolution of the mid-nineteenth century that the child and the adult were seen as having contrasting physiologies, the child's being geared toward growth, the adult's remaining fixed and static.

The child whom Gerry and the NYSPCC sought to protect was thus a contradictory mix, one part romantic, one part modern, a combination of a fixed, innocent character with a fluid, developing body. This manifold nature is an enduring feature of conceptions of the modern child, the product of a process in which "we do not so much discard old conceptions of the child as accrue additional meanings around what remains one of our most culturally potent signifiers."[10] For all its prominence as a focal point for reform efforts, the figure of the child was unstable, open to a variety of interpretations. As such, it was as likely to divide as to unite Americans, as Gerry knew only too well.

The view of childhood as distinctive, rather than as an immature form of adulthood, had emerged in the wake of challenges to the doctrine of original sin, which characterized children as innately depraved. This secularization of the concept of childhood brought a shift in focus from spiritual health to development and growth, a process seen as driven more by nature than by God. The work of the philosopher John Locke provides a common marker of the beginning of this redefinition of childhood; his book *Some Thoughts Concerning Education* went through twenty-six English editions before 1800, establishing it as the eighteenth century's leading child-rearing guide. Locke is credited with giving authority to the idea that the child was a tabula rasa, possessing a blank nature at birth, capable of neither good nor evil until the child developed a will and the capacity to resist her or his impulses.

European romanticism went further in challenging the doctrine of original sin, arguing that a child's original nature was innocence, a state of natural goodness. The opening sentence of Jean-Jacques Rousseau's *Emile* asserted that "God makes all things good; man meddles with them and they become evil." Rousseau urged that children be allowed to develop "naturally," "according to certain laws whose natural progression must be respected above all," without interference with the impulses, the "methods of seeing, thinking and feeling," that set them apart from adults. Romantics thus insisted that childhood be treated as distinct from adulthood: "Nature would have them children before they are men." It was not until the early nineteenth century that mainstream American Protestants joined in the repudiation of the concept of original sin. Evangelical revivals brought a rejection of predestination, in favor of a vision in which God made human beings free moral agents, in which evil did not come from an innate human depravity, but came rather from freely willed decisions to do wrong. The new theology gave the child the potential to be good, if parents instilled and nurtured virtue.[11]

In the course of the nineteenth century, the notion of childhood innocence became bound up with a burgeoning middle-class domesticity. This ideology held that the child's place was in the home, in the sphere, and care, of his or her mother, who was charged with shielding the child from influences that threatened its innocence, and with providing it with moral tutelage. Cut off from the public sphere, and domesticated, the child's distinctive innocence assumed a broader form. No longer involved in wage labor, children began to be seen as being characterized by incapacity and dependence. Removed from the public gaze, children appeared to be without sexuality. Consigned increasingly to the schoolroom, children took on the trait of ignorance. Purity, incapacity, and ignorance: by the last quarter of the nineteenth century, many upper- and middle-class Americans perceived these as the traits that constituted the innocence particular to childhood.[12]

While prior to the last decades of the nineteenth century childhood was seen as having a distinctive nature, its boundaries remained plastic and nebulous. Broadly speaking, an individual who retained the innocence and dependence particular to childhood remained a child until, and even beyond, the age of majority of twenty-one years, his or her physical maturity and chronological age notwithstanding.[13] By the same token, the loss of innocence or the display of autonomy ended childhood with equally little regard either to an individual's physical maturity or her or his age. Given that childhood's distinctive innocence depended on the ability to locate a break between it and adulthood, the lack of a clear boundary created uncertainty about the status of particular young people. Middle- and upper-class Americans were preoccupied with the vulnerability of childhood, with an image of innocence as a state of emptiness that made children particularly susceptible to harmful influences — bad examples, impure knowledge, the suggestions of others — that could corrupt their character before they had attained the strength of will and moral rectitude that came with adulthood. As a result, adults listened carefully to children, alert for language that signified knowledge and corruption.

Fears about the child's openness to evil influences betrayed a recognition that children could behave like adults and develop adult understanding and knowledge. To borrow James Kincaid's compelling phrase, the loud insistence on the innocence of the child created a "subversive echo: experience, corruption, eroticism."[14] That recognition of the child's potential corruption, fuelled by submerged layers of beliefs about children—enduring faith in the innate depravity of children and in the child's close connection to a primal, disorderly Nature—gave urgency to the middle-class concern to preserve childhood by sheltering children within the home.[15]

In the second half of the nineteenth century, an explosion of information about physiological development in human beings, stirred by the Darwinian revolution, added a further dimension to the distinction between children and adults, one that provided the basis for drawing a more definite boundary around childhood. Romantic visions of the child's lack of development and growth had been framed not in terms of the body but in relation to nature, in images of the child as a kitten, bunny, or lamb, or as a blossom or flower bud. Portraits diminished the corporeality of the child's body, firmly differentiating it from the adult body by drawing attention to the face, with its big eyes and downy cheeks, and to chubby feet and arms, the parts least associated with sexuality, and by shrouding the rest of the body in special costumes or wafting clothing. After Darwin, the child's body attracted more intense scientific study, a scrutiny and measurement of the corporeal form from which romantics averted their eyes, and new meanings were given to its difference from the adult body. A gaze shaped by an evolutionary perspective saw the child's body in terms of motion, with a physiology directed toward growth and development. The adult body, by contrast, appeared static, its physiology fixed, operating to maintain what had already developed.[16]

By the 1870s, the increased attention to the physiology of children's bodies convinced physicians that children and adults were sufficiently different to require children's medicine to be established as a new specialty within the field of medical science, pediatrics. Delivering his presidential address to the American Pediatric Society in 1889, the year after its founding, Abraham Jacobi, gave voice to that vision: "Pediatrics does not deal with miniature men and women, with reduced doses and the same classes of diseases in smaller bodies. . . . There is scarcely a tissue or an organ which behaves exactly alike in the different periods of life. . . . There are anomalies and diseases which are encountered in the infant and child only. There are those which are mostly found in children, or with a symptomatology and course peculiar to them."[17]

Concern with biological development tied childhood more closely to bodily immaturity, in the process reducing the plastic scope of childhood. As physicians refined their theories about growth into a formalized conception of stages of development in childhood, one that fixed age norms to growth stages and occurrences of specific diseases, childhood also began to be tied to chronological age. By 1920 these findings had been codified into developmental indices such as height-weight charts, which showed the mean weights of same-sex and same-age children of equivalent heights. Employed by pediatricians and public health officials, and used in the better baby contests that were a feature of agricultural fairs across the United States in the 1910s and 1920s, those charts helped spur ordinary white Americans to see children in terms of age, to measure them against developmental norms, and to adopt "new convictions about precisely how the young should live and grow." The new norms were derived from research on white middle-class children, and organizers informally, and sometimes formally, excluded African Americans from participating in the better baby contests that employed and popularized them.[18] It is perhaps not surprising then that African Americans continued to run "beautiful baby" contests, which measured appearance against standards of beauty, rather than following whites in abandoning beautiful baby contests in favor of "better baby" ones.[19]

The late-nineteenth-century coupling of physical development with the older notion of innocence was a somewhat uneasy one. While the logic of development suggested a continuous relationship between childhood and adulthood, innocence implied a dichotomous relationship between the two age groups. A more consistent notion of childhood, one that also saw a child's mind in developmental terms, would not take hold in the United States until the early twentieth century. The relative inattention to the child's mental development reflected a lack of interest on the part of nineteenth-century alienists. They had little to do with children, and little to say about them; when they did discuss the child, with regard to the related problems of masturbation and precocity, they showed little of the concern with her or his distinct nature displayed by other professional groups.[20]

In the absence of a discussion of mental development, notions of physiological development could be combined with the idea of childhood innocence only by relying on the romantic construction of puberty. Physiological development followed a logic that suggested a gradual emergence of sexuality in childhood that ran counter to the absence of sexuality that was a central component of innocence. Romantic constructions of puberty bridged that conceptual gap. For Rousseau, puberty represented a second birth, a period of drastic change that required careful oversight. Such characterizations of puberty as a metamorphosis, an abrupt reformation of the body that introduced sexuality and recast the child as an adult, allowed upper- and middle-class Americans to successfully amalgamate the new emphasis on biological development with the existing domesticated concept of childhood innocence.[21]

Although NYSPCC officers interwove physical development and innocence in their descriptions of children, the Society formally defined those it aimed to protect in terms that gave preeminence to the new concern with physiology. The 1875 act that established the NYSPCC as a privately chartered corporation to enforce laws "relating to or affecting children" did not define childhood.[22] Left to decide for itself the meaning of "children," the Society took a different approach than that taken by the previous generation of child savers. The reformers who had established asylums, prisons, and "placing-out" programs in the early decades of the nineteenth century had relied on social markers to define the children that came within the scope of their work. In limiting themselves to orphaned, abandoned, and dependent children, they used the lack of a home and an absence of parental authority to determine the objects of their concern.[23] The directors of the NYSPCC, by contrast, looked to physical development, as interpreted by physicians, and employed age to delimit the objects of the Society's work. Children, the NYSPCC determined, were individuals who had not yet reached sixteen years of age. Elbridge Gerry explained the selection of the age of sixteen as the upper limit of childhood as "the result of a long and careful medical investigation into the relative physical strength of children."[24] On other occasions, he added a gender-specific justification: sixteen was the age by which "the female function is presumed to [have begun]" in most girls.[25] The Society's definition was not as straightforward and uncontentious as Gerry's statements imply. The degree of physical development and occurrence of puberty that formed the basis of that definition did not take place uniformly, but at a range of ages. The age the Society opted for was the age at which physicians believed most individuals had developed strength and reached puberty, but when it was employed to define childhood, that age became universalized. The transformation in robustness and sexuality introduced an element of inconsistency into the definition of childhood, in that an individual who had developed the traits of adulthood earlier than most others would still be defined as immature, as a child.

How much of a threat this incongruity posed to the legitimacy of the definition depended on where the age chosen by the Society lay in relation to the range in which maturity was attained. The closer that age was to the upper end, the greater the number of individuals whose physical development would be at odds with their formal status. Early-nineteenth-century girls had not begun to menstruate until age fifteen or sixteen, but by the end of the century menarche was occurring at a younger age, a trend that would continue and, by the 1990s, cause the average age to fall to twelve years.[26] American boys also reached adult size and strength at younger ages, with the average fifteen-year-old in 1920 two inches taller and fifteen pounds heavier than his counterpart in 1880.[27] Definitions of childhood in New York law reveal that other reformers employed ages that were in line with the earlier ages at which American children were reaching puberty. A child was required to attend school only until his or her fourteenth birthday. Between 1886 and 1898, a child had to wait until he or she reached thirteen years of age to work in a factory; after 1899, a child had to wait a further year, until he or she turned fourteen. It would not be until the early twentieth century, when legal definitions of childhood reflected psychological development as well as physical growth, that age sixteen became a common boundary of childhood, employed most influentially in the juvenile justice system.[28] To choose sixteen as the end of childhood in the last quarter of the nineteenth century, as the NYSPCC did, was to stretch the scope of the concept of childhood.

Initially, the NYSPCC presented the threats to those it defined as children in terms of "cruelty"—physical abuse at the hands of adults. NYSPCC officers stressed the need to "rescue" children from "constant abuse and cruelties practiced on them by the human brutes who happen to possess the custody and control of them." In doing so, they appealed to the increased humanitarian sentiment and sensitivity to violence and suffering evident among middle-class Americans in the decades after the Civil War.[29] Such appeals also took on a material and visual form. A visitor to the Society's rooms was shown first "the chamber of horrors, which is something like a hardware shop and something like an arsenal—crammed with knives, hatchets, scissors and even firearms that have been used on child victims," and, following that, "the innocents' gallery, with its photographs of poor, abused little wretches still bleeding."[30]

But once it began working in the neighborhoods of New York City, the Society soon found itself dealing more often with neglect and sexual behavior, and with policing the movements and activities of children, experiences that broadened its officers' vision of what dangers the developing child faced.[31] They saw working-class children as exposed, vulnerable to a range of perils and temptations that existed in the urban environment beyond the shelter of a home.[32] Middle-class New Yorkers saw evidence of these threats all around them whenever they traversed the city's streets. Rather than the bourgeois city imagined by early-nineteenth-century reformers such as Charles Brace, with "streets free for trade and respectable promenades, emancipated from the inconveniences of pickpockets and thieves, the affronts of prostitutes and hucksters, the myriad offenses of working-class mores," New York City in the late nineteenth century continued to be disorderly, its streets filled with beggars, street venders, prostitutes, and gangs.[33] "Girls of tender years" who ventured into those spaces found themselves, in the accounts of NYSPCC officers, assailed by "lewd men" and initiated "into vice and immorality" by already corrupted girls. "Numerous temptations" beset both girls and boys. "Allurements and promises held out by wretches whose sole object [was] to make money by their fall" "decoyed" girls "into the downward path," while "associations with others of vicious character, often their seniors" taught boys "profanity and a total disregard of all moral and social duties" and led to their "committing offenses requiring the stringent hand of the reformatory institution."[34] Even when children survived the streets, they went to factories and succumbed to the entertainments being offered by dance halls, dime museums, and theaters, crossing into the adult worlds of work and leisure. In those spaces, interaction with adults brought premature knowledge, while participation in adult activities overtaxed children's bodies.

Child protectors increasingly traced these threats to a single cause: the failure of working-class Americans to adopt the ideology of domesticity and its attendant commitment to sheltering childhood innocence. Responsibility for that failure rested with working-class parents. On the Society's tenth anniversary, looking back to the moment of the NYSPCC's founding, Gerry conjured images of "impecunious parents," who "drove [their children] from their miserable homes at all hours of the night to beg and steal, . . . play on musical instruments, [and] peddle flowers and small wares to the passer-by all too often as a cover for [prostitution]"; of drunken parents who "sent [children] out at night to procure liquor"; of parents who endangered their children's health by having them trained as acrobats, or "drilled in juvenile operas and song and dance variety business."[35] In their more charitable moments, NYSPCC officers attributed such behavior to "lax" attention to the distinctions between children and adults, as in the case of the mother who saw no harm in her daughter selling newspapers in Battery Park at night but, after a man had tried to lure the girl to a brothel, "thinks differently now, poor woman."[36] More often, they blamed the failure to shelter children in the home on a depraved humanity. "Only those who are degraded far below the level of brute creation (for brutes have no vices)," Gerry told the National Conference of Charities and Corrections in 1882, "by a shameless submission to degrading passions compel such little children, by their pitiful condition, to extract alms from the compassionate for their support, or for the procurement of the means of vicious indulgence."[37] Beginning in the 1880s, Gerry also linked the behavior of parents to their "foreign and anti-American notion" of children as "merely the property of the parents to be utilized as they see fit for their pecuniary gain and profit." That view, he argued, had its origins in a lack of domesticity, in the fact that "very many of those who come to this country seeking a *home* are unfamiliar with the meaning of that word in the American sense."[38]

Gerry's descriptions of parents reflected the increased sense of threat felt by the middle and upper classes as they confronted the working classes in the years after the Civil War. The "tenement classes" that reformers had worried about in the pre–Civil War decades had evolved into the "dangerous classes."[39] Riots, increased violent crime, and pervasive labor unrest carried working-class "depravity" into the wider society, turning back efforts to bring working people closer to middle-class mores. New waves of immigrants from southern and eastern Europe brought in to the working class a population that had even less in common with native-born middle-class Americans than had native-born and northern European workers. The Manhattan neighborhoods policed by the NYSPCC were filled with workers who dressed differently, spoke languages other than English, and practiced Catholic and Jewish faiths rather than Protestant religions of the middle class.

In the context of this transformation, and as Darwinism became popularized, middle-class Americans began to code class-based differences as "racial." "Human races were assumed to have evolved from simple savagery, to advanced and valuable civilization," a process so far accomplished only by Anglo-Saxons and other "advanced" white races. Linked to the millennial striving for human perfection, this racial vision "conflated biological human evolutionary differences with moral and intellectual human progress." The threatening traits of workers and immigrants highlighted by Gerry became markers of their membership of less evolved, less civilized races. Unlike Anglo-Saxons, they had not learned to control their passions, nor did they seek to protect their children from the world of work, to secure them in the domestic sphere, as did members of "advanced" white groups. Explicit mentions of African Americans are absent from NYSPCC rhetoric in this period, despite blacks' long-standing presence in Manhattan. But that did not mean that blacks were outside the framework on which reformers relied, that they were seen in fundamentally different terms from other members of the working class. White, middle-class Americans saw African Americans in terms of the same racial hierarchy they applied to ethnic whites, attributing to blacks the same traits of brutality, lack of self-control, and the failure to adequately differentiate adults from children, though in a more pronounced form.[40]

Faced with what they perceived as the failure of the working-class family and the increasingly threatening otherness of the working class itself, child protectors went to radical lengths in their efforts to protect childhood from the perils assailing it. Early-nineteenth-century reformers had "spread their nets wide to catch a variety of dependent children." They did not, however, reach beyond the boundaries of parental authority, even if they sometimes did not inquire too carefully into the stories of children who claimed to be orphaned or abandoned.[41] Although some state legislatures passed school attendance laws and child labor laws that impinged on the authority of parents, efforts to enforce those laws were piecemeal at best. Early-nineteenth-century reformers were, as Gerry put it, reluctant to "meddle" in relations between parent and child in the face of a "general supposition, or rather presumption . . . that every parent knew and did what was best for the welfare of the child and that no outside person had any right to interfere."[42] The NYSPCC showed no such reluctance. As Gerry was fond of pointing out, it would reach into the midst of the family: in a direct challenge to parental authority, the Society "seizes the child when it is in an atmosphere of impurity, or in the care of those who are not fit to be entrusted with it, wrenches the child out of these surroundings, brings it to the court, and submits it to the decision of the court—unless, on the other hand, it reaches out that arm of the law to the cruelist, seizes him within its grasp, brings him also to the criminal court and insures his prosecution and punishment."[43]

When the NYSPCC dealt with children, its focus was on keeping children from contact with the adult world. Despite Gerry's initial claim that, because "ample laws" already existed, the Society did not have to fashion laws that intruded into relations between parents and children, the Society did draft and promote legislation to erect barriers between childhood and adulthood. A variety of such laws, sponsored and enforced by the NYSPCC, regulated where children could go, preventing individuals under sixteen years of age from entering brothels, any place that sold intoxicants, opium dens, theaters, movies, dance halls, and billiard, pool, or bowling halls unless accompanied by their parents. Another set of laws restricted what children could do, prohibiting girls from selling newspapers at night, preventing all children from begging and rag picking and other dangerous occupations, outlawing the selling or receiving of obscene publications, the pawning or selling of junk, and the buying of intoxicants, tobacco, and firearms and other dangerous weapons. The laws also required child theatrical performers to be licensed.[44]

Within the legal system, the NYSPCC established procedures and facilities that limited children's contact with adult criminals. The New York Police Department required its officers to notify the Society whenever they arrested or took into custody a child under sixteen years of age.[45] Empowered by court orders issued by magistrates, the Society took custody of child victims, child offenders, and child witnesses.[46] The NYSPCC housed those children until the courts were done with them, a period of time—in the case of children whose testimony was required in a prosecution—that could stretch to several months. For those children required to testify, the Society obtained a room, staffed by two agents, in each of Manhattan's police courts, where children could wait apart from adult defendants and witnesses. In the Criminal Court Building, where felony cases were tried, the Society had two rooms, which allowed it to separate boys and girls.[47]

Once the courts decided a child's fate, the Society had nothing more to do with that child, thereby avoiding both the burden of the child's care and a debilitating, divisive competition with the existing sectarian institutions that cared for children. But NYSPCC officers could not resist claiming that they had worked some of the transformation from "little creature" to little child. "Miserable little creatures are brought in [to the Society's building] at all hours from the street," Gerry wrote; "their garments, saturated with filth and vermin, are promptly removed and destroyed; they are thoroughly washed and cleansed in a lavatory prepared for that purpose, and then, dressed in clean clothes, and fed, if hungry, with a substantial meal, they are at night, perhaps for the first time in their lives, placed in comfortable beds."[48] Pairs of engravings, and later photographs, that illustrated the NYSPCC's *Annual Report* captured that transformation. A typical example from the Society's second *Annual Report*, entitled "Ellen Connors—(Condition When Found)," shows a girl, only partially dressed in clothes that are little more than rags, with disheveled hair, and scars on her arms and face. She stands awkwardly, against an ill-defined background, gazing toward the viewer with a dazed expression. On the facing page, however, Ellen appears transformed. The caption locates Ellen "in her new home," safe within the domestic sphere that middle-class ideology deemed appropriate for a child. She is neatly dressed in respectable, even fashionable clothes. Her face is clean, her hair neatly presented, and she is unmarked. Looking confidently toward the viewer, Ellen stands in the conventional pose of portraiture, against a background containing the furnishings of a respectable home.

When the NYSPCC dealt with adults who had committed crimes against children like Ellen, its focus was on ensuring that those men and women were successfully prosecuted. For Gerry, law enforcement work constituted the Society's main role; it had been "instituted for the express purpose, and for none other, of applying the arm of the law to the protection of the helpless."[49] He expressed no confidence in the power of "exhortations . . . made upon . . . duties as parents, guardians and custodians of the helpless" to change working-class behavior. Since offenders "uniformly turn a deaf ear" to such entreaties, Gerry argued, only the "certainty of conviction [and] the dread of that conviction" would "keep in check the brutal passions of those who regard helpless little children as entitled to no consideration."[50] Gerry's stance was in keeping with a weakening faith "that an intrinsic human morality could provide the engine for a fundamental transformation of society" that marked middle-class thought in the period following the Civil War.[51] It also reflected late-nineteenth-century racial ideology. Anglo-Saxon Americans believed that members of the so-called less advanced races lacked the capacity, during the span of their lives, to develop the civilized traits that would bring their behavior into line with that of their betters. Such a vision could justify more punitive actions than the methods of deterrence promoted by Gerry, and was used in that way against African Americans, particularly in the South.[52] Despite the NYSPCC's claim that it had no vindictive purpose in enforcing the law, that it aimed only to inspire "wholesome fear," the Society's officers sometimes allowed a more punitive language and tone to slip into their public statements.[53] On a number of occasions, Gerry expressed a desire to "fasten the grasp of the law upon the offender" and teach him or her a lesson, either through a term of "penal servitude" or appropriate corporal punishment, "pain [being] the only thing to which [the human brute] is not insensible."[54]

Although Gerry imagined that the Society's law enforcement work involved the NYSPCC's becoming "a hand affixed to the arm of the law by which the body politic reaches out and enforces the law," the NYSPCC was more than an appendage to the legal system.[55] It became, rather, a "component part of the city government."[56] The New York State Penal Code and the Code of Criminal Procedure installed the NYSPCC "as part of the legal machinery of the state," "substantially, and mainly, . . . a branch of the Police Department, the District Attorney's office and of the Criminal Courts."[57] The 1875 "Act of the incorporation of societies for the prevention of cruelty to children" gave the NYSPCC the power to bring complaints "for the violation of any law relating to or affecting children," and to aid in presenting to the courts the law and the facts. The act also required "magistrates, constables, sheriffs and officers of the police" to aid the Society in its law enforcement work.[58] In addition to its agents' powers of arrest, and the rooms provided for them in court buildings, the Society's counsel and attorney were also authorized to represent both the state attorney general and the district attorney for New York County.[59] In the turn-of-the-century United States, there was nothing unusual about the state's granting such powers to a private organization. In fact, the American state made a practice of delegating its authority to voluntary agencies and individuals, thus establishing a close relationship between the middle class and the state, a relationship that contributed to the middle class's willingness to give the state more legal power to respond to social change.[60] Researchers working for the Russell Sage Foundation found that, by the first years of the twentieth century, "to many [West Side] families the functions of the court and 'the Gerry,' as the society is called after its founder, were indistinguishable."[61]

The presence of the NYSPCC introduced a modern, middle-class voice into the legal culture of New York City, one that sought to use the law to promote new ideas of childhood. At the same time, the Society's efforts to increase the effectiveness of prosecutions enhanced the ability of working-class New Yorkers to articulate their understanding of the law and their concepts of childhood. Not all the adults charged with crimes against children had been apprehended by the Society's agents; in fact, most were reported by members of the working-class communities from which they came. Moreover, once the NYSPCC established its place in the legal system, it became a focal point for complaints about children and concerns as to their welfare, many of which came from the inhabitants of working-class neighborhoods.[62] For all the resentment working-class New Yorkers felt at the intrusions of NYSPCC agents, they were still prepared to have recourse to the Society. In addition, the NYSPCC's superintendent observed in 1916, "requests for co-operation and for direct action pour in from schools and churches, aid societies, social and charitable and friendly agencies." He went on, in the somewhat superior tone characteristic of the NYSPCC's public statements, to note that "the City Departments are always glad to avail themselves of the Society's help in their activities, and in particular, the Department of Education has numerous times proven itself a great and good friend in closely and effectively co-operating with the Society."[63]

The Society's agents helped ensure that legal action was taken against the men and women that working-class New Yorkers alleged had committed a crime against a child. The city's police could not be relied on to take such action. Often hostile to immigrants and African Americans, New York police were notoriously corrupt; one commentator described them as "political henchmen," prepared "to 'let off easy' all who are protected by the favor of political leaders," and open to bribes from everyone else.[64] The powers of arrest granted to the NYSPCC, and the requirement that police officers notify the Society when they arrested someone for an offense against a child, took responsibility for acting on reports out of the hands of police. An NYSPCC officer's involvement not only increased the likelihood that a report would lead to the offender's appearance before a magistrate; it also improved the chances that the magistrate would hold him or her to appear before the grand jury. Ordinary New Yorkers who appeared as parties to a case found it difficult to influence what happened in a magistrate's court. "Cases come on with great rapidity, sometimes one a minute," sociologist Mary Roberts Smith reported in 1899, "averaging from forty to seventy per day in the different district courts." "In addition," Smith noted, "there is the confusion created by a dozen or two police officers, five or six police clerks, roundsmen, attendants, prisoners, and a motley audience of onlookers in the court, all of whom talk more or less continuously. What the magistrate says can seldom be heard more than ten feet away, while the witnesses and prisoners must come close to the desk to be heard at all." Not surprisingly, Smith concluded that "in the midst of such confusion, noise, and incessant movement no one can hope to understand the procedure of the court without some legal training, and perhaps not even then without a close connection with the court itself." In the case of child victims, however, "an officer of the Society comes into court with them to suggest to the magistrate where they should be sent."[65]

Magistrates would not dismiss or hold for trial any case involving a child without a written report on the child's surroundings and history from the NYSPCC.[66] The Society did its most important work in interviewing the child victim, a task in which it had considerably more experience than did the changing cast of legal officials who worked in the city's courts. While they had victims in their care, NYSPCC officers recorded and carefully checked the children's statements, seeking "to determine the truth of their story and to corroborate their evidence." Keeping children in custody helped safeguard that testimony, shielding child victims from "threats, corruption or other methods [that] could be successfully utilized to destroy their evidence and to blunt their memory as to the facts of the case."[67]

Most magistrates were happy to rely on the Society not only to gather information on a case, but also to determine its disposition. In part, that attitude reflected the extent to which magistrates were inundated with other matters, and lacked the time or the inclination to attend to the details of the law raised by cases concerning children. Many were also not particularly well qualified to make such decisions themselves. Until 1895, magistrates were not required to have any legal training. Even after the legislature required that magistrates be members of the bar with five years in legal practice, political ties remained a more important qualification. The mayor appointed magistrates for ten-year terms. The clerks with whom magistrates worked were also political appointments, men rewarded for their service to the party, and often lacked the experience, training, and other qualifications required for their positions. Until 1910, assistant district attorneys (ADAS) were not present at arraignments in the magistrates' courts. As a result, an NYSPCC agent was often the only person present in a courtroom with any knowledge and experience of the law and its workings as they pertained to crimes against children.[68]

When a magistrate held that there was sufficient cause to believe a defendant was guilty, an NYSPCC agent would then oversee the next stage of the prosecution of that individual. The agent worked with an ADA to put together a case to present to the grand jury, and, if necessary, at trial. The position of ADA was a part-time one, dispensed as political patronage; like most employees of the district attorney's office, ADAS were either ward politicians or the friends and relatives of such men. They rarely held the job for more than a short time. Each change of control invariably brought a flood of resignations from staff members with ties to the outgoing DA, followed by his successor's appointment of new personnel with the appropriate political affiliations. One reformer judged the ADAS who staffed the office in the 1890s, when it was controlled by the Tammany Hall machine, to be "drones who weren't expected to do much more than draw their salaries, demonstrate their loyalty to the Organization and keep their mouths shut."[69] Such men were obviously ill equipped to handle the legal challenges of prosecuting a man for a sex crime against a child. C. C. Carstens, president of the MSPCC, complained that children's testimony was commonly so "poorly used" by district attorneys that prosecutions were "futile."[70]

To avoid such an outcome, the NYSPCC not only gathered "evidence and information" but also, in the words of its superintendent, "carefully assimilated, analyzed and put [it] into legal form for the action of the District Attorney."[71] In the most straightforward sense, this meant creating a trial brief for the prosecutor, which is to say, a summary of the statements of each of the prosecution's witnesses. An examination of the briefs, which survive in the district attorney's case files, reveals, however, that NYSPCC agents did more than organize and summarize the information they had collected. They shaped the evidence into the form required to win a conviction, making it conform to jurors' understandings of the alleged offense, as much as to the legal definition of that offense. In this way, the Society facilitated prosecution and conviction, literally transforming a complaint into a legal case. They generally left to an ADA, however, the actual task of conducting a prosecution.

To win convictions, NYSPCC agents and ADAs had to persuade two groups of jurors, neither inclined to follow the letter of the law in making their judgments about a case. Under New York State statute, eligibility for jury service was restricted to men, between the ages of twenty-one and seventy, who were citizens residing in the city, who owned real or personal property worth at least $250, who were of sound mind, who could read English, and who had no criminal record. Clergymen, lawyers, teachers, physicians, journalists, firemen, and engineers — among quite a few other professionals — could claim an exemption from jury service.[72] Members of both grand juries and trial juries were drawn from this pool, but, since service on a grand jury lasted at least a month, the two panels differed somewhat in their composition. Many grand jurors were well-to-do businessmen, for whom the long term of service involved little hardship; several such men remained on the grand jury for several years. The task of the twenty-three men on the panel was to review the cases presented to them by ADAs, and to decide whether the evidence would, "if unexplained and uncontradicted, warrant a conviction by the trial jury." If a grand jury determined that the evidence was sufficient, an indictment listing the charges against the defendant would be issued, and he would be committed for trial. If the grand jury found the evidence to be lacking, the charges against the defendant were dismissed. Petit juries decided the guilt of men tried in the New York County Court of General Sessions, the court that dealt with men and women charged with felonies. Those panels tended to be composed of New Yorkers from the lower ranks of the social scale, "retail cigar and newspaper dealers and small tailors from the East Side," whose lives were better suited to the shorter period of time required to serve on a petit jury than the time involved in being a member of a grand jury.[73]

Many New York City jurors believed, despite the oath they swore to uphold the law and base their verdict on the evidence, that the jury's function was to render what one former ADA labeled "substantial justice." Jurors "frequently feel by no means confident that the punishment will fit the crime," the ADA complained, "and are anxious, so far as they can, to dispose of the case for themselves." Influenced by sentiment and easily impressed by collateral matters, such jurors were less likely to follow the law than to exclaim, "Oh, let him go! He's only a kid. Give him another chance!" The press, and even some judges, encouraged that attitude and lauded juries that "tempered justice with mercy."[74] Winning an indictment or a conviction from a panel of New Yorkers thus required more than attention to the law; it necessitated attention to jurors' own understandings of the nature and harmfulness of particular acts.

New York City juries, together with prosecutors and judges, recognized such a narrow range of circumstances as sexual violence that few of the small number of men charged with rape were convicted and punished. In the case of men charged with assaults on adult women, that situation did not change significantly during the first half of the twentieth century. From 1906 to 1955, only 30 percent of the men charged with the rape or attempted rape of a female over eighteen years of age were convicted.[75] By comparison, the conviction rate for all felony prosecutions in the years from 1896 to 1932 was never less than 75 percent, and usually over 88 percent. That average is inflated by high rates of conviction in burglary, robbery, and larceny cases, but even charges of assault and murder produced convictions in more than half of all cases.[76] The low rate of conviction in rape prosecutions initiated by adult women was partly mandated by the law. It was not that the state's law defined rape so as to include only a limited set of circumstances. To the contrary, the state penal code adopted in 1881 defined "an act of sexual intercourse with a female against her will or without her consent" as including not only acts when a woman's resistance was forcibly overcome but also acts "when her resistance is prevented by fear of immediate and great bodily harm, which she has reasonable cause to believe will be inflicted upon her."[77] However, in 1886, the state legislature effectively backed away from providing women with such broad protection by amending the rape law to require that the complainant's testimony had to be corroborated by other evidence before a man could be convicted. Common law had not required such corroboration. If a jury "cautiously scrutinized" a female's testimony, considered "the manner in which she testifie[d], the consistency of her testimony," and whether the surrounding circumstances supported her account, and, as one appellate court decision put it, was "satisfied of the truth of her evidence," her testimony "was alone sufficient evidence to support a conviction."[78] John Wigmore, the leading American authority on the laws of evidence, did not consider a law requiring corroboration to be necessary, and in the late nineteenth century only one other state legislature joined New York's in applying the requirement to rape.[79]

New York's adoption of a corroboration requirement helped the state earn a reputation for being, as one historian recently put it, "relentlessly hostile to female accusers," a judgment that seems somewhat harsh given the way that the courts applied the law.[80] The state's higher courts read the statute as imposing a strict standard. Their decisions held that the supporting evidence had to corroborate every material fact of the crime and connect the defendant to it, but the evidence did not have to be convincing or conclusive in and of itself to establish the commission of the crime by the defendant.[81] Yet, at the same time, as the New York State Law Revision Commission noted in 1937, the state's higher courts "refrained from attempting a rigid definition of what constitutes sufficient corroborating evidence."[82] That approach helped keep the dockets of the appellate courts full of appeals against convictions on the grounds that there had been no corroboration, most of which resulted in the conviction being overturned, a pattern that hardly suggests that the requirement was the insurmountable obstacle to conviction at trial that it is often portrayed as being.[83]

In New York City, however, the corroboration requirement alone did not produce the low rate of conviction. Jurors and judges also employed a narrower definition of rape than that provided in the state's law, and on occasion they paid little regard to the evidence presented to them. The opinions of appellate courts and the decisions of grand juries and prosecutors express an understanding of rape as a physically violent assault or an attack involving multiple assailants, where no prior relationship between victim and defendant existed.[84] That concept required evidence of extensive injury to establish the use of force—unless a woman had also been robbed, her loss of property thus establishing her lack of consent. Judges and jurors also gave men very broad access to women they knew. The existence of even a relatively casual relationship led courts to assume a woman would consent, unless she was white and the man accused of raping her was nonwhite.

Only if a woman had suffered "observable injuries," New York DAs believed, would a jury consider that she had been assaulted and had resisted to the limit of her capacity—that she had been raped. In my sample, most of the handful of men convicted of the rape of an adult woman had inflicted grievous injuries.[85] When a woman had not suffered such wounds, a rape prosecution rarely produced an indictment, let alone a conviction.[86] Grand juries did not see injuries such as a knife wound, scratch marks on a woman's neck, bruises on her body, or even a fractured jaw, as establishing either that a man had used force to complete an act of sexual intercourse with a woman or that she had resisted him to the utmost of her ability.[87]

If a woman knew her assailant, judges and jurors required her to display far more resistance to establish her lack of consent than they did if he was a stranger to her. Only if a man had promised to marry a woman prior to having sexual intercourse with her did he risk forfeiting his sexual access to her. New York was one of thirty-five states that had a crime of seduction in their statute books, a law that punished a "person, who under promise of marriage, seduces and has sexual intercourse with a female of previous chaste character."[88] The seduction law's focus on promises of marriage meant that it not only encompassed acts that occurred within relationships but also included no requirement that women behave in specific ways, such as resisting to the limit of their capacity. From 1886 to 1955, in the cases for which details survive, more than one in every three women who made a charge of seduction in Manhattan described being subject to physical force and violence.[89] Only 16 percent of seduction prosecutions resulted in convictions, but an equal number were resolved by the marriage of the parties.[90] Although a "strange signification by modern standards," the seduction law extended the reach of understandings, and legal definitions, of sexual violence.[91]

Presented with a nonwhite man charged with assaulting a white woman, jurors showed far less concern about a woman's physical injuries or her relationship to her assailant. Had twenty-seven-year-old Juan Bana not been Mexican, there is little chance that he would have been convicted of raping twenty-year-old Clara Maguire. Bana knew Clara prior to the night of the alleged rape; in fact, he and Clara had eloped two and a half years earlier, but they had failed to marry because of a quarrel over whether they would travel in the same sleeper car. For eighteen months, Bana worked in Cuba. On his return, he arranged to meet Clara and took her to dinner. During the meal, Clara felt ill after drinking something Bana had given her, and she asked to leave. When they had walked two blocks, Clara could no longer stand up. Bana took her to the nearby Astor Hotel, after which Clara claimed to remember nothing until she was awoken in the middle of the night by Bana's efforts to have sexual intercourse with her.[92] She screamed and struggled, before once again losing consciousness. When Clara awoke the next morning, Bana tried to again have intercourse with her, but on this occasion Clara was able to stop him. She then had Bana take her home, but she did not tell her sister what had happened until that evening; the police were not called until the following night, after Bana failed to keep an appointment with Clara and her family. The physician who examined Clara found her hymen ruptured, and she was "very nervous and excited," but he observed no signs of physical injury. The house detective at the Astor Hotel testified that Clara appeared drugged or drunk when she arrived at the hotel. Bana said that she was drunk; not wanting to take her home in that condition, he had merely put Clara in bed and slept next to her. He did not touch her at all. Given the lack of witnesses as to what happened in the hotel room, the intimate relationship that had existed between the couple, and Clara's lack of physical injuries, a jury and judge would ordinarily have dismissed Clara's charge that she had been raped. However, the interracial nature of this encounter meant that this was not an ordinary case.[93]

In sentencing Bana, Judge Edward Swann offered an account of the case that revealed the suspicion of and hostility to females that ran through all facets of the legal response to a woman's charge of rape. The judge laid most of the blame for what had happened on Clara and her father. Clara had been "very careless . . . and totally oblivious to the fact a young man such as this man is, or any young man, will go just as far as a young woman will let them go and no farther." Going out all night with Bana once, when they eloped, Judge Swann claimed, "was enough to lead any young man on to try more." Swann admonished Clara's father for not exerting more control over his daughter: "When you put a young woman in the City of New York and allow her to go in that particular section, the Tenderloin section, she cannot play with tar without being defiled." Bana drew condemnation from Judge Swann only for taking advantage of Clara's drunkenness, and even that criticism was tempered by the comment that Bana himself was probably drunk.[94] Such suspicion of women could even lead jurors to ignore compelling evidence of a man's guilt.[95]

Given such outcomes, it was clear to the NYSPCC that to secure the punishment of men who sexually assaulted girls it needed to persuade juries and judges that girls were different from adult women who charged rape. That working-class New Yorkers did not share the Society's understanding of childhood complicated that task. Whereas working-class New Yorkers saw children as characterized by a distinctive innocence, the NYSPCC also emphasized bodily immaturity and age as factors that defined an individual as a child. The Society's agents found those different concepts easiest to reconcile in cases involving young girls under eleven and boys. But in cases involving girls of between eleven and sixteen years of age, working-class New Yorkers pushed prosecutions toward outcomes other than those sought by the NYSPCC. As a result, older understandings reappeared in the new concepts of childhood and sexual violence articulated in and around New York City's courtrooms.

The Act of Violence on a
Child of Tender Years

Nine-year-old Jane Gardner must almost have reached the entrance to her school, at 150th Street and Tinton Avenue, when she heard the man call out. He was in the hallway of a building across the street. Identified later as a twenty-seven-year-old driver named Walter Bailey, the man told her that he could not see very well, and asked if she could read him the names under the bells. She did so, but the name Bailey said he was seeking was not on the list. At his request, Jane then asked a woman across the street if she knew who lived in the building. When she said she did not, Bailey asked Jane to come with him to another house on the street in order to continue the search. When the list of names in the hallway again did not include the one he sought, Bailey suggested that they go down into the basement to find the janitor. There was no one in the basement, which gave Bailey the opportunity to pick Jane up, lay her down on a box, and take down her drawers. He then unbuttoned his trousers, leaned over her and, as her affidavit put it, "pushed something between her legs and against her privates. It hurt her and she began to cry." At this point, Bailey heard a noise in the yard, and after instructing Jane to wait where she was, he left the basement. Instead, Jane went upstairs, where she met a woman in the hallway. Still in tears, she told the woman, and two other tenants from the building, who joined them on the street, what Bailey had done. After searching for him without success, they took Jane to her school and reported to the principal what she had told them.[1]

Anita Lanza, another nine-year-old girl, was assaulted closer to home. Sometime about 1 June 1886, she was playing on the stairs of her building at 37 Crosby Street. At around six o'clock in the evening, another tenant, Raffaele Nicolini, took hold of her and carried her to his room. Once there, he sat Anita on his lap, pulled up her clothes, and, as her affidavit stated, "pulled out his penis, put it in her privates and kept it there for a little while." She tried to scream, but he stopped her. Afterward, Anita fell sick with a vaginal discharge. When it did not go away, she told her mother what had happened.[2]

These examples are typical of the sexual assaults on young girls in late-nineteenth-century Manhattan. When approached by their assailants, just as many girls were close to home, in hallways, bathrooms, and yards, and within apartments, as girls were playing or walking in the street.[3] Most assaults took place in basements, accessible but out-of-sight spaces that offered seclusion and protected the identity of the men. Men's apartments represented the next most common location. Rooms offered men even greater privacy than did basements, but they made identification easier. Less frequently, men assaulted girls in the hallways or on the roofs of apartment buildings, risking discovery by janitors and tenants. Men often persuaded girls to accompany them to these spaces by requesting help, as did Walter Bailey, although most asked them to run errands. Girls agreed to help strangers as readily as they did men they knew—neighbors, boarders, employees of their parents, and even relatives—whom they had often previously assisted with child care, errands, or other household tasks.[4] Other men, such as Raffaele Nicolini, did not go to that trouble, calling to girls to come with them or simply taking them by the hand and leading them, or picking them up and carrying them.[5] Only a few men found it necessary, in order to secure a girl's cooperation, to offer her money, or gifts like candy, or thread and buttons, or the opportunity to see something special.[6]

Although the rhetoric of the New York Society for the Prevention of Cruelty to Children (NYSPCC) recognized no divisions within childhood, deeming all those under sixteen years of age as having the same nature, in practice these crimes against young girls were treated differently from other sex offenses against children. The law, working-class communities, and jurors regarded young girls as distinct from boys and older girls. Those distinctions within childhood formed part of the statutes that the NYSPCC undertook to enforce. The definition of rape as an act of sexual intercourse with a female ensured that boys would not be treated in the same way as girls. The law also distinguished young girls from girls who were between ten and sixteen years old. Any act of sexual intercourse with a girl younger than ten years of age was rape, whereas when an older female was involved, only acts in a limited range of circumstances were defined as rape.[7] After 1887, when the New York State Legislature raised the age of consent to sixteen years, that distinction disappeared from the rape statute, only to be restored, by another means, in 1892. In that year, adopting an amendment proposed by the NYSPCC and purity reformers, legislators created two degrees of rape, a lesser offense based on the age of consent and a more severely punished offense that included "the act of violence on a child of tender years." That form of rape was defined as an act of sexual intercourse with a female when "by reason of mental or physical weakness, or immaturity, or any bodily ailment, she does not offer resistance."[8] By virtue of an appellate court decision in 1852, which ruled that the state's incest statute applied only to acts that involved mutual consent, the definition encompassed acts committed by male relatives as well as unrelated men.[9]

While the legal definitions of rape and incest identified a group of children, they did not determine who would be included in it. The law's promoters described the victim as a "child of tender years," but the actual statue included no reference to age. NYSPCC rhetoric presented all those younger than sixteen years of age as possessing the immaturity to which the law did make reference. In practice, however, the law was applied only to cases involving girls ten years of age and younger, whose small size indicated obvious physical weakness, and who had not yet reached puberty, and consequently were mentally weak in the sense of lacking sexual knowledge and understanding.[10] Although the NYSPCC sought to extend the law's purview to include girls in their teens, the group treated most unambiguously as children was essentially the same group previously encompassed by the old age-of-consent criterion, those ten years of age and younger. Moreover, despite their shared concern to protect these young girls, the NYSPCC and the New Yorkers who served on juries did not perceive them in the same way. For the Society, physical immaturity was enough to define a girl as a child. Jurors, however, also expected a child to lack understanding, a trait that revealed itself in passive behavior and the use of "childish" language. Thus, when jurors confronted a girl in court, they listened to her as well as looked at her; and they paid more attention to what they heard than to what they saw, and little, if any, to her age.

In June 1891, the playmates of a four-year-old girl sought out her father to tell him that a man they did not know had just taken her into a cellar. He rushed to investigate and, on finding the pair, attacked the man, Patrick Kennedy. As the father hurried his daughter home, a crowd of the family's neighbors pursued Kennedy, "shouting, pushing and howling at each other in their attempt to get at [him]," according to the *Morning Journal* reporter at the scene, and crying all the while, "Lynch the fiend! I'll get the rope! Let me at him! I'll kill him!" The commotion attracted a police officer, who, as soon as he had dragged Kennedy away from the infuriated mob, took him to the scene of the alleged assault to confront the witnesses, and then to the local station house. While this was happening, a crowd was following, growing to three or four hundred strong, "so large as to almost block the street." "Women as well as men assail[ed] [Kennedy] with their tongues" and bombarded him with sticks and stones. At one point the girl's mother pushed her way through the crowd, struck Kennedy several times in the face, tore several clumps of hair from his head, and "denounced him . . . in unmeasured terms," all to the cheers of the crowd.[11]

This was not the only reported occasion on which working-class New Yorkers responded violently to crimes against young girls. The district attorney's scrapbooks contain a number of newspaper accounts, most from the 1880s and 1890s, describing the behavior of crowds roused to violence by charges that a man had raped a small girl.[12] New York City's press clearly seized on such outbursts, seeing in them an opportunity to embellish the middle-class image of the working class as violent, lawless, and uncivilized, with the women as vicious and foul-mouthed as any man. Press accounts presented the crowds as mobs, driven by unrestrained passion and pursuing vengeance rather than the maintenance of law and order. Setting the tone, the headlines gave prominence to lynching, the most familiar symbol of extralegal justice. "'LYNCH HIM,' CRIED THE MOB," read the headline in one newspaper; "POLICE FIGHT MOB TO PREVENT LYNCHING" trumpeted another.[13] But press reports hinted that such outrage was not entirely indiscriminate. In describing the girl that Patrick Kennedy assaulted as "the neighborhood pet," the *Morning Journal*'s correspondent suggested that the immaturity of the victim, and the helplessness that went with that condition, played a role in stirring the community to action.[14] The city's neighborhoods rarely responded in this way to crimes against older girls or women.[15] Other forms of injury to young children, however, did incite communities to act. In the first decades of the twentieth century, for instance, crowds set upon drivers who accidentally killed children in the streets. The deaths of adults, however, did not prompt so intense a response.[16]

It was not only when New Yorkers were swept up in an angry crowd that they paid particular attention to young girls. Individual witnesses, typically janitors, who in the course of their work came across assaults taking place in hallways and cellars, also reacted, intervening without apparent equivocation and bringing men before the authorities.[17] Underpinning these reactions was a practice of watching young girls and of following men in the company of girls. One woman took note when she heard a male neighbor call to a five-year-old girl playing in the yard. She watched as he showed her a coin and then took her into his room. She followed, and listened, and when she heard the girl cry out, she began hitting and kicking the man's door. There was no response, but she stayed outside the room; and when the door opened, and the man pushed the girl out, she tried to grab him. Perhaps because such awareness of the dangers children faced, and the efforts made to protect them, did not fit the NYSPCC's picture of working-class communities, the agent who prepared the brief in this case omitted any mention of the woman's actions, including only her account of what she had seen the man do.[18]

There is some evidence that sexual acts with young girls had not always prompted such emphatic reactions. Historians Christine Stansell and Marybeth Hamilton Arnold found a more ambivalent, suspicious response in New York City prior to the Civil War. In a case from 1816, for example, a male lodger heard his landlord's ten-year-old niece cry out and saw another lodger having intercourse with her, but he reacted with indecision instead of outrage. After watching for several minutes, he decided to dress and inform the landlord rather than intervene.[19] His uncertain reaction and the defense of such behavior as "a legitimate and benign, if slightly illicit, form of play"—offered not only by accused rapists but also by New Yorkers who witnessed their acts—led Stansell to argue that "men's erotic attention to girls . . . was not a discrete and pathological phenomenon, but a practice that existed on the fringes of 'normal' male sexuality."[20] Late-nineteenth-century reactions, by contrast, suggest that sexual activity with young girls now appeared both distinctive and more pathological, reflecting a sharpened awareness of the differences between children and adults, a recognition of their incommensurate sexual natures. It is significant in this regard that when New Yorkers paid attention to endangered or assaulted girls, and reacted to their victimization, they were responding to what they saw. A girl's small stature and physical immaturity connoted a greater degree of vulnerability than it had early in the nineteenth century.

Despite the attention paid to young girls, most sexual assaults went unobserved. It was the physical signs and marks that a sexual act left on a girl's body that brought most cases to the notice of parents and the legal system. The role of bodily signs in prompting the report of sexual assault is peculiar to cases that involved young children. Marks and injuries inflicted on older girls and adult women offered evidence to support a charge of rape, but they rarely instigated it. A young girl's silence heightened the importance of bodily signs. Only just over one in ten girls followed Jane Gardner in immediately telling someone she had been assaulted.[21] Some later explained that they had remained silent because their assailants had threatened to kill them if they told anyone.[22] Others, including Anita Lanza, claimed to have said nothing out of fear of their parents' reaction. Despite such expressions of shame, many girls did not seem to understand what had happened to them, or at least did not understand it as something significant enough to tell their parents about. They judged their experiences in terms of the hurt, the physical injury, they suffered; a fleeting experience of pain did not warrant reporting. If, on the other hand, the pain or discomfort persisted, a girl would tell her mother about it.[23] More often, a mother noticed the pain before her daughter brought it to her attention, and then questioned the girl about the cause of it.

If a mother found her daughter's genitals not only sore and inflamed but also bleeding, she showed little hesitation in going to the police to report that the girl had been assaulted.[24] More often, she found a vaginal discharge, which, unlike bleeding, was not a clear sign of sexual assault. In the cases that made it into the legal system, working-class parents investigated the causes of the discharge themselves. Even when, after her condition was discovered, a girl told her parents what had happened, the parents were not always prepared to rely entirely on what the girl said; at the least, they wanted to discover the nature of the injuries before they decided what to do. Nor were they prepared to let the NYSPCC conduct the investigation for them (as the parents would have known, the Society employed its own doctors). When Frances Flannery discovered that her seven-year-old sister Mary was suffering from a discharge, she considered attributing it to "chafing." But, uncertain about her judgment, she decided to consult a neighbor, who thought the discharge resulted from an "attempt to wrong the child." Still not certain, Frances took Mary to a doctor. He diagnosed the discharge as the product of venereal disease and, after Mary finally described what had happened to her, urged Frances to report the case to the NYSPCC, which she then did.[25] Although Frances's decision to turn first to a woman neighbor before going to a physician suggests that medical expertise did not enjoy unchallenged authority in working-class communities, it was increasingly common for working-class families to regard doctors as being able to authoritatively read bodily signs.

Part of the importance of bleeding as a sign of sexual assault was that it was seen as indicating a ruptured hymen. In this regard, New Yorkers did not see any difference between the body of a prepubescent girl and that of an adult. "The vital point of interest to [parents]," as Gurney Williams, a police surgeon in Philadelphia put it, "is the question, has or has not the child been entered? Is she still a virgin?"[26] In the cases that appear in the legal system, the doctor did find the hymen ruptured; when he found it intact, many New Yorkers judged a girl to not be sufficiently harmed to warrant recourse to the law.[27]

Based on the numerous instances in the district attorney's case files in which a physician played a key role in the reporting of a sexual assault, it might appear that the medical profession's growing expert status contributed to the legal system's increased concern with child victims. However, doctors often betrayed the trust that parents placed in their knowledge and ability to read a child's body. In 1894, William Travis Gibb, who for over twenty-five years performed medical examinations on children for the NYSPCC, complained that most doctors treated cases of vaginal discharges in children without inquiring about the cause, which they assumed to be vaginitis, thereby allowing indecent assaults on children to go unreported.[28] Doctors' ready assumption that a discharge was vaginitis grew out of their belief that "bad diet, uncleanliness, scrofuloustaint, and epidemic influences" made the condition common in the children of the poor.[29] Until the 1890s, as the voluminous discussions of the topic in medical jurisprudence textbooks attest, doctors had great difficulty in reliably distinguishing the discharges produced by venereal disease from those resulting from vaginitis.[30] Even after bacteriological examinations made it possible to identify gonorrhea, doctors were not always prepared to attribute its presence to sexual activity, particularly in the case of middle-class girls, because such a diagnosis would have pointed to incest. Instead, they developed the concept of "innocent" infection and attributed the presence of gonorrhea to bad sanitation, along with unclean bathrooms and toilet seats, rather than to sexual violence.[31]

NYSPCC officers and assistant district attorneys (ADAS) took the complaints made by New Yorkers and turned them into cases, shaping them into a form they judged would allow them to win a conviction. What made a case compelling was dictated by the law and by jurors' understandings of the crime. Those two frameworks were related, but they did not precisely overlap, creating a complex tangle that prosecutors had to negotiate if they wished to steer a case through the legal process successfully. The role of NYSPCC officers in that work, visible in the trial briefs they prepared for ADAS, centered on the victim's story. A striking turn of phrase used by an agent in a brief prepared in 1916 captured what their work involved. "She tells in her own way," he wrote, "how he opened her drawers, took her on his lap, put his finger into her privates, and then tried to force his penis into her privates until he was interrupted by her father's entrance."[32] The agent's statement highlights the point that the way a girl told her story was not the way that an NYSPCC officer recorded it. Her statements provided the details, but the emphases, structure, and much of the language came from the NYSPCC officer. In the brief, he summarized the girl's statements in a form that he thought jurors would recognize as an account of a rape. When a case went to trial, the ADA not only had to present a girl's story in that form, shaping her testimony with his questions; he also had to be concerned with the girl herself. In a courtroom, how she testified was as important as what she said in determining whether a jury would see her as a child victim. Jurors focused particular attention on a girl's language.

In the brief prepared for the ADA prosecuting Raffaele Nicolini for the rape of nine-year-old Anita Lanza, the NYSPCC officer handling the case offered the following summary of her statement: "The prisoner seized hold of witness and carried her in his arms to his room in said premises . . . After he had brought her into the room, he sat on a chair, took her on his lap, pulled up her clothes (she had no drawers on that day), pulled out his penis, put it in her privates and kept it there for a little while. She tried to scream but he would not let her. He did not give her any money."[33] This brief is typical in casting the defendant as the actor and the girl as acted upon—picked up, carried, having her clothes lifted, and her body penetrated. Admittedly, the advantages of size, strength, and authority that adult men had over young girls like Anita certainly left the latter little scope for struggle, but clearly the concern of NYSPCC officers preparing briefs was to emphasize the girls' passivity. If Anita had been an adult, such passivity would have been treated as evidence of her consent; to establish that she had not consented, a woman had to resist to the limit of her physical ability. But the law defined an act of intercourse with a girl who was mentally or physically weak or immature as rape when she did not resist. The existence in New York law of second-degree rape, a lesser offense based on the age of consent, helped ensure that a girl had to be passive in order to be seen as a genuine victim. The law defined any act of intercourse with an underage girl as second-degree rape, in effect recognizing that the girl might consent and denying her the ability to do so. If a young girl had resisted in any way and failed to prevent the act of intercourse from taking place, her actions would have been seen as consent, and would have brought her within the definition of second-degree rape. Only when she did nothing at all did she fall within the ambit of first-degree rape.

The law required more than simple passivity. An act of sexual intercourse with a girl who did not resist was rape, *provided* that she was physically or mentally weak or immature. Any of those traits identified a girl as a child in the eyes of the law. Prosecutors perceived jurors, however, as believing that childhood required all of those characteristics. The young girls involved in such prosecutions were small, and thus physically immature, but jurors did not see in their appearance a guarantee that they possessed "mental weakness," the ignorance and innocence of a child. Passivity, in addition to establishing the behavior required to fit a girl to the law, could also go some way toward satisfying jurors that she was the kind of girl provided for in the law. To encourage jurors to see a girl's passivity as a sign of her lack of understanding, NYSPCC officers emphasized particular details when they summarized a girl's statement.

No brief failed to make specific mention of a girl's underwear. Anita Lanza wore none when she was assaulted, which meant that underwear had no place in her statement. Nonetheless, the NYSPCC agent made parenthetical mention of her underwear when he summarized her statement, implying that the story would be missing a crucial element without such a reference. Jane Gardner did wear underwear, and the agent who summarized her statement took care to mention that Walter Bailey had removed that item of clothing.[34] Once a girl's underwear was taken off, the encounter assumed an unambiguously sexual character. If she removed her own underwear, that action was taken as indicating her understanding and consent. The agent's summary also made specific mention of the fact that Anita Lanza screamed; what was significant here was precisely when she had screamed, and what that implied about why she did. The brief prepared in the case of Jane Gardner makes that significance more explicit. When Bailey "pushed something between her legs and against her privates," the NYSPCC officer took care to note, "it hurt her and she began to cry."[35] According to prevailing beliefs about rape, an adult woman screamed when a man attempted to rape her because she understood what he meant to do and sought to prevent it. A child, lacking such understanding, cried out only after a man had sexually penetrated her, in response to the physical effects of what he had done. Immediately after the mention of Anita's scream, the NYSPCC agent stated that the perpetrator "did not give her any money." Although adults dispensed gifts in daily life to garner children's affections, if a man gave a girl anything in the context of a sexual assault, that would have indicated that the girl understood sexual intercourse to have an exchange value, thus casting her in the role of a prostitute. New Yorkers were familiar with the child prostitute from the city's streets and were constantly reminded by reformers that a girl "young in years" could be "advanced in vice."[36] That Anita received nothing confirmed her innocence.

At trial, jurors looked for a girl's physical immaturity, and listened for signs of her mental immaturity and innocence. Girls aged ten years and younger appeared physically immature, so prosecutors did not have to concern themselves with what jurors saw. Of primary concern to ADAS was the need to ensure that what jurors heard fitted their understanding of childhood. The ADA's first objective was to shape a girl's testimony so that it emphasized her passivity, and this the prosecutor accomplished by structuring his questions to highlight the actions of the defendant. It was easier for ADAS to take this approach with young girls than with older females. They could not ask women leading questions, questions that suggested the answer they sought, whereas judges allowed, as one put it in 1911, that in the case of a young girl "it is entirely proper, in view of the youth of the witness, to lead her a little bit."[37] The result was exchanges such as this, from a trial in 1891:

Q.: What did he do when he came there, when you first saw him?
A.: He came in the closet.
Q.: He came into the closet?
A.: Yes sir.
Q.: Did he say anything to you?
A.: No sir.
Q.: Did you say anything to him?
A.: Yes sir.
Q.: Tell us what you said to him?
A.: I wanted to push him away and said "go away."
Q.: Did you try to push him away?
A.: Yes sir, and he was too strong for me.
Q.: Did he take hold of you?
A.: Yes sir.
Q.: Did you see him turn the key in the door?
A.: Yes sir.

By the Court. [Questions from the bench.]

Q.: Tell me what he did to you?

A.: He took out his privates and put it into mine.

Q.: What else did he do?

A.: He stayed there about half an hour and then he went out.

Q.: Now go on, what else?

A.: And then me and my two cousins went out.[38]

While the ADA twice questioned this girl about what she said and did when the defendant assaulted her, he buried the answers to those questions in a narrative about "what he did." When the trial judge picked up the questioning of the girl, he continued, with some tenacity, to pursue the issue of what the defendant did to her.

It mattered to jurors what language girls used when they testified, particularly when they described sexual intercourse. To be regarded as a child, it was necessary that a girl "not know the meaning of the wrong done her," as one ADA put it during a particularly florid summation.[39] The girl's language was scrutinized for signs showing how well she understood what had happened to her.[40] How she spoke could overshadow how she looked. When a girl spoke like a child, that could have a visible impact on those listening to her. A reporter for the *Sun* described how one girl "told her fearful story in such a simple, childlike way that before she finished half the people in court had tear-filled eyes."[41] If a girl used language that contradicted her childish appearance, the impact could be just as powerful, if less visible. Writing in the *Philanthropist*, a social purity journal, in July 1907, in response to calls for sex education, a mother dramatized that impact. "I looked at my little girl of seven, and I said to myself: 'Think of that child knowing anything on that subject. It is impossible.' But my husband said: 'Try it out. Question Ethel very carefully and see.' I did, and then it came my turn to be horrified! She told me a story of practices and talk in her primary class that were unspeakable. And my little girl of seven, my child, sir, had heard and knew—not the truth, but the most unspeakable truths!"[42] Her eyes told her one thing about the character of her daughter, that she was a "little girl" and therefore innocent; her ears conveyed a different message, one that irretrievably recast her impression of the girl's character.

What this mother, and judges and jurors, expected of an innocent child was that she would speak in a manner different from that of an adult, that she would use vague, simple, and euphemistic language.[43] Girls typically testified vaguely that the defendant "did something to me" or "done bad," or else they used the more descriptive, but sexually inexplicit, phrases "he took out his thing and put it in me" or "he put his privates in my privates." For prosecutors seeking to make a case, there was a tension between their fear of compromising such language and their need to clearly establish that the offense had taken place. As one doctor complained, the less descriptive phrases made it unclear whether a girl was describing sexual intercourse or simply a hand being put up her dress.[44] ADAS sought to negotiate that tension, first, by asking leading questions that provided girls with language that was appropriate, yet still had a clear meaning for jurors, and, second, by convincing judges to allow girls to point to the parts of the body that they referred to in their testimony. An ADA pursued the former approach in a trial in 1916:

Q. You say you went into the back room?
A. Yes.
Q. And then he pushed you on the couch; is that right?
A. Yes.
Q. And then he unbuttoned his pants?
A. Yes, sir.
Q. After he unbuttoned his pants, did he do anything more?
A. Yes, sir.
Q. What did he do after he unbuttoned his pants?
A. He put it in me.
Q. You mean he put his private parts into your privates?
A. Yes, sir.

At this point, the defense attorney, Solomon Sufrin, objected to the form of the questioning. In an attempt to frustrate the ADA's strategy, Sufrin repeatedly argued that, because of the way in which the prosecutor had interrogated the girl, "she personally did not say a thing."[45] Defense attorneys also strove to thwart prosecutors by eliciting, or drawing attention to, instances in which girls used "bad language," as in words such as "prick," or "adult language," as in references to "sexual intercourse" or "connection." They argued that such language revealed understanding, with the suggestive nature of bad language also arousing sensuality, undermining the hierarchy of reason over desire, and thereby contributing to the creation of an immoral character.[46] That argument drew strength from a middle-class predisposition to believe that girls who grew up in immigrant, working-class homes and communities, as those who appeared in child rape cases invariably did, fell into "degenerate habits and associations" at such a young age that, as Jane Addams put it, they "cannot be said to have 'gone wrong' at any one moment because they have never been in the right path even of innocent childhood."[47] No matter how young they were, in other words, working-class girls were unlikely to be children.

A further tension surrounded what a girl said in court. While the display of a lack of understanding was necessary for a girl to be seen as falling within the scope of the rape law, it could also lead to her testimony being given little or no weight as evidence. Since the seventeenth century, the growing recognition of the distinctions between childhood and adulthood had resulted in the giving of less weight to what children said. Courts initially continued to allow a child to testify, but they discounted her testimony when it came time to weigh the evidence. Later, they began to prevent those younger than ten, or sometimes fourteen, years of age from testifying at all.[48] In the case of turn-of-the-century New York, the Code of Criminal Procedure required judicial examination of all children twelve years of age and younger; only if a judge determined that a child had sufficient intelligence could she testify. The judge then had to determine whether the child could give sworn testimony, a decision that hinged on whether a girl understood the nature of an oath.[49]

To ascertain their level of understanding, judges asked girls about their families and schooling and about what would happen to them if they lied. In trials, judges decreed that girls as young as five years of age had sufficient intelligence to testify. However, such girls could not give sworn testimony. When girls as young as seven years old answered that they would go to hell if they lied, they were allowed to give sworn testimony.[50] For a defendant to be convicted, unsworn testimony had to be supported by other evidence, a requirement that imposed a heavy evidentiary burden on prosecutors and made winning a conviction difficult. After 1886, less was at stake when a girl swore an oath in New York than elsewhere in the United States. In that year, the state legislature enacted a law requiring that the female complainant's testimony had to be corroborated by other evidence before a man could be convicted of rape, seduction, or abduction.[51] Even if a girl could give sworn testimony, the corroboration requirement ensured that her words would not provide sufficient evidence to convict her assailant.

At first glance, the corroboration requirement seemed to aggregate girls and women, to break down the distinctive treatment of young girls, which, as I have shown, emerged in the process of prosecution. However, it is only when the corroboration requirement is considered in isolation that it appears to apply without distinction to prosecutions involving adult women and those involving young girls. When the requirement is read alongside the rape law, differences surface. The "act of violence on a child of tender years" did not need to involve all the elements of the definitions of rape that applied to adult women. As a result, corroborating all the material facts of the crime was a lesser burden in cases that involved young girls. Because all acts of sexual intercourse with a prepubescent girl constituted rape, prosecutors only had to find additional evidence that an act of intercourse had taken place and that the defendant had perpetrated it. They did not have to furnish evidence that it had taken place without the girl's consent.

Medical evidence offered a ready source of confirmation that an act of sexual intercourse had taken place, notwithstanding the uncertainty in which courts tried to garb the testimony of physicians. Examinations of prepubescent girls involved in rape cases typically found an inflamed and excoriated vulva, not the ruptured hymen and dilated vagina typically found in examinations of pubescent girls and adult women, a difference that reminded jurors of a girl's physical immaturity. Outside the legal system, most doctors who found those signs concluded without hesitation that a girl had been sexually penetrated. Inside the legal system, they could not offer that opinion. Since doctors were, as one court put it, "constrained to admit, what any person of ordinary intelligence knows without the aid of expert testimony, that there are other causes which might have produced such inflammation," judges reasoned that medical training did not provide the certain knowledge required of an expert. As nonexpert witnesses, doctors were only permitted to describe the conditions they found, to state "what effect might result from a rape," and to answer questions about what might have caused the conditions they described. Judges asserted that "it was for the jury to determine whether the inflammation which the [physician] testified to was the result of rape or some other cause."[52]

While doctors with limited experience of the legal system struggled to conform to these rulings, those who routinely examined girls for the NYSPCC developed a protocol for presenting the results of an examination of a girl's body that revealed evidence of sexual intercourse.[53] They testified to having found "signs of penetration of her genital organs by some blunt instrument."[54] On rare occasions, a defense attorney attempted to exploit that ambiguous language by suggesting that the signs of penetration had been produced by masturbation.[55] But jurors gave no indication that they took seriously the possibility that the "blunt instrument" was anything other than a penis.[56]

A girl's testimony as to the identity of the man responsible was more difficult to corroborate. Appellate courts held that only eyewitness testimony or circumstantial evidence could confirm her identification. Such evidence was not generally available in cases involving young children. In just over half of the cases in which prosecutors secured indictments from the grand jury, they either presented no corroborative evidence whatsoever or depended on evidence of the opportunity to commit the crime, or on a form of evidence peculiar to cases involving children, namely, a girl's affliction with venereal disease.[57] New York's higher courts expressly stated that neither opportunity nor the presence of venereal disease had any value as corroboration.[58] Initially, some appellate court decisions did treat opportunity as corroboration, holding that not to do so would make the requirement so "exacting [that] in most cases [it] would be impossible of fulfillment."[59] But ultimately the state's higher courts denied to evidence of opportunity any value as corroboration, on the grounds that such evidence was so easily obtained that it would "practically nullify the protection to which by this section of the law a defendant is entitled."[60] In regard to venereal disease, in 1913, the New York State Court of Appeals held that evidence that a girl suffered from gonorrhea was "not evidence of intercourse with any particular man." It made no difference that the defendant also had the disease. "Gonorrhea," the judges insisted, "may be contracted without intercourse; therefore, it is of less value, if such be possible, than pregnancy as corroborative evidence."[61]

Prosecutors were less deterred by the corroboration requirement when the victim was a young girl than when she was an adult woman. In light of the "facts, and the melancholy circumstances," of cases involving young girls, the approach of the NYSPCC, as Elbridge Gerry described it, was that "all doubtful cases of this character should be resolved by the verdict of a jury."[62] The district attorney's office was not prepared to go quite so far in testing the corroboration requirement as was the Society. Securing an indictment was one thing: it allowed ADAS to try to negotiate a guilty plea, which they managed to do in four cases in my sample where they had insufficient evidence, including one in which they had no evidence to corroborate the girl's identification of the defendant.[63] Continuing with the prosecution when a plea bargain failed was another matter. On three occasions when they had insufficient corroborative evidence, ADAS dismissed the indictment. However, those cases amounted to only one indictment in every sixteen. By contrast, they declined to prosecute one in every four men indicted for the rape of an adult woman.[64]

Over time, ADAS' experiences with judges and jurors gave them good reason to go through with a trial, notwithstanding their inability to find corroborative evidence. At trial, it was the judge's responsibility to determine, as a question of law, whether evidence was corroborative in nature.[65] In the fourteen trials for which I have evidence in the period 1886–1926, the only evidence the ADA presented to corroborate a girl's identification of the defendant was either evidence of opportunity or evidence that the girl suffered from venereal disease. In just one of the fourteen trials, an incest case, in which the defendant was the victim's uncle, and which relied on evidence of opportunity, did the judge follow appellate court rulings that this evidence did not constitute corroboration; he therefore directed the jury to acquit the defendant.[66]

While judges determined whether evidence had legal standing as corroboration, whether that evidence was sufficient to satisfy the requirement of corroboration was a question of fact, not law, and therefore up to the jury to decide.[67] Jurors consistently decided that evidence of the opportunity to commit a child rape was not alone sufficient to support a conviction. They acquitted the defendant in all four cases in my sample that relied on that evidence as corroboration.[68] Proof that a girl was suffering from venereal disease, however, was to them more compelling. In two of the five trials in which the ADA relied solely on such evidence, the defendants were convicted, Raffaele Nicolini being one of them. In a third case, the jury could not agree on a verdict, indicating that at least some of its members were prepared to convict the defendant.[69] Juries also convicted defendants in two other cases that relied on a combination of evidence of venereal disease and of opportunity.[70]

Evidence that the victim suffered from venereal disease was almost exclusively a feature of cases involving girls — as opposed to women — suggesting that its particular power as evidence came in part from its intrusion into childhood. To be sure, medical evidence of any kind was compelling, as we saw in regard to signs of penetration. Despite the efforts of judges to deny it, by the late nineteenth century, medicine had begun to assume the "privileged status in the hierarchy of belief" that it now occupies, notwithstanding the somewhat uncertain nature of medical knowledge.[71] Juries appeared unconcerned about the possibility that a girl could have contracted venereal disease by some means other than sexual contact, so long as the defendant shared her condition. The fact that evidence of his affliction commonly came in the form of a refusal to submit to a medical examination — one could be performed only if the defendant gave permission — can only have added weight to the corroborative power of a girl's condition; a refusal would appear to be an admission of guilt as well.[72] But this evidence also had a symbolic dimension. The presence of disease linked with sexuality in a child's body was not so much an illness as a form of corruption. A child's body was imagined as pure, as a blossom or bud, and venereal disease corrupted that purity: it introduced sexuality, in the sense that it made a girl aware of her sexual organs in a way that contradicted the ignorance required of an innocent child. The body of a girl afflicted with venereal disease thus precisely mirrored the corruption of innocence that middle-class Americans saw resulting from a child's exposure to sexuality. That which was written on her body was, they feared, that which had happened to her nature. Whatever its formal legal status, evidence that a girl suffered from venereal disease carried significant weight with juries because it perfectly fitted the crime as they understood it.

Prosecutors won one further conviction without having provided evidence to corroborate the girl's testimony, but in this instance the outcome had little to do with childhood or with how the jury saw the victim. The circumstances of the case were no different from those of the cases I have already discussed; the defendant, however, was far from typical. Ten-year-old Elsie Russell, who, since her race is not identified in the case file, was almost certainly black, testified that Thomas Lawrence, a nineteen-year-old African American elevator operator, approached her on East Ninety-seventh street and offered her 50 cents to carry a small bag one block to a room. According to the NYSPCC officer's summary of her statement in the brief, when they got to the room Lawrence took Elsie on his lap and put his penis between her legs. When she "commenced to scream from pain," he "put his hand over her mouth and held her"; after she "cried and begged him to let her go home," Lawrence released her, but only after he placed a pistol to her head and threatened to shoot her if she told her mother. Elsie returned home crying and immediately told her mother what had happened. A medical examination found evidence of penetration, but the brief contained no evidence that even placed Lawrence and Elsie together, let alone corroborating her identification of him.[73] However, Lawrence's race provided all the confirmation that the jury needed to convict him. Racist images of African American men as beasts, creatures consumed by a sexual desire that drove them to rape, were well entrenched in whites' minds by the late nineteenth century. They came to the surface even more readily when the victim was white. The NYSPCC superintendent described a case in 1911 as an "aggravated" one simply because it involved "a young colored man . . . and the victim was a white child."[74] In that case, the defendant's conviction was supported by evidence of opportunity and venereal disease, but Lawrence's fate suggests that the verdict likely had as much to do with the color of the defendant's skin.

If the age of the victim had little effect on how juries responded when the defendant was a black man, when he was white it was a different matter. The corroboration requirement reflected a suspicion of females; prosecutors' ability to win convictions with little corroborative evidence suggests that juries were less suspicious of girls than women. That is confirmed by what did not happen in cases involving young girls. There are no cases in which juries acquitted defendants in the face of overwhelming, corroborative, evidence, as happened in prosecutions involving adult women.

In determining the outcome of prosecutions, the jurors, prosecutors, and judges ultimately expressed their attitude toward crimes against young girls. The overall pattern of such outcomes provides the final indication of the distinct status of crimes against young girls. Grand juries indicted a far greater proportion of the men accused of assaulting girls than of those men charged with the rape of an adult woman: almost all when the alleged victim was a child compared with barely half when she was an adult. Trial juries voted to convict in similar proportions, although the evidence was generally far stronger in cases involving adult women.[75] Moreover, juries typically convicted the defendant of rape if the victim was a girl and of a lesser offense if the victim was a woman.[76] As we have seen, ADAS discharged a far smaller proportion of the men indicted in cases involving young girls than they did of the men indicted in cases involving adult women. In my sample, ADAS, NYSPCC agents, and judges, who had to be in agreement for a plea bargain to be effected, accepted only one plea of guilty to a misdemeanor from a defendant charged with an assault on a young girl; all fourteen of the other guilty pleas were for felony offenses. By contrast, one in every three men who pled guilty to an attack on an adult pled to a misdemeanor.[77] Finally, judges handed out longer sentences to men whose victims were girls, something closer to the maximum both for those convicted of rape and for those convicted of lesser offenses.

As the NYSPCC intended, some young girls in New York were clearly brought within the protection of the law, and the men who assaulted them did indeed feel "the iron hand of the law." The Society succeeded in those tasks because its agents were able to align their efforts with the understandings of childhood displayed by the New Yorkers who served on juries and the judges who presided over the city's courts. By emphasizing girls' passivity and lack of understanding, and taking care that girl victims spoke like children, prosecutors ensured that juries and judges did indeed treat physically immature girls as children. However, the Society sought to do much more than protect young girls. It wanted to deal with boys and pubescent girls in the same way, to extend to those groups the same protection from sexual assault by men provided to young girls. In regard to both groups, NYSPCC agents found it more difficult to reconcile the Society's understanding of childhood with the notions of working-class New Yorkers. Efforts to treat boys in the same manner as girls proved to be at odds with a belief that boys were active by nature and not subject to the passivity that typified girls. In the case of pubescent girls, it was their mature appearance, not their character, that obstructed efforts to present them as children. While the NYSPCC's efforts to extend the duration of childhood were ultimately stymied, the Society did in time change how the courts treated both boys and older girls.

The Crime against Nature

It was just after 8:00 A.M. when nine-year-old Peter Williams knocked on the door of the fourth-floor apartment at 313 West Nineteenth Street. He and his eight-year-old brother Alfred were delivering newspapers; their parents owned a confectionery and newspaper store just down the street. John Cantor, a forty-three-year-old singer, opened the door and brought both the newspaper and the boys into the apartment. Cantor put Peter on the bed and, ignoring his struggling, "unbuttoned his trousers, took out the boy's penis, and sucked it." He then gave the boy five cents, before doing the same thing to his brother. When Peter and Alfred left, Cantor told them not to tell their mother what had happened, and to come back again, promising them a new suit of clothes if they did. The boys did not tell their mother and did not return to Cantor's apartment, but, several days later, he came to the family store to ask their twelve-year-old brother Richard to run an errand for him on Ninth Avenue. "Not for a million dollars," Richard declared. After Cantor had left, the boys' mother asked Richard why he had refused to run the errand. He replied that on one occasion on which he had delivered a paper to Cantor's apartment, the man had thrown him on the bed, pulled down his trousers, and "put his thing into [my] behind," afterward promising to take him to the Hippodrome, and warning him not to tell his mother what had occurred. After hearing their brother's story, Peter and Alfred told their mother what Cantor had done to them. She promptly had him arrested.[1]

In circumstances and nature, there was little to distinguish acts that gave rise to charges of sodomy in turn-of-the-century New York City from sexual violence against young girls. Most sexual assaults on boys took place in similar locations and situations, in the victims' own homes, in locations around those homes, such as basements, hallways, and toilets, or in the rooms of their assailants. Boys were also assaulted further from home than young girls, reflecting the greater distances over which they roamed, and the fact that some of those assaulted were older, between eleven and sixteen years of age. Their assailants were adult men, who took advantage of the power they could exert on children.

What distinguished sodomy cases from rape cases was the nature of the sexual act that occurred: anal and oral intercourse, rather than vaginal intercourse. The older label for such acts, the "crime against nature," marked them as nonprocreative, and they were further distinguished by descriptions that almost without fail employed adjectives such as "vile," "filthy," "wicked," and "diabolical." New York's sodomy statute referred to such acts as "the detestable and abominable crime against nature."[2] Notwithstanding this rhetorical effort to distance oral and anal acts from sexual intercourse, those acts formed interchangeable parts of the sexual practices of men involved in relations with girls. In 1901, for example, a fifty-nine-year-old man first tried to have vaginal intercourse with thirteen-year-old Laura Gold, but he could "only get his penis into her private parts a little way." It was only then that he had anal intercourse with her, telling Laura that "she was too small to do it the other way."[3] Men who failed in their attempts to have sexual intercourse with young girls also had girls perform fellatio on them.[4]

Even though many of the men who sexually assaulted girls clearly saw their sexual satisfaction as more important than the act by which that release was achieved, legislators held the opposite opinion. The law was framed to emphasize the act, not who was involved or the circumstances in which it took place. The legal definition of rape encompassed only acts of sexual intercourse. Sexual assaults that involved oral or anal acts were not rape, but sodomy. Whereas the rape law included only acts of sexual intercourse committed in certain circumstances, the sodomy law defined any anal or oral act as a crime, even those that involved no violence or coercion. Moreover, it was just as criminal to "voluntarily submit" to an act of sodomy as it was to perpetrate it. Since the sodomy law made no mention of age, or any provision for immaturity, a child faced the same requirement that an adult did to demonstrate that his or her involvement had been involuntary in order to avoid being treated as an accomplice.

Despite the statute's failure to make special provision for children, in New York City almost all those charged with sodomy had committed acts involving individuals younger than eighteen years of age.[5] The statute had none of the gender specificity of the rape law, declaring that any person could commit sodomy, and that both males and females could have the act perpetrated on them.[6] However, in New York City, gender was a feature of how the law worked. In practice, sodomy was an offense committed by men.[7] Those men targeted boys; three out of every four victims in sodomy cases were males under eighteen years of age.[8]

Prosecutors presented sodomy cases differently from the way they did rape cases. Only some of that divergence is explained by the definition of the crime. Despite the gender blindness of the statute, in New York City's neighborhoods, and in the legal process, boys were treated differently from girls of the same age, who had experienced assaults of a similar nature. Their different treatment was the result not of boys being the same sex as their assailants, but of their masculinity. New Yorkers understood boys, unlike girls, as able to resist their assailants without compromising their status as innocent children. That perception made it easier for prosecutors to present boys to juries and judges as victims rather than accomplices. Exactly what juries heard when they listened to children, and on what basis they, and prosecutors, made their determinations about the outcome of cases, is difficult to reconstruct from the surviving evidence. Trial transcripts for sodomy cases do not survive, and the case files generally contain fewer documents than do files for rape cases. Nonetheless, sodomy prosecutions reveal how New Yorkers' concern with the intrinsic differences between males and females fragmented the singular vision of childhood held by the New York Society for the Prevention of Cruelty to Children. Where the NYSPCC saw children, most New Yorkers saw boys and girls.

"Momma, momma! He tried to take my pants off!" As Joey Cohen screamed these words, he flung himself into the arms of an old apple peddler. A minute or two before, the boy had gone into a hallway with a man, "a bum in moldy, wrinkled clothes, . . . with a rusty yellow face covered with sores," who had offered him a chance to earn a nickel. The man followed Joey out of the hallway, knocking the peddler down as the peddler grabbed at him. The boy's struggles attracted a crowd. A "fat, snub-nosed little Jew in a flannel shirt and cap" hit Joey's assailant on the jaw, and then, after the fleeing man reacted by stabbing him, two Italian laborers, brandishing the shovels they had been using to dig a sewer, barred the assailant's way. The ensuing scene was captured by Mike Gold in his autobiography: "Every one, even the women, kicked, punched and beat with shovels the limp ugly body on the sidewalk. One told the other what this man had done. It turned people insane. If a cop had not arrived, the pervert would have been torn into little bleeding hunks."[9] On this occasion, New Yorkers responded to an attempt to sodomize a child in the same way that they did to an attempted rape. Such outbursts, however, were sufficiently rare that none were reported in the press.

It was not that New Yorkers were unprepared to act, or saw nothing to react to, when faced with a boy threatened by a man. They showed the same willingness to investigate and intervene themselves, without recourse to police, that was evident when girls were assaulted.[10] It was a lack of opportunity, not a lack of inclination, that made such action against men who assaulted boys an infrequent occurrence in New York City. A man with a boy attracted less attention than did one in the company of a girl, and provoked little of the suspicion that marked New Yorkers' response to men in the company of girls. While a man attracted notice whenever he talked or walked with a young girl, one accompanied by a boy drew attention only in certain contexts, or if he had the appearance of "a degenerate." It was around bathrooms that New Yorkers became most suspicious of a man with a boy. A building superintendent, who gave a man with a four-year-old boy the key to the water closet, became suspicious enough to investigate when the man had not returned twenty minutes later. She found him "on his knees on the floor [while] the child was standing on the frame of the closet [with his drawers unbuttoned]."[11] A man's "degenerate" appearance could also trigger concern, although it was police officers rather than community members who responded to that cue.[12]

Just as often, however, it was a matter of simply happening upon the man and the boy in the act, not of following a suspicious-looking adult in the company of a youth.[13] The limited attention that men and boys attracted in the city's streets and neighborhoods at least partly explains the gap between the number of men prosecuted for crimes against boys and the number prosecuted for crimes against girls. More men were charged with sodomy with boys than were accused of sodomy with girls. But 50 percent more were prosecuted for the rape of girls under eleven years of age than were charged with sodomy with boys in that age group, and over forty times more men were accused of the rape of a teenage girl than were charged with sodomizing a teenage boy.[14]

As with child rape, most acts of sodomy went unobserved. This being the case, physical symptoms suffered by children who had been assaulted were crucial in bringing instances of sodomy within the legal system. Oral acts rarely left a physical trace, although one mother was led to question her eleven-year-old son when he returned home "having his cheeks besides his lips covered with what seemed to be human semen."[15] Anal acts, however, could cause children physical injury and produce persistent pain or discomfort that, as in the case of girls who had been raped, attracted the attention of their mothers. On 14 September 1916, David Goldman complained to his mother that he had pains in his bowels and his rectum was sore. On examining him, she discovered that his rectum was inflamed. After applying a cold bandage, she asked him what had caused his injuries, and David related how Michael Tannenbaum had anally penetrated him three times in the last four days. His mother relayed this to the boy's father, who took David to the NYSPCC to report what had happened.[16] New Yorkers saw injuries to the anus as being as clear in meaning as a lacerated and bleeding vagina, and did not take a child to a doctor before reporting an assault.[17] So self-evident a sign of sexual assault were injuries to the anus that when two police officers brought a boy to NYSPCC officer Robert Dimond at the Second District Magistrates' Court, he examined the boy himself, and finding his anus "raw, with a lot of matter exuding from it," he directed the officers to arrest the Chinese laundryman whom the boy had identified as his assailant.[18]

Despite the clear signs left by anal acts, cases of sodomy received relatively little attention from reformers. The NYSPCC's concern with sexual assaults on girls did not distinguish oral and anal acts, its descriptions typically referring to a "criminal assault" and not offering further details, on the grounds that it was "neither necessary or desirable."[19] Sodomy was discussed only in regard to boys, but even here such acts remained very much in the background.[20] The vices that reformers saw threatening boys were those of theft and idleness; sex, the primary danger faced by girls, was considered very much a secondary hazard for boys.[21] Even in discussions of the sexual dangers boys encountered, exposure to female prostitutes received far more attention than did assaults by men or older boys, or "perversion," as such assaults were referred to in re-form writing.[22] But cases of sodomy can be glimpsed. The "Details of Cases" provided to illustrate the NYSPCC's work included a handful of examples of the "brutal and unnatural crime" against young boys, which the Society's super-intendent also referred to as "the most detestable of crimes," "a most heinous crime," and "the vilest of crimes."[23] One undercover child labor investigator in New York City reported that a seventeen-year-old night messenger told him that he and his colleagues were most afraid of "men who try to 'Suck you off.'"[24] The Russell Sage Foundation study of boys on New York's Middle West Side (west of 42nd Street) noted that the neighborhood had "many sexual perverts," who "furnish[ed] an actual menace to the children."[25]

NYSPCC agents and deputy assistant district attorneys emphasized different aspects of sodomy cases than was their practice in handling child rape cases. In the brief prepared for the DADA prosecuting John Cantor for his assaults on the Williams boys, the episode with which this chapter opened, the NYSPCC officer handling the case offered the following summary of nine-year-old Peter's statement: "He seized Peter, put him on the bed, unbuttoned his trousers, took out the boy's penis and sucked it. The boy struggled to get away but the man was too strong for him. When he released the boy the prisoner gave him 5¢. He then took hold of Alfred and said, 'Come.' Alfred said, 'No.' The prisoner said, 'It is very nice; every boy likes it.' He then did the same to Alfred as to Peter."[26] This brief is typical in its attention to both the force employed by the man and the efforts of the boy to resist.[27] The NYSPCC officer displayed a particular interest in the boys' struggle, throwing it into sharp relief by describing, on the one hand, Cantor's actions and, on the other, the boys' efforts to resist them.

This treatment is in stark contrast to the concern of NYSPCC agents to cast a girl as passive, as an object acted upon, that was so evident in their presentation of child rape cases. Yet there is little in the statements of boys to suggest that the quality of men's actions in sodomy cases were sufficiently different to prevent NYSPCC officers from using the same language they used to represent men's actions in child rape cases. Instead, prosecutors' differing presentations of these cases was in part a response to the statute they were employing, that is, the statute relating to sodomy. That law did not make the allowance for age that the rape law did, thus requiring children to actively demonstrate their lack of consent in the manner expected of adults.

In the period before 1927, a handful of states did begin to establish a more age-sensitive response to sexual acts other than vaginal intercourse. Nine states passed laws that dealt with acts other than intercourse and encompassed both boys and girls, while not applying to adults, thereby treating children primarily in terms of their age.[28] This legislation took two forms. Beginning with California in 1901, five states enacted laws that punished anyone who committed "any lewd or lascivious act . . . with the body, or any part or member thereof, of a child under the age of fourteen years, with the intent of arousing, appealing to, or gratifying the lust or passions or sexual desires of such person or such child."[29] A second group of states punished anyone who took "indecent and improper liberties with the person of a child" under sixteen years of age.[30] Some uncertainty existed as to the precise nature of the acts referred to in these laws, with the result that convictions for both categories of sex crime were sometimes overturned on the grounds that the laws were too vague.[31] Whatever act the new laws referred to, it was not sodomy; as such, these pieces of legislation supplemented rather than replaced existing laws. That they were adopted in such an ambiguous form, and in only a handful of states, indicates that, while turn-of-the-century articulations of the new ideas of childhood and development could provide the basis for an age-specific view of sexual violence, they did not create a strong imperative to let go of the long-held gendered visions of children and sexuality, as reflected in rape and sodomy statutes.

In New York, as in most states, it remained the case until the 1920s that sodomy was the only offense that covered acts other than vaginal intercourse and that could be applied to men who sexually assaulted boys. Until the late nineteenth century, New York's sodomy law did not specify what act it punished. Instead, as was common throughout the United States, it simply prohibited "the detestable and abominable crime against nature, with mankind or with beast," hinting, by going on to specify that "any penetration, however slight, is sufficient to complete the crime," that the act referred to was anal intercourse. By 1892, as a result of two amendments promoted by the NYSPCC, New York's law declared to be guilty of sodomy any "person" who "carnally knows in any manner any animal or bird;" or "carnally knows any male or female person by the anus or by or with the mouth;" or "voluntarily submits to such carnal knowledge." Elaborated in this way, the crime of sodomy included acts by and against females as well as males and encompassed the oral acts of fellatio and cunnilingus, as well as anal intercourse.[32] Both the mention of specific acts and the inclusion of oral acts in addition to anal acts became features of sodomy laws throughout the United States in the early twentieth century, either by legislation or judicial decision.[33] However, it was the final clause of New York's statute that caused the prosecutors to present sodomy cases differently from rape cases. That clause allowed for a child to be treated as a victim.[34] But the status of being a victim was contingent on a child's demonstrating that he or she had not consented to the act, rather than, as it was in rape prosecutions, on his or her age or immaturity. This construction was the same as that applying to adult women in the rape law, but it did not have the same effect of narrowing the range of circumstances to which the law applied. While a woman's consent was a defense against a charge of rape, a man was guilty of sodomy even if the person on whom he had committed the act had consented to it.

However, the criminalizing of voluntary submission did restrict prosecutions in a way that those who drafted the law had not intended. In 1902, the New York State Supreme Court ruled that the amended statute made any person who submitted to an act of sodomy an accomplice. The Code of Criminal Procedure stipulated that an accomplice's testimony did not provide the basis for a conviction. As a result, the court's decision meant that, when prosecutors failed to establish that a child had not consented, they had to provide, before a man could be convicted of sodomy, "such other evidence as tends to connect the defendant with the commission of the crime." This corroboration requirement, however, was not as demanding as the one the legislature applied to rape, seduction, and abduction. Courts required less conclusive evidence to meet the corroboration test in the case of accomplice testimony, and prosecutors could avoid that test entirely by establishing that a victim's submission had been involuntary.[35]

In dwelling on the force employed by a man, and a child's efforts to resist, prosecutors were responding to the requirement imposed by the sodomy statute to establish involuntary submission. However, in cases that involved girls, they failed to sustain that approach. Only in cases involving boys did NYSPCC officers highlight a child's resistance. When they summarized a girl's statement, NYSPCC officers followed the approach of casting the man's actions as forcible, but, as in rape cases, they presented the girl as a passive object. Fourteen-year-old Elizabeth Bell's statement, for example, described various attempts she had made to prevent thirty-four-year-old Arthur James, a boarder in her home, from performing acts of cunnilingus on her. She first told him to desist and drove him from her room. When she later awoke to find him performing cunnilingus on her, Elizabeth pushed him away and fought with him when he took her into his room and laid her on the bed. None of these actions appear in the NYSPCC officer's summary of her statement; in that account, only James was active. He first "got hold of her and put his mouth to her privates." Later he "took her to the bedroom, put her down on the bed and again committed sodomy upon her by placing his mouth on her privates."[36]

The NYSPCC's approach reveals that, in addition to responding to the law, the way in which prosecutors' presented sodomy cases was shaped by the preeminence of gender in ordinary New Yorkers' understanding of childhood. Awareness of the intrinsic differences between males and females eclipsed attention to their age. The male nature of boys caused them to be regarded as eager and impulsive, aggressive to an almost brutish extent, and as such instinctively resistant to adult authority in a way that girls were not.[37] A boy's resistance to a man's attempts to sexually assault him could be seen as an expression of his male nature, and not always as a sign of sexual understanding and lost innocence, as was the case with girls. When New Yorkers did regard a boy's innocence and childhood as compromised, they nevertheless perceived the boy differently than they would a girl of compromised virtue.

When jurors determined that a boy was an adult rather than an innocent child, it did not cause them to suspect that he had consented to participate in an act of sodomy. Rather, jurors still saw the failure of his efforts to resist an assault as the product of a disparity in strength, or of his circumstances, and still regarded his resistance as evidence that he had been coerced. The NYSPCC officer handling the case involving Peter Williams exemplified that attitude when he noted that the resistance of the nine-year-old boy had failed because "the man was too strong for him." In the case of a girl, such was the suspicion of female sexuality that almost any failed effort to resist was liable to be judged evidence of consent. That distrust extended even to those involved in oral and anal acts, which, although considered "unnatural," were understood as behavior to which a female might consent in return for money. In casting girls as passive objects in order to mitigate such suspicions, rather than highlighting their efforts to resist, NYSPCC officers pursued a strategy that reflected the catch-22 in which female victims of sodomy found themselves. In a sodomy case, unlike in a child rape case, such passivity could be also interpreted as evidence of voluntary submission, triggering the corroboration requirement, and making the winning of a conviction difficult, if not impossible.

The manner in which DADAS presented children in sodomy trials reveals an effort to have both boys and girls speak without displaying understanding; it also suggests that prosecutors were less concerned about whether a boy spoke like a child. Exactly what went on during trials is difficult to establish given the lack of any surviving transcripts, but in trial briefs and statements taken by prosecutors, girls used the same vague, simple, and euphemistic language that they had in rape cases. In describing how Martin Schultz anally penetrated her, nine-year-old Helen Powers recounted that he "played with his fingers about her hole where she peas [sic] and then he put his thing, which is between his legs, up her back hole where she dirties."[38] By describing her body in terms of its nonsexual functions, and Schultz's genitals in terms of their appearance alone, Helen made clear what Schultz had done without using any sexual or adult words or phrases. That presentation was consistent with prosecutors' efforts to present girls in sodomy cases just as they did in rape cases. To describe anal acts, boys used language similar to that of girls. In 1926, ten-year-old James Murphy related how Harold Carlson "tried to put his thing in my behind, but it would slip out."[39] However, boys described oral acts using less euphemistic language than that expected of girls in rape cases. A boy typically stated that a man "sucked his penis."[40] Some stated, as did Richard Waldron, that the man "sucked him off."[41] Such language could reflect the character of oral acts, which allowed little scope to distinguish a simple description of what was done, such as "he sucked my penis," from a statement that conveyed a sexual meaning for that act, such as he "sucked me off." It could also reflect a relative lack of concern about whether boys displayed sexual understanding.

While a girl's sexual understanding led to the presumption that she possessed an adult sexuality and would consent to sexual activity, that logic did not apply so straightforwardly to boys who were involved with men. The adult sexuality that was attributed to a boy who displayed a sexual understanding did not make him likely to submit to oral and anal acts with other males. As George Chauncey has revealed, submission to penetration was a female role in working-class cultures. Only those males who displayed inverted gender behavior, effeminacy, were regarded as likely to consent to being penetrated; expressions of sexual understanding indicated that a boy was not a child, but they did not cast him as a "female," but rather as an adult male. As such, he would have consented only to taking the insertive, masculine role in sexual relations with another male. Thus boys who manifested a lack of innocence did not trigger the broad suspicion that was directed at seemingly knowing girls, and they were more readily presented as victims.[42]

In contrast to the distinction made in the rape statute between girls younger than eleven years and older girls, victims of all ages fell within the scope of the sodomy statute. However, the law's failure to recognize any distinctions based on age was at odds with the circumstances of the cases dealt with by the courts. Cases that involved older boys often took place in strikingly different circumstances than did those involving younger boys, and they left little ambiguity about the boy's voluntary submission. Fifteen-year-old Richard Waldron knew forty-year-old Michael Fleischer from his daily trip to meet his mother at the end of her day's work in a silk mill on 132nd Street, where Fleischer was the superintendent. Sometime in 1924, while Richard was playing in the street outside the mill after the employees had gone for the day, Fleischer appeared at his office window and called out to the boy to come up. Inside the office, Fleischer gave Richard money and "sucked him off." In the following two years, he often called Richard into his office or took him to his house. Sometimes Fleischer "jerked him off"; on other occasions he "sucked him off." He always paid him.

Richard never reported what was happening to anyone. Only after the mother of another boy overheard her son talking about getting money from Fleischer did the case come to light. The NYSPCC officer did not present the case in terms of force and resistance. The only gesture in that direction in the brief was the omission of any expression of consent by Richard. Summarizing the boy's statement, the officer wrote, "One day [Fleischer] called him into the office, after the employees had gone, and gave him either 25 cents or 50 cents, and then either 'jerked him off' or 'sucked him off' or both."[43] The brief recorded what Fleischer did, and the exchange of money, but not how Richard responded. That approach echoed NYSPCC officers' presentation of young girls as passive objects, but in this case Richard is not objectified to the same degree as were those girls, who were picked up, carried, undressed, and penetrated. In failing to paint Fleischer's actions as dominating the events, the NYSPCC officer left spaces in the picture he provided into which jurors could impute voluntary submission. The fact that prosecutors were as successful in steering such cases through the legal process as they were with cases involving younger boys, and had more success than they did with cases of sexual intercourse involving girls of the same age, provides further evidence of jurors' tendency to focus on gender rather than age.

Consistent with their presentation of children in sodomy cases as victims rather than accomplices, prosecutors were not concerned, as they were in rape cases, about producing evidence to corroborate a child's testimony. Corroborative evidence was at hand in the cases that had been reported by a witness. But when there was no witness, prosecutors pursued a case when they had no corroboration other than medical evidence that the child had been subjected to a sexual act. Such medical evidence could not establish the identity of a child's attacker, and none of the children in sodomy cases had a venereal disease, which in rape cases served at times as corroboration. Nonetheless, prosecutors regarded physical evidence of an act as adding sufficient weight to a child's testimony for juries to credit her or him. Since oral acts left no physical signs, medical evidence was available only in cases of anal penetration. None of the prosecutions that relied on a child's testimony involved an oral act; all of the sodomy cases dismissed by the grand jury did.[44]

Prosecutors' attitude toward evidence of anal penetration derived at least in part from physicians' testimony that such evidence was more certain and more compelling than evidence of vaginal penetration. The same doctors working with the NYSPCC whose testimony in rape cases was carefully phrased to describe only what they had found, and to avoid any opinion or conclusion about the cause of those conditions, rarely followed that approach in sodomy cases.[45] After stating that he had examined a ten-year-old boy at the center of a 1906 case and found "the anus stretched and the sphincter relaxed," Samuel Brown concluded that "in my opinion an act of sodomy has been committed."[46] William Travis Gibb, who examined most of the children involved in sex crimes from the mid-1890s into the 1930s, also drew conclusions about what he found in his examinations of a child's anus, stating that the conditions he found "would be produced by an act of sodomy."[47] Such an approach was not simply the idiosyncratic behavior of a handful of New York physicians; it was echoed in medical jurisprudence textbooks. The authors of those texts identified the abrasions and tears of the mucous membrane of the anus, and the more severe lacerations and inflammations that NYSPCC doctors found, as the signs to be expected after the first anal penetration, particularly in children. Medical jurists did not baldly assert that those signs could result only from an act of sodomy, but they failed to draw attention to the equivocal nature of these signs, or to qualify them with discussions of the various acts or conditions that could have caused them, as they did when discussing evidence of rape.[48]

In responding differently to signs of anal penetration than they did to those of vaginal penetration, prosecutors and physicians drew on understandings of gender. Anal acts were generally associated with males. In my sample, few of the instances of anal acts—only four of thirty—involved girls, and those cases made up only 22 percent of the prosecutions involving girls, compared with just over half of those that involved boys.[49] A male body was not as difficult to decipher as a female body, sexual activity marking its surface rather than leaving traces within it. Nor, in regard to sexuality, were males subject to the same degree of suspicion as were females, as is evident in the lack of equivocation in medical jurists' discussion of signs of anal penetration. Textbooks warned physicians that signs of rape could have been fabricated, produced to support a false accusation, which they traced to a particularly female propensity to lie about sexual behavior either for revenge or material gain, or to protect their reputation. Medical jurists included none of those arguments in their discussions of sodomy, discussions in which they implicitly dealt with a male subject, one whose gender provoked less suspicion.

Prosecutions relying on a child's testimony could also be undone by the youthfulness of the victim, and of the witnesses, which might make it necessary for their evidence to be corroborated.[50] As in rape cases, it fell to the judge to determine whether a child could testify and swear an oath. The treatment of young victims was inconsistent, but legal officials appeared more reluctant about swearing in girls. Grand juries displayed little of the wariness of the testimony of young children required of judges; only one of the cases they dismissed involved a victim young enough for his ability to take an oath to have been an issue. As in rape prosecutions, when DADAS could not negotiate a plea bargain, they balked at taking to trial all of the cases in which the grand jury had handed down indictments. They discharged seven of the sixty men indicted by the grand jury for sodomy, a slightly higher proportion than in child rape cases, with all but one of those cases involving young children whose ability to give sworn testimony was subject to judicial scrutiny. Most of those cases involved female victims, with defendants charged with acts with girls discharged in far greater proportions than those who assaulted boys—one in four compared with one in sixteen—and in far greater proportions than men charged with raping girls.[51]

Those proportions suggest that DADAS accorded boys a considerably greater degree of credibility than they did girls. But despite this cautious approach, prosecutors still ran afoul of trial judges. In a trial in 1911, the judge directed the acquittal of the defendant on the grounds that the nine-year-old victim and his seven-year-old sister, the only witness, were too young to give sworn testimony. The directed acquittal of a second man, accused of anal intercourse with a nine-year-old girl, likely resulted from a similar determination.[52] In both cases, without the child's testimony, the DADA did not have enough evidence to make a case.

Notwithstanding those setbacks, DADAS relying on the victim's testimony had success in trials until the appellate court ruled that children who voluntarily submitted were accomplices. Before that 1902 decision, three of the four cases tried on that basis resulted in convictions; both cases tried after it ended in acquittal.[53] The appellate court's ruling subjected victims to increased scrutiny and suspicion. By the 1920s, that shift was also evident in the behavior of grand juries, who displayed a new concern with corroboration. In two cases involving assaults on ten-year-old boys—one in 1921, the other in 1926—grand juries opted to transfer the defendant to the court of special sessions, the court that dealt with misdemeanors, on the grounds that there was no evidence to corroborate the testimony of the victim.[54]

Looking at the outcome of sodomy prosecutions in general, we can see that it is gender rather than the nature of the act that looms largest in the response of jurors, prosecutors, and judges. While the conviction rates for cases involving young children were on a par with those in child rape cases, men charged with sodomizing older children were convicted in higher proportions than men accused of having sexual intercourse with girls in their teens. Significantly, that gap stems from the fact that a smaller proportion of the men accused of intercourse with an older girl were convicted than were the men alleged to have assaulted a younger girl. In sodomy cases, the victim's age had no such impact on the outcome. Courts found it more difficult to see physically mature, pubescent girls as victims than they did in the case of younger girls. But older children involved in "unnatural acts" did not attract the heightened suspicion directed at those involved in adult heterosexual intercourse.

Overshadowing the divergences between rape and sodomy outcomes are differences based on gender. Men charged with sodomizing boys were convicted in higher proportions than men who assaulted girls, although the courts dealt with only a small number of the latter. The gap between the conviction rate in sodomy cases involving older boys and that in rape cases involving teenage girls was even larger than that between sodomy and rape cases involving girls. Men accused of sodomy with boys between eleven and seventeen years old were 50 percent more likely to be convicted than were those accused of the rape of a girl from the same age group. Once convicted, men who had been indicted for sodomy with older boys received different treatment at the hands of judges than did those who had been indicted for rape. Almost all those charged with sodomy and convicted of a misdemeanor received a prison term, whereas judges suspended the sentences of nearly half of the men charged with rape who were convicted of misdemeanors. In the case of men convicted of a felony, those who had been charged with sodomizing a boy generally went to prison for at least five years, while those who had been charged with rape typically received a suspended sentence or spent no more than a year in prison.[55] Overall, judges established a pattern in which sex crimes against teenage boys were more harshly punished than those committed against teenage girls.

Those outcomes reflected the attention to gender that was evident in turn-of-the-century New York City's neighborhoods and throughout the legal process. Instead of a single group of children, New Yorkers saw two different groups: boys and girls. They gave less thought and attention to the sexual dangers faced by boys. Boys were expected to resist adult authority, and they were not considered likely to consent to homosexual activity, even when they had lost their innocence. Consequently, most New Yorkers considered boys' accounts of sexual assault by men to be credible.

In addition to the impact of gender difference, a far less pronounced fracture within the NYSPCC's broad vision of childhood is evident in the outcomes of sodomy cases. A distinction between the treatment of those who assaulted young boys and those who assaulted pubescent boys is apparent in the offenses for which men accused of sodomy with boys were convicted. Nearly half of the convictions in cases involving boys older than ten years of age were for misdemeanors, compared with only a third of the convictions in cases where the victim was younger than ten years of age.[56] That discontinuity reflected the relatively more active role of older boys, which had the effect of making their submission appear more voluntary. In regard to boys involved in sodomy, the distinctions that emerged between older and younger boys did not push them so far apart that they were seen in entirely different terms. Men charged with assaulting pubescent boys were convicted in the same proportions as those whose victims were young boys. But this was not the case with girls. Understandings of femininity created a much sharper distinction between young girls and pubescent girls. Despite the efforts of the NYSPCC to contain that tension, it caused their vision of a single, extended childhood to fragment even further. As female childhood was distinguished from male childhood, it fractured into two distinct age groups.

To Throw Absolute Protection around
Females of Less Than Sixteen Years of Age

Around midday on 2 September 1886, a note was delivered to the headquarters of the New York Society for the Prevention of Cruelty to Children (NYSPCC). It contained a request from the police that the Society send an officer to the Fifth District Court at two o'clock that afternoon. When Officer Charles Knolls responded, a court officer informed him that a fifteen-year-old Jewish girl named Ruth Levy had been held for examination, on her mother's complaint that she was a juvenile delinquent. Knolls then went to the prison to see Ruth, and from her he learned that the previous Saturday night, afraid to go home at a late hour, she had instead slept in the apartment of a former neighbor on Lexington Avenue. It was not the first time she had stayed out all night; nor was it the first occasion on which her mother had turned to the courts for help in controlling her. Three months earlier, Ruth had spent twenty days in the New York Juvenile Asylum, committed there by her mother. The "whole cause of the trouble," Ruth explained, was that her mother objected to her frequent visits to the Harlem Beach Baths.

Mrs. Levy had good cause to be concerned. Ruth described to Knolls a papered-over door that connected the "Ladies Toilet" in the Bathing Pavilion to the office of its proprietor, twenty-one-year-old Louis Fletcher. She had seen many girls go through the partition into Fletcher's office, and claimed that he had "done 'it' to a great many girls under and about 16 years of age";

Ruth, however, denied that she had been one of them. With her story recorded in his notes, Knolls set out to investigate its truthfulness. He first visited the neighbor with whom Ruth had stayed, who confirmed that she had taken the girl in at about 10:45 on Saturday evening, as she had on many previous occasions. From there he went to the home of Norma Sheppard, one of the girls identified by Ruth as having had sexual intercourse with Fletcher. Sheppard angrily denied Ruth's story and demanded to "face [Ruth] and give her the lie." Norma did concede, however, that Elizabeth Flynn, the soda water stand attendant at the Pavilion, had told her that Ruth and several other girls had had intercourse with Fletcher. When Officer Knolls tracked down Elizabeth at her home on 109th Street, she denied telling Norma any such thing, but said that she had heard similar stories from other girls.

At this point, Knolls had heard enough. He returned to the prison to confront Ruth with what he had been told. She confessed that she had indeed had sexual intercourse with Fletcher. One Monday afternoon early in August, a friend of hers, fourteen-year-old Esther Hunter, had gone into Fletcher's office at the Pavilion, and had returned shortly after to beckon Ruth in, ostensibly so that Fletcher could show her a pair of roller skates. Once she had been led inside by Esther, Fletcher took hold of Ruth, pulled her on to his knee, and had sexual intercourse with her. Esther saw the "whole business." Questioned by Knolls, Ruth claimed that Fletcher had not attempted anything similar prior to that Monday, nor did he do so on any of the visits she made to the Pavilion in the week after the assault. She insisted that she had struggled with him, and claimed to have been too afraid to tell her mother what had occurred. Ruth also again implicated Norma, Elizabeth, and dozens of other girls in acts of sexual intercourse with Fletcher. When Ruth was brought before a police court justice the following day, Officer Knolls, who was in attendance, made a complaint charging Fletcher with abduction.[1]

The NYSPCC became involved with Ruth Levy because she fell within their definition of the state of childhood, being younger than sixteen years of age. Her social situation conformed broadly to the position expected of a child. Living with her mother, and having no occupation, Ruth clearly remained both subordinate to parental authority and dependent, and hence innocent in the sense of being incapable of looking after herself. Yet neither the circumstances of the assault nor the girl's character conformed to those that were common in child rape cases. As was typical of many cases involving older girls, the assault occurred away from Ruth's home, in an adult, sexualized, "disorderly" space, where men and women "caroused" and "mingled freely." Brothels and assignation houses, which rented rooms for an evening, were other common locations for such occurrences; cases also began at picnics, skating rinks, and bars. Like Ruth, some girls chose to go to such places on their own, rather than being taken to them by men. Others ran away from their homes, ignoring the authority of their families. Such independence was generally coupled with understanding; their language and their behavior during sexual activity revealed that these girls knew what sexual intercourse was. Most did not even look like children; reporters and court officials described them as "well developed." None of those divergences from the behavior that defined childhood ultimately mattered to the NYSPCC. The Society gave age a significance that transcended other signs of childhood. By employing sixteen years as the boundary of childhood, they extended the category to include pubescent girls like Ruth, who displayed a mix of the characteristics of a child and those of an adult.

But the Society did not take the same approach to prosecuting Fletcher that they took against men who assaulted younger girls. The charge made against him was not rape but abduction. In 1886, the age of consent in the rape statute was ten, and the clause relating to immaturity had not yet been added; so when females aged between eleven and sixteen years made a charge of rape, they faced the same questions about force and resistance that were directed at adult women. However, the NYSPCC had progressively reshaped the offense of abduction until it offered, as the appellate court put it, "absolute protection" to females under sixteen years of age. With a definition that encompassed a broad range of circumstances and utilized age, the statute provided protection similar in scope to that given to young girls. However, in employing a legal category for cases involving older girls that was different from the one applied to acts with girls under the age of consent, the Society created the basis for the treatment of girls aged between eleven and sixteen years of age as a discrete group.

In 1886, all but one of the victims in abduction cases came from the eleven-to-sixteen age group; and all but two of the cases involving victims aged between eleven and sixteen years were prosecuted as abduction.[2] Although these girls did not conform to prevailing conceptions of childhood, abduction prosecutions proved to be as successful in securing convictions as were those for child rape. But while the Society did extend legal protection to older girls, it was not able to shield them as effectively as it did younger children. A conviction for abduction carried a far lighter penalty than did one for rape. In effect, the NYSPCC achieved an extension of childhood up to sixteen years of age, but not a seamless merging of older girls and young children. A distinction still existed within childhood, but it was a fissure rather than a break.

In 1887, purity reformers expanded the legal protection provided to girls in their teens by successfully campaigning for an increased age of consent of sixteen. According to the amended law, a man who had sexual intercourse with an older girl could be prosecuted for rape and be subject to the same severe punishment meted out to someone convicted of sexual intercourse with a younger girl. The new law therefore appeared to presage the disappearance of the distinction between the two groups of children. In practice, however, it had the opposite effect. Enforcing the new age of consent put pressure on the cracks that already existed within the extended definition of childhood envisioned by the NYSPCC, and set in train the fragmentation of childhood into two discrete age groups. In the process, the new law progressively eroded the absolute protection provided to older girls.

On 19 April 1886, Hannah Steiner made the journey from her apartment on East Houston Street to the local police court. Her fourteen-year-old daughter, Eva, had not been home in several days, and, her husband having left her five years earlier, Hannah Steiner had decided to seek the court's help in locating her. Appearing before a Justice Gorman, Hannah related how, the evening before her daughter failed to return home, a letter addressed to Eva had been delivered. On opening it, Hannah had read a plea from someone named Michael Sharp that Eva return to his rooms the next evening. A day or so earlier, Hannah had found the thirty-five-year-old dry goods salesman's card in Eva's possession. Justice Gorman issued a summons for Sharp to appear before him, which the NYSPCC officer delegated to investigate the case delivered to the address on Sharp's card. Sharp duly appeared the next day, but while admitting he knew Eva, denied knowing her whereabouts or having ever "used her for immoral purposes." Confronted with the letter he had sent to her, his denials wavered, and he promised that, if paroled, he would learn Eva's whereabouts from her friend Kitty and produce her in court the next afternoon. Sharp fulfilled his pledge, having found Eva on the corner of Ludlow and Houston streets, and convinced her that since "her mother had made trouble," she must come with him to court. But the girl paid less regard to his plea to her that she not "give him away." Once in the NYSPCC's care, she recounted how he had approached her when she was crying in the street after having lost her wages, and had convinced her to go to his room, where he attempted to have intercourse with her. Sharp had not succeeded on that occasion, but several days later, when Eva took up his invitation to return with a friend, he had intercourse with both girls. He then gave them picture frames, fans, and stockings.[3]

This example highlights how the paths by which abduction cases made their way into the legal system differed from those taken by rape and sodomy cases involving younger children. The physical conditions, presence of venereal disease, and doctors' examinations crucial to the reporting of those cases did not play a part in instances of alleged abduction. Bodily signs and symptoms were crucial when the victim had only a limited capacity to act and was as much an object as a subject. They were less important when a girl displayed subjectivity. It was a girl's actions as much as what her assailant did that attracted attention. Most reports were precipitated by girls failing to return home on time, staying out all night, or leaving their homes.[4] By leaving home, they exposed the tensions in middle-class understandings of childhood. The shelter of the domestic sphere prevented puberty from transforming a girl's identity, keeping her "unencumbered with sexuality" and "free from the burdens of adult sexual life," an innocent child, until marriage.[5] Once a girl left that shelter, her physical maturity was exposed, and her purity thrown into doubt. Moreover, by leaving, she had acted in a way that contradicted the dependence and subordination expected of children.

On the few occasions when an arrest resulted from the testimony of a witness, that witness had not come upon an act in progress, nor had he or she simply reacted to the sight of a girl with a man. The witness had become suspicious because of the nature of the place where the girl appeared. Locations such as brothels, assignation houses, public amusements, and neighborhoods like Chinatown would arouse the concern of passersby. In those highly charged contexts, New Yorkers did not always, before reacting, look closely at the girls they saw in the company of men. In the experience of the superintendent of the NYSPCC, a man who came upon a young white female in Chinatown quickly associated her presence there with "visions of Chinese vice," "of gambling, opium infatuation, and things much worse — much worse. He pictures these places as dens of vice and sinks of depravity; he fills them with Chinese demons whose special delight is to devour fair maidens, like that ancient god of mythology. Indignant and horrified he rushes to the authorities and writes to the Society." Attempting to encourage more circumspection, the superintendent described how the NYSPCC's investigations revealed that those passersby had been "deceived by the short hair, short dresses and small figures of certain habitués of these quarters." The Society's officers found no young girls.[6]

They were less certain that the situation was the same in the city's brothels. In the 1880s and 1890s, the NYSPCC mounted a campaign of surveillance, raids, and prosecutions intended to clear the city's disorderly houses of young girls.[7] The Society's officers not only arrested men who tried to enter brothels with girls who appeared to be younger than sixteen years of age; they also created a threat of prosecution that caused the proprietors of such houses themselves to scrutinize girls before admitting them. When Donald Stewart presented himself at 23 Bowery in the early evening of 25 August 1886, and asked for a room, he was turned away. The clerk looked carefully at his companion, a thirteen-year-old domestic servant named Annie Garretty, a member of the family with whom Stewart boarded, and decided that she was "too young." Unfortunately for Stewart, the clerk went further than refusing him a room. As the couple set off down the street, the clerk alerted two police officers, who arrested both Stewart and Garretty.[8]

While the case files make it clear that a girl's location was crucial in attracting attention to her, reporters embellished press accounts with portrayals of girls as innocent children, whose appearance attracted notice. Although Donald Stewart's arrest had been precipitated by the clerk's actions, a newspaper report described it as the result of the police officers' suspicions having been aroused by "the character of the place and the innocent appearance of the girl."[9] The *Morning Journal*'s reporter offered the most elaborate description of the scene. "At about 9:30 o'clock Wednesday evening," his report began, "Officers Selig and Reap, of the Eldridge Street Station, saw a hard-visaged specimen of humanity, whose clothes looked like a second-hand, marked-down suit from a junk shop, standing in the hallway of the hotel entrance of the notorious lodging-house and concert dive, No. 23 Bowery, holding by the hand a pretty little girl about thirteen years of age. The girl was a bright but innocent-looking little thing, and now and then glanced up into her companion's face with a trusting ingenuous expression, which the officers thought, from the man's appearance, wholly misplaced, and suspecting the fellow's intentions they at once arrested him."[10] That Stewart would admit to having had intercourse with Annie on three previous occasions, and that she would testify to having accompanied Stewart and her older sister to 23 Bowery a year earlier, gives a far less innocent impression of any exchange between them. Later, the reporter characterized Annie as a "little fairy in petticoats." His colleague, writing for the *New York Times*, marked her innocence by describing her as wearing a white dress, an attire somewhat removed from the one in which she appeared in the *Morning Journal*: "a faded checked calico [dress], which reached almost to her shoe tops and disclosed bright red hose."[11] The gap between these reports and Annie's appearance is emblematic of the challenge that prosecutors faced in securing the conviction of a man involved with an older girl. Reporters seeking to stir public sentiment against Stewart had to exaggerate Annie's innocence. Only then could she be presented as a victim.

When preparing a brief in an abduction case, NYSPCC officers did not show the concern about presenting a girl as innocent that is evident in the writings of newspaper reporters. In the brief prepared as part of the prosecution of Louis Fletcher, the NYSPCC agent handling the case offered this detailed summary of Ruth Levy's statement:

> Is 15 years of age, and was in the habit of going to the Harlem Beach Baths. On or about the afternoon of August 9th, about 3 o'clock, she went there with a girl named Esther Hunter, and as witness was sitting at a table in the Pavilion, looking at the people bathing, the prisoner came out and said to Esther Hunter, "It is low tide; come into the Ladies' Toilet and I will let you in." Then Esther went by the private door which adjoins the ladies' toilet, into Fletcher's room. This ladies toilet room is papered, but the part covering the door is loose and can be easily pushed aside. Esther went into this room and stayed about 15 or 20 minutes, and then the prisoner came out and said it was high tide and beckoned witness to come into his room, and witness went in the ladies' toilet, and prisoner let witness in through the partition into his room. A man named Charlie and Esther were in the room. When witness got in the prisoner tried a pair of skates on her, and the skates were a little too small, and the prisoner slipped them off. Prisoner put his hand up witness' clothes. Witness was sitting on his lap. After the prisoner had tried skates on witness, the prisoner put her on the bed, which had a white spread over it and a blanket and two pillows, and in the presence of Esther and Charlie, he had sexual intercourse with her. The girl named Elizabeth Flynn came into the room and saw witness on the prisoner's knee. Witness saw a number of other girls who she knew were in the habit of going into this room with the prisoner, whose names she will mention.[12]

At first glance, the author of this summary appears to have taken the same approach that NYSPCC agents took when preparing briefs in child rape cases; they, too, emphasized the girl's passivity. Ruth is rendered an object manipulated by Fletcher, who brought her into his office, tried a pair of skates on her, put his hands up her clothes, placed her on the bed, and, finally, had sexual intercourse with her. To achieve that impression, the agent omitted any mention of the sustained efforts at resistance that Ruth described in her affidavit. In that statement, recorded in the third person by the court clerk, she recounted how, when Fletcher put "his hand under deponent's clothes and felt of deponent's limbs and privates" while helping her try on a pair of skates, she "objected and ordered said Fletcher to stop, but said Fletcher pulled deponent on to his knees, deponent screaming, and succeeded in unbuttoning deponent's drawers, having previously pulled up deponent's clothes, said Fletcher did then and there have sexual intercourse with deponent."[13]

However, the officer's approach to summarizing Ruth's statement differed from the way in which he would have presented a rape case in not including details that would help jurors attribute her passivity to her lack of understanding. He makes no specific mention of her underclothes and how they came to be removed, records no expression by Ruth that she had been hurt, and fails to make clear that she received nothing from Fletcher. Ruth's statement had mentioned one of those details, describing, in the passage quoted above, how Fletcher removed her underwear. She had also not spoken of getting anything from Fletcher after he had sexual intercourse with her. Only the third detail, an expression of being hurt, was absent from Ruth's statement. She did scream, but before Fletcher had intercourse with her. That timing rendered her outcry a sign that she understood what Fletcher was trying to do to her, a recognition that was incompatible with innocence. Nonetheless, the agent's failure to include signs of a lack of understanding in his summary was clearly not simply a reflection of their absence from Ruth's statement. Instead, his omissions indicated his lack of concern about presenting Ruth as innocent.

The agent's emphasis on Ruth's passivity enabled him to highlight Fletcher's actions, in order to ensure that the case appeared to match the circumstances covered by the abduction statute. Louis Fletcher's assault on Ruth Levy would not have fallen within the scope of the abduction law as it stood at the time of the NYSPCC's formation. However, in the intervening years, the Society had expanded the meaning of abduction from an offense limited to prostitution to one that applied to any act of sexual intercourse with an underage girl. The earliest form of the offense appeared in the Revised Laws of 1829. It provided that "every person who shall take away any female under the age of fourteen years, from her father, mother, guardian, or other person having the legal charge of her person, without their consent, either for the purpose of prostitution, concubinage, or marriage," faced a punishment of up to three years in prison, a fine not exceeding $1000, or both.[14] Decisions by the state's higher courts included within the scope of the law those who employed force, threats, and deceit and who committed acts against a girl's will.[15] At the same time, they limited the law to acts committed for the purpose of promoting a criminal practice, such as prostitution, and thus excluded "vice of a private character."[16] In the 1881 codification of New York's penal law, the 1829 law was combined with a statute from 1848 that punished anyone who "shall inveigle, entice or take away any unmarried female of previous chaste character, under the age of twenty-five years from her father's house or wherever else she may be, for the purposes of prostitution," and a law prohibiting the taking of a woman with the intent to compel her to marry.[17] The resulting combination was named abduction. The commissioners who drafted the code also raised the age in the law from fourteen to sixteen years and changed the statute's language by substituting "sexual intercourse" for "concubinage."[18] The new language significantly broadened the scope of the statute, from acts done in the context of cohabitation to any act of intercourse. In 1884, the legislature made it even more difficult to escape the law's scope by removing parental consent as a defense in cases involving sexual intercourse and prostitution, and by providing for the punishment of any parents who did provide such consent.[19]

In 1885, the appellate court handed down a decision that ran counter to this trend to expand the statute's scope, provoking a final rewriting of the law. Before the court was the case of a fifteen-year-old girl, who had appeared at the defendant's saloon, announced that she had come to stay, and remained a month, during which time she had sexual intercourse with several men. Those circumstances, the judges determined, did not constitute abduction; only those acts of sexual intercourse that involved "a taking of her person by some active agency" fell within the law. In adopting that position, they excluded from the law acts "where the female is merely received, or permitted and allowed to follow a life of prostitution without persuasive inducement by the person accused."[20] In other words, an act to which a girl consented was not abduction. Elbridge Gerry quickly countered by promoting an amendment that augmented the word "take" with a string of additional verbs, defining as guilty of abduction any person who "takes, receives, employs, harbors or uses, or causes or procures to be taken received, employed, harbored or used, a female under the age of sixteen years, for the purpose of prostitution; or, not being her husband, for the purpose of sexual intercourse; or, without the consent of her father, mother, guardian or other person having legal charge of her person, for the purpose of marriage."[21]

In this form, the statute, labeled "the Gerry law" by the New York press, achieved the breadth that the NYSPCC desired. Appellate courts recognized that the legislature "intended to throw absolute protection around females of less than sixteen years of age, against the evil of sexual intercourse to which their tender years may be exposed," including protection against girls' "lending themselves for purposes of sexual intercourse."[22] Even in its revised form, however, the offense of abduction was still framed in terms of a man's actions, requiring prosecutors to establish that a defendant had taken an active role in shaping the events of a case. It was that obligation that NYSPCC agents sought to address by rendering girls as passive.

The lack of attention to innocence was also in part a reflection of the abduction statute. The offense did not hinge on the victim's having displayed the subjective traits of immaturity, and physical and mental weakness, employed in the definition of child rape. A girl needed only to be younger than the age specified in the statute to fall within its scope; her physical or mental state or development was not relevant. Accordingly, the NYSPCC agent's summary began with the information most important in establishing Rachel as a victim in the eyes of the law, stating that she "is 15 years of age."

An additional explanation as to why NYSPCC agents did not try to present older girls as innocent can be found in the trial setting. Prosecutors could not sustain an image of girls as innocent children once jurors saw and heard them. Ruth Levy's appearance did not have this effect on those who saw her. Newspaper reporters variously described Ruth as "a pretty girl, tall for her age," with "short and curly hair" and as "a very pretty, plump girl with dark hair and eyes."[23] Typically, though, observers found a girl's appearance more difficult to reconcile with their visions of childhood. A French girl at the center of one abduction case struck the reporter writing for the *Morning Journal* as "a woman in appearance, [although] only a child in years, having just passed her fifteenth birthday." According to his account, the jury had had a similar reaction; its members "could hardly believe that the womanlike girl was under 16."[24]

If observers thought Ruth Levy was an innocent child, her testimony would have quickly disabused them. As in other comparable cases, when the magistrate and defense attorney questioned Levy about sexual intercourse, they used "adult" words and phrases that gave a meaning to the act, rather than the simple, descriptive language of children.[25] During Fletcher's attorney's cross-examination of Ruth Levy, the following exchange occurred:

Q. Did you have connection with any other man?
A. No sir.
Q. Sure about that?
A. Yes sir.
Q. Do you know what the word connection means?
A. Yes sir.

Q. What does it mean?

(No answer).

Q. Nobody else had connection with you?

A. No sir.

Q. Are you sure about that?

A. Yes sir.[26]

This dialogue presents a striking contrast to those that took place in child rape cases. The attorney did not have to elicit adult language from Ruth in order to claim that she possessed sexual knowledge; he was able to assume from the outset that she understood the meaning of an adult term like "connection." For her part, Ruth made no effort to claim otherwise. In response to the question "Did [Fletcher] insert his person into you?" she claimed that she did not understand what was being asked of her, but her subsequent answers made clear that she was asserting an ignorance of that particular euphemism, not of the meaning of the act.[27] The term that Ruth did understand—that is, "connection"—was the expression most often used in the questioning of older girls, though it was sometimes supplemented with references to "sexual intercourse" and to a man "having something to do with her."[28]

If a girl displayed sexual knowledge, this triggered a form of scrutiny not evident in child rape cases, a concern with a girl's demeanor and a judgment as to whether she displayed shame. Evidence of shame most often came in the form of blushing. When Ruth's friend Esther Hunter recounted an assault that took place in the hallway of a tenement house by a man she met at a picnic, the reporter for the *Star* wrote that her "rosy cheeks grew crimson and her voice was scarcely above a whisper." Such a display signified that a girl was pure, if not totally ignorant, possessing some qualities that inclined New Yorkers to see her as a victim. A girl who testified without manifesting such signs, as did a fifteen-year-old in "giving the most damaging evidence against her own character" with "not a blush on her cheek," revealed herself as having an immoral, bad character, one that increased her culpability in the eyes of those who watched her.[29] Observers did not always read a girl's reactions in the same way. Having studied Ruth Levy, the reporter writing for the *Sun* determined that she did "not seem to care very much about the notoriety she was receiving." To the *World*'s reporter, by contrast, she "looked as though she felt her shame deeply."[30] Superintendent Jenkins of the NYSPCC was not prepared to venture a judgment, commenting only that Ruth was "greatly distressed over the affair, but whether from shame or the restriction of her liberty it was difficult to say."[31]

Prosecutors showed little concern about the impact of older girls' appearance and language on the willingness of judges and jurors to apply the law to men charged with abduction. Rather than objecting to how Ruth Levy was cross-examined, the prosecutor, Superintendent Jenkins of the NYSPCC, offered "to admit Ruth was not as pure as she might be, but this was not admitted as evidence and the Superintendent took back his statement."[32] Nor did prosecutors raise objections when an attorney took his lead from the apparently unchildlike appearance and understanding of a girl and treated her as if she were an adult woman making a charge of rape. Fletcher's attorney went to great lengths to establish that Ruth's efforts to resist Fletcher fell short of the resistance required of an adult woman to establish her lack of consent. In only twice telling Fletcher to stop, and in not continuing to scream or biting him, despite his failure to cover her mouth, she had failed to resist to the limit of her physical ability, the standard set by the state's courts in rape cases. The attorney also drew out that Ruth had not immediately reported the assault, as required by law of an adult woman, instead staying around the Pavilion for an hour. In fact, she told no one of the attack until she made her admission to Officer Knolls.[33] Neither of these issues was relevant at law, but they did raise questions in the minds of jurors as to whether a man deserved to be punished, particularly if his alleged victim did not appear to them to be an innocent child entitled to protection regardless of the circumstances. In failing to object to this line of questioning, prosecutors held to the belief that a girl's age was sufficient to establish that she was a victim. They clearly expected that jurors would follow the law by giving precedence to that objective criterion.

In practice, prosecutors often found it difficult to establish a girl's age. The problem they encountered was that age did not matter to working-class New Yorkers in the way that it did in the abduction statute. Mrs. Levy did testify that her daughter Ruth was born in Germany on 11 October 1870. But her subsequent testimony that she did not know even the years in which her five other children had been born, let alone the precise dates of their birth, eroded her credibility. Such vagueness was common. Mrs. Levy did not have a birth certificate for Ruth, nor could she quickly or easily obtain one, a situation shared by many immigrants. Neither could she refer to an entry in the family Bible, a form of documentary evidence that working-class families more often possessed. It had long been lost, and, in any case, it had not contained a record of Ruth's birth because, when it had occurred her family "had a great deal of trouble," and they had forgotten to make an entry.[34] Even had Mrs. Levy been able to produce a Bible that recorded Ruth's birth, the court might not have accepted it as evidence of the girl's age. In ordering a new trial in another case prosecuted in 1886, the state supreme court expressed doubts about the admissibility of the girl's family Bible, citing decisions holding that such a document could only establish an individual's pedigree, not his or her age.[35] Only early in the twentieth century did the penal code recognize Bible entries as evidence of age.[36]

In 1884 the state legislature had made provision for cases in which documentary evidence of age was lacking. A child could be "produced for personal inspection, to enable the magistrate, court or jury to determine the age thereby"; alternatively, a court could have a child examined "by one or more physicians, whose opinion, shall also be competent evidence upon the question of age."[37] A court decision in 1877 had confidently held that "in most instances the indications of age are so unequivocal and decided that not the least risk can be encountered in acting upon them."[38] However, such certainty often proved elusive in New York City courts. One-third of the girls involved in abduction cases in 1886 were fifteen years old, including Ruth Levy, who, if her mother is to be believed, was only one month short of her sixteenth birthday at the time she appeared in court.[39] When a girl was so close to the legal age, discovering from "ordinary observation" how old she was required, as one supreme court judge remarked, "such fine discriminations" that it had only "slight value" as evidence.[40] On the only occasion on which a deputy assistant district attorney (DADA) tried to use medical evidence to establish a girl's age, two doctors testified that they could not precisely determine such a thing from an examination of her body.[41] George Baker's attorney persuaded the state supreme court that Lizzie Silver's appearance was an unreliable sign of her age. The NYSPCC had manipulated the girl's appearance, he alleged, to make her look young, "placing the complaining witness (who had formerly worn a long dress, and with her hair so arranged as to rest upon the top of her head) upon the witness stand 'in short clothes, with her hair braided in a child-like way [hanging down her back].'" The Society indignantly denied any intention to mislead. Its staff had simply replaced Lizzie's filthy dress with a clean one from among those donated by the NYSPCC's supporters, Superintendent Jenkins protested, and they had done nothing to her hair.[42]

Such debates over clothing and hairstyles highlight how inspections to establish a girl's age returned prosecutors to the position of relying on subjective criteria rather than an objective trait as the basis of their cases. Given the difficulties they faced in presenting older girls as innocent children, that situation could leave them unable to win a conviction. John Lindsay, the DADA charged with prosecuting George Baker, found himself in that predicament. Faced with the fact that "by her appearance [Lizzie] might readily be taken to be a person of eighteen or nineteen," he concluded "that it would be useless to again place the defendant on trial."[43]

Even when a girl's age could be established, some New Yorkers clearly felt uneasy about placing so much weight on it in defining what was criminal. The *Morning Journal*'s reporter gave voice to that unease in an account of a case involving a fifteen-year-old girl who "had the appearance of being at least seventeen years of age," commenting that "had the girl been a few months older, the prisoner would have been called on to plead to a lesser crime."[44]

Whatever misgivings New Yorkers had about the significance of age, they were not enough to save Louis Fletcher. At the conclusion of the hearing, his attorney moved to have the charges against him dismissed, arguing that insufficient corroboration had been produced. The magistrate denied the motion and held Fletcher for the grand jury; it, in turn, voted two indictments against him. After many delays, Fletcher eventually pled guilty to one charge in return for the NYSPCC's support of his request to be sent to the Elmira Reformatory, rather than the state prison.[45]

Despite the difficulties prosecutors encountered in presenting cases, their success in convicting Louis Fletcher was not an anomaly. In fact, the conviction rate for abduction prosecutions in 1886 was essentially the same as for rape prosecutions involving younger girls.[46] Those convictions came in part because abduction was defined in terms that made corroborative evidence relatively easy to find. Where the rape and sodomy statutes focused narrowly on the sexual act, the offense of abduction was extended to encompass "taking" and the intention to have sexual intercourse, allowing evidence of opportunity that was not corroborative of a rape charge to fulfill the requirement when the charge was abduction. Witnesses, in effect, had to see less in order to provide corroboration: to simply find men in hotel rooms with girls, observe men and girls entering assignation houses, or encounter girls in a brothel keeper's house.[47]

The relatively light punishment provided for abduction—imprisonment for up to five years and a fine of up to $1,000—compared to prison terms of between five and twenty years for rape and sodomy—also helped produce convictions. Juries considered such a punishment appropriate for the relatively limited wrongdoing they perceived, and it likely encouraged defendants to agree to plea bargains. Judges offered further encouragement, rarely feeling the need to apply the full extent of the punishment the law provided, in contrast to their treatment of men convicted of child rape. The longest prison term given to a man convicted of abduction was four years and two months, in a case in which the victim was "not right in head." Louis Fletcher and

Michael Sharp received sentences of around two years, and three others terms of eighteen months or one year. The final man had his sentence suspended. There is little to distinguish this pattern of punishments from those the men would have received had they been convicted of a misdemeanor; the sentences certainly had little in common with the severity with which judges punished men who had assaulted young girls.

Whether child protectors and DADAS could have sustained their success in winning convictions was never tested. After 1886, they no longer relied on the abduction statute when they prosecuted men involved with older girls. In 1891, only 40 percent of the men accused of having sexual intercourse with a teenage girl were charged with that offense.[48] The remainder faced a charge of rape, as prosecutors made use of the new age of consent of sixteen years adopted by the state legislature in 1887. The age of consent offered girls more protection, by providing for longer sentences, and was almost as broad in scope as the abduction law, punishing all acts of intercourse if not the intention to have intercourse. By 1896, the proportion of cases prosecuted as abduction had dropped to one-third, a downward trend that continued in the twentieth century. Only when a man had involved a girl in prostitution or forced her into marriage did prosecutors charge him with abduction. As a criminal charge pertaining to sexual acts in other circumstances, the offense of abduction had been overtaken by the increased age of consent.

Signs of that impending encroachment are evident in 1886. Newspaper reports described Gerry's abduction law as one that increased the age of consent in a way parallel to an English law passed the previous year.[49] That legislation had come in the aftermath of the scandal provoked by "The Maiden Tribute of Modern Babylon" (London: *Pall Mall Gazette*, 1885), W. T. Stead's controversial exposé of child prostitution and the traffic in young girls between England and brothels on the Continent. Across the Atlantic, Americans too had "felt the thrill of horror that Stead awakened," as one commentator put it; and when the British parliament increased the age of consent to sixteen years, they had been prompted to look at their own laws.[50] Following the publication, in December 1885, by the Women's Christian Temperance Union (WCTU) of an article by Georgina Marks revealing that American laws set the age no higher than ten years, and in some states as low as eight years,[51] an increased age of consent became part of the agenda of American purity reformers.

The initial concerns of the clergy, women's rights advocates, and former abolitionists who made up the social purity movement in the United States had been somewhat narrower, focused on defeating moves in the 1870s to institute state-regulated prostitution in American cities. The reformers' success in achieving that goal, and the example of their counterparts in Britain, led them to adopt the more ambitious objective of abolishing prostitution and purifying and perfecting society. As purity reform groups pursued that aim through campaigns for moral and sex education, child rearing, social hygiene, and the promotion of a single moral standard for men and women, their ranks were swelled by middle-class social reformers, physicians, and philanthropists. In the 1880s, the New York Committee for the Prevention of State Regulation of Vice was the organizational heart of the movement. Led by former abolitionists Abby Hopper Gibbons and Adam Powell and physician Emily Blackwell, among others, the committee published a journal, the *Philanthropist*, edited by Powell, that helped coordinate purity reform throughout the United States.[52]

In January 1886, Powell used his editorial in the first issue of the journal to launch petitions asking the New York State Legislature and the United States Congress to raise the age of consent.[53] In the absence of such a law, he wrote, "vicious and designing men" were able to "pursue their evil ways" with impunity, leading astray young and poor girls to satisfy their lust, and creating "flagrant spectacles of vice [and] abandoned girls in their teens in the streets." That argument evoked the by-then familiar scenario of seduction as the tragic first step in a career in prostitution, a trope that had been employed by moral reformers since the early nineteenth century. Powell went on to make a second, less familiar argument, one that painted a scenario of sexual violence rather then seduction.[54] He asserted that, unless the age of consent was increased, whenever a ten-year-old girl was "assaulted and overpowered, if it be shown that she did not resist to the uttermost limit of exhaustion, the man (?) who assaulted her may still successfully plead 'consent.'" Although Emily Blackwell touted the effectiveness of this scenario in "excit[ing] indignation even among the majority of persons of vicious life," purity reformers rarely used it after 1887 because it was at odds with the ways in which they otherwise defined those in need of protection.[55] Powell's image rendered the girls in need of protection as physically immature, and hence as incapable of the effective resistance expected of an adult woman. Yet, in the same passage, he linked the age of consent to the age of majority, twenty-one years, pointing to the discrepancy between the legal protection given to a minor's property and that given to her person. In the process, Powell invoked a female subject whose physical maturity precluded the possibility of what was legally defined as sexual violence.[56]

Purity reformers linked the age of consent to the age of majority far more often than they invoked the scenario of sexual violence, demonstrating how their perspective differed from that of the NYSPCC and the child protection movement. They saw innocence primarily in terms of incapacity, with those who needed protection characterized by dependence and a subordinate social role that reflected the fact that they were "incapable in the most insignificant things of independent judgment and action."[57] Absent from the purity reformers' vision was a concern with physiological development, so evident in NYSPCC rhetoric. In fact, it was their political opponents who raised the issue of physical maturity and, arguing that "nature fixed the age of consent," sought to tie the age of consent to the onset of puberty. Although this position echoed the terms employed by the NYSPCC, it fixed the boundary of childhood at twelve or fourteen years of age, rather than the age of sixteen favored by the Society. And physical maturity did not have a leading place in the arguments made against an increased age of consent. Legislators who opposed purity reformers gave most of their attention to questions of character, rather than physical maturity, arguing that if the age of consent was increased, "unchaste and designing young women" would "inveigle young men into illicit relations and then use the law to extort blackmail from them."[58] In five states such arguments produced a range of new offenses designed to punish females who had intercourse with boys, statutes that sought to have females share responsibility for acts their proponents portrayed as fornication, and that treated adult women, especially prostitutes, as posing the same threat to boys that adult men did to girls.[59] Such legislative action highlights the way in which debates about an increased age of consent left unchanged the relationship between age and gender, treating only girls as victims of rape and boys as the prey of fallen women.

In New York, purity reformers and their allies in the WCTU and the Knights of Labor overcame such efforts to defeat or deflect their campaign. In 1887, the state legislature raised the age of consent to sixteen years, making it one of two dozen legislative assemblies around the nation to adopt a higher age of consent in the 1880s. However, rather than increasing the legal protection provided to teenage girls, the new law made it more difficult to convict and deter men. In February 1888, the *Philanthropist* reported prominently on the first successful prosecution using the new law.[60] In the coming months, that success proved to be the exception. In March 1891, when the NYSPCC proposed amending the statute, the Society was struggling to secure convictions even in "cases where the evidence of guilt on the part of evil men was conclusive."[61] The problem they faced was that the age of consent formed part of the rape statute. Juries expected a case of rape to involve force and violence, Elbridge Gerry reported, in explaining the need for a change in the law. Even some judges expressed the opinion that violence had to be proven in age of consent prosecutions. Since most cases involving teenage girls entailed little or no violence, and sometimes involved expressions of consent, the expectations of jurors went unmet, leaving them unwilling to convict the men involved of rape. That those men faced a minimum sentence of five years in prison if convicted only made juries, in Gerry's experience, more likely to acquit them, particularly when jurors decided that the girl had a "bad character."[62] A sentence of five years seemed disproportionate to the degree of criminality involved in having sexual intercourse with such a female. One consequence of the breakdown of prosecutions involving older girls was that, in contrast to the situation when men were charged with abduction, cases involving older and younger girls no longer produced a similar proportion of convictions.

To make the statute enforceable, Gerry, Adam Powell, and ex-judge Noah Davis fashioned an amendment that, when enacted by the New York State Legislature in 1892, reinscribed in the law the distinction between older and younger girls that the increased age of consent had removed. Gerry's preferred solution was to return to an age of consent of ten years, thereby using the abduction statute in cases involving girls aged between ten and sixteen years. However, purity reformers, who Gerry felt did not understand the difficulties his Society encountered in the courts, rejected that approach on the grounds that it "diminish[ed] the protection toward the female." Instead, the amended law "divid[ed] the crime of rape into two degrees — first where violence is used, second where it is not." Rape in the first degree replicated the existing definitions, except that relating to the age of consent; sexual intercourse with a woman under the age of consent "under circumstances not amounting to rape in the first degree" became second-degree rape. Second-degree or statutory rape was a lesser offense, carrying a sentence of not more than ten years in prison, rather than the five to twenty years applicable to first-degree rape. Since removing any mention of age from the definition of first-degree rape left no provision, as Gerry put it, to punish "the act of violence on a child of tender years," these amendments were coupled with a new clause that defined as first-degree rape any act of sexual intercourse with a female when "by reason of mental or physical weakness, or immaturity, or any bodily ailment, she does not offer resistance."[63] The new rape statute clarified the relationship between the age of consent and other forms of rape, and removed the confusion about the role of force in the offense, something that had proved an obstacle to securing convictions. In addition, the reference to immaturity opened the way for teenage girls to be treated differently from younger girls: second-degree rape recognized teenage girls as sufficiently immature to warrant protection not available to adult women, but insufficiently immature to warrant the protection the law gave to physically immature, prepubescent girls. The law, in short, recognized two distinct forms of childhood rather than the single extended childhood created by the age of consent.

Despite their support for the new law, purity reformers had not yet adopted the vision of childhood articulated by the NYSPCC. In 1895, a purity reform group, the White Cross and Social Purity League, succeeded in winning a further increase in the age of consent, to eighteen years.[64] Although many of the older girls whom reformers encountered conspicuously displayed and expressed their sexuality and proved "impatient of restraint . . . and not readily amenable to advice from the older and more experienced," the reformers argued that these attitudes indicated that they needed to be protected from themselves.[65] However, since the amendment set the upper limit of childhood at two years beyond the boundary employed by the NYSPCC, the Society did not support the change.

It was only in 1896, when Powell floated the idea of a further increase in the age of consent, to twenty-one years, that Gerry directly challenged purity reformers' view of childhood. In letters published in the *Philanthropist*, Gerry complained that the age was already set beyond the time at which "a girl became a woman." After the onset of puberty, he argued, a girl lost "the helplessness of the child victim" that "implied violence" and "ensured conviction." Her "physical weakness" gave way to "physical strength," childish ignorance was replaced by "a higher intelligence and greater strength of will," and innocence gave way to "a mental inclination or possibly sexual desire." Gerry claimed that jurors, too, considered puberty to have "practically nullified" a girl's immaturity, causing most cases to appear to them to be instances of "simple fornication." As a result, "the nearer the child . . . approached to sixteen, the greater became the danger of a disagreement of the jury, if not of an actual acquittal; especially if the girl presented an appearance of maturity." When the girl was sixteen or seventeen years of age, securing a conviction was almost impossible. It was absurd, Gerry advised, to even try to prosecute a man for consensual sexual intercourse with an eighteen- or nineteen-year-old female, as reformers were proposing to do.[66] Reformers took heed of Gerry's warnings and shelved plans to effect a further increase in the age of consent, probably influenced as much by his insights into jurors' attitudes as by his vision of childhood.

In 1913, however, when the editors of *Vigilance*, the journal of the American Purity Alliance, canvassed support for the fixing of a uniform age of consent at eighteen, leading purity reformers gave voice to an understanding of childhood that recognized the distinct nature of pubescent girls. In reject-ing such a high age of consent, they echoed Gerry by arguing that public opinion—by which they meant the opinions of the men on juries who had to enforce the law—did not see girls in their late teens as children and would not enforce an age of consent of eighteen years. Now, however, the reformers themselves shared that view. Ada Sheffield, a member of the Massachusetts Board of Charities, reflecting the view of the other leading purity reformers who responded to *Vigilance*, saw "the average girl of sixteen" as possessing an essentially adult understanding: she "may not realize beforehand what is the full price that must be paid for wrong-doing—few of us do," Sheffield argued, ". . . but she does know, in the great majority of cases, that she ought not to be unchaste." "A girl of sixteen," Sheffield boldly asserted, "is not a child."[67] But neither was she an adult.

This was a significant shift from the conception that middle-class reformers like Sheffield had articulated in the 1890s, one that caused them to no longer seek the "absolute protection" of older girls. It was born partly out of exposure to the ideas of the child study movement and the writings of G. Stanley Hall. Just as crucial, but less well appreciated, was the contribution made by those ordinary Americans who shaped the way in which the law relating to the age of consent actually worked. As reformers used Hall to argue that, despite their failure to act like children, girls in their teens were not equipped to be adults or to take responsibility for their sexual behavior, ordinary Americans continued to insist that those girls had the maturity to marry and to be moth-ers. Although before the 1930s reformers' arguments generally failed to win over jurors, some of the distinctions between adults and girls in their teens that they sought did emerge. The age of consent provided underage girls who attempted to deal with the social consequences of sexual activity, such as loss of reputation and pregnancy, with legal avenues that older females did not have, and it generated a new concern among working-class men to discover a young female's age. Even if it did not happen in the way reformers envisioned, the law did play a constitutive role in changing the meaning of childhood.

The Age of Consent

chapter five

Making Right a Girl's Ruin

On the evening of 28 July 1911, Olive Smith found blood on the underwear of her fifteen-year-old daughter, Helen. Although she had just returned from a job in Mount Kisco, which had kept her out of town for some time, Olive knew that Helen's last period had ended only two weeks earlier. She therefore sought out the girl and asked her what had happened during her absence. Helen told her that she had been assaulted. Two days earlier, while staying with her cousin on West 134th Street, as she regularly did when her mother was away working, Helen had been sent to buy groceries. On her way out of the building, she had passed Malcolm Lewis, a seventeen-year-old elevator boy who lived on the same floor, standing in his doorway. He asked her in, but she declined. When Helen returned from her errand, she found Lewis still standing by his open door. He repeated his invitation, which she again refused, but as she went by, Lewis grabbed her and forced her into his apartment. Helen was then pulled into a rear bedroom and forced onto a bed. Although she punched Lewis repeatedly, she could not prevent him from removing her underwear and having sexual intercourse with her. The only person she had told about the assault was her cousin's daughter, Helen, who had seen her a few minutes after it happened, and asked why her face was so red.

Olive Smith, on hearing this story, did not seek out a police officer or set off for the local court. Instead, she chose to go to the rooms where Malcolm Lewis lived. Finding both Lewis and his mother there, she demanded to know what he had done to her daughter. Both of the Lewises "refused to admit or deny anything." Olive's response was to declare that she would bring Helen to confront Lewis, but when she returned with the girl, only Mrs. Lewis was there to face her. Malcolm had gone downstairs and refused to face Helen. Olive Smith then informed Mrs. Lewis that she would give her a day or two to "think it over." According to Helen, her mother wanted to see what Mrs. Lewis "would do about the matter." On 31 July, having heard nothing, Olive took Helen to the Fifth District Court in Harlem and charged Malcolm Lewis with rape.[1]

Olive Smith clearly did not see the punishment provided in the rape statute as the only, or even the most desirable, response to what had happened to her daughter. She turned to the courts only after Lewis and his family refused to acknowledge what he had done to Helen. Making a complaint against Lewis was a way of putting pressure on him to do something, and as such was a means to an end as much as an end in itself. For Olive Smith, and for many other working-class New Yorkers from a variety of different racial and ethnic groups, the significance of the increased age of consent was that it made it easier to use the law in this way. A charge of rape or seduction could only be used to put pressure on a man if he had had sexual intercourse with a girl in certain circumstances. A charge of statutory rape, on the other hand, could be made whatever the situation in which the act had taken place.[2] The new offense of second-degree rape was thus drawn into a working-class legal culture that saw the formal law as an adjunct to extralegal efforts and a criminal charge as a stage in a process that began outside the courts. Working-class New Yorkers overlaid their own investigations, confrontations, and negotiations on the legal processes of arrest, arraignment, indictment, and disposition, consciously using the law for their own purposes.[3]

Olive Smith's statement does not make clear what she wanted Malcolm Lewis to do, but it is likely that she wanted him to marry Helen. That this was the way in which working-class New Yorkers preferred to respond is suggested also by the case of Elizabeth Tedesco. In August 1931, less than two weeks before her sixteenth birthday, Elizabeth decided that her family was being too strict with her, so she ran away from her Brooklyn home. Several days later, she saw a sign advertising the Strand Dance Roof, a taxi-dance hall, and, after dancing there all night, she applied for a job as one of the hostesses. With a photograph paid for with money borrowed from the woman in whose house she was staying, and wearing a gown loaned by one of the other hostesses, Elizabeth started work the next day. Several days later, a patron of the taxi-dance hall, Angelo Bonelli, a twenty-year-old assistant cutter from Long

Island, and his friend Marty asked Elizabeth and Angelina Guida, another runaway girl working at the Strand whom Elizabeth had befriended, to go out with them. After the two couples had had a meal, Bonelli and his friend invited the girls back to a hotel to play cards and have some fun. Since the men promised they "wouldn't touch" the girls and "weren't a bit fresh," Elizabeth and Angelina thought they would be safe and agreed.

Elizabeth and Angelina had misjudged the men. Once in the hotel rooms, Bonelli dragged Elizabeth into one room and locked the door. When she resisted his efforts to have intercourse, he threatened to punch her in the jaw, chased her around the room, and fought her until he got her down. At this point, Elizabeth fainted, and Bonelli "ruined" her. During the night, Bonelli had intercourse with Elizabeth several more times, leaving her "sore all over." Next door, after Angelina "put [her] legs together" and resisted Marty's re-peated efforts, he eventually gave up trying to have intercourse with her. In the morning, the men told the girls to keep their mouths shut about what had happened, and gave them ten cents so they could get back to their own rooms.

Two days after Bonelli assaulted her, Elizabeth's married brother Paul found her at the Strand Dance Roof. After he had urged her to "tell the truth" about her time away from home, she told him what Bonelli had done. Paul took Elizabeth and Angelina home with him, but the following evening all three returned to the dance hall together with some of Paul's friends. They waited outside until Bonelli emerged, whereupon Paul confronted him and asked him if he was "willing to do right by [Elizabeth]." Having talked the matter over with Paul and the others at Elizabeth's family home, Bonelli agreed to marry Elizabeth the next morning. However, when they reached City Hall, Bonelli told the clerk he had been kidnapped and forced to come there. The clerk called the police, who arrested Bonelli, and put Elizabeth in the custody of the New York Society for the Prevention of Cruelty to Children (NYSPCC). There is no evidence that the two ever married: Bonelli maintained his refusal to marry Elizabeth even after being prosecuted for statutory rape, pleading guilty to misdemeanor assault, and being sentenced to one year in the New York City Reformatory. Elizabeth's fate is unknown.[4]

In seeking marriages for teenage girls, working-class families were not treating them as children. Elizabeth Tedesco described Bonelli as "ruining" her, using an adult term that conveyed an understanding of the consequences of sexual intercourse outside marriage. A female who lost her virginity or became pregnant, whatever the circumstances, was ruined, both physically, in having lost her hymen, and socially, in having lost her respectability, and, therefore, her prospects of marriage. Families sought a girl's marriage to save her from that ruin, to secure her future. In doing so, they signaled that they saw a girl as ready to assume an adult role. In allowing teenage girls to marry, working-class parents showed the same concern with physical development that jurors and newspaper reporters evinced in abduction cases: a girl's ability to bear children and to gain employment was seen as establishing her maturity.

The law allowed working-class families to treat girls as adults in that way. Until 1926, New York was one of eleven states that had no statute establishing a minimum age of marriage, leaving in effect the common law ages of twelve years for girls and fourteen years for boys. The state legislature did, however, raise the age at which parental consent was no longer required, first in 1887, and then again in 1896, when it was set at eighteen years for females and twenty-one years for males.[5] Those measures subordinated girls in their teens to their parents, denying them the freedom of choice in marriage enjoyed by adults, but, crucially, defining them as capable of marriage, unlike younger girls. By not simply extending the prohibition on a girl's marriage, those changes created a fluid boundary between childhood and adulthood. After her twelfth birthday, a girl became a potential adult, even though she only attained that status absolutely on her eighteenth birthday. This inconsistency between marriage law and the age of consent reveals the limitations of analyzing only a single statute or offense. By pulling out a single thread from the fabric of the law in that way, we lose sight of the larger pattern, which in this case is one in which the status of teenage girls as children was less clearly, or easily, established than the increased age of consent suggested.

It was the support of legal officials that allowed families to use a charge of statutory rape as a means of achieving the outcome of marriage. In the case of prosecutors, that attitude reflected in part their inability to present a girl, who cast herself as ruined and sought marriage, as an innocent child. They also followed the lead of judges. Many who presided over the city's criminal courts saw teenage girls as mature and gave little indication of having been influenced by the vision of childhood expressed by the NYSPCC. They also continued to display a "Victorian" sensibility that emphasized female chastity and tolerated male sexual license. Although such notions put judges at odds with social workers and with young women who sought to express their sexuality, they tended to ally judges with proponents of the view that a "ruined" girl should be able to make right her condition through marriage.[6] It was also the case that, unlike efforts by families to institutionalize "problem girls" or to obtain support from social agencies, a marriage imposed no burden on the legal system, and could even save the state the cost of imprisonment or of providing support for an illegitimate child. In part then, working-class New Yorkers gained access to the law because judges—rather than adhering to a coherent system of normative values and beliefs, as much legal history presents them as doing—"improvise[d] solutions to immediate and intractable conflicts, using the imperfect materials of an inherited and changing legal order."[7]

Working-class efforts to use the law to make right a girl's ruin occurred on a large enough scale to affect the way in which legal officials and jurors understood teenage girls, and also to influence the meaning of the age of consent. Thirty percent of statutory rape cases for the years 1896 to 1926 included an effort to resolve a case by means of a marriage or by a financial payment in lieu of marriage.[8] In practice, in many prosecutions using the age of consent, reformers, prosecutors, and other New Yorkers confronted teenage girls quite unlike their younger, prepubescent sisters, girls who seemed to require less protection than did young children. By instigating those cases, working-class families helped to produce an increasingly sharp division between prepubescent and pubescent children.

Throughout the first half of the twentieth century, working-class New Yorkers continued to use the language of ruin to describe premarital sexual intercourse. Girls and their families generally spoke of a man who took a girl's virginity as having "ruined her," described the sex act itself as "her ruin," and referred to the victim as a "ruined girl." Sociologist Ruth True reported in 1914 that working-class parents on New York City's West Side told her that " 'you've got t' keep your eye on a girl. . . . [Y]ou never can tell, if you don't keep watch, when a girl's goin' to come back an' bring disgrace on you.' . . . The sting of her shame is felt to be keener than any boy can inflict." Pregnancy magnified the consequences of a girl's ruin. Illegitimacy continued to carry a strong social stigma throughout the first half of the twentieth century, with the result that a ruined girl passed on her loss of respectability to her child.[9] While generally shared by the white working-class populations of New York City, the notion of ruin apparently held less sway among their African American neighbors. Some middle-class observers argued that blacks placed less value on virginity and marriage than European cultures commonly did, pointing to evidence that they engaged in cohabitation and serial monogamy. But not all African American workers shared that attitude. In Philadelphia, for example,

W. E. B. Du Bois also found a "respectable" working-class whose concerns more closely approximated those of most white workers.[10]

After the turn of the twentieth century, working-class families found the task of preventing a girl's ruin increasingly difficult. Forced by low wages to depend on contributions from all family members, parents did not have the option of keeping their daughters at home, "under the protection of parents and family connections, until mature age [and marriage]," the middle-class ideal as purity reformer Emily Blackwell expressed it.[11] As the female work-force quadrupled between 1870 and 1910, an increasing proportion of teen-age girls sought paid work, as many as three-quarters by the 1890s, up from around half in the middle decades of the nineteenth century. Increasingly, those girls found themselves not exchanging their homes for the homes of middle-class employers, in which they could live and labor as domestic ser-vants, but traversing, instead, the city's streets to factories, department stores, and offices. "Never before in civilization," lamented social reformer Jane Addams, "have such numbers of young girls been suddenly released from the protection of the home and permitted to walk unattended upon city streets and to work under alien roofs."[12]

Once their daughters ventured into the public arena, parents could not easily protect or police them. This was true even of Italian parents, who sub-jected pubescent girls to especially strict supervision. It might have been the case, as sociologist Josephine Roche asserted in 1914, that "the old-country custom of close watchfulness" over a girl was only relaxed "during her hours of work," but work proved to be a significant chink in the armor of parental surveillance. Italian girls who struck up acquaintances with, or were assaulted by, men they met on the way to and from work appeared in the city's courts, as did girls who used going to work as a cover for meetings with men, and others whose female co-workers helped them run away from home.[13] Other, less strictly supervised, girls even more easily found their way to urban spaces, such as hotels, furnished rooms, parks, stores, movie theaters, and saloons, where their families and communities had only a limited ability to police or investigate their sexual encounters. Increasing numbers also left their homes entirely, becoming runaways.

If a teenage girl's ruin could not be prevented, it might still be made right by marriage. Marriage could bring both respectability and at least nominal eco-nomic security. Ruth True found that, among the Irish, Italian, and German communities on New York City's West Side, "marriage — even a common law marriage — is accepted as removing any stigma that might attach to an irregu-lar relationship"; working-class New Yorkers from other ethnic groups and neighborhoods who appear in the case files echoed that attitude. A marriage made right premarital sexual intercourse by rewriting that sexual encounter as a courtship, thereby resituating what had happened within the boundaries of respectability, and removing any blot on the family name. Marriage also, at least formally, offered the opportunity to shift the burden of providing for a girl from her family to the man who had ruined her.[14] Middle-class reformers often lamented that the marriages of ruined girls, particularly marriages into which the man had been forced, lacked any substance and often quickly collapsed; but even a brief marriage, one that existed in form only, did win for some girls a degree of respectability in their communities.[15] When a man's wedded state or other circumstances made his marriage to the girl he had ruined impossible, working-class families commonly sought a financial settlement from him as an alternative. Payment of a lump sum, or regular payments for the support of a child, went some way toward ameliorating a girl's dependency, but, except when the money allowed a pregnant girl to be sent away from her community to have her child, it failed to restore a girl's respectability.

In the eyes of working-class parents, marriage was as much an option for a girl in her teens as for an adult woman. According to Ruth True, families on the West Side found that marriage at "sixteen is a bit early, but [that] eighteen or nineteen is a good age and further delay is considered needless." A mother did not view her fifteen- or sixteen-year-old daughter's marriage with displeasure, nor did it disturb her to see the girl assume "the incessant struggle for existence which makes up the career of the wife of a casual laborer."[16] On the other hand, for Josephine Roche, True's collaborator in the West Side study, whose outlook was shaped by new ideas about childhood and development, a sixteen-year-old bride provided a portrait of incongruity: "The dark, frail little bride in her elaborate costume looked like a child playing at 'dressing up.' . . . She was only sixteen, and Nick, who walked beside her bearing his head like a young prince instead of the butcher's helper that he was, had barely turned nineteen. One could not help but reflect that if [the little bride] had been living in Gramercy Park instead of on the West Side . . . [she] might be heading the freshman basketball team with years of care-free development ahead of her, instead of facing the imminent trials of child-bearing with the probable addition of factory labor."[17]

Yet even Roche did not deny the girl's capacity to be a married woman; she might have more development ahead of her, but she nonetheless could bear children and perform labor. Only a shift in emphasis separated that understanding from the one expressed by working-class parents, who looked to the capacities that a girl had rather than to the growth still ahead of her. The only limit that understanding imposed on the notion of ruin related to physical maturity, not age. To be ruined, a girl needed to have developed to the stage where she could be penetrated sufficiently for her hymen to be ruptured. As a result, the concept of ruin was at odds with efforts to include teenage girls in the category of childhood, serving instead to distinguish pubescent girls from those who had yet to reach menarche.

The notion of ruin that can be glimpsed in the New York County district attorney's files encompassed a more extensive range of circumstances than has generally been recognized. Working-class families sought a girl's marriage when she lost her virginity, even if she had lost it to a man she had not known before he "ruined" her. Families more often made efforts to arrange a marriage or a financial settlement when a girl's ruin extended beyond the loss of virginity to pregnancy.[18] The Tedesco family was not unique in adhering to a concept of ruin that made no more allowance for the circumstances in which a girl lost her virginity than it did for the duration of her relationship with the man responsible for her condition. Elizabeth's family regarded marriage as the solution for her situation, even though the prospective husband had brought about her ruin through the use of force. In fifteen cases, or 17 percent of the cases I found that involved extralegal efforts, the girl alleged that the defendant had forced her to have sexual intercourse.[19]

Even more strikingly, seven of the girls who stated that they had been raped themselves sought marriage. Seventeen-year-old Susan Russell, for example, charged that Peter Waldstein, a twenty-six-year-old Russian salesman, had put drugs in her wine and, once she lost consciousness, had had intercourse with her. In return for his promise to marry her, however, Susan agreed not to tell her brothers about the assault and regularly went with Waldstein to hotels for the purpose of having sex. Only when she became pregnant, and Waldstein refused to go through with the marriage, did Susan tell her brothers. They confronted Waldstein, who threatened to have them arrested for blackmail; instead, Susan and her family had him arrested and charged with rape. As in other similar cases, the middle-class deputy assistant district attorney (DADA) saw Susan's willingness to remain involved with Waldstein as inconsistent with her claim that he had coerced her. In the terms in which most working-class immigrants viewed sexuality, however, Susan's behavior was entirely consistent: once ruined, a girl had little prospect of marriage to anyone other than the man who had ruined her. It was thus no easy matter for a ruined woman to spurn a man who had coerced her, contrary to what middle-class prosecutors may have thought. Moreover, the firm distinction made by prosecutors between coerced and consensual intercourse did not exist in the culture of working-class youth. Violence against women constituted an unexceptional part of the sexual behavior of young men; it was common even in sexual relationships into which girls willingly entered. In this sexual culture, the fact that a man had coerced a girl did not necessarily represent an obstacle to their marriage. In the event, Waldstein did eventually marry Susan Russell, whereupon the DADA dropped the charges against him.[20]

Girls who had not been coerced also on occasion initiated extralegal efforts to pressure their sexual partners into marriage. Most of those girls were pregnant, and they shared with their families the concern that their children be made legitimate and have financial support.[21] In speaking and acting in those ways, girls testified to the extent to which belief in ruin crossed generational lines.

The concept of ruin made a man responsible for a girl's condition and put the onus on him to "do the right thing." When confronted, almost all the men in my sample admitted to having had sexual intercourse with the girl in question, but in only approximately one-third of the cases did men or their families propose that the case be settled through a marriage.[22] There is some evidence to suggest that the reason why a greater proportion of the men charged with statutory rape did not propose marriage was that different cultures held men responsible for a girl's ruin to different degrees. In a sociological study of the community of Greenwich Village carried out in the 1920s, Caroline Ware argued that, regardless of their class and degree of Americanization, Italians believed that "if a boy got a girl into trouble, the fault lay with the girl's father who had not protected her." The Irish, by contrast, were "more ready to lay responsibility on the man."[23] In African American migrant communities, and the rural southern communities from which they came, the relative lack of stigma attaching to extramarital sexuality and pregnancy meant that men felt little pressure to marry girls with whom they had sex.[24]

A further explanation for the failure of more men to propose marriage is a double standard that limited male responsibility for sexual acts with a girl who had already lost her virginity. As late as the 1930s, sociologist William Whyte reported that, in an Italian slum district of a city in the eastern United States, "a man who takes her virginity from a 'good girl,' seriously affecting her marriageability, will marry her because he is responsible. . . . [If a girl] enjoys a good reputation, her family will be able to exert a good deal of pressure to force a marriage. If he makes her pregnant, marriage is hardly to be avoided. The promiscuous girl is less desirable socially, but there is also less risk in having relations with her. Only pregnancy can impose a responsibility and . . . such entanglements may frequently be avoided."[25] Even in the case of a girl who had already lost her virginity, becoming pregnant outside marriage compounded her ruin. She passed on the stigma of illegitimacy to her child, and she suffered the same economic pressures that a "good girl" did. But, since her earlier sexual activity had damaged her social standing, the man who had made her pregnant felt less social pressure to make right her ruin than the man who had made a "good girl" pregnant. Some men who agreed to "do the right thing" were motivated by their earlier promise to marry a girl should she become pregnant. But most proposed marriage in order to avoid legal punishment.[26]

When a girl's family refused an offer of marriage, as they did in 9 percent of cases, the case files indicate that the family was usually motivated by concerns as to how effectively the marriage would make right the daughter's ruin. Some parents rejected an offer of marriage because they did not think the man could adequately provide for their daughter. In other cases, parents objected to the bad character of the man, which usually meant that he had served time in prison. Ethnicity also operated as an obstacle to marriage. Jewish parents, for example, often regarded Italian and Irish men as inappropriate husbands for their daughters. The parents of one African American girl refused to allow her to marry a "West Indian negro" on the grounds that he was not, like her, a "real American."[27]

Strikingly absent from the reasons parents gave for opposing the marriage of their daughters is the daughter's young age. In only one case, in 1916, did a father reject a man's offer to marry his daughter on the grounds that "she was rather young."[28] However, at that time he did not know that the man had "ruined" his daughter; knowledge of her situation would likely have changed his response. Moreover, the girl was only thirteen years of age, probably barely pubescent. Marriages of twelve- and thirteen-year-old girls appear relatively infrequently in the legal record, reflecting those girls' limited physical maturity. By age fourteen, when many had also entered the paid workforce, no such ambiguity about a girl's capacity for marriage existed.[29]

The extensive range of circumstances that fell within the ambit of working-class New Yorkers' concept of ruin, together with their reliance on physical maturity to define the end of childhood, helps explain why such a high proportion of statutory rape prosecutions involved efforts to enforce marriage. For ordinary New Yorkers, any act of premarital sex ruined a girl. It did not matter if an unmarried girl had had no previous relationship with the man with whom she had sexual intercourse, or if a girl had been forced to have sex. New Yorkers saw the consequences as the same. As long as the girl was at least twelve years old, and physically mature, they believed that her condition could be made right by marriage to the man in question. Only within the category of cases in which a girl had sexual intercourse with a man in return for money, or some other form of payment, are there no examples of efforts to arrange a marriage.

Working-class girls and their families began their pursuit of marriage and financial settlements by using informal, extralegal, and local means. In early-twentieth-century New York City, neighborhood ties, particularly among women, helped to police sexual behavior. Families conducted their own investigations, sometimes with the assistance of doctors, and confronted men whom girls alleged had "ruined" them. Only when those informal efforts failed did working-class New Yorkers look to the legal system in order to apply additional pressure through the threat of imprisonment. The extralegal measures appear only on the margins of existing accounts of the efforts to police female sexuality, which has the effect of overstating the role of the legal system. What has been largely overlooked is the extent to which the extralegal actions of working-class New Yorkers took place in the shadow of the law, rather than apart from it, and as a result affected how the legal system responded to the sexual activity of teenage girls.

In the early twentieth century, working-class New Yorkers continued to display a degree of interest in their neighbors' activities and a willingness both to help parents maintain authority over their children and to intervene when they observed suspicious behavior. Charles Morris, a twenty-four-year-old shipping clerk, owed his conviction for statutory rape in 1896 to such community policing. Morris met Ethel Katz, a fourteen-year-old schoolgirl, on the street and, over the following weeks, took walks with her, before asking her to come to his room. Morris went into his building first, and had Ethel follow a short time later. However, the janitress who was scrubbing the steps saw through this subterfuge, spoke to the landlady, and sent a male tenant to tell Ethel's mother that they believed the girl "was in a room with a man." When Mrs. Katz arrived, the landlady took her to Morris's room, and when Morris, responding to Mrs. Katz's knocking, opened the door, Mrs. Katz caught sight of her daughter. When Morris refused to let her in, she went to fetch her husband, but the parents returned too late to catch Morris.[30]

On the more frequent occasions when members of a family did not actually catch a couple in the act of consensual sex, unlike Mrs. Katz and her neighbors, they often conducted their own investigations, seeking to determine whether a girl had been ruined. One form of investigation was to take a girl to a trusted family doctor. As they did in the case of younger girls, parents turned to doctors as experts, able to authoritatively read bodily signs and to tell them the "truth" about what had happened to a teenage girl. Although the objective was sometimes the same as when a young girl was involved—to determine, that is, whether the hymen had been ruptured—families more often used doctors in quite a different way: to impel a girl to tell the truth, rather than to have the physician speak for her. Parents and siblings asked doctors to confirm their suspicions that a girl had lost her virginity, or become pregnant, and used his diagnosis to persuade the girl to tell them what had happened. In 1911, for example, an Italian woman, visiting her sister's family, noticed the "condition" of her fourteen-year-old niece and became suspicious. She called the girl's physical appearance to her brother-in-law's attention, and he took the girl to a doctor. The doctor diagnosed her as five months' pregnant. Only then, in the doctor's office, did the girl admit that her stepmother's father had been forcing her to have intercourse with him.[31]

As we have seen, when a family established that a girl had been ruined, they often confronted the man who was responsible. Olive Smith's trip to the local district court makes it clear that the legal option of lodging a charge of rape lay in the background of extralegal efforts to force a marriage: when a girl or her family asked a man to "do the right thing," they were offering him a choice between marriage and prosecution. As sixteen-year-old Mary Marcus put it, in testimony in the magistrates' court in 1911, "if he married me then there would be no trouble now."[32] In effect, and regardless of whoever initiated them, extralegal efforts to make right a girl's ruin through marriage took place not so much outside the legal system as in its shadow. Most men caught having sexual intercourse with teenage girls were aware of the options available to them. Many followed Paul Covello in proposing marriage "if that would get him out of trouble."[33]

The use of the shadow of the law was a well-established part of working-class legal cultures in the United States long before the early twentieth century. Historians have found evidence that, in the eighteenth century, pregnant single women and their families began initiating fornication prosecutions in an effort to secure private maintenance and compensation settlements from the man responsible. In part, they did so because of local authorities' decreasing interest in prosecuting such cases.[34] In nineteenth-century Philadelphia, as part of poor and working people's regular recourse to criminal courts to resolve everyday quarrels with neighbors, friends, and co-workers, unwed mothers continued to initiate prosecutions for fornication and bastardy in an attempt "to use the threat of court action to gain a private settlement."[35]

Reconstruction gave African Americans in the South the opportunity to use the law in the same way.[36]

The absence from my sample of middle-class families reflects an equally long-standing rejection of recourse to criminal law in middle-class legal cultures. Cornelia Dayton locates the origins of that attitude in the eighteenth century, when elite and propertied householders moved from "a communal ethos — by which one revealed and repented all sin — to an ethic of privacy in which middle-class respectability was preserved by shielding the family name from public exposure."[37] In the late nineteenth and early twentieth century, when middle-class Americans failed in their informal efforts to arrange marriages or financial settlements in response to premarital sexual behavior and to out-of-wedlock pregnancy, they turned not to criminal courts but to private networks, to organizations such as the Women's Christian Temperance Union and to private maternity homes and reformatories.[38]

Although some New York families succeeded in arranging marriages without formal recourse to the law, the efforts of others to force men to "do the right thing" flowed into the courts. Even after a man's refusal to marry a girl caused her or her parents to charge him with rape, the wronged girl's family continued to pursue marriage within the legal system. One father, confronted by a female social worker seeking his consent to the marriage of his nineteen-year-old son to the fifteen-year-old girl he had impregnated, declared he would not let his son marry any girl who appealed to the court, but generally working-class New Yorkers did not see the fact that a girl had charged a man with rape as an obstacle to the couple's marrying later.[39]

Despite the increased opportunities that the higher age of consent provided for working-class families to use the law as a lever, a threat, or a bargaining chip, immigrant New Yorkers did not always succeed in taking advantage of that potential. In her snapshot of a typical day in New York City's magistrates' courts, reformer Kate Claghorn described an Italian woman who came to make a complaint that a man had "done something to her little girl." The mother found herself unable to get anyone in the courtroom to understand what it was that he had done. "The chief clerk knows a little Italian, translates a few words, and gives up," Claghorn recounts. "It turns out that she is speaking the Sicilian dialect. No one in the court knows that language; the chief clerk tries again, and in a few seconds the case is discharged." Not surprisingly, the woman left the court "boiling with rage." Claghorn's presumption that her frustration would lead the woman to take the law into her own hands, and land her back in court as a defendant, reflects stereotypes of Italians as hot-blooded and violent more than it does the alternatives available to working-class immigrants.[40] Actually, many immigrants responded by turning to one of a variety of extralegal tribunals established in their communities to hear cases that they were unwilling or unable to take to court.[41]

Nonetheless, many working-class families did successfully use the law to apply pressure on men to go through with a marriage. Men who offered to marry a girl, or agreed to a marriage proposed by her or her family, typically did so at the time of their arrest. Of those who did not, most suggested or accepted marriage after being arraigned in the magistrates' court; only a few waited until a grand jury indicted them, at which point they faced the prospect of spending a long period in prison while awaiting trial. Michael Lione held out until he faced the prospect of conviction for statutory rape. After keeping company with seventeen-year-old Donna Gallo for six months, Lione forced her to have intercourse with him. He told her, "I done this so that I know you are my true wife. I know that you have to marry me." Because of Lione's promise to marry her, Donna told no one about the rape, but a month later Lione told Donna's mother. Lione then stopped visiting the family, who eventually had him arrested. At his trial, Lione testified that he had called on Donna, but he denied that he had talked to her of marriage or had had intercourse with her. As the evidence against him mounted, however, Lione changed his position. He pled guilty to second-degree assault and agreed to marry Donna.[42]

Working-class New Yorkers' efforts to pressure men into marriage survived within the legal system, and often succeeded, because of the crucial support they received from legal officials. In the second half of the nineteenth century, a concern to make the law less accessible to personal use, and more effective in controlling specific populations, had led to institutional and structural changes that placed control of the process of criminal justice in the hands of salaried city officials: professional police, district attorneys, and magistrates. Although historians have argued that these officials helped create rigid boundaries between formal and informal legal sites, discourses and practices, legal officials in Manhattan, particularly the judges whose decisions provided a lead for prosecutors, facilitated the continuous relationship between informal and formal legalities sought by working-class New Yorkers.[43] Studies of courts in Wisconsin, New York, California, and North Carolina have highlighted instances in which legal officials ignored the wishes and authority of parents who had come to the legal system for help in controlling their daughters, and in which judges displayed hostility toward girls who expressed their sexuality. The case files in my sample show that there was another side to those attitudes. Many of the judges who presided over New York City courts shared with working-class families the beliefs that girls who had sexual intercourse outside marriage were ruined, that marriage was the only way to remedy that condition, and that girls in their teens were sufficiently mature to enter into a marriage. Those beliefs sometimes led judges to disregard legal rules and stretch legal categories, or to endorse the efforts of others to do so, in an effort to obtain that remedy.[44]

Officers of the NYSPCC were the first legal officials encountered by most of those working-class New Yorkers who had lodged a charge of rape with the aim of pressuring a man into marrying a ruined girl. The Society's view of teenage girls as children in need of protection, and its commitment to law enforcement and the punishment of offenders as the only effective means of protecting children, could have been expected to lead NYSPCC officers to obstruct working-class efforts to use the law to pressure men into marriages. In practice, however, its officers proved more pragmatic, adapting themselves to the attitudes of the DADAs and the judges, who had the greatest influence on how a case would be resolved. When a man who admitted impregnating a fifteen-year-old girl asked one NYSPCC officer "what was the customary thing to do in these cases," the officer replied, "sometimes they married and sometimes they stood trial."[45] NYSPCC officers did not so much encourage or endorse marriage in statutory rape cases as act as intermediaries in the efforts of others to achieve that end. Most often that meant simply directing the parties involved in a prosecution to the district attorney's office. When Joseph Angelico, an eighteen-year-old Italian errand boy, was charged with the rape of fifteen-year-old Maria Ferranti and released on bail, he approached the Society, which had the pregnant Maria in custody, and sought to marry her. The superintendent of the NYSPCC responded by sending Angelico to the DADA, a referral that began a process by which the families involved resolved the case through the marriage of Joseph and Maria.[46]

In a typical pattern of action, the DADA, after meeting with Angelico and both families, recommended to the judge that the couple be allowed to marry. When the couple supplied him with proof of their marriage, the DADA obtained the judge's permission to recommend to the grand jury that the charge against Angelico be dismissed.[47] When circumstances made it difficult for a marriage to be performed, DADAS sometimes went beyond telling families what they needed to do: they would help with the process by obtaining documents such as birth certificates and arrange for the couple to be issued a marriage license. On rare occasions, they went as far as putting pressure on a man to go through with a marriage. In one case in 1906, a DADA told a man to produce a marriage certificate within two days or face prosecution for rape. There is little direct evidence as to DADAS' motives for such actions. When the man threatened with prosecution in 1906 later filed for divorce on the grounds that the prosecutor had coerced him into marriage, the district attorney's office defended itself by asserting that the DADA "had merely followed the precedent established in the police courts and the Court of General Sessions in similar cases."[48] That statement, the most explicit expression of prosecutors' attitudes that the case files offer, suggests both that the district attorney's office was not committed to enforcing the law when the parties sought a marriage and that, in supporting marriages, DADAS followed the lead of magistrates and trial court judges. There is no evidence that they gave any consideration to the girl's age.

In addition to a DADA's endorsement, working-class families had to have the support of both a grand jury and a judge in order to secure a marriage and to extract a couple from the legal system. Grand juries, inclined as they were to follow their own ideas of who should be prosecuted, did not always follow the lead of a DADA. Although that break with the prosecutor most often involved rejecting his recommendation to indict a defendant, grand juries did also opt to issue an indictment when they had been directed to dismiss the charges. In fact, had a grand jury taken that action, it would have been following the letter of the law; under New York law, marriage per se was not a defense that nullified a charge of statutory rape. When the parties to a case had married, however, grand juries followed the recommendations of DADAS and dismissed the charges.

Although the case files contain little direct evidence of jurors' attitudes, in one surviving transcript, from April 1916, a grand jury focused on marriage in its consideration of a statutory rape case. Early in the hearing, seventeen-year-old Sadie Brumberg told the foreman that, after an extended sexual relationship with Joseph Rosen, she had become pregnant and had had a child. The foreman and several other jurors then questioned Sadie and the other witnesses at length about why the couple had not married. Sadie claimed Rosen had initially promised to marry her, but he had then demanded $200 from her family to go through with the marriage. Sadie's brother and father told the grand jury that they opposed her marriage to Rosen. The arresting officer testified that Rosen had revealed nothing to him about his attitude concerning such a marriage. Eventually, the grand jury did indict Rosen, but the questions its members asked clearly showed their willingness to see the case resolved through marriage rather than by Rosen's imprisonment.[49]

A marriage settlement also required the support of a judge. Magistrates and trial court judges in the criminal courts generally cooperated with a family's efforts to pressure a man into marriage. Arthur Towne, the superintendent of the Brooklyn SPCC, and Bertram Pollens, the senior psychologist at Rikers Island Penitentiary and the author of a popular book on the sex criminal, both described judges as not only sympathetic to efforts to arrange marriages but also active in their support of those efforts. Pollens offered an account of a magistrate who claimed that four out of five statutory rape cases could be resolved through marriage and who attacked the NYSPCC for unnecessarily dragging couples into the courts.[50] Not all judges acted in this way. Commentators also observed a lack of uniformity in the attitudes and decisions of the judges who presided over the city's criminal courts. Moreover, judges in the juvenile courts, who were often allied with child protectors and shared their modern idea that childhood extended beyond puberty, more frequently opposed the marriage of teenage girls than did those who sat in the criminal courts.[51]

Judges' motives are less clear than are their actions. The available evidence suggests that judges who supported efforts to bring about a marriage did so because they saw the situation of the girls who appeared before them in the same terms that working-class families did: the girls were ruined, but they had the capacity to marry, and, by entering into marriage, they could make right their condition.[52] Judges' belief that teenage girls were capable of assuming the adult role of being a wife reflected the degree of attention they paid to the physical maturity of the girls who appeared in their courtrooms, as well as their understanding of the cultural beliefs of southern European immigrants to the United States. Judges frequently commented on the physical maturity of adolescent girls and stressed the incongruity between a girl's mature appearance and the law's treatment of her, on the basis of her age, as an immature child. Ideas about the different, more sexual, nature of southern and eastern Europeans added to judges' inclination to see immigrant girls as mature enough to marry. As Judge William Gold of the Niagara County Children's Court remarked in 1927, "A person must recognize that both the Italian girl and the Polish girl mature much younger than the average American girl. I had a girl come into my office, she was Polish, not quite fifteen, she weighed one hundred-thirty-five pounds, a strong robust girl."[53]

Judge Gold went on to tell his colleagues that "everybody knows the Italian girls marry early in life, and I think there is less immorality among the Italian people because of that fact. . . . I feel it is my duty to grant that [Italian] girl the right to be married."[54] His comments reflected a tendency on the part of New York City judges to see early marriage as a laudatory element in the cultures of immigrant groups. In Judge Gold's case, his support for the marriage of Italian girls derived at least in part from his belief that early marriage could contain the sexual nature of Italian immigrants, a nature that would otherwise manifest itself in socially dangerous sexual activity. Arthur Towne, in generalizing about judges' support for the marriage of teenage girls, also attributed the bench's respect for early marriage as a cultural practice to an assumption that such marriages "must be part of Nature's wisdom."[55]

Judges' support for marriage also reflected a belief that marriage effectively made right a girl's ruin. Michael Lione had agreed to marry Donna Gallo only after he realized that the jury would convict him of statutory rape. Nonetheless, the presiding judge felt that, given the support for the marriage of both sets of parents and Lione's previous good character, "there is no good reason why two young people cannot live happily together." He then gave Lione a suspended sentence, warning him that if he did not treat his wife as a husband should, he would send him to jail.[56] These comments reveal that the judge believed that marriage made right a girl's ruin by providing her with the social identity of a wife and with a future, a life of happiness, if not of wedded bliss, that reintegrated her into respectable society. The judge did recognize that a gap existed between the formal state of marriage that the law provided and the relationship that effectively made right a girl's ruin. He noted that the couple's parents would need to support them, and he warned Lione that imposing a suspended sentence allowed the court to supervise and, if necessary, punish his behavior. Reformers such as Arthur Towne, however, argued that the gap between form and substance made marriage ineffective as a response to a girl's ruin. Towne lamented the fact that, once the charges against men had been dropped, they often mistreated or abandoned their wives, leaving them to face the same struggle to support themselves that they had confronted before their marriage.[57] The judge in the Lione case, by contrast, was typical of his colleagues in taking the view that there was "no good reason" to believe that marriage would fail to make right a girl's ruin.

If a girl had become pregnant, judges saw marriage as a good solution on the grounds that it prevented her ruin from being passed on to her child, in the form of the stigma of illegitimacy. "It always seemed to me harsh for us to refuse to give a name to an unborn child," Judge Scripture remarked, in 1930, to the general assent of his colleagues from children's courts throughout New York State.[58]

Both the beliefs that judges exhibited and those that they did not help explain why they supported working-class efforts to secure a marriage. To act on their beliefs, judges had to step outside the rape statute, outside formal legal categories and rules. But we do not hear judges lamenting that the formal law restricted them from acting to help families. Rather than appearing to be constrained by statute and precedent, they seem willing to improvise a solution, particularly one that employed a legal form, marriage, which reflected long-standing custom and which cost the state nothing. Even judges in the children's court balanced the modern view of the immaturity of teenage girls (the premise on which their court had been founded) with a willingness to improvise. As one judge told his colleagues in 1927, "You can't lay down any hard and fast rules, you have to get the facts, you have to study them and see what is best for the welfare of the girl, the child involved, and if you do that there will be some instances, as you well understand, where they ought to get married."[59] Judges also showed little sensitivity to modern concepts of childhood and sexuality, the ideas that persuaded social workers to reject forced marriage. Older ideas remained so entrenched in the criminal justice system that, as Ruth Alexander has argued, even the psychiatrists and social workers who became affiliated with the courts after the 1920s reinforced rather than overturned the courts' emphasis on female sexual purity.[60] Because modern ideas were less influential in the criminal courts, concepts of ruin and of marriage as the means of making right that condition appear to have survived among judges in these courts to a greater degree than they did among their colleagues in the juvenile courts or among the staff of maternity homes and reformatories.

By the 1920s, marriages finalized after a man's conviction also enjoyed the support of probation officers. John Nicessa, a nineteen-year-old Italian factory worker, was arrested in 1926 after the parents of Ruth Feinberg, the fifteen-year-old schoolgirl with whom he had been keeping company for a year, discovered that the couple had started having sexual intercourse. Nicessa professed a desire to marry Ruth, and both sets of parents, who had sanctioned the relationship, supported that outcome. In light of Nicessa's intentions, and because he convinced investigators from the Probation Bureau that his sexual behavior was the "climax of his affectionate interest" in Ruth, rather than the result of "deliberate viciousness," the judge opted to place him on probation for five years. Two weeks later he married Ruth, and a year later she gave birth to a baby girl. When the marriage ran into trouble, Nicessa's probation officer repeatedly intervened to sustain it. After the child's birth, when Nicessa started spending his evenings at a local speakeasy, rather than with his family, his mother-in-law visited the Probation Bureau on her daughter's behalf. The result was a letter warning Nicessa that "further violation of probation would not be tolerated by the Department." When Nicessa stopped working five months later, in the aftermath of his daughter's death, the probation officer could not prevent his sixteen-year-old wife from leaving him. But the officer did attempt several times to reconcile the couple, notwithstanding the fact that Nicessa's family believed that the different "racial characteristics" and "psychology" of the couple made such a reconciliation impossible. The two did, however, begin seeing one another again, and Ruth became pregnant. When Nicessa delayed setting up a home for them, it was the Probation Bureau to whom seventeen-year-old Ruth appealed for help in forcing Nicessa to keep his promise. A meeting was arranged, at which the probation officer identified the root of the problem as Nicessa's membership in a club, which his wife feared would lead him to neglect her. When Ruth accepted her husband's promise to give up going to the club if it interfered with his family life, the probation officer felt confident that he had placed their relationship on a firmer footing. In December 1928, in recommending Nicessa that be discharged, the probation officer reported that "harmonious relations" once again existed in the marriage.[61]

Since probation officers had the opportunity to bolster only a handful of relationships, their efforts did little to assuage reformers' growing concern about the frequency of marriages that took place following prosecutions for statutory rape. In the 1920s, that unease spurred a campaign to raise New York's age of marriage. That proposal took the authority to allow the marriage of a girl in her teens out of the hands of both parents and judges. In doing so, it brought marriage practices into line with the age of consent, solidifying the status of teenage girls as children. It was not simply that a girl in her teens was too young to assume the adult role of a wife, social worker Arthur Towne of the Brooklyn spcc argued in 1925; her immaturity would render marriage ineffective as a response to her situation. Despite a teenage girl's physical maturity, she had not yet had the "opportunity for the stabilizing of emotional reactions, for the orientation of the individual as a social being, and for the acquiring of moral standards." A teenage girl's marriage therefore could produce a catalog of social problems, Towne argued, including "improvidence, incompatibility, non-support, abandonment, abuse, exploitation, infidelity, separation, divorce, [and] improper rearing of offspring."[62] In mounting this argument, Towne and his colleagues granted that the physical maturity of teenage girls gave them some of the characteristics of adults, a view with which working-class families had repeatedly confronted them. But social workers did not attach the same significance to that physical maturity. It may have made those girls different from younger girls, but it did not make them adults. Individuals in their teens still retained an immature nature that marked them as children.

Campaigns against "child marriages" in New York did win changes in the state's marriage law, but not amendments that removed either the fluidity of the age of marriage or the inconsistency between it and the age of consent. The minimum age for getting married was raised in 1926, but only to sixteen, not to eighteen, the age of consent. The amended law also continued to allow fourteen- and fifteen-year-old girls to marry, provided that they obtained the permission of a children's court judge.[63] Despite the arguments of Towne and others, legislators treated the differences between girls in their teens and younger girls as significant enough for older girls to warrant only some, but not all, of the protection accorded to little children. They could not look past the fact that some teenage girls were physically capable of marriage and adult sexuality. Girls who married, or sought to marry, cast a shadow over their peers, making those who had been forced into acts of intercourse, or who had responded passively to a man's sexual advances, somehow undeserving of the treatment and protection that younger girls received. However, while jurors, acting on that perception, returned proportionally fewer indictments and convictions than they did in cases involving younger children, they none-theless did indict and convict some men, rather than entirely nullifying the law. Reformers also held to the idea that if a teenage girl was not a child, neither was she an adult. This response to statutory rape prosecutions would provide one foundation for a reconceptualization of children in their teens. Reformers would take the lead in that transformation, seizing on G. Stanley Hall's writings to explain the behavior of girls as the product of psychological immaturity. That immaturity distinguished a girl in her teens from an adult woman and marked her as an adolescent, as something different.

Making Adolescents

On the morning of 4 January 1916, Rosa Colletti, a fifteen-year-old embroidery factory operative, and eighteen-year-old Anna Belsito, Colletti's friend and co-worker, determined to escape any further beatings at the hands of their mothers, ran away from their parents' homes in the Bronx. Two nights later, as the girls ate dinner in a restaurant, they were approached by twenty-year-old Louis Morelli. Morelli talked with them for a while, and then took them to his furnished room. Later that evening, he told Anna to leave but invited Rosa to stay. Rosa and Morelli then had sexual intercourse. Some time after that, Morelli's roommate, James Torcello, arrived home and joined Rosa and Morelli in the room's only bed. In the days that followed, the two men went to work while Rosa "kept house"; in the evenings, Morelli brought Rosa food and took her out to various entertainments. On one occasion, Torcello had intercourse with Rosa while Morelli slept. At 2:00 A.M. on 20 January, two detectives, tipped off by Anna, whom they had arrested for soliciting, found Rosa and the two men in bed, and took all three into custody. Morelli admitted to the officers that he was living with Rosa and that he had had intercourse with her. He also claimed that he wanted to marry her. Unmoved by his offer, the police charged him with statutory rape.[1]

The encounter between Rosa and Morelli fell in the middle of the spectrum of acts that appeared in statutory rape prosecutions in the first quarter of the twentieth century. In one-third of all statutory rape cases, as in the Morelli case, it is not possible to determine if the girl consented to have sexual inter-course or was coerced. Another third of cases involved more clearly consen-sual acts. There is little ambiguity, for example, about what happened between Harry Donovan and sixteen-year-old Ellen Wilson. After meeting at a dance at 125th Street and Lexington Avenue, they had seen each other regularly for several years, before having sexual intercourse on 7 May 1916. On that evening, Donovan took Ellen to the vestibule of his hallway, where they had intercourse "standing up against the wall." Ellen acknowledged that she had "consented to the act," aware that, although Donovan had promised to marry her "if he found [her] straight," she "was supposed to get married before he touched [her] at all." They had intercourse once more soon thereafter, in his room, and then did not see each other until they met on 89th Street several weeks later. In the interval, Ellen's sister told their father that Ellen had been "ruined," but, despite his entreaties, she refused to tell her father "the truth." Some time later, she left home, first staying with a friend, then with an aunt, and finally, once she had found work, in a rented room. Following their meet-ing on 89th Street, Donovan tried to return Ellen to her father's home, but she cried and refused to go, ultimately convincing him to come with her instead. For two months they lived together, passing themselves off as married, until Ellen was discovered and arrested. Donovan, like Louis Morelli, was charged with statutory rape.[2]

While Ellen Wilson consented to have sexual intercourse, sixteen-year-old Catherine Vance clearly did not. Catherine's case is representative of the final third of statutory rape prosecutions. She and a young child were alone in the rooms on West 36th Street in which her family lived, when her half uncle William Buchanan came to visit in April 1915. For an hour, he sat in the kitchen reading, saying nothing to her until, the house having become dark, Catherine went to light the gas. Then he grabbed her from behind, pulled her into the bedroom, and threw her on the bed. When she went to scream, Buchanan threatened to kill her, leaving her too afraid to make any outcry, although she struggled with him all she could. However, she could not stop him from having sexual intercourse with her. The assault over, Catherine told Buchanan that she would tell her mother what had happened, to which he responded that if she did, "he would tell my father that it was I who wanted him to do it to me." Evidently afraid of how her father would react, Catherine "never said a word to anyone," even after Buchanan assaulted her on three further occasions. Only when she became pregnant, and was made aware for the first time of "how a child was born," did she cause the arrest of her half uncle.[3]

That Buchanan, Donovan, and Morelli were all charged with statutory rape highlights how, by the second decade of the twentieth century, that offense was used against practically all men accused of sexual intercourse with a girl aged from eleven to seventeen years regardless of the circumstances of that act.[4] Such an approach flew in the face of the statute, which defined statutory rape as including only acts involving underage girls that took place in circumstances not amounting to forcible, or first-degree, rape. Prosecutors' practice of including men who committed acts of incest among those charged with second-degree rape also broke with the prevailing interpretation of the state's incest law: that it applied to all incestuous acts that did not involve force.[5]

In focusing on the victim's age alone in determining which cases to prosecute as statutory rape, prosecutors reflected, and gave weight to, what they took to be jurors' perception of teenage girls as distinct from prepubescent girls. As Arthur Train, an assistant district attorney (ADA) in New York City in the first decade of the twentieth century, saw it, jurors "frequently feel by no means confident that the punishment will fit the crime, and are anxious, so far as they can, to dispose of the case for themselves."[6] In jurors' judgment, all acts with a teenage girl were by nature less violent, less criminal, than any act with a younger girl. The workings of the age of consent thus had the effect of sharpening the differentiation between girls in their teens and young children. That the age of consent nonetheless left in place some distinctions between teenage girls and adults is most strikingly evident in the treatment of cases involving incest. In the case of teenage girls, prosecutors used the legal notion of the age of consent to redefine incestuous acts that did not involve force as a form of sexual violence.[7]

Confronted by girls who did not behave like innocent children, and by working-class families, prosecutors, and jurors who did not treat them in the way that they did younger girls, reformers were forced to abandon their view of teenage girls as simply children. To articulate their sense that, if not children, those in their teens were nonetheless not adults, reformers needed a new framework, a new set of terms. That need made them receptive to the ideas contained in psychologist G. Stanley Hall's encyclopedic *Adolescence*, a two-volume work published in 1904.

Despite the relative slimness of the case file put together by the New York County District Attorney's Office for the prosecution of Louis Morelli, it contains not just one account of Rosa Colletti's story, but three. There is Rosa's statement to the officer from the New York Society for the Prevention of Cruelty to Children (NYSPCC) who investigated her case. There is that officer's summary of Rosa's statement, as contained in his investigation report. And there is a later and fuller summary that the officer made in the trial brief he prepared for the deputy assistant district attorney (DADA) who prosecuted Louis Morelli. Rosa's statement describes an encounter with Morelli in which she set some of the terms of their subsequent relationship. When Morelli asked, in the restaurant where they first met, whether she wanted to become his "friend," Rosa, taking the initiative, replied that he would first need to obtain a furnished room. But when Morelli said that he had such a room, it was Anna, not Rosa, who suggested that they go to see it. It was also Anna who, by agreeing to leave without Rosa, created a situation in which Rosa was left alone with Morelli. Rosa's statement as to what happened next is opaque, making it difficult to determine whether Morelli compelled her to remain and later have intercourse with him. The NYSPCC officer's initial summary of Rosa's statement omitted her conversation with Morelli in the restaurant, as well as the other details of their relationship before and after they had intercourse. Rosa was presented, instead, as a passive object whom Morelli "brought" to his home to "perpetrate an act of intercourse upon." In his second summary of Rosa's statement, the officer did include the restaurant conversation, but, as he recounted it there, Rosa played no role when the terms of her relationship with Morelli were being set. In this second narrative, Morelli told Rosa that "if she would be his friend he would take her to stay with him in his furnished room."[8]

The NYSPCC officer's two renditions of Rosa Colletti's story evinced a clear concern to make her appear passive. Had he charged Louis Morelli with abduction, as was the Society's practice at the end of the nineteenth century, presenting Rosa in that way would have been enough to make a case. The abduction statute required only that the jury be convinced that the man was the active party. But the charge made against Morelli was rape, and the rape statute also made the reason for a girl's passivity a relevant factor. If passivity resulted from her physical or mental weakness, or her immaturity, traits that marked her as a child, then the man who had sexual intercourse with her was guilty of first-degree rape. If she lacked those characteristics, and was therefore not a child, then he was guilty only of statutory rape.

In keeping with the NYSPCC's view of girls in their teens as children, turn-of-the-century prosecutors lodged a charge of first-degree rape against a man accused of having intercourse with a teenage girl. However, a teenage girl's statement, as opposed to one by a prepubescent girl, proved more difficult to present in a way that would lead jurors to regard her as a child. NYSPCC officers who summarized a young girl's statement could highlight a number of details that would encourage jurors to see her passivity as stemming from a lack of understanding. None of those details can be found in either the investigation report or the brief prepared by the officer presenting the case against Louis Morelli, because Rosa made no mention of them in her statement. Morelli did not remove her underwear; Rosa undressed herself, before getting into bed. She did not claim to have been hurt, or that she had cried out in pain, when Morelli was having intercourse with her. In fact, Rosa made no mention of any reaction on her part. But she did admit to receiving something in return for having intercourse with Morelli, namely, a room, meals, and a trip to the theater, an exchange that would hardly have suggested to jurors that she had no understanding of the value of sex. The NYSPCC officer in charge of Rosa's case could thus present her as passive, but could do nothing to encourage jurors to see her passivity as stemming from a childish lack of understanding.

The same problem faced NYSPCC officers responsible for cases involving girls, such as Catherine Vance, who had been coerced or assaulted. As they did in child rape and abduction cases, NYSPCC officers presented those girls as being passive by omitting the accounts they gave of being physically assaulted and of putting up resistance. The summary of Catherine Vance's statement contained in the brief described how William Buchanan "picked her up and carried her into a bedroom and assaulted her." After the assault, Buchanan "made her keep quiet about the affair by threats of bodily harm." Those threats are the only mention of force the NYSPCC officer included in his summary. Absent is any reference to Catherine's account of being "grabbed around the neck and waist from behind," of Buchanan's threatening to kill her, and of how he "pulled" her into the bedroom and threw her on the bed, holding his hand over her mouth. Also excluded are her accounts of screaming when he attacked her and of how she "struggled with deft. [sic] all [she] could." Having rendered Catherine passive in this way, the NYSPCC officer could do nothing more to portray her as a child. In her statement, Catherine did describe how Buchanan "pulled up her clothes," but the inclusion of this detail would have entailed referring to her struggles with him, and hence would have undermined the implicit claim that she was passive. Catherine explicitly stated that she felt "no pain" when Buchanan had intercourse with her; and, as with Ruth Levy, the timing of her screams, before the assault, meant that jurors were liable to interpret them as evidence that she understood what was happening. Although she made no mention of obtaining anything from Buchanan, in all likelihood Catherine would have been seeking money from him to help support her child, a circumstance that made it difficult to use her earlier failure to receive any payment as evidence of her innocence.

NYSPCC officers faced even greater difficulties when a girl clearly consented, as did Ellen Wilson. The NYSPCC officer who prepared the brief of the case against Harry Donovan represented Ellen as playing a passive role in her sexual acts with Donovan, but he could not avoid placing that passivity in a context that diminished its weight as a sign of childishness. Summarizing her statement, the officer wrote that, after Ellen let Donovan know where she was living, "he came to her room, and on June 22nd had sexual intercourse with her the first time in that room; that she had sexual intercourse with him on previous occasions elsewhere, but she cannot fix the dates; that from the time the defendant came to her furnished room until the day she was located and arrested, August 20th, the defendant lived with her in that room and frequently had sexual intercourse with her." Donovan is cast as the active agent in this account; the sexual acts happened because he came to her room and because he stayed on there with her. Omitted are any details of acts prior to that time, acts to which Ellen stated she had consented. However, other details of the events preceding the acts described in the brief, in which Ellen plays an active role, cannot simply be left out in this way. To place Ellen in the room she would share with Donovan, the NYSPCC officer had to recount how she had left home, stayed with an aunt and a friend until she found work, and then used her first paycheck to rent a room of her own. Neither that behavior nor her subsequent actions in passing herself off as Donovan's wife gave her the appearance of a child. And her statement contained no details that the officer could highlight to counter that impression.[9]

In court, prosecutors continued to face the dilemma that they had encountered in abduction cases: that what jurors saw and heard was at odds with what they expected from a child. DADAs reacted by taking into account a girl's physical development when they made decisions about whether to pursue a prosecution. In recommending the dismissal of the charges against a defendant in 1901, a prosecutor expressed his concern that "the girl is very large; indeed in her physical appearance she would easily pass for a full-grown woman, and certainly appears to be fully 18 years of age. . . . [F]rom the appearance of the girl I seriously doubt whether a jury would be willing to accept the statement of her parents [that she is sixteen years of age]."[10] As New York City's population of southern and eastern European immigrants swelled in the early decades of the twentieth century, racial ideas further exacerbated this situation. The children's court judges discussed in the previous chapter were not alone in being influenced by the notion that girls from those ethnic groups reached physical maturity at a younger age than native-born or Anglo-Saxon girls did.[11] When jurors looked at an immigrant girl, her ethnicity made them even more likely to regard her physical development as a sign of maturity, making it unlikely that they would see her as a child.

Whereas DADAS prosecuting men for abduction had shown little concern with how the alleged victim spoke, believing that jurors would follow the law and pay attention only to a girl's age, when they came to present statutory rape cases they were more inclined to emphasize that a girl spoke like a child. However, prosecutors could not bring the language of girls in their teens into line with the testimony of prepubescent girls. When teenage girls attempted to speak like children, defense attorneys aggressively challenged them. Relying on the presumption that intelligence came with physical maturity, attorneys insisted that girls in their teens could use adult language; if they did not know what sexual intercourse was before the events of the case, their experience would have provided them with an understanding of it. In a case in 1916, for example, one attorney objected that fourteen-year-old Maria Stadler was allowed to testify in euphemistic language and was whispering to the stenographer. "This girl is not a baby," the attorney complained. "This girl had a child. She knows what happened, where it happened, how it happened, and she ought to tell her story before the jury." When the attorney cross-examined Maria, she testified that Nicolo Alberti, the man accused of raping her, had "put his private thing into my privates." The defense attorney then attempted to ask Maria what a "private thing" was, in order "to show this girl never used these words before" and to find out "where she got this language from," but the district attorney objected. Instead, at the judge's suggestion, the defense attorney asked her "if she knows any other name for it." "I can't say it no other way," Maria answered. She was then confronted with a transcript from an earlier paternity proceeding against Alberti, in which she had testified that he had "sexual intercourse with me." Maria denied that she had used this language.[12] Faced with the prospect of this type of attack, NYSPCC officers and DADAS increasingly encouraged teenage girls to use the phrase "sexual intercourse," rather than the more euphemistic language employed by younger girls.

To make a case for statutory rape, prosecutors attempted to argue that a teenage girl who used adult language did not, in fact, have an adult sexual understanding, but remained essentially a child. They did this firstly by invoking the girl's virginity, whenever they could, in order to emphasize that, at the time the defendant had intercourse with her, she had possessed the innocence and purity of a child. After establishing her virginity by asking a girl if she had bled following intercourse with the defendant, a DADA would draw out statements designed to show her lack of understanding of the act at the time it took place. After Catherine Vance had testified about William Buchanan's assault on her, the prosecutor asked her, "Now, Catherine, up to the time that this happened to you, did you know what the defendant was doing or trying to do to you?" She answered that she did not. To be absolutely sure that the jury understood the significance of that testimony, the prosecutor restated his question. "You didn't know, as I take it, what sexual intercourse was; is that right? No, sir, I did not. Or how it was done? No sir."[13] In pursuing this approach, prosecutors accepted defense characterizations of girls in their teens as intelligent enough to speak like adults in the aftermath of their sexual experience, but they sought to shift the focus back to the girls' previous innocence. As one DADA put it in a particularly florid summation in 1901, "She is but a girl . . . She was a virgin when this man met her and she had no guile; she knew not of this sin. How is it today? Ah, he has blighted and blasted her life." Such rhetoric aimed to persuade jurors that, if a girl did not display the language and understanding of a child, her behavior was a reflection of what the defendant had done to her, not a sign of her corrupt, and untrustworthy, character.

The prosecutor just quoted followed up with a second, and frequently used, line of approach, invoking images of middle-class childhood, and of the jurors' own children, in order to argue that the degree of understanding that teenage girls possessed, as revealed through their language, was not that of an adult. "Your children of fourteen are going to school, not yet out of grammar school," the prosecutor pleaded, "and yet my learned friend would have you believe [that this fourteen-year-old girl] was a mature woman, with all the senses and judgment of a woman."[14] Even if a girl's language displayed some degree of understanding, so this argument went, her social role implied that that understanding was immature. Schoolgirls, Jane Addams noted, "have never broken the habits of childhood."[15] Prosecutors tried to establish that teenage girls were children by suggesting that their understanding of what was happening to them was so immature that they could not be taken to have given consent, and so limited that it rendered them as passive as children.

The substance of what teenage girls said in court also disrupted prosecutors' efforts to present them as children. Elements of their statements omitted in summaries and briefs were not so easily excluded from their testimony. So much was omitted from the story of an Ellen Wilson or a Catherine Vance, in order to make her appear to be a child, that it was more difficult to sustain the appearance of childhood at trial than was the case with a younger girl. Accounts of force and resistance, such as those provided by Catherine Vance and approximately one in every three complainants, did the most damage to prosecutors' claim that a girl was an innocent child, implying as they did an adult knowledge of the meaning of a sexual act.

Yet such testimony also provided the element of physical violence that, Elbridge Gerry had complained, some judges and jurors saw as necessary for an act to constitute rape. Until the amendment to the rape law in 1892, which introduced second-degree rape into the penal code, some judges had argued that force was a necessary element in statutory rape cases. By the early twentieth century, that misapprehension had been corrected: judges instead consistently stated that force was not a necessary part of the crime, although only rarely did they exclude such testimony, as had Judge Otto Rosalsky in a trial in 1906. When seventeen-year-old Donna Gallo testified that Michael Lione had threatened her with a revolver and covered her mouth to prevent her screaming, Rosalsky interrupted, "Well, that I cannot allow." "The charge is rape in the second degree and here is evidence of force," Judge Rosalsky declared, before going on to instruct the prosecutor not to "attempt to introduce any evidence as to force because it is not admissible in a charge of rape in the second degree . . . , that is, having sexual intercourse with a female, not the wife of the defendant, under the age of eighteen."[16] More often the presence of such testimony went unremarked upon. That silence was likely to have been, in part, a reflection of legal officials' perception that the force and resistance described by teenage girls fell short of what courts saw as constituting rape in the case of adult women, and thus was not out of place in a case of statutory rape. As a rule, no evidence existed to corroborate a girl's claim to have been coerced, so such a claim carried no formal weight in establishing a defendant's guilt: he could not be convicted on the basis of the girl's testimony alone.

But while legal officials understood that any act of sexual intercourse with a teenage girl constituted rape, many New Yorkers clearly did not. Men confronted by NYSPCC agents or police officers frequently admitted to having had intercourse with a teenage girl, but they did not think that they were thereby confessing to rape. Some responded to the charge of statutory rape by admitting to having had intercourse but denying that they had forced the girl to participate, just as many men did when accused of the rape of an adult woman.[17] In 1901, sentencing such a man, who "little knew the serious consequences of [his] act at the time [he committed it]," a judge commented that unfamiliarity with the statutory rape law was widespread in New York City's neighborhoods. "It is such a serious offense and yet it is an offense that is committed every day in the week, and I think very largely through ignorance." Men seemed unaware, he lamented, that "to have any intercourse whatever with a girl under the age of eighteen [is rape]," and "whether she consents, whether she is paid for it, whether she solicits or not, does not matter."[18]

But there was more to those men's behavior than simple ignorance of the law. They also clearly saw girls in their teens as adults, as able to engage in sexual activity, and showed little concern about establishing a girl's age before having sexual intercourse with her. Ernesto Colon, an eighteen-year-old black West Indian, born and raised in Puerto Rico, revealed himself to be "rather puzzled by the strict standards imposed upon him here," when questioned by Dr. Leslie Luehrs, of the Neurological Institute, as part of a Probation Department investigation in 1927. "He was accused of rape although as a matter of fact the girl with whom he had sex relations was perfectly willing," Luehrs wrote in his report, "and in his former environment this would not have led to real difficulties."[19] Over time, the NYSPCC's activities in working-class communities made some New Yorkers aware of how the state's law defined rape and childhood. But each new wave of immigrants and migrants added to the ranks of men unaware that sexual relationships considered legitimate in the countries or regions from which they came were deemed criminal in New York.

The misconceptions about the legal definition of rape shared by many New Yorkers played a crucial role in providing prosecutors with the corroboration they needed to convict a man of statutory rape. As in child rape, prosecutors were required to find additional evidence of the occurrence of the act and a girl's identification of the defendant as the man responsible.[20] They relied on medical evidence to corroborate the act, just as they did in other sex crimes. The corroboration of a girl's identification, however, most often came in a form almost never seen in other sex crimes: an admission by the defendant. Two of every three prosecutions in the years 1906 to 1926 relied on such a declaration to provide corroboration.[21] NYSPCC practices reflected the pivotal role of a man's statement in the case against him. Its manual, *Instructions for Officers and Staff*, impressed upon agents the importance of taking note of any statement a defendant made during his arrest because "frequently such testimony by the officer is the sole corroboration of a child's charges against an adult."[22]

The confusion about the legal import of sexual language that prompted many men to admit to statutory rape could also lead to disputes about the meaning of their statements and the value of those statements as corroboration. In the trial of Michael Lione in 1906, the debate over the statement he made to the relatives of seventeen-year-old Donna Gallo had two dimensions: the court interpreter's translation of the words he allegedly used and the meaning of those words. According to the interpreter who translated their testimony, both Donna's mother and grandmother stated that Lione had told them that he had "deceived" Donna and would marry her. Questioned by the defense attorney about his translation of the grandmother's testimony, the interpreter described "deceived" as a "literal translation" of the Italian word she used. When questioned further, Donna's grandmother explained that she understood the word as meaning "dishonored."[23] Lione's attorney held to the original translation, arguing at the close of the prosecution's case that since to "deceive" a girl did not mean to have sexual intercourse with her, his client's alleged statement did not provide corroboration and the charge against him should be dismissed. Judge Rosalsky denied the motion, leaving it to the jury to decide the meaning of Lione's words.[24] Other defendants contended that saying they had "insulted," "fooled with," or "done wrong to" a girl did not amount to an admission of having had sexual intercourse with her.[25] Lower court judges and juries rarely appeared to take such linguistic sleight of hand seriously. Appellate court judges, on the other hand, often interpreted such language more literally. In *People v. Page*, the authority most often cited on this issue, the state court of appeals ruled that the defendant's admission that he had "insulted the girl" had no value as corroboration, since "it is entirely possible for a man to insult a woman without committing or attempting or intending to commit the crime of rape." In a similar vein, a court in 1923 argued that, while the defendant's statement that he had "fooled with her" "might imply an admission that he had been guilty of indecent familiarities, it did not imply a confession of the crime of rape in either degree."[26]

Other defendants explained an apparent admission of culpability by saying that they had misunderstood the "proper," "scientific" sexual language used by legal officials. In 1921, when Paulo Rossi, a twenty-year-old Italian immigrant, was charged with the rape of Holly Gardener, the two arresting officers asked him if he had had sexual intercourse with the fourteen-year-old girl, and he said that he had. However, at his trial, Rossi claimed that he had only "told [the] officers he went out with her twice," that he did not know what "rape" meant, and that he thought "sexual intercourse" meant "social." Evidently the jury did not find Rossi's explanation convincing; he was convicted of second-degree rape.[27] In an attempt to deny defendants the opportunity to mount this sort of defense, NYSPCC officers resorted to posing the crucial question in a variety of ways. After one defendant had been made to listen to a girl tell her story, the officer asked him first if her statement was true, then "if he had committed an act of sexual intercourse with the girl," and, finally, "if he had 'screwed' the girl."[28]

Jurors showed more concern than they did in child rape cases that a girl's testimony was corroborated by a man's statement or some other evidence. Whereas almost half the child rape cases in which the grand juries voted for an indictment did not include corroborative evidence, only one in every six indictments for rape cases involving teenage girls was based on evidence lacking corroboration.[29] In cases that involved incest, jurors paid slightly less attention to the corroboration requirement, but even then only one in three indictments involved no corroboration.[30] DADAS were equally unwilling to ignore the corroboration requirement by going to trial when they had insufficient evidence. In rape cases where there was no evidence to corroborate the testimony of a teenage girl, when they could not negotiate a plea bargain, prosecutors opted to discharge just over half, 58 percent, of the defendants.[31] However, in cases involving younger girls, when there was a similar lack of evidence, they discharged only 18 percent of the defendants.[32] That gap would have been even greater if not for instances in which prosecutors took cases of statutory rape to trial against their better judgment. On at least two occasions, DADAS appear to have been pressured by officers of the Florence Crittenton League into not discharging defendants. Both prosecutions ended in acquittal.[33]

An acquittal was the typical outcome when prosecutors tried cases despite a lack of corroborative evidence. Trial juries acquitted two-thirds of the defendants, compared with just over half of those in child rape cases with a similar lack of evidence.[34] Trial judges were also more active in policing the corroboration requirement for proving statutory rape, directing the jury to acquit defendants in 40 percent of the cases in which no corroborative evidence was presented, a step they took in only 7 percent of child rape cases.[35] In the handful of cases that ended in convictions, the success of the prosecution had more to do with the status of the defendant than with the court's perception that the girl involved was a child in need of protection. Two of the men were police officers; two others were foremen charged with assaulting girls under their supervision. All four had abused the authority granted to them, an action that appeared to outrage judges and jurors alike. The final man convicted despite a lack of evidence was Chinese, a victim of long-standing American fears about the threat that nonwhite men posed to white girls.[36]

As had become apparent to ADAS when they had prosecuted men for abduction, even when sufficient evidence was presented, jurors had misgivings about relying solely on age to determine whether a girl deserved protection; they required some other evidence of her immaturity or innocent character. Jurors found little such evidence in the appearance of the girls they encountered in court or in what they heard those girls say. Some defense attorneys did worry that a juror who was "a father of children" would be predisposed to see a girl in her teens as a child, like his own daughter.[37] However, more often jurors saw teenage girls in a very different light: as other people's children, sharing little if any of the childishness of their daughters. They grew up in environments that jurors, generally drawn from the upper ranks of the working class and from the middle class, saw as denying them a childhood. For social investigator Ruth True, the "most noticeable" trait of the West Side girls that she studied was their "precocious development." "In spite of the essential helplessness of their age," she concluded, "they acquire a surface hardihood which marks them out from normal children." They also acquired sexual knowledge by way of what they saw in overcrowded bedrooms and heard in "the idle talk of the kitchen, the stoop and the street," information that led many "to surrender their chastity and even to participate in gross immoralities."[38]

Once jurors determined that the girl before them was not a child, they looked to her character. When juries saw no evidence that a girl had a bad character, they generally followed the law and indicted and, to a lesser extent, convicted men who had been charged with statutory rape, although generally on less serious charges. When they saw what they regarded as signs of a bad character—evidenced by previous sexual experience, extensive sexual knowledge, or the exchange of sex for some kind of payment—they generally nullified the law, either dismissing the case or acquitting the defendant regardless of the evidence.[39]

In the questions they directed at girls who appeared before them, members of grand juries revealed the importance that they attached to a girl's character, despite its irrelevance in the legal definition of statutory rape. In 1916, two seventeen-year-old stenographers, Anne Francis and Maria Grosz, told a grand jury that when they went to Frank Haller's office seeking work, he and another man had intercourse with them. Anne's testimony, that Haller had forced her into his office to have intercourse, provoked a series of questions from jurors about whether Haller had paid her for having intercourse with him or intimated that having sex with him formed part of the job he had offered her. A juror also asked Anne if Haller was the only man who ever had sexual intercourse with her; when, after initially insisting he was, she admitted having had intercourse once prior to her encounter with Haller, she was again asked whether she was paid. Maria Grosz then testified that, while Haller had Anne in his office, another man got "fresh" and attempted to have intercourse with her in an adjoining room, before making Maria "do it French," "put it in [her] mouth." She was asked how she knew what "French" meant—she claimed the man told her—and about her sexual activity several years earlier with a sixteen-year-old boy. All the questions asked by the jurors displayed a concern with circumstances central to an assessment of the girls' character, but irrelevant to the legal definition of statutory rape. Despite the partial corroboration of Anne's testimony provided by Maria, the grand jury dismissed the charge against Frank Haller. Their decision reflected a judgment that Anne and Maria had "bad" characters, rather than a weighing of the evidence against Haller.[40]

Trial juries confronted with "bad" girls like Anne and Maria commonly displayed the same unwillingness to punish defendants. In a case tried in 1901, the jury heard fourteen-year-old Beth Reilly testify that she had intercourse with Robert Palladino, a twenty-nine-year-old Italian shoemaker, in the rear room of his shop on Roosevelt Street. After Palladino "got through with her," he gave her twenty cents, which Beth divided with her fourteen-year-old friend Gillian Jarrett, who had witnessed the act. The two girls later returned to Palladino's shop, and Beth again had intercourse with Palladino while Gillian watched, and received the same payment of twenty cents. Gillian, however, refused to have intercourse with Palladino, and when his helper tried to drag her into bed, the girls ran out of the shop. Despite the corroboration of Beth's story provided by Gillian, the jury could not agree on a verdict, forcing the DADA to discharge Palladino.[41]

The pattern of fewer indictments and convictions in statutory rape prosecutions than in child rape prosecutions laid bare the law's failure to extend to teenage girls the same legal status as that possessed by children and the same degree of protection accorded their younger sisters. On the other hand, jurors' willingness to convict some men, rather than entirely nullifying the law, did change the status of teenage girls. It removed them from the ranks of adult women, who could obtain legal redress only when they resisted a physically violent sexual assault to the limit of their strength.[42]

In the face of these outcomes, prosecutors backed away from presenting adolescent girls as simply children, indistinguishable from younger girls. In 1896, all the men alleged to have had intercourse with a teenage girl were charged with first-degree rape, on the basis of the girl's immaturity. In 1921, none of those accused of the same act faced that charge, prosecutors indicting them instead for second-degree rape.[43] In changing their practice, prosecutors treated teenage girls as lacking the immaturity of their younger sisters, a difference that diminished the degree of legal protection offered to them.

Later in the legal process, prosecutors further reduced that protection by accepting pleas of guilty to lesser offenses from men indicted for second-degree rape. In the 1910s and 1920s, as plea bargains determined the outcome of an increasing proportion of cases, prosecutors allowed the punishments imposed on men who had sexual intercourse with teenage girls to become progressively less severe.[44] Until 1926, the vast majority of defendants pled guilty to a felony, but over time that offense shifted from second-degree rape or abduction, both of which carried a punishment of up to ten years in prison, to second-degree assault, which carried a maximum sentence of only five years in prison.[45] In 1906, 65 percent of defendants pled guilty to rape or abduction rather than assault; in 1921, the proportion fell to only 16 percent.[46] That shift accelerated further in 1926. Only one man entered a plea of guilty to second-degree rape, while three out of four defendants were allowed to plead guilty to a misdemeanor, carrying a maximum sentence of a year's imprisonment, rather than to a felony.[47] NYSPCC officers, as well as DADAs, were implicated in these outcomes; the prosecutor required the Society's endorsement of any plea bargain he negotiated. Judges too were involved, having the final say in whether a guilty plea was accepted.[48]

The judiciary's support for this view of teenage girls as different from younger girls is also evident in the conduct of trials, in rulings on which charges would go to the jury, and in the sentences given to men convicted in rape prosecutions. The judge presiding over a trial in 1911 listened to the twelve-year-old girl with whom Alberto Passantino had repeatedly had intercourse testify that she had visited him and that Passantino had paid her after each act. At the end of the prosecution's case, he dismissed the charge of first-degree rape, leaving Passantino to face a charge of second-degree rape. The ADA made a half-hearted objection that the girl's immaturity warranted the charge of first-degree rape. "The girl was of considerable intelligence, as shown by my own examination," the judge responded, "[and] was fully aware of what she was doing."[49]

Judges also looked to a girl's character when they came to impose sentences. In a case in 1916, a defense attorney who wished to gather evidence of the "notorious character" of the complainant was granted several adjournments by the judge presiding over his client's sentencing. Alluding to evidence he had gathered that a variety of men had had intercourse with the girl, one of whom had contracted venereal disease, the attorney characterized her as "wrong in character, abnormal in her tendencies, and, therefore, she was bad afterwards, she was bad before and she was bad at her birth, and she is bad now, and she sends word that, when she gets out of the hospital, she will paint Yorkville red."[50]

When probation officers conducted a pre-sentencing investigation, their assessments of the harm a girl had suffered showed a similar concern with her character rather than with her age. Two twelve-year-old girls, who, after meeting a forty-two-year-old Italian shoemaker in a movie theater on East 25th Street in 1926, visited him on over a dozen occasions to have intercourse in return for money, were described as having been "chaste" before those events took place. It was "obvious" to the probation officer that "they have undergone a physical, mental, and moral experience of the harmful variety, the impression of which will never be obliterated." No such sympathy was extended to sixteen-year-old Josephine Lovetro, who was "seduced" and then brought to New York City by a twenty-seven-year-old man boarding in her Philadelphia home. An investigation found her "not of a chaste character" prior to this seduction and her family as being without "any high ethical standards of conduct." "It is difficult, therefore," the report concluded, "to discover in this case circumstances which aggravate the offense."[51]

Judges dispensed sentences that reveal a diminishing concern with the circumstances of statutory rape cases and a changing sense of the seriousness of the offense. In the years before 1916, men like Harry Donovan, convicted of acts with girls who consented and showed that they understood what they were doing, received more lenient treatment than men convicted of nonconsensual acts. The typical sentence for men like Donovan was an indeterminate period of incarceration in the Elmira Reformatory—between one year and the maximum for the offense, with release dependent on reformation—or a suspended sentence rather than confinement in the state prison. Judges sent men who had coerced girls, or had sexual intercourse with girls who displayed neither consent nor understanding, to prison for periods of between four and ten years. By 1916, sentences of that length were no longer typical. Judges instead usually sent men to the penitentiary for no more than a year, or suspended their sentence, with little regard for the circumstances of the offense.[52] These punishments fell far short of those judges gave to men convicted in child rape prosecutions. Those who pled guilty to a misdemeanor in 1926, a plea rarely accepted in child rape cases, fared even better. Almost half had their sentences suspended.[53] In imposing these sentences, judges failed to extend the protection they provided young girls to girls in their teens, in effect failing to treat them as children. Nonetheless, they did grant such girls a degree of protection that they did not provide to adult women.

By the 1920s, reformers too had backed away from treating teenage girls as simply children. But like jurors and legal officials, they did not regard them as adults. Seizing on G. Stanley Hall's notion that the years around puberty formed a unique stage of life—namely, adolescence—they reconceptualized teenagers as having a nature unlike that possessed by either adults or younger children. For much of the first two decades of the twentieth century, social reformers had continued to cling to a conception of girls in their teens as childish in nature and explained their unchildlike behavior as the product of forces in their environment. A naturally innocent girl succumbed to overwork, poverty, lack of family, and the constant temptations of the theater and the dance hall. By the 1910s, reformers saw an additional threat: the white slave trade. As part of "the business of securing white women and selling them or exploiting them for immoral purposes," Edwin Sims, the United States district attorney for Chicago, explained, "pure, innocent, and unsuspecting" girls were "forced unwillingly to lead an immoral life," becoming "actually slaves . . . owned and held as property and chattels."[54] However, when municipal vice commissions and social investigators went looking for white slaves, they returned largely empty-handed. The girls and women they found participated in sexual activity without being coerced. As this evidence gradually redirected the search for explanations for the behavior of teenage girls to forces within them, Jane Addams tried to argue that they were nonetheless victims of white slavers. A girl was subjected to "shameful experiences," Addams wrote, that eventually would "become registered in every fiber of her being until the forced demoralization [became] genuine. She is as powerless [then] to save herself from her subjective temptations as she was helpless [earlier] to save herself from her captors."[55] But reformers found few to whom this scenario applied, forcing them to more fully examine the role of factors originating within teenage girls in accounting for their sexual behavior.

In *Adolescence*, G. Stanley Hall's massive study, reformers discovered a more compelling endogenous explanation for a girl's behavior. Beginning in the 1880s, Hall's pioneering work had fostered the emergence of the child study movement in the United States, in the process extending the analysis of development to include cognitive as well as physiological factors. The new approach to children's psychology derived from observational studies in which researchers looked for "the 'nascent periods' of the various powers and interests of the mind, the schedule of times at which they grew most rapidly and hence were most impressionable."[56] Hall placed particular emphasis on the teenage years as a distinct phase of life, initiated by puberty, a physiological change that brought a "rapid spurt of growth in body, mind, and feelings and a new endowment of energy," broke up the stable personality of the child, and initiated a period of storm and stress, which he labeled "adolescence." One of the upheavals of adolescence was the appearance of heterosexuality. Hall's vision of sexual development coupled physiological maturity with psychological immaturity and posited sexuality as a deep unconscious instinct that the child did not understand, and that needed to be sublimated in order for an individual to successfully attain civilized adulthood. If a girl failed in that task, her sexual instincts became the "psychic foundation and background upon which the colossal and . . . ever more youthful evil of prostitution is built." An emphasis on gender differences persisted within this framework, with males and females going through very dissimilar processes of development. For girls, adolescence was about developing reproductive capacity and the higher instinct of motherhood; male adolescence, by contrast, was directed toward mental and physical growth and the attainment of reason, rational will, and morality. Boys required physical activity to ensure their growth; girls had to avoid it at all costs lest they deplete their capacity to bear children.[57]

Hall's ideas recast current understandings of extended childhood so as to recognize the presence, in the years of puberty, of only a qualified immaturity, an immaturity that reformers distilled down to the trait of psychological immaturity. As Judge Ben Lindsey, the leading juvenile justice reformer of the early twentieth century, put the matter in 1925, teenage girls were "physiologically awake with the desires of maturity without the intellectual restraints and sophistication of maturity. They are women with the minds of children; and for many of them, the burden and the responsibility are too much. . . . Sex overwhelms them before their minds and their powers of restraint and judgment are mature enough to cope with it."[58] In effect, reformers changed their approach to sexually active girls to bring it into line with their view of teenage girls as adolescents. In the Progressive Era, they sought, by promoting preventive reforms — sex education, the regulation of amusements, the establishment of girls' clubs led by educated women, the passing of laws that bolstered parents' ability to discipline their daughters — to "fortify the innocence of childhood" against the threats brought by puberty.[59] If Hall, and the psychologists and psychiatrists who followed him, "invented" adolescence, it was working-class girls, and the men who sat on juries, who created a space, even a need, for that new concept, helping at once both to anchor and to disseminate it.

Reformers' vision of girls in their teens as adolescents struggling to maintain their innocence during the upheavals brought on by puberty provided a rationale for continued enforcement of the age of consent. By 1930, the prosecution of statutory rape had made many Americans aware that, in the eyes of the law, teenage girls were not adults, altering, in the process, social relations in New York City.

Bruno Bizella and Peter Klein encountered Ruth Filakovsky in a cafeteria on 14th Street, in December 1930, one month after she had run away from home. Unlike Louis Morelli fourteen years earlier, in his encounter with Rosa Colletti, Bizella and Klein asked about Ruth's age. The fifteen-year-old girl answered that she was nineteen, a lie intended, as she later admitted to a DADA, to make Bizella and Klein understand that she was "old enough." Satisfied that Ruth was an adult, Bizella and Klein offered her a ride in their car, a ride that ended at an address in Broome Street, where Ruth had sexual intercourse with both men. As did many men in New York City by 1930, Bizella and Klein asked the age of the girl with whom they were seeking to have sexual intercourse because they recognized that even a girl who appeared to be sexually mature and to desire sex had to be eighteen years of age in order to engage in sexual intercourse. The slang term "jailbait," which first appeared in the 1930s to describe underage girls like Ruth, shows clearly that ordinary Americans understood the role of the law in constituting teenage girls as unable to consent to sexual intercourse and, therefore, as sexually distinct from adult women. The neologism reminded men that prison awaited those who, holding to older ideas, paid attention to a teenage girl's physical maturity and sexual desires rather than to her age.[60]

The Age of the Child

chapter seven

Crimes against Children

On 21 March 1937, the body of nine-year-old Einer Sporrer was found in a burlap bag on a stoop in Brooklyn. One of the police detectives called to the scene remembered that two months earlier he had arrested Salvatore Ossido, a twenty-six-year-old barber whose shop was nearby, for an attack on a young girl. Within hours Ossido had confessed to enticing Einer into the back room of his shop, striking her with a hammer, and, after she was dead, raping her.[1] Two similar crimes occurred in quick succession four months later. On 31 July, a neighbor found the naked body of eight-year-old Paula Magagna in the cellar of the Brooklyn tenement house where her family lived. She had been raped and strangled with a clothesline. Five days later, Lawrence Marks, under arrest after being accused of "annoying" another girl, confessed to Paula's murder. The forty-nine-year-old unemployed hospital orderly, only recently released after completing a sentence for a sexual assault on a child, admitted luring Paula into the cellar by asking her to show him the gas meters, and then raping and killing her.[2] With Marks's crime still filling the city's newspapers, the naked body of four-year-old Joan Kuleba was found in the cellar of a deserted house in a swamp near South Beach, Staten Island. She had been strangled after an attempted rape. Simon Elmore, the thirty-nine-year-old painter who found Joan's body, eventually admitted he had committed the crime. He had used a grasshopper in a milk bottle to persuade Joan to go into the house.[3]

The press associations picked up the stories of these crimes and distributed them to newspapers throughout the United States. Sex crimes also featured in radio news broadcasts. These media reports spawned general articles on sex crime in weekly and monthly periodicals, as well as feature articles and series in newspapers. Community groups, the mayor of New York City, and the state legislature all launched investigations into sexual violence and proposed legislative action. After a pause during World War II, the pattern in which a sensational crime provoked a broad discussion of sex crime would be repeated in communities throughout the United States until the 1960s, giving concerns about sexual violence a prominent place in the media and in popular culture.[4]

While some of the general statements by politicians and commentators who responded to the panic over sexual violence referred to crimes against "women and children," it was offenses involving children that preoccupied Americans in these years.[5] That focus is unsurprising given that the child-centered culture of the American middle-class reached a new peak in the postwar suburbs. During the baby boom, the child became, as historian Elaine Tyler May has shown, "the key to a personally fulfilling life, compensat[ing] for frustrations at work, boredom at home, and unfulfilled promises of sexual excitement."[6] Since the child served as a bulwark against the terrors of the age, any threat to the child was bound to provoke intense anxiety.

For all its resonance with the concerns that had brought the New York Society for the Prevention of Cruelty to Children (NYSPCC) into being, the sex crime panic was not simply a continuation of the anxieties of the early twentieth century. One sign of that disjuncture was the NYSPCC's failure to play a prominent role in midcentury efforts to protect children. Representatives of the Society are conspicuously absent from the records of experts called on to take part in investigations of sex crime or to give evidence to those inquiries. Clearly, they had lost much of their status as experts on both children and the law. In their place, politicians and the public looked to psychiatrists, psychologists, and social workers as the new experts on childhood and to district attorneys and judges as experts on the law and the workings of the legal system.

The legal officials now viewed as experts were different from their predecessors, who had been politicians and party loyalists rather than legal professionals. Thomas Dewey, elected DA for New York County in 1938, following his successful campaign against organized crime, and his successor, Frank Hogan, did away with cronyism in the DA's office. Hogan's pursuit of a rational, ordered, and nonpartisan approach to law enforcement and his emphasis on the judicial nature of prosecution made the office a model for prosecutors throughout the country. Although the NYSPCC continued to be involved in prosecutions, it now had less influence over how prosecutors approached and disposed of cases. Part of the broader transformation of the American state into an administrative state, which centralized state power rather than delegating it to private groups, the Society's changing role also reflected a shift away from beliefs that the NYSPCC promoted.

Signaling the waning influence of the NYSPCC, the child victims who haunted midcentury Americans were different from those whom the Society and other late-nineteenth-century child protectors had seen as children. Adolescents were regularly excluded from discussions of sex crime, dismissed as being too close to maturity to be victimized to the same extent as children. The midcentury child victim was not only different in age from the injured party of earlier decades, but also different in nature. For the first time, psychology featured in characterizations of children who had not reached puberty, replacing the emptiness previously associated with innocence. That focus helped cast males and females in the same terms, as children rather than as boys and girls, with an emphasis on their shared immaturity rather than on their different genders and bodies.

The notice paid to the psyche of prepubescent children grew out of a broad concern with psychology evident in the 1920s, and from a new interest in the child's mental development in both psychology and psychiatry. Psychiatrists in the mental hygiene movement had the most to say about sexuality, articulating a notion of psychosexual development that identified sexual instincts in prepubescent children. In tracing how those desires developed through a series of stages into mature heterosexuality, that vision produced a proliferation of new sexualities specific to childhood. However, even as popular discussions began to address the psychological effects of sexual activity, they did not take up the related concept of psychosexual development or adopt the characterization of children as sexual. Instead, the popular view continued to present child victims in terms of innocence. A child might no longer be "a negligible psychological creature," to use psychiatrists Lauretta Bender and Abram Blau's dismissive characterization of older ideas, but, despite that recognition, in the eyes of many Americans the child retained an innocent character.[7] Here, as in the late nineteenth century, new ideas accrued around older conceptions of childhood, rather than forcing them to be abandoned. And, again, that process produced tensions between the different elements that made up visions of childhood.

The sex crime panic, then, changed the context within which efforts to prosecute sexual violence took place. New York's response to the sex crime panic gave a prominent place to psychiatrists' concept of the sexual child, but it also revealed a continued commitment to an older vision of the child as innocent. In public discussions of sex crime, those two perspectives appeared to be confluent streams, and they rarely came into conflict. However, in practice, the tensions between the concepts of the sexual child and of the innocent child became clear. In the legal system, the belief in childhood innocence proved to be an obstacle to the acceptance of new efforts to protect children from sexual violence, and it ultimately limited the protection that the law gave to children.

Public reaction to the child murders in New York was immediate. "Word of Ossido's confession spread through the thickly populated neighborhood, mostly foreign-born," the *Daily News* reported. "By the time detectives led the shivering Ossido from his establishment, a crowd of 2,000, the majority of them parents, had gathered." While the *New York Times* reporter noted only that "police had some difficulty in pushing their way through with the prisoner," Al Binder of the *Daily News*, in a style reminiscent of turn-of-the-century accounts, described a crowd "roused to lynch madness." "'I'll slash his throat myself,' shouted one middle-aged man, brandishing a knife. Police overpowered him. Others in the mob, many of them women, tried to claw and strike the prisoner."[8] Salvatore Ossido, Lawrence Marks, and Simon Elmore were not the only targets of such violence. Austin MacCormick, the New York City commissioner of correction, complained that the public concern had reached such an extent that "for a while it was utterly unsafe to speak to a child on the street unless one was well-dressed and well-known in the neighborhood. To try to help a lost child, with tears streaming down its face, to find its way home would, in some neighborhoods, cause a mob to form and violence to be threatened."[9]

Using terms that echoed, even sharpened, the emphasis on crimes against children, national weekly and monthly magazines reflected New Yorkers' fears that "a wave of sex crimes . . . was in full surge" throughout the nation. In August 1937, *Time* magazine described such crimes as "appalling examples of pedophilia [*sic*]," which it defined as "the lust of mature men for prepubescent children." The term served not only to medicalize sex crime but also to mark the distinction between crimes against children and those involving adults.[10]

Four days after the discovery of the body of Joan Kuleba, the New York

State Legislature announced the first official response to the murders, the appointment of a joint legislative committee to take up the broad subject of sex crimes.[11] In the final three months of 1937, the Joint Legislative Committee to Investigate the Administration and Enforcement of the Law, chaired by Senator John J. McNaboe, heard testimony from psychiatrists, police officials, district attorneys, and other professionals. Once it began its work, the Joint Committee quickly narrowed its focus to crimes against children. "As I look at it," Assemblyman Ira Holley commented on the first day of hearings, in asking a witness to define sex crime, "the sex crime that practically brings us here is more or less the rapist with children."[12]

As the hearings progressed, the Joint Committee expanded its investigation beyond rape to include other sexual acts with children. For example, Senator McNaboe questioned district attorneys appearing before the Joint Committee primarily about the incidence of the crimes of carnal abuse and of impairing the morals of a minor, offenses that punished men who handled or fondled a child's genitals. Several prosecutors echoed McNaboe's terms in their answers, distinguishing crimes against children, which they labeled "pervert" crimes, from sex offenses involving adult women.[13] They did not count statutory rape among the pervert crimes. Psychiatrists, prosecutors, and police officials all insisted that sexual intercourse with a teenage girl was not an offense akin to a sexual act with a younger child.[14] In framing its recommendations, the Joint Committee remained true to its title, addressing the need for tighter administration and stricter enforcement of the law, particularly the procedures for dealing with mentally abnormal offenders.

Two investigations of sex crime subsequently undertaken in New York City followed the Joint Committee in focusing their attention on crimes against children. The Citizens Committee on the Control of Crime undertook its investigation in response to the "belief that a 'wave' of sex offenses was sweeping" New York City. Concerned with the workings of the legal system, and primarily statistical in nature, the Citizens Committee's subsequent report, published in 1939, also drew attention to the young age of the victims. In a section headed "Babies among the Victims," the report's authors remarked, "Of all the aspects of this problem of sex offenses, there is none that can stir the observer more deeply than the age of the victims." When the report went on to stress the need to make more adequate provision for offenders whose crimes suggested mental abnormality, the Citizens Committee still had those victims in mind, identifying men involved in "carnal abuse, impairing morals, [and] sodomy" as the criminals who should be presumed to be abnormal.[15]

The Citizens Committee urged Mayor Fiorello La Guardia to appoint a body to look beyond the figures and the procedures that they had described and investigate the work of prisons, hospitals, and parole and probation commissions.[16] In 1939, he did create the Mayor's Committee on Sex Offenses, but it did not pursue the agenda proposed by the Citizens Committee.[17] Instead, the Mayor's Committee decided "that a broader and more comprehensive study of sex crimes passing through our courts was necessary before sound conclusions could be reached as to the extent of the sex crime problem and the methods of dealing with it."[18] That the sex crimes the Mayor's Committee had in mind were those involving children is evident from the way it framed its subjects as "the serious threat to the children of the city" represented by the sex offender and the "implied threat to children" represented by the increase in sex crimes.[19] Notwithstanding the slightly broader definition of the "problem of sex crime" provided in the Mayor's Committee's *Report*—as crimes that "involve[d] elements of violence, abnormality, and threats to the sexual integrity of women and children"—the focus on crimes against children is evident in its recommendations and analysis. In concentrating its proposals on ways to deal with "mentally abnormal" offenders, the Mayor's Committee was concerned with "men who tamper sexually with children."[20]

It also recommended legal reforms to address the failure of New York law to "sufficiently provide for the cases in which children are the victims of sex crime."[21] The statutes that troubled the Mayor's Committee were those relating to impairing the morals of a minor and carnal abuse, the same offenses that had been singled out by both the Joint Committee and the Citizens Committee. Statutory rape was again excluded, on the grounds that the offense encompassed acts quite different in character from crimes against children. While "no account is taken in the rape statute of the age of the offender," the *Report*'s authors complained, "there is a wide disparity in social damage and individual perversity between sex intercourse or sex play between boys and girls of similar ages and the same type of acts on the part of mature men and young girls."[22]

Amid all the discussion of the mental state of men who committed sex crimes, the first American psychiatric study of victims took place, in New York City, in 1937. The study, conducted by Lauretta Bender and Abram Blau of Bellevue Hospital, examined the cases of sixteen "prepuberty children," girls and boys between the ages of five and twelve, referred by the courts for observation in the Children's Ward of the Psychiatric Division at Bellevue following sexual relations with adults.[23]

After a lull in the panic about sex crime during the nation's involvement in World War II, New York's experience was repeated throughout the United States. Although no further sensational crimes took place in New York, its citizens were caught up in the controversy, and its government was moved to action. The discovery of nine-year-old Shirley Jean Coxey on the morning after Thanksgiving in 1945, "dead, ravished, her body pitifully torn," was one of the first of a series of child sex murders and sex crimes against children reported extensively in local newspapers. By 1950, Howard Whitman could write in *Collier's* magazine, "Most American cities have had their Shirley Jeans. In Chicago it was six-year-old Suzanne Degnan, in Cleveland eight-year-old Sheila Ann Tuley, in Detroit a six-year-old boy named George Counter, and—within the same 48 hours last November—seven-year-old Glenda Joyce Brisbois in Burley, Idaho, and six-year-old Linda Joyce Glucoft in Los Angeles."[24] It was the latter two crimes, the murders of Glenda Brisbois and Linda Glucoft, that lifted the national concern about sex crime to new levels. In faraway Detroit, the least sensational of the city's newspapers, the *Detroit News*, devoted a week of banner headlines to the murders, local sex crimes, and FBI statistics. It also twice published stories about past sex crimes in the city and elsewhere in the state, three times editorialized on sex crime, and launched an eighteen-part series examining how to deal with sex criminals.[25]

General articles on sex crime published by weekly and monthly magazines fanned local anxiety about sex crime into a national controversy and maintained the focus on crimes against children. In "How Safe Is Your Daughter?", an article published in *American Magazine* in July 1947, J. Edgar Hoover referred to the need to prevent crimes against "women and children." However, almost all of Hoover's numerous examples involved child victims, a focus echoed in the title of the article and in the image that appeared opposite that title. The term "daughter" could be read broadly to include adult women, but, in the context of this article, the stronger association was with children. The image alongside the title depicted three white girls, the eldest apparently in her early teens. All are neatly attired in short dresses that marked their immaturity and middle-class status. Screaming, with looks of horror on their faces, they are fleeing an enormous male hand that reaches out for them from the top back corner of the frame. Adult women are nowhere to be seen.[26]

Just as had happened in New York City in 1937, the postwar concern with sex murders quickly broadened to include lesser sexual offenses, but only those that involved children. Howard Whitman described how, in the wake of the "murders on front pages," "St. Louis woke with a start to the rest of it: the scores upon scores of children led into alleys and molested on their way to school, the girls and boys lured into garages with the promise of roller skates and obscenely handled, the children forced or bribed—in their ignorance — into acts of perversion. And the rapes."[27] Once awakened, the public reacted. In St. Louis, as in New York before it, meetings were held, growing from local Parent-Teacher Association gatherings into citywide meetings of several hundred people, eventually producing a new civic organization, and a legislative agenda targeting "mentally ill sex offenders."[28]

In ten states, public officials responded to this pressure by appointing commissions to study sex crime and sex offenders. Many of these state investigations were modeled on the New York Mayor's Committee on Sex Offenses, and their reports generally echoed its findings, extending the discussion of mentally abnormal offenders and what to do with them.[29] This official response fed into campaigns for legislative action, the adoption of so-called sexual psychopath statutes, that allowed offenders identified as mentally abnormal to be transferred to psychiatric care for an indefinite period, until declared cured. To talk about the sexual psychopath was also to talk about child victims. A crime against a child remained the most significant sign of mental abnormality, and most state laws used the commission of such offenses to identify men who would be subject to commitment and treatment.[30]

The reliance on psychiatric language in the new laws reflected the extent to which Americans looked to psychiatrists to explain and prevent sex crime, an approach that provided increased support for research studies. Six states provided funding for such studies, with the largest undertaken in California and New York. Most, including David Abrahamsen and Bernard Glueck's work at New York's Sing Sing Prison, took sex offenders as their subjects. But the California study and a handful of smaller projects focused on victims, who were, without exception, children.[31]

The children who dominated discussions of sex crime were different in nature from those who had concerned Americans earlier in the century. In declaring that "boys as well as girls may be the victims of sex crime," the New York Mayor's Committee did more than draw attention to an overlooked group. The Mayor's Committee's claim signaled a shift toward treating boys and girls as children, united by age more than they were divided by gender. Particularly in the postwar period, male victims attracted unprecedented notice. Among the sex murders that became sensational cases were the death of three-year-old Charles Bradley at the hands of Joseph Bortnyak in Chicago in 1947, Theodore Hilles's murder of six-year-old George Counter in Detroit in 1949, and the killing of twelve-year-old Ellis Simons by sixteen-year-old Seymour Levin in Philadelphia, also in 1949.[32] Boys also figured as victims of the sex crimes that attracted attention in the wake of those cases. "The naive parents who felt safe because their children were *boys*," one reporter wrote, "learned—some with a shock—that 20 per cent of the victims are boys."[33]

But more was occurring than a simple recognition that boys were vulnerable to sexual assaults by men. By the end of the 1940s, politicians and public officials began to recast the sex crime panic to stress the age of the victims rather than their gender. The two articles that FBI Director J. Edgar Hoover wrote for *American Magazine* illustrate that shift. The first, "How Safe Is Your Daughter?", instanced several examples of crimes against women and girls to support its call for the psychiatric and medical treatment of offenders. In "How *Safe* is Your Youngster?", published eight years later, in 1955, one-third of the examples Hoover employed to support the same call involved male victims. Among them was the case of "a 31-year-old pervert [who] criminally molested a 12-year-old newspaper delivery boy three different times in a suburb of a large Eastern city."[34]

This shift took place in the context of a broader age segmentation of American society, which diminished many of the differences that had existed in the experience of boys and girls. Increasingly, boys no longer enjoyed the greater independence, freedom of movement, and earlier access to the workplace that had distinguished their experience from that of girls. Instead, boys joined their sisters in being restricted to schools and the domestic sphere. Postwar anxiety that the American boy had become a "sissy," lacking in masculinity as a result of spending too much time with his mother and the female teachers who predominated in schools, suggests that the shared experiences of childhood were perceived as eroding gender differences.[35]

The new concern with psychology played a crucial role in bringing the new emphasis on age rather than gender into understandings of sexual violence. NYSPCC rhetoric had presented the consequences of sex crime in terms of physical wounds and a stunting and warping of physical growth. Such effects were conceived of in terms of gender and served to foreground differences between boys and girls. Boys and girls suffered different injuries—to the anus in the case of a boy, to the vagina in the case of girl—and these injuries had different physical consequences and meanings. A girl's sexual identity was harmed in a way a boy's was not; a ruptured hymen signified lost virginity, and other damage to the genitals threatened a diminished capacity for childbearing. Midcentury accounts made little reference to such physical injuries, focusing instead on the psychological effects of sex crime.[36] Those discussions took no account of gender; their subject was the child. "These things the children survive," Howard Whitman noted in *Collier's* magazine, "but with what trauma? With what long-smarting scars of frightfulness? With what psychological wounds?"[37] Of growing concern was that psychiatrists could not offer an immediate answer to those questions, because the "mental damage" caused by a sex offense "may lay hidden under the surface of conscious mental life," as the Mayor's Committee put it, "and may take a long time to develop and reveal its disastrous effects."[38]

The recurrent use of metaphors of physical injury to convey psychological damage signaled the newness of Americans' concern with child psychology: "scar" and "wound" appear more often in popular discussions of sex crime than does "trauma." Only in the 1920s had the advice provided to parents by physicians and other experts begun to address the child's emotional health and psychology. Earlier advice had been preoccupied with physical health. *Infant Care*, the United States Children's Bureau's widely distributed pamphlet, presented proper feeding and the nursing of ills as the only things with which a mother had to concern herself.[39] Pediatricians and public health officials supplemented that advice with height-weight charts to allow parents to measure their child's physical growth against developmental norms. Arnold Gesell, a physician and psychologist at Yale University, insisted that "standards of mental health are as legitimate and as feasible as standards of physical status," and he maintained that it was "possible to lay down for various ages of infancy and childhood certain concrete minimum essentials of mental health expressed in tangible behavior terms." In 1925 he did just that, in a text called *Mental Growth of the Preschool Child*, and those psychological norms were quickly integrated into child-rearing advice.[40] The concern with the psychological dimensions of childhood also seeped into discussions about a range of issues. Warnings about the effects of paid work on children, for example, had long centered on physical injuries and the disruption of growth and development. In the 1920s, reformers also warned of psychological effects. Dr. C. Floyd Haviland cautioned, in a 1929 pamphlet, that child labor led to "the development of malformed child personalities which are the forerunners of ill-balanced, partially integrated and poorly adjusted adult personalities."[41]

The psychologists whose work informed this concern with mental and emotional development had broken with the child study movement associated with G. Stanley Hall. They dismissed child study as "too idiosyncratic" to "amount to a science of children": it was "anecdotal and unsystematic"; it neglected "important factors like the influence of surroundings"; and it varied "in method from person to person." The new professional child psychologists, of whom Arnold Gesell was the best known, observed large numbers of children in university-based clinics, "under controlled, experimental, almost laboratory conditions." Gesell famously isolated his subjects in softly lit observation domes, outside which his researchers clustered. Based on their observations, they elaborated child study's "nascent periods" into developmental norms: "standard[s] based upon the average abilities or performances of children of a certain age on a particular task or a specified activity," arranged in a unified sequence along an axis of time.[42] By the 1930s, child psychology was also becoming increasingly preoccupied with mental testing, using IQ tests, pioneered in the United States by Lewis Terman, a student of Hall.

Child psychologists had little to say about sexuality. It was psychiatrists in the mental hygiene movement, another group that had its roots in observational child study, who articulated a concept of psychosexual development.[43] Part of the turn-of-century movement of psychiatry out of the asylum, mental hygiene drew its conceptual basis from dynamic theories of mental illness that focused on functional disorders of the mind and emotional maladjustment, rather than on physiological conditions. This was a developmental framework in which personality matured from infancy until it became, in the words of William Alanson White, superintendent of St. Elizabeth's Hospital in Washington, D.C., "firmly established, structuralized" in adulthood. It followed, White argued, "that the foundation of those defects which later issue in mental illness are to be found in the past history of that development." Moreover, efforts to maintain mental health, "to reinforce the weak points in character," were also best directed at children, whose personalities were "peculiarly plastic."[44] Mental hygiene's orientation toward childhood took its practitioners first to clinics attached to juvenile courts. In the 1920s, with the support of the Commonwealth Fund, practitioners also moved into child guidance clinics that cooperated with social welfare agencies and schools as well as courts, and they provided adult education classes for middle-class parents increasingly anxious to obtain child-rearing advice from medical experts.[45]

Mental hygienists made a more pronounced break with the romantic child than did child study or the field of child psychology that succeeded it.[46] They repudiated the innocent prepubescent child in favor of Freud's sexual child. Rather than presenting puberty as the transformation that introduced sexuality, mental hygienists instead endowed children with manifest, unique forms of sexuality that emerged progressively throughout childhood as preliminaries to sexual maturity. In so doing, they challenged Americans to recognize that children possessed a "sexual instinct." In *The Mental Hygiene of Childhood*, a seminal text published in 1925, William Alanson White asserted that "people are loath to see and to acknowledge . . . that the infant of two, three, and four years of age has sexual feelings" because "they do not want to believe it." "An unbiased observation of little children," by contrast, found inescapable evidence of their "sexual desire, for it is expressed over and over again in their conduct and what they say."[47]

White and his colleagues wanted Americans to open their eyes not only to the existence of child sexuality but also to its distinctive nature. "Sex, no more than any other part of life, springs fully fledged into life," sociologist Ernest Groves and his wife Gladys counseled in their *Sex in Childhood*, a text published in 1933 that distilled the ideas of mental hygiene for parents. "Rather, it develops from immature forms, which grow out of preliminary capacities, accompanied always by attitudes which are a mixture of personal history and present reactions to other people's attitudes." Applying a developmental framework to sexuality in this way replaced a singular understanding of sexuality, based on adult experience, with a proliferation of sexualities that varied from the "mature" form. The Groveses laid out four distinct forms of sexuality, each based on traits that came to the forefront at a particular stage of a child's development. Infancy, the first two years, saw a period of "oral supremacy," with the mouth as a "pleasure zone," and, later, an interest in the anal. The child from ages three to six, "the pre-school child," became for the first time "acutely aware of his [*sic*] genitals." The next stage, from six to ten years of age, was characterized by "sex latency" and "sublimation, or the redirection of sex energy into other forms of personal expression." With puberty came "new intensities of impulse" and a renewed focus on genital interests, coupled for the first time with a "supreme interest in members of the opposite sex."[48]

Where to situate homosexuality within such a framework was a particularly contentious issue. Some psychiatrists and writers, such as the Groveses, saw homosexuality as an "aberration," a departure from psychosexual development and a distortion of "normal" heterosexuality.[49] Others, more strongly influenced by psychoanalysis, like William Alanson White, saw it as an "intermediary stage," one that preceded adolescence.[50] The latter position gained in prominence in the postwar period, expressed in a range of government publications. In *A Citizen's Handbook of Sexual Abnormalities and the Mental Hygiene Approach to Their Prevention*, a pamphlet distributed in 1950 to every household in Michigan, Samuel Hartwell endeavored to make this concept credible to a lay audience. "Many mature adults have difficulty in remembering that they went through such an experience," Hartwell admitted. But "if they can be realistic in remembering their youthful experiences," he insisted, "they will usually find that they, like most young people, had crushes or deep demanding friendships with someone of their own sex."[51]

For all that mental hygienists disagreed about the place of homosexuality in childhood, they largely concurred in presenting child sexuality in racialized terms. Midcentury studies recognized that African American children possessed sexual desire, but they did not present them as progressing through a series of stages preliminary to sexual maturity. Instead, psychiatrists and physicians argued that black children "engage[d] quite freely in sex conduct" at all ages, spoke freely about their sex life, and "[did] not appear to have any moral sense."[52] As such, they were always already sexual, indistinguishable from adults. If African Americans had no childhood in the sense that they never went through a process of sexual development, in another sense they never left childhood. The singular sexuality attributed to African Americans was not mature heterosexuality but rather an immature form, in keeping with persisting white images of blacks as a childish race. Scientific racial thought had buttressed that notion, with psychologists contributing the argument that African American children learned as readily as whites did until puberty, at which point their intellectual development ceased. This left them to become, in G. Stanley Hall's words, "adolescents of adult size," perpetually characterized by traits such as "love of pleasure and of music and dancing"; "lack of will power"; "impulsiveness and general emotionalism; fearfulness and a concomitant sense of dependence."[53] As part of that conception, scientific racial thought also portrayed African American adults as having the immature sexuality of adolescents, as having the same lack of the powers of restraint and judgment needed to prevent sex from becoming overwhelming that Judge Ben Lindsey attributed to teenage girls.

Since they believed African American children were neither innocent nor capable of developing mature heterosexuality, psychiatrists in the mental hygiene movement showed little concern that they might be harmed by sexual experiences prior to puberty. They did, however, worry about the ways in which a white child's progress toward sexual maturity might go awry. "If the process proceeds smoothly, well and good; but," William Alanson White cautioned, "if at this point or that, there is too long a tarrying at some source of erotic interest, then that portion of the personality remains relatively infantile in its pleasure-seeking activities." "Such an infantile area, making its demands upon the adult," he warned, "leads to repressions with subsequent distortions and resulting deformations of the personality."[54] The Groveses restated that argument in "non-technical language," rather than in "the vocabulary of the specialist."[55] "The pleasure-urge that is imperfectly gratified in its season, whether by overindulgence or too stringent curtailment," they admonished, "is a dead weight that impedes the normal progress through the usual experiences of emotional growing up."[56] The Groveses also highlighted other threats to a child's development. "Some mishap occurs in the developing life of the child which leads to emotional tension along the lines of sex," they counseled parents, "something shocking, something that leads to fear or conflict, which turns the child away from wholesome progress toward sex maturity, with consequences of physical, nervous, or emotional significance."[57]

Mental hygiene writers were quick to point out that the effects of such experiences were contingent on how parents responded. Parents who saw "only the moral issue when confronted with these situations [would] be handicapped by their own unhappy associations with sex," Douglas Thom, director of the Massachusetts Division of Mental Hygiene, informed readers of his *Everyday Problems of the Everyday Child*. Such parents would only "confuse the child by their own doubts, misgivings, and obvious embarrassment," or they would hold the child up to "ridicule and shame" that would serve only to "stimulate a feeling of degradation," providing "the nucleus for breakdowns in later life." Better to "approach the matter frankly and unemotionally," to not give it undue attention, and to provide the child with "occupation and diversion" that will allow the experience "to drop into the background" and be forgotten.[58]

The experiences that mental hygienists had in mind were accidental or incidental stimulation of pleasurable physical sensations, masturbation, misinformation provided by "bad playmates," sex play with other children, and the sight of adult sexual behavior. Sexual relations with adults received no attention in prewar mental hygiene writings or in the work of contemporary psychoanalysts, such as Melanie Klein and Helene Deutsch.[59] The midcentury sex crime panic altered that perspective, producing psychiatric studies focused on children who had experienced sexual acts with adults. The researchers found that those children had suffered "anxiety, guilt, or psychic trauma," but not on the scale expected, by which they meant not to the extent imagined by those who saw children as innocent.[60] Sexual experience was entirely foreign to the innocent child, whose nature was devoid of sexuality, and its introduction was therefore corrupting and impossible to ameliorate. Sexuality was not so alien to the developing child. As Lauretta Bender and Alvin Grugett put it, "Overt sexual activity in childhood with adult partners was in one way a deflection of the normally developing sexual impulses."[61] In "deflecting" impulses already present, such activity did less harm to a developing child than the introduction of impulses did to one imagined as previously free of sexuality. In their 1937 study, Bender and Abram Blau had found that only nine of the sixteen children examined had been affected by their experience.

Three of the younger children "manifested a tendency to revert to infantile sex practices, and to fixate on onanistic genital preoccupations." Three others "reacted with a form of intellectual bewilderment and preoccupation." The final three, "repeat offenders," displayed a "misanthropic attitude." Most importantly for Bender and Blau, these effects could be ameliorated, something not possible for an innocent child whose nature had been corrupted. With psychiatric treatment, the children "seemed to be able to give up the sexual interests, preoccupations and activities under normal circumstances, with minimal degrees of neurotic features."[62] Bender and Grugett's follow-up study of these children fourteen years later confirmed that conclusion. It found that the children displayed no "maladjustments rooted in [their] experience" and had not "again needed social correction or attention because of sex activities."[63] Like other mental hygienists, those who studied victims attributed much of the responsibility for what harm children did suffer to their parents' "emotional upset."[64]

Studies of victims gave most of their attention not to how children had been affected by sexual acts with adults, but to how the children had behaved during those encounters. Struck by the fact that their subjects did not resist "and often play[ed] an active or even initiating role" in their encounters with adult men, Bender and Blau concluded that they did not "deserve completely the cloak of innocence with which they have been endowed by moralists, social reformers and legislators."[65] That focus exposed the limits of mental hygiene's break with older visions of childhood. The concept of psychosexual development, articulated by psychiatrists, endowed children with sexual instincts and desires, expressed in acts distinct from those that defined mature heterosexuality. However, it did not accord them subjectivity. The sexual child was only obeying his or her natural impulses, not exercising will or conscious choice. She or he was imagined as being possessed by sexuality, by the process of development, rather than as possessing sexuality. His or her status as a child thus remained contingent on passivity. If a girl was active in any sense when involved with an adult in sexual intercourse, her actions put her at odds with understandings of childhood and prevented her from appearing to be a victim.

Joseph Weiss and his colleagues, for example, relied on the standards courts employed in regard to adult women when they divided children into "those who took part in initiating and maintaining the relationship," whom they called "participant victims," and those who did not, whom they labeled "accidental victims." Accidental victims were girls assaulted within the same narrow set of circumstances that courts saw as indicating that an adult woman had been coerced, namely, when "the offender was a stranger, the act occurred only once, the child received no remuneration for it, and she told her parents of the incident soon after it occurred." Sixty percent of the subjects of the study attracted the oxymoronic label "participant victim." Those children were participants because their encounters with adult men involved circumstances that in the case of adult women would be deemed consensual: they were victims because the law categorized them as such, because they had been referred to Weiss and his colleagues by district attorneys. These girls had been involved in more than one sexual encounter, had "received some type of remuneration such as candy, money or movie tickets," "knew the offender for some time before the incident," and "kept their sex relationships with the offenders secret from their families."[66] In an earlier account of the study, Weiss also interpreted "simple compliance with the offender's wishes" and being "threatened by the offender with punishment if they did not participate" as evidence of "participation."[67] To see these children simply as victims, psychiatrists would have had to perceive them as possessing an immature subjectivity and will, which gave their behavior different meanings than the same acts had in the case of adults.[68] Without that recognition, a child who was not passive in an encounter with an adult took on an appearance of maturity and was judged by standards applied to adults, notwithstanding psychiatrists' recognition that the child possessed unique, developing sexual instincts and desires.

When *Science News Letter* summarized Bender and Blau's findings for a popular audience, neither the sexually developing child nor the sexualized "participant victim" was discussed. Instead, child victims were repeatedly referred to as "little," an adjective associated with innocence. The writer reported the psychiatrists' observation that many of the girls were particularly "charming" and "attractive," but not their conclusion that such personalities were a sign "that the child might have been the actual seducer rather than the one innocently seduced." The writer similarly sheared the child's participation of any sexual connotation. "It may not always be the 'offender' who first seeks the acquaintance in cases of sex attack," the writer reported, "but rather the child who is anxious to be friendly to the strange adult." In fact, Bender and Blau had suggested that the child's behavior was determined not by an urge to be friendly but by a desire to get "some form of satisfaction" of her "sex urges." In the report on the two psychiatrists' work, the "cloak of innocence" that they had been so anxious to remove from child victims remained firmly in place.[69]

That short item in *Science News Letter* reflected the way in which child victims were represented in popular writings on sex crime. Even as those discussions articulated a new awareness of the psychological effects of sexual assault, reporters, commentators, and public officials failed to adopt the concept of psychosexual development. Instead, they continued to see children as devoid of sexuality, as innocent. Nowhere is this more apparent than in the press coverage of child murders. The *New York Daily News*, the city's leading tabloid, for example, illustrated its stories about the girls killed in 1937 with photographs showing them in clothes and situations that emphasized their innocence: Paula Magagna in her confirmation dress, playing with dolls; Joan Kuleba in a swimsuit frolicking at the beach; and all of the girls in the company of their parents. Their funerals, attended by crowds of several thousand, were presented as pageants of innocence. Reports gave a prominent place to the girls' "playmates," who were invariably dressed in white. Eight girls so garbed preceded Joan Kuleba's coffin. Forty followed the hearse from Paula Magagna's home to the church, where a choir of fifty girls sang hymns. Thirty-five girls from Einer Sporrer's marching club, a unit of the German-American Bund, raised a Nazi salute over her coffin as it was carried out of the church, and again as she was buried. Representations of young male victims employed the same tropes. Beneath a front-page headline that announced that his killer had confessed, the *Chicago Sun* placed a photo of a victim dressed as a cowboy, sitting on a pony; another boy was pictured in a sailor suit. High school boys acted as pallbearers at the funerals of both Charles Bradley and George Counter. Charles Bradley's funeral also gave a prominent place to "12 little children" who had been his playmates, while George Counter's featured a children's choir.[70]

Popular images of children as innocents are also evident in debates over how children could be protected from sexual attacks. Discussions of the factors that precipitated an assault treated children as objects, with no role in initiating the encounter, and not as seducers who aroused male desire. Instead, some argued, it was a child's appearance, not her behavior, that triggered men's sexual instincts. At a meeting of more than a thousand residents of the Ridgewood neighborhood (in Brooklyn/Queens) where two of the murders occurred, speakers warned parents "not to permit little girls to roam the streets in scanty attire such as so-called 'sun-suits' or open-work play suits."[71] While Police Commissioner Lewis Valentine labeled this warning "hysterical," it struck a chord with other New Yorkers.[72] Several wrote to Mayor La Guardia blaming the sex attacks on the "scanty clothing" worn by girls. According to one correspondent, scanty clothing meant that "if one of those lust fiends see [*sic*] a child like that, they in there [*sic*] lust don't see the child but the woman."[73]

To avoid the possibility that their child might inadvertently invite an assault, parents were urged to warn them against behavior that could lead to encounters with strange men. In New York City, Assistant Chief Inspector of Police John Lyons counseled parents to instruct children "not to talk with or accept gifts from strangers." The Children's Protective Association in St. Louis cast its warnings in broader terms, "educating" children "to take no short cuts, to avoid alleys, not to loiter, and to flee from any man who offered them candy, gum, comic books, or roller skates." A pamphlet distributed to Detroit schoolchildren offered gendered warnings: girls should "NEVER go with strangers when they ask for directions," while boys should "NEVER wait around toilets."[74] All of these appeals were directed at innocent children, boys and girls unable to understand the nature of the threat that lurked in the proscribed spaces and encounters. Although they gave children directions on how to act, the warning did not provide them with the knowledge and understanding that would have allowed them to protect themselves. Frustrated psychologists and psychiatrists complained that warnings couched in those terms actually harmed children, whom they saw as being in the midst of sexual development rather than innocent. Thus A. R. Mangus, a researcher involved in the California Sexual Deviation Research project, cautioned that warnings "may have harmful effects on the social and emotional lives of some children by creating vague fears and anxieties about mysterious, unexplained dangers and by creating a sense of alienation and estrangement from people."[75]

Efforts to minimize the damage done to children who had been assaulted likewise portrayed those children as innocent. The primary concern here was parents' unwillingness to report assaults, out of fear of the "attendant notoriety and publicity" to which their children would be subjected, as Martin Littleton, the Nassau County DA, put it. He told the Joint Committee that in his experience parents believed that a trial "exposed" a child, thereby destroying his or her innocence. Required to take the stand, a girl is "put in the position of having to stand there and give a most detailed explanation of her most private affairs, which children are taught generally are unmentionable, and there she is exposed to the upturned faces of the morbid crowd in the courtroom." This scenario was dangerous to the child only if talking about sexuality, particularly in a public context, was harmful, a logic that required a child to be otherwise ignorant of sexuality. Littleton also claimed that parents believed that such a "harrowing" experience would render a child "unfit for the future, [and unwilling] to go back to school," and would leave him or her "marked for all time."[76] What he was describing was a notion of such children as ruined. Unlike the situation that obtained earlier in the century, this status was grounded not in a physical condition, such as a ruptured hymen, but in a psychological condition. Despite that distinction, the idea that appearing in court was a harmful experience only made sense if a child was normally free of sexuality, in this case in the form of sexual feelings and sexual knowledge, rather than merely innocent of the experience of sexual intercourse.

Littleton suggested two frequently proffered solutions. The first recommended that a "private trial in which the public is excluded" should be held in sex crime cases involving child victims, a suggestion that other witnesses echoed, but which does not seem to have been adopted.[77] His second proposal was that the publication of the names of child victims should be abandoned. That plan enjoyed broad support from those who appeared before the Joint Committee, and from public officials like J. Edgar Hoover. While efforts to legislate a ban ran afoul of constitutional protections, many newspapers, including the *New York Times* and the *Daily News*, did choose to withhold the names of victims and their families.[78]

One further means of extending the legal protection of children was discussed in New York: the removal or modification of the state's corroboration requirement. Proponents of that approach found themselves drowned out by critics who regarded children's testimony with suspicion.[79] But the child invoked by those who opposed reform was not the desire-filled figure that psychiatrists worried about. They imagined a child without a fully formed psychology, open to manipulation, unable to reliably separate fact from fiction. "Kiddies are naturally suggestible," warned Judge Franklin Taylor, defending the corroboration requirement in the aftermath of the arrest of Salvatore Ossido, the man who murdered Einer Sporrer in 1937. As a result, "stories of this type come readily to their inventive minds because their parents have often warned them against strange men." Judge Taylor also claimed that "many children are habitual liars," liable to "prevaricate to avoid punishment and scoldings from parents and teachers."[80] Such views found support in the new wave of legal psychology texts published in the 1920s and 1930s. Drawing on turn-of-the-century European research, Ralph Brown, in his 1926 *Legal Psychology*, argued that when lawyers "create an idea of what the child is to hear or see," "the child is very likely to hear or see what [he or she] desired." Given that the "fertility" and "vividness" of children's imagination led them to confuse "the world of make-believe" with "stern reality," he also questioned whether it was ever possible to place faith in children's truthfulness.[81] On rare occasions, some of the language of psychoanalysis and mental hygiene did slip into these conceptions of children's unreliability, but it was the psychologically immature, but innocent child, not the sexual child, who dominated the discussion of the reliability of children's testimony.[82]

Only in discussions of the effects of homosexual assaults can the sexually developing child be glimpsed. Writing in *Coronet* magazine in 1950, Ralph Major referred to a boy rescued from his contacts with an adult man "in time to prevent his complete conversion to the unfortunate cult."[83] Although he chose to render it in religious terms, Major clearly derived his sense of how the boy might have been affected by his experience from the concept of psychosexual development. Bertram Pollens, senior psychologist at New York's Rikers Island Penitentiary, argued, for example, that if a boy "happens to be seduced by a homosexual . . . and he finds the relationship satisfying, he may become fixated in that direction and it may be next to impossible to change the direction of his sexual drive after that."[84] Behind this vision of boys being transformed into homosexual men lay a notion of homosexuality as a stage, a point at which a seduced boy's development might be arrested if his desire had become "fixed" on male sexual objects. "In some people," Major noted, "homosexuality may represent a passing phase in emotional development—a temporary protest against conservative morals or a craving for self-expression carried to bizarre extremes."[85]

This notion of the psychological effects of homosexual acts introduced a gender difference into the consideration as to how sexual contacts with men affected children, highlighting how the new emphasis on age subordinated, rather than excluded, concern with such differences. The separation of sexual desire from the gender identity that developed in this period of childhood development gave a different meaning to a girl's experience. In a complex process unpacked by George Chauncey, shifts in middle-class culture, and changing medical discourse, made the object of an individual's desire, rather than being an inversion of gender conventions, the basis on which gay men were distinguished from other men. It also provided the foundation for the division of individuals into heterosexuals and homosexuals on the basis of the sex of their sexual partners.[86] Sexual acts, and an individual's role in an act, assumed a lesser importance in that vision of sexuality. As a consequence, a girl involved in an oral or anal act with a man was not regarded as having been harmed to the same extent as a boy would have been. Although such an assault involved a girl in an "unnatural" act capable of distorting her development, it did not involve an "abnormal" sexual object, an individual of the same sex, and thus did not push her outside the bounds of heterosexuality.

Boys who were in danger of developing into homosexuals thus appeared among the innocent children who dominated popular representations of the victims of sex crime, a combination that hints at the tensions at work in the midcentury sex crime panic. On the surface, a new understanding of sexual violence came to the fore in these years. Child victims dominated discussions of sex crime, as they had in the preceding decades, but such victims were now often portrayed in different terms. The effects of their experiences were cast in psychological rather than physical terms. Where earlier visions of children had been divided along gender lines, these victims were seen in terms of their age and shared immaturity, with gender differences taking a secondary place.

However, beneath this surface lay rival notions of children's nature and of precisely which sexual acts caused damage. That tension was rarely evident in media discussions of sex crime, preoccupied as they were with sex murder, an act that did obvious and incontestable damage irrespective of how a child's character was imagined. But, after the New York State Legislature created a new offense, carnal abuse, the competing ideas came to the surface in the legal system. The new crime provided increased punishment for men who handled a child's genitals or who made genital contact without penetration. Those acts only appeared sexual, and damaging to children, when seen from the perspective of psychosexual development, rather than from the point of view that children were as a rule innocent. Ironically, given the anxieties expressed in the sex crime panic, by the late 1950s the clash of these perspectives caused sex crimes against children to be treated as less harmful than sexual assaults on adult women.

Child Molestation

In 1927, the New York State Legislature, for the first time in almost one hundred years, created a new felony sex crime. They did so at the urging of Societies for the Prevention of the Cruelty to Children from throughout the state, whose officers drafted the bill, in consultation with the New York County district attorney, in an effort to "give further protection to little children."[1] The new offense, carnal abuse of a child, provided a punishment of up to ten years in prison for any male who "carnally abuses the body or indulges in any indecent or immoral practices with the sexual organs of a female child ten years or younger."[2] The state's appellate courts defined "indecent or immoral practices" as any acts that involved an object or a man's hand, rather than his genitals. Carnal abuse of the body, the other form of the crime, they interpreted as referring to an act involving a man's genitals "short of intercourse," namely, an act that did not involve penetration of a girl's sexual organs.[3]

In enacting the new law, the state legislature attributed to those acts more damage to children than had previously been recognized.[4] That additional harm had literally not been visible to legislators before. Handling the genitals and acts that did not involve genital penetration caused little, if any, physical injury, the defining feature of earlier concepts of sexual violence. Nor did they do significant damage to a child's innocence. Innocence was defined in reference to a singular sexuality centered on sexual intercourse, a penetrative act that left physical signs or caused bodily injury. From this perspective, acts such as touching and fondling were not sexual acts, and they did not introduce sexuality into a child's nature in the way that the experience of intercourse did. The injury that justified treating carnal abuse as a felony was not physical but psychological. Evidence of such injuries came from psychiatrists and psychologists who, the Michigan *Report of the Governor's Study Commission on the Deviated Criminal Sex Offender* noted, "offer substantial evidence that the traumatizing effect of a sex offense which may be considered minor may be as great as that of a sex offense involving physical force or violence."[5] However, the law recognized only children as suffering those effects. In the case of adults who had reached sexual maturity, "acts consisting of indecent familiarities, not amounting to sexual intercourse or an attempt to have sexual intercourse" remained a misdemeanor, assault in the third degree.[6]

In making that distinction between children and adults, the state legislature drew on notions of psychosexual development. From this perspective, acts of carnal abuse were part of a range of sexual behaviors that expressed the forms of sexuality appropriate to different stages of development. As such, even when they caused no physical injury, those acts affected how a child's sexuality developed. Subsequent amendments to the statute further elaborated that developmental framework. A 1929 amendment defined the same acts as a lesser crime, a misdemeanor, when committed with a girl between eleven and sixteen years of age.[7] That amendment distinguished prepubescent and pubescent children, characterizing an adolescent, an individual at a more advanced stage of sexual development, as less affected by acts of carnal abuse than a young child would be. In 1933, the statute was amended again so that both forms of the offense applied to male children as well as female children.[8] The new amendment placed children of both sexes within a common developmental framework, putting their shared age ahead of their different gender.[9]

In drawing on understandings of psychosexual development to craft a gender-blind law targeted at men who committed genital acts other than intercourse, New York was at the forefront of a nationwide wave of legislative action to expand definitions of sexual violence against children. Nevada, North Dakota, and Minnesota had enacted similar laws in the late 1920s, and Vermont followed suit in 1937; another twenty-one states passed laws of a comparable nature between 1948 and 1958, in the midst of the sex crime panic.[10] Seven states joined New York in using the term "indecent and immoral practices"; seven others persisted with the "lewd and lascivious" language that was popular early in the century; and another seven combined the two definitions.[11] A new, even more explicit vocabulary of fondling and touching distinguished the laws of the remaining four states. Texas, which pioneered this approach, made it unlawful for "any person with lascivious intent to intentionally place or attempt to place his or her hands, or any portion of his or her hand or hands upon or against a sexual part of a male or female under the age of fourteen years, or to in any way or manner fondle or attempt to fondle a sexual part of a male or female under the age of fourteen." The law also prohibited the placing of hands on or the fondling of the breast of a female under the age of fourteen.[12]

At first glance, the New York County DA's case files appear to indicate that the new notion of sexual development had won out over the older idea of innocence not only in the law but in New York City's streets and courtrooms as well. From 1931 to 1946, cases of carnal abuse made up two out of every three prosecutions involving sex crimes against children younger than eleven years of age. In the first half of the 1950s (data from 1951 and 1955), that proportion fell, but carnal abuse cases still constituted half of the total prosecutions.[13] Although most crimes against boys continued to be cases of sodomy, with carnal abuse cases making up only one-third of the total, cases that involved boys were no longer presented differently from crimes involving girls, and they produced increasingly similar outcomes.[14]

A closer examination, however, dispels the impression of change. Almost half of the carnal abuse cases involved acts that earlier in the century had been treated as rape. A reinterpretation of penetration, an unintended consequence of the new law, caused those cases to be categorized as carnal abuse and led to an almost complete disappearance of rape prosecutions. When it came to deciding the outcome of prosecutions, most New Yorkers continued to treat acts of carnal abuse as less harmful than rape or sexual assaults that caused physical injury. New Yorkers were not alone in taking that position. Many Americans continued to see physical injury as the defining feature of sexual violence. In 1951, the Committee on Legislation of the Michigan Governor's Study Commission on the Deviated Criminal Sex Offender observed, "In general, it may be stated that laymen assess the nature of the offense with regard to the physical harm caused the victim."[15] By the late 1950s, the blunted impact of new ideas of psychosexual development was reflected in a new label applied to sex crimes against children: "child molestation."

The four children arrived at the restaurant on 103rd Street and Broadway early in the evening of 14 September 1941. Nine-year-old Amy Burton took her ten-month-old sister Margaret out of the baby carriage she was pushing and followed her ten-year-old brother George and Josephine Wolf, a ten-year-old friend, inside. Using the money their father had left for them at the restaurant, they bought doughnuts and then went outside to play tag on the sidewalk. While Amy and George were still inside, a man followed Josephine outside, called her over, and asked, "Do you play between your legs?" She said no. After returning to the restaurant for a glass of milk, the children set off for home. The man, a twenty-six-year-old clerk named Martin Dickens, followed them. At 104th Street and Amsterdam Avenue, he caught up with the children. Pulling Josephine on to his lap, Dickens placed his hands under her dress and in her pants, and asked, "Do you want to go down the cellar with me?" She again said no. Dickens continued to walk with them, giving Josephine a nickel. At 107th Street and Columbus Avenue, after Josephine had parted company with the group, he suggested to Amy that they go through an opening in the fence of the Lion Brewery. When she did as he asked, Amy told the grand jury, Dickens "took out his thing and put his hand under my dress." She ran back through the fence and told her brother what had happened. The two then rushed home.[16]

Elizabeth Abel, an adult woman sitting at her window on the second floor of the building opposite the brewery, saw Amy go through the fence with Dickens. She quickly got dressed and rushed downstairs in time to see Amy emerge from the fence and disappear around the corner. Abel then followed Dickens for half an hour, until he entered a tavern on 106th Street and Manhattan Avenue. Sending a girl to call the police, she went to get Amy, whom she knew from the neighborhood, so that the girl could identify Dickens. When the police arrived, they found Dickens, Amy, and Josephine surrounded by a crowd. The officers quickly put Dickens in a squad car, and removed him to the Twenty-fourth Precinct.[17]

It only took the sight of a girl going through a gap in a fence with a man to send Elizabeth Abel running for the door. She felt compelled to act even though Dickens had not forced Amy behind the fence, and the girl had not appeared distressed. Such a reaction reflected the heightened anxiety about crimes against children that marked the midcentury sex crime panic. The children who provoked that anxiety did differ from their counterparts earlier in the century, reflecting the shift in Manhattan's population. Increasing numbers of African American and Hispanic children filled the neighborhoods earlier dominated by European immigrants. For all the discussion among whites of those children's lack of innocence, especially the sexualized character of blacks, assaults on them produced reactions from their communities that matched what occurred in immigrant communities.

But the evidence that midcentury New Yorkers, as compared with the city's inhabitants of forty years earlier, had a different awareness of what constituted sexual violence is ambiguous. Elizabeth Abel and the crowd that joined her did target a man for committing an act, the touching of a child's genitals, that would not have triggered such anxiety at the turn of the century, when intercourse was the only sexual act considered harmful to a child. However, it is not at all clear that they were aware of that fact. Elizabeth Abel had acted without knowing what Dickens had done to Amy Burton.

Most witnesses at least saw the man whom they reported do something to a child, but even in that circumstance it is not clear that they knew precisely what he was doing when they took action. As in the preceding decades, New Yorkers paid less attention to boys. Witnesses reported none of the handful of carnal abuse cases involving young boys and only a small proportion of the cases of sodomy.[18] It was men in the company of girls, and particularly a man with his hands under a girl's clothing, that aroused suspicion.[19] But it was also the case that carnal abuse took place in the same circumstances found in child rape. Girls playing or walking in the street were approached by strangers and taken to hallways or apartments. They were assaulted in parks and by store owners in their shops, janitors in cellars, neighbors in hallways, and family friends and relatives in their own homes. Consequently, New Yorkers' willingness to report men they observed touching a child's genitals is at best ambiguous evidence that they had adopted a new view of sexual violence centered on development.

Cases in which a child told an adult, usually a parent, that she had been assaulted, are a better guide to whether new ideas had been adopted. That situation provided parents with an opportunity to establish what had happened to a child before deciding how to respond. Tellingly, very few carnal abuse cases made their way into the legal system without having been witnessed. What makes that phenomenon particularly striking is that it is the reverse of the pattern in child rape cases in the preceding decades, most of which were reported by parents. Part of the explanation for the lack of parental action lies in the fact that touching and genital acts short of penetration less often caused the sorts of physical injuries that prompted children to tell their parents about being raped or sodomized. This was especially true of cases in which a man touched or fondled a child's genitals. But even that circumstance does not explain the almost complete absence of prosecutions based on a child's report. Of the twenty cases of this nature in my sample for which it is possible to identify how they came into the courts, a witness reported all but five.

One of those five cases, an example from 1931, is particularly suggestive of attitudes in New York City's working-class neighborhoods. Margaret Marcus learned from her seven-year-old daughter Gail that a neighbor, a fifty-three-year-old Syrian peddler named Abraham Gans, had taken her into his apartment. Once inside, Gail told her mother, he put her on the bed, took off her bloomers, "and then he shake it" and "leaked" on her legs. Margaret Marcus did not contact the police or the New York Society for the Prevention of Cruelty to Children (NYSPCC). It was nearly three weeks before the Society, on receipt of an anonymous letter, found out what had happened. Mrs. Marcus instead took Gail to be examined by a doctor. What she wanted from him, she later told a magistrate, was "a letter as proof of the fact that the little girl is in no danger." What the doctor gave her reveals that the danger that concerned Margaret Marcus was "ruin," that she saw the effects of sexual assault in terms of physical injury. "To whom it may concern," Dr. Moses Kupperman wrote, "Gail Marcus was examined by me on October 10th and I am happy to state that the hymen was found intact, although the labia showed some irritation." Assured that Gail was still a virgin, her mother felt no need to take any further action. Notwithstanding what the law said, she felt that no damage had been done. It took the appearance of an NYSPCC officer at her door to change her mind.[20]

This continued focus on physical injury appears to be echoed in cases involving boys, although it is difficult to judge that with any certainty, given the small number of such cases in my sample. Of the eight carnal abuse files, only two record how the case came into the legal system.[21] Neither involved a witness, but they do offer contradictory evidence as to how parents regarded nonpenetrative acts with boys. In one, the mother of six-year-old Angel Ramirez immediately took action when her son reported being assaulted, but the man, a thirty-three-year-old Cuban neighbor named Martin Bailey, had done more than simply touch the child. He also had the boy touch his penis, and then Bailey masturbated in his presence. Although neither of those acts fell within the definition of carnal abuse, they certainly caused Bailey to appear more of a threat to Angel, making it difficult to see Mrs. Ramirez's response as grounded in new ideas about the harm done by sexual experiences that caused no physical injury.[22] More telling is the second case. Nine-year-old Roger Goodman told his mother that while he and a friend of his were in Sakura Park (on the Upper West Side), a man who had offered to show them some wrestling tricks had touched his penis. She noticed that "his penis was not of its normal coloring," but the apparent physical injury was not sufficient for her to report what had happened to Roger. When the man repeated his behavior several months later, the boy himself reported it to a police officer in the park.[23]

The signs that attitudes toward childhood and sexuality had not changed may at first seem at odds with the dominance of carnal abuse prosecutions in the cases involving child victims.[24] On the surface, that pattern suggests that New Yorkers were overwhelmingly concerned with the acts that were newly defined as sexual violence. However, a look behind the figures reveals that it was not the acts appearing in the legal system that changed, but their categorization. Almost half the total number of carnal abuse cases involved acts that had previously been classified as involving penetration and been prosecuted as rape or attempted rape.[25] As such, their presence in the legal system was not evidence of a change in attitude. In December 1941, for example, Mary Howard opened the door of her apartment at 2558 Eighth Avenue and found John Richardson lying on the couch on top of Sarah Hunt, the six-year-old daughter of a neighbor, whom Howard was minding while the girl's mother went shopping. When she pulled Richardson away, she noticed that Sarah's underwear had been removed. As Richardson got up from the couch and fled the apartment, Howard saw that his penis was also exposed. Sarah said that while the Howard children were playing in another room, Richardson entered the apartment, placed her on the couch, removed her underwear, and, after inserting his finger in her genitals, "he put his privates in me." Her story, and what Howard had seen, would certainly have led Howard to say that the child had been raped. The visit they made to Harlem Hospital appeared to confirm that impression. An examination found what the NYSPCC agent who prepared the brief characterized as "evidences of assault upon the child," namely, "erythema of [the] vulva." Nonetheless, the charge laid against Richardson was carnal abuse rather than rape or attempted rape.

This recategorization came about because the enactment of the carnal abuse statute had the unintended consequence of forcing a reinterpretation of the meaning of penetration. The prosecuting attorney wrote on Richardson's case file that no penetration had taken place.[26] So too did prosecutors presented with medical evidence of a lacerated vagina.[27] Prior to the 1930s, physicians examining young girls had interpreted an inflammation, such as erythema of the vulva, and excoriated external genitals as signs of penetration. They did so on the basis that a prepubescent girl was unlikely to suffer the ruptured hymen that signified penetration in the case of pubescent and adult females. As Clifton-Edgar and Johnston noted in a leading medical jurisprudence treatise, "Not only the deep situation of the hymen, but the narrowness of the pubic arch and of the soft parts oppose the introduction of so large a body as the male organ in erection and protect the membrane from injury."[28] If a young girl's hymen could not be ruptured, then any sign of genital contact, any injury to her external genitals, became a sign of penetration, and the absence of any injury, a sign of attempted penetration. That interpretation of a girl's body provided no way for a medical examination to distinguish the nonpenetrative acts defined as carnal abuse from an act of rape, or even attempted rape. An inflammation could be the result of penetration, to the extent that it was possible, or of an attempt at penetration, or simply of genital contact without any attempt to achieve penetration, the result of a man's placing his penis between a girl's legs or against her genitals.

To distinguish carnal abuse from rape, physicians — and the legal officials who relied on their evidence — had to abandon the recognition of the different nature of a girl's body and employ the same measure of penetration that they did in the case of adolescents and adult women, a ruptured hymen. A medical examination in a carnal abuse case from 1936, for example, which an assistant district attorney (ADA) summarized as having "revealed no evidences of any injury to the genital organs," had found that the "anal orifice and hymen were intact."[29] This reinterpretation of penetration led to an almost complete disappearance of prosecutions for the rape and attempted rape of young girls.[30] Men had not stopped committing such assaults, but those acts no longer fell within a definition of rape now framed in terms of an adult body.

The carnal abuse statute did not have the same impact on the meaning and prosecution of sodomy, which remained the most common charge leveled against men who assaulted boys. Almost all of the men charged with carnal abuse had handled a boy's genitals. In my sample, the two cases involving genital acts with boys and the two cases involving anal acts with girls reveal no sign of a reinterpretation of anal penetration. What distinguishes those cases from the ones prosecuted as sodomy is the absence of any physical injury. In other words, the carnal abuse cases indicated no signs of penetration whatsoever.[31] The divergent impact that the carnal abuse statute had on the definitions of rape and sodomy appears to be at least in part rooted in the body. Anal penetration produced no injury equivalent to a ruptured hymen, either in terms of its social meaning or in terms of its character as an internal injury that could be accorded greater significance than external injuries. No scope and means were thus available for reinterpreting anal penetration. Moreover, the treatment of anal and oral acts was already marked by the age segmentation that developed in regard to other sex crimes. Sodomy was a charge employed almost exclusively against men who committed acts with children. Just as they had been earlier in the century, adults involved in anal acts, particularly men involved in same-sex acts, were typically prosecuted for disorderly conduct.[32]

After the 1930s, the definition of sexual violence thus came to replicate the increased age segmentation emerging in American society. Although the legal categories set in place by the NYSPCC and its allies defined some crimes by reference to age and others by reference to particular acts, in practice, age alone came to dictate how a crime was categorized. Whereas rape was a crime committed only against adolescent and adult women, all sexual crimes against prepubescent girls were treated as carnal abuse. That segmentation provided for increased punishment of nonpenetrative acts at the cost of diminished punishment of what had been previously regarded as penetrative acts. It also left a crime against a prepubescent girl as a lesser offense, a felony punished by a maximum sentence of ten years rather than the twenty years provided for rape.

In practice, the categorization of any sexual act with a prepubescent girl as carnal abuse resulted in their being treated as even lesser offenses, as misdemeanors. It was not jurors' failure to see prepubescent girls as children worthy of protection that produced those outcomes. NYSPCC agents and prosecutors successfully presented girls as children. What they could not do was show that a girl had suffered the physical injury that defined an act of sexual violence from the perspective of those who saw children as innocent.

NYSPCC agents and ADAS continued to present young girls just as they had earlier in the century: as passive. Such a portrayal fitted both competing visions of children's nature, neither of which regarded subjectivity as compatible with childhood. However, presenting a girl as innocent also required additional details in order to characterize her passivity as evidence of the lack of understanding central to innocence. Given the nature of the acts defined as carnal abuse, one of those details, crying after being hurt, was lacking. Ultimately, that absence did not prevent prosecutors from presenting the victims as innocent, but it did highlight that girls who had been subject to carnal abuse had not suffered the physical injury necessary to bring what had been done to them within older understandings of sexual violence.

In the case that opened this chapter, Amy Burton's testimony about the indecent and immoral practices that Martin Dickens had committed on her is summarized in the brief as if he alone had played an active part. "Again he followed them until they reached 107th Street at Columbus Avenue," the NYSPCC agent wrote. "Here the defendant told her to accompany him through the opening in the fence at the Brewery. He then exposed his naked penis, told her to 'play with it,' and placed his hand under her dress and in the vicinity of her private parts. She then ran out to the street." Only in fleeing does Amy have an active role in that account; until then she is entirely overshadowed by Dickens and what he is doing. The act that he committed did not require removing the girl's underwear, a key detail in rape cases. However, the description of his reaching under her dress without her resistance served a similar function as a detail indicating that the victim's passivity derived from a lack of understanding. The NYSPCC agent could not underscore Amy's innocence by emphasizing her failure to receive anything from Dickens. Amy testified that while he was walking with them, he had promised her a nickel, suggesting a motive for following him through the fence that implied understanding rather than ignorance. Not surprisingly, the agent omitted that detail from the brief. More significantly, he also made no mention of Amy's crying or being hurt. Like the girls in twenty-eight of the thirty carnal abuse cases in my sample that involved indecent and immoral practices, Amy did not cry.[33] Her silence, even more than the lack of any medical evidence in the brief, expressed clearly that the act committed by Dickens had done her no physical injury. The absence of her crying did little damage to her claims to innocence, but it meant that the treatment of Dickens's behavior as a sexual assault only made sense in relation to the more expansive vision of sexuality associated with psychosexual development.

References to crying and injury were also absent in most instances when NYSPCC agents presented cases involving genital acts. Again, that gap reflected the nature of the act. In three out of every four such cases, the man committed an act that did not inflict pain or cause physical injury.[34] In the brief of the case against Eddie Padilla, a forty-six-year-old Colombian janitor, the NYSPCC agent recorded that eight-year-old Mary Tyler had stated that on "February 25, 1941, she, with Alice Lindenfeld [a ten-year-old friend], visited Padilla at his apartment at 170 Henry Street, in accordance with his invitation. On their arrival, the defendant instructed them to accompany him to the basement, and there placed her on a bed, pulled down her bloomers, and placed his naked penis upon and against her naked private parts, in the presence of Alice." He then did the same thing to Alice, before giving both girls "a small sum of money" and sending them home.[35] The agent not only cast the girls as passive during the sexual act—objects placed on the bed, undressed, and subject to genital contact—but also in the lead-up to the act. It was Padilla's invitation that brought the girls to his apartment and his instructions that caused them to go the basement. However, the summary offered little to encourage jurors to see Mary's passivity as a sign of innocence. Padilla was identified as having removed the girls' bloomers, but the girls had also received money from him. The NYSPCC agent had little to work with in regard to those details. Testifying before the grand jury, Mary had described an earlier visit to Padilla, with her younger brother, during which he had committed the same act and given her the same payment. Nor could the agent refer to Mary's crying. On neither occasion did Padilla cause Mary any injury. Asked what he did, Mary told the grand jury, "He put it between my legs." The DADA, Arnold Bauman, then asked, "And did it touch your number one?" Mary initially said no, but when queried again by Bauman, she answered, "Sometimes."[36] That genital contact did not cause Mary to cry out, and it left no marks. As a consequence, prosecutors were unable to offer evidence that Mary had suffered the physical damage central to older notions of sexual violence.

In court, ADAS were able to sustain their portrayal of girls as children. The nature of the acts prosecuted as carnal abuse, and a change in language, made it easier for girls to speak in a way that displayed the lack of understanding expected of an innocent child. Unlike in earlier decades, evidence of how girls appeared in courts can only be found in legal records. Despite the extensive coverage of sex crime in this period, the media rarely offered detailed accounts of court proceedings. Instead, most cases received only a few lines in newspaper accounts that briefly described the offense and often focused on the defendant, a relative silence that at least in part reflected the efforts of legal officials and politicians to discourage the kind of publicity that dissuaded parents from reporting assaults on their children. Transcripts of hearings in the magistrates' courts and before grand juries, along with the notes prosecutors took during trials, reveal that girls simply described the elements of what had happened to them. Typical was eight-year-old Gladys Cordova's statement: "Then he put his hand under my clothes and he touched my skin all over. And he put his fingers between my legs."[37] Defense attorneys had challenged girls in child rape cases to characterize, rather than simply describe, what had been done to them, attempting to get them to use terms like "connection" and "sexual intercourse" that indicated understanding. However, in carnal abuse cases, they were unable to contest the testimony of girls on those grounds. No adult, sexual term existed to characterize touching and nonpenetrative genital acts, no phrase like "sexual intercourse" that attributed a meaning to the act.

Unable to scrutinize how girls described acts, attorneys and jurors were left to focus on the terms a girl used to describe genital organs. After the 1930s, that language changed. Girls in previous years had used terms like "privates" or "private parts" and had described a man's penis as a "thing," or simply as "it." In the 1930s, girls still typically used such expressions, and attorneys continued to make an issue of that vocabulary. Testifying in the magistrates' court, Sarah Hunt said, "He put his privates in me." Immediately, John Richardson's attorney asked how she came to use that term and whether the ADA had told her to use it. Sarah responded that the prosecutor had used the word in questioning her, at that time telling her where her privates were. But she insisted that the ADA had not told her to use that language when she testified.[38] It was not just that "privates" was considered an adult term, and could indicate that someone had influenced a girl's testimony, as the attorney suggested. The term also had sexual connotations; genitals were private because of their sexual function, because reticence was necessary in discussing sexual activity. Terms such as "thing" and "it" had no such specific connotations, but their very vagueness left listeners free to give them sexual meaning.

By contrast, the language that girls began to employ in the 1940s and 1950s was unambiguously devoid of sexual meaning. They variously referred to their genitals, and a man's penis, as a "wee wee," "pee pee," "wetter," or "number one."[39] Those terms all focused on elimination. Since it made no reference to the sexual functions of genital organs, such language allowed little scope for defense attorneys or jurors to construct a picture of a girl as one possessing sexual understanding. In that way, girls who used those terms were even more effectively distanced from adult sexuality, and marked as innocent, than those who used the older childish idioms.

While NYSPCC agents and ADAS continued to approach assaults on girls just as their colleagues had earlier in the century, they changed their method in cases that involved boys. No longer did they emphasize a prepubescent boy's resistance to a man's efforts to commit an act of sodomy, an emphasis that had distinguished their treatment of cases involving boys from those involving girls. In the period from 1930 to 1955, the adult understanding connoted by such resistance provoked a suspicion that a boy might have consented. Age alone was insufficient to convince jurors that a boy was a child; they also looked for a lack of understanding, which would be manifest in his passivity and in his language. Over time, ADAS and NYSPCC officers began to portray boys in sodomy cases in the same manner as they did girls in carnal abuse and rape cases, that is, as objects in narratives in which only the defendant acted, and in which, at most, only passing mention was made of force.

In 1955, for example, an ADA showed that kind of concern with a boy's passivity and lack of understanding in his summary of seven-year-old John Messenger's statement. One afternoon, when Messenger was watching television in the apartment of his building's janitor, he was joined by twenty-six-year-old Frank Johnson, the building's handyman. "After a while [Johnson] asked him to step into the next room," the ADA wrote. "There the defendant first removed his own trousers and then took off Messenger's trousers. Defendant took Messenger's penis into his mouth. After completing this act the defendant told him not to tell anything to his mother."[40] In that summary, the boy is entirely overshadowed by Johnson, his one action, acceding to the handyman's request to go into room, having been omitted. As in the presentation of cases involving girls, the detail that Messenger did not remove his trousers is highlighted in an effort to emphasize his lack of understanding. Since Johnson committed an oral act, he did not inflict any injury, so the ADA had no scope to highlight Messenger's reaction. Nor did he mention the boy's failure to gain anything from the act, in part because he had received something from Johnson: access to the janitor's television.[41] Both gaps in the portrait of innocence that the ADA painted paralleled those in presentations of female victims of the same age. Prosecutors' presentation of crimes against boys thus revealed the same diminished concern with gender evident in broader discussions of sex crime.

In 1950, in a pathbreaking move, New York legislators amended the sodomy statute in order to bring the law more closely into line with the diminishing attention being paid to a child's gender. The revised law used the same language and structure as the law on rape. In place of a definition of sodomy that emphasized the act and made no mention of age, the statute now employed the same age of consent and gave boys the same protection from violence that the rape law did in the case of girls. In effect, although boys still did not fall within the scope of the rape statute, the law now treated all children assaulted by men in the same way.[42] It would be more than a decade later, after this approach had been endorsed by the American Law Institute and incorporated in the Model Penal Code, that other states began to narrow their sodomy laws to apply only to cases that involved violence and children.[43] Illinois, in 1961, was the first state to adopt the Model Penal Code; eighteen others would revise their sodomy laws by 1976. What has drawn attention in these laws is the decriminalization of consensual acts between adults—New York's law only went as far as reducing such acts to the status of a misdemeanor. Yet these laws also extended definitions of sexual violence to include forcible acts of sodomy, and they did so in a form that distinguished crimes against children from those against adults.[44] It was in those terms that Governor Thomas Dewey presented New York's law, explaining it as intended to address the "rigid provisions of the existing definitions," by introducing "distinctions between crimes involving force or the abuse of children and those which do not contain those elements."[45]

For a brief period, the sodomy and carnal abuse statutes shared another feature that distinguished the legal treatment of sex crimes against children from those against older females: the absence of a corroboration requirement. In 1952, the New York State Court of Appeals ruled that a twelve-year-old boy had not been forced to commit sodomy with his teacher and was therefore an accomplice in the act. That ruling returned prosecutors to the position of either having to establish that a child in a sodomy case had been coerced or having to provide corroborative evidence.[46] Neither the courts nor the state legislature imposed a similar corroboration requirement on carnal abuse prosecutions, but, thanks to the youth of the victims and to jurors' increased skepticism about the weight that should be given to children's words, prosecutors nonetheless had to provide additional evidence to make a case. One in every three carnal abuse cases involved a victim who was six years of age or younger, children that magistrates and grand juries determined were too young to understand an oath. Since unsworn testimony had no value as evidence, additional evidence was required to prosecute those cases.[47]

When a victim could give sworn testimony, the practice in sodomy cases in the earlier period, when the law likewise did not require corroboration, had been for grand juries and ADAS to prosecute men with no additional evidence other than a physician's findings. After 1930, in both carnal abuse and sodomy cases, grand juries proved less willing to place that weight on a child's words, and instead proceeded only when they had corroborative evidence. Among the forty-eight indictments for carnal abuse in my sample, only two were based on the sworn, but uncorroborated testimony of a child; the DA ultimately discharged both men.[48] Just one of the twenty sodomy indictments relied on the combination of sworn testimony and medical evidence common in the earlier period; that evidence also proved compelling to the ADA who took the case to trial and to the trial jury that convicted the defendant.[49] Twice grand juries did indict men for carnal abuse when presented with nothing more than the unsworn, uncorroborated statement of a young child, but in both instances it appears that it was the race of the accused, rather than the words of the victim, that made an impression on the jurors. One defendant was an Indian, described by the child as "a dark man but not a nigger," the other a Syrian. The DA discharged both men, clearly uncertain that a judge would be so blinded by racial feeling that he too would overlook the lack of evidence in these cases.[50]

Ultimately, the reluctance of grand juries to indict men for a felony based entirely on a child's word did not prevent ADAS from mounting carnal abuse prosecutions. Other evidence did exist to corroborate their statements. Witnesses reported most of the carnal abuse cases that came into the legal system. Few sodomy cases involved witnesses, but in almost half the defendant admitted committing the offense.[51] Those statements were not due to the ignorance of the law, the confusion about language, or the efforts to pursue extralegal outcomes that motivated admissions in statutory rape cases in the preceding decades. Many of those who made admissions claimed to have been drunk, a condition, they said, that left them either unaware of what they were doing or unable to control their behavior. Drunkenness made the men less responsible for their actions, and a claim of intoxication might have been an effort to avoid some of the stigma attached to the accusation that one had engaged in sexual activity with a child. It also made the crime appear to be an aberration, making a man appear less dangerous, and diminishing the likelihood that his actions would lead to his being regarded as a sexual psychopath. Aberrant behavior might also draw a lesser punishment. Regardless of its effect on his punishment, coupling an admission with a claim of drunkenness did nothing to diminish the admission's value in establishing a man's guilt.

Despite this weight of evidence, a smaller proportion of the men in my sample who were prosecuted for carnal abuse were convicted than those prosecuted for sodomy, or even rape, of young children.[52] But that figure gives a misleading impression of how jurors responded to the new offense and to young victims. It could prompt one to overstate the degree to which they nullified the law and condoned the behavior that it sought to punish. Half of the men whose prosecution for carnal abuse did not result in their conviction neither had the charges against them dismissed nor won an acquittal. Instead, they were transferred by the grand jury to the court of special sessions, to be tried for a misdemeanor offense.[53] Jurors' decision to transfer a man to this court recognized that the act he had committed was one that warranted punishment but not the degree of sanction that was provided in the carnal abuse statute. Jurors' actions defined carnal abuse as a lesser offense, continuing the treatment of those acts as misdemeanors, as had been the practice before the new law. A handful of the men that grand juries transferred could not have been prosecuted for carnal abuse. In those cases, witnesses were typically too far away to see whether a man with his hand under a child's clothes actually had his hand on the child's genitals.[54] As the law stood, the grand jury could have dismissed such cases. Instead, they treated the defendants as if they had committed a lesser offense, directing that they be prosecuted for impairing the morals of a minor.

The decision to transfer defendants also demonstrated how treating carnal abuse as a lesser offense freed grand juries to rely on a child's testimony, something they were not prepared to do when the consequences for a defendant were greater. "Oftentimes you can secure conviction on a misdemeanor where it was a question of a small girl's word against a man of some substance in the community," Charles Tracy, the Montgomery County district attorney, told the Joint Legislative Committee to Investigate the Administration and Enforcement of the Law in 1937. "If it was a felony," he went on, "that might be an argument against securing the conviction."[55] That reaction further underlined the trend toward giving less weight to children's testimony that had begun in the seventeenth century. With recognition that children developed through various stages of understanding and intelligence, simply being able to swear an oath no longer established that a child was as reliable and credible a witness as an adult. Concepts drawn from child psychology, which was being popularized in this period, also figured in that assessment. One magistrate, for example, referred to the possibility that a ten-year-old girl's testimony was a "figment of imagination."[56]

Trial juries also treated carnal abuse as a lesser offense. All of the men convicted by juries were found guilty only of a misdemeanor. That perception of acts of carnal abuse went hand in hand with an emphasis on childhood innocence, as the trial of Martin Dickens, the man whose case opened this chapter, makes clear. Dickens faced a jury that included six women — New York women won the right to serve on juries in 1937 — but their presence did not produce any change in attitudes toward child victims.[57] In the courtroom, the defense broke down the appearance of Amy Burton as a passive, innocent child that prosecutors had striven to create, in the process diminishing the weight her testimony carried with the jury. Under cross-examination, Amy described approaching Dickens in the restaurant to tell him he was handsome and looked like a rich man. In testifying that "I knew when I saw him hold Josephine in his lap he wanted to do something dirty," she also displayed some sexual understanding. That statement likely ensured that the jury saw the circumstances in which Amy ran away from Dickens as further evidence of a lack of innocence. Amy testified that she started to run when she saw his "number one," before she realized that Dickens was putting his hand under her dress. Since she had not been hurt, a jury might have surmised that she understood that an attempt to have sexual intercourse might follow Dickens's action. At the same time, the defense attorney presented a parade of witnesses to attest to his client's good character, including his employer, his fiancée, and several members of his church. In effect, their testimony added weight to Dickens's words. The ADA, clearly feeling that the balance of the evidence had shifted in favor of Dickens, withdrew the felony charge. But the jury's concern went even further: it acquitted Dickens of impairing the morals of a minor.[58]

Trial jury verdicts and grand jury votes influenced the decisions that judges, ADAS, and NYSPCC agents made in negotiating plea bargains. The result was that, in my sample, only one of the men who admitted, or were convicted of, committing indecent and immoral practices was found guilty of a felony offense. All of the other ten defendants received misdemeanor convictions, the same punishment that they would have faced before the enactment of the carnal abuse statute. In other words, the new law brought almost no change in the punishment of indecent and immoral practices. However, it did lead to lesser punishments for genital acts. Only six of the seventeen, or 35 percent, of the men found guilty of committing nonpenetrative genital acts were convicted of felonies, and only one of the five men found guilty in rape prosecutions was declared a felon. That proportion falls far short of the pattern in the earlier period, when fourteen of the fifteen men found guilty in child rape cases had been convicted of a felony.

The years after 1930 also saw an erosion of the gender differences that had existed in the disposition of men convicted of crimes against young children. Men convicted as a result of sodomy prosecutions no longer received sentences that were more severe than those handed out to men convicted of sexual acts with girls. Only one in five men convicted of sexual acts with young boys in the years before 1930 received a prison sentence of a year or less, but, in the years from 1931 to 1955, judges showed four in every five men such leniency.[59] Even when faced with a defendant convicted of a felony, judges opted to impose a short sentence. Between 1886 and 1926, judges had sent two-thirds of the fifteen men convicted of a felony to prison for at least five years; in the period from 1931 to 1955, not one of the seven men convicted of a felony received a term longer than five years.

By the late 1950s, a new language of sexual violence was emerging, one that captured how little understandings of acts with prepubescent children had been changed by the concept of psychosexual development. In those years, the term "child molestation" began to appear regularly in the American media. An article published in *National Parent-Teacher* in 1957, for example, opened with examples of "assaults" on both girls and boys, and then quickly moved to define the problem not simply as "sex murders and brutal assaults" but as "the whole range of sex offenses against children." The authors labeled that grouping "child molestation."[60] By prefacing the term "molestation" with the word "child," the phrase signaled the importance now given to age in determining the character of an act, both in regard to whether it was sexual and to whether it constituted sexual violence. In addition, that coupling replaced the gendered language of sexual violence of Victorian America with a gender-blind language that reflected modern sexuality's emphasis on development. Child molestation also expressed the new breadth of understandings of sexuality, recognizing more acts than those encompassed by the older language of rape and its euphemisms. However, in encompassing the "whole range" of acts, the new language displaced rather than supplemented discussions of crimes against children in terms of rape.

The term "molestation" also connoted a less harmful act than that associated with the older language of rape. In more general usage, it referred to an act that was annoying or vexatious, rather than one that caused injury. Following World War II, psychiatrists and sexologists, including Alfred Kinsey, adopted the term precisely because of those connotations, using it to convey the limited harm that they believed children suffered as a result of sexual activity with adult men. Since "child molestation" was applied to the whole range of sexual acts, and not simply to nongenital acts, this usage did more than minimize the psychological damage newly recognized as attending sexual activity for children. It also played down the harm long associated with physical injuries that children suffered as a result of sexual activity.

To argue, as Philip Jenkins has done, that the appearance of "molestation" in cultural discourse was a product of more liberal and tolerant attitudes toward sexuality is to fail to probe beneath the surface of that discourse.[61] New ideas accrued to older notions of childhood without changing core meanings. New language, new laws, and new patterns in the prosecution of sex crimes gave an appearance of change that masked how the concept of innocence circumscribed the impact of the vision of the sexually developing child on social relations and legal practice. When they looked at both prepubescent children and sexuality, Americans placed more stress on age and on psychology, in the process giving less attention to a child's gender. But they retained a vision of sexuality as sexual intercourse, and they still saw prepubescent children as innocent.

chapter nine

Sex Play

On 8 July 1946, Assistant District Attorney (ADA) Aloysius Melia rose to present the case against Rodney Moore, a twenty-three-year-old African American, to the First Grand Jury. The charge was statutory rape; the alleged victim, fifteen-year-old Thelma Becton. Thelma told the assembled jurors that Moore had been her "boyfriend" since the previous summer. Around December 1945, "of her own free will," she started having "sexual relations" with him. By January, she was pregnant, and, in March, Thelma left home to live with Moore. She was still with him when the police arrived to arrest Moore in June. It was not something Thelma had sought; the police officer was acting on her aunt's complaint. The case file does not make clear what had prompted the woman to go to the authorities. Perhaps she had discovered that Moore and Thelma were not married, as she had previously thought: the ceremony that she and the girl's mother had witnessed was a fraud, performed by a man the couple had met at a party. Her presence at the alleged wedding was the only thing Thelma's aunt mentioned in her testimony to the grand jury, other than the girl's age. Detective Young, who followed her, testified that Moore had "admitted" everything that Thelma and her aunt had related. Moore also expressed a wish to marry Thelma, Young reported, and would do so as soon as she turned sixteen years of age. The detective's testimony concluded ADA Melia's presentation to the grand jury. Rodney Moore was present, having waived his right not to appear before the grand jury, and wanted to testify.

However, the grand jury "did not wish to hear him." Instead, they moved quickly to dismiss the case.[1]

Thelma Becton and Rodney Moore were black, one of an increasing number of nonwhite couples who appeared in the legal system after 1930, as African Americans and Puerto Ricans poured into Manhattan.[2] Thelma's consent and active participation in their sexual activity featured more prominently in the ADA's account than in the rendering of similar behavior in the first quarter of the century. Pregnancy was also a far more common condition among the girls involved in statutory rape cases when Thelma appeared before the grand jury than it had been thirty years earlier. Rodney Moore, unlike men in the previous generation of defendants, had sought to appear before the grand jury, even though, by his own admission, he was guilty. He clearly understood the statute as a law that the grand jury, and even the prosecutor, might not enforce. And the grand jury proved him right. Far more often than in the earlier period, grand juries nullified the law, dismissing statutory rape cases even when presented with overwhelming evidence of the defendant's guilt. Moore's desire to marry Thelma might have won him a dismissal even in the earlier period, but most of those whom grand juries freed did not make such a proposal. Notwithstanding the broad protection still provided by the law, jurors offered girls in their teens less protection than they had in the first quarter of the century, and little more protection than they provided to adult women.

A new understanding of adolescence contributed to this shift. The concept of sexual development brought a sexualization of adolescence, a transformation that has attracted far less attention from historians than the "invention" of adolescence.[3] Whereas G. Stanley Hall's adolescent had to be chaste in order to successfully attain adulthood, mental hygienists argued that adolescents had to express their sexuality in order to complete their development. "Young people need to do some tentative investigating to learn what their feelings are," the staff of the Child Study Association told parents in 1952, "and this need may involve them in some tentative physical experimentation."[4] Adolescence focused children's sexuality on their genitals, but the sexual activity appropriate in those years was not intercourse but acts popularly labeled "petting." This category was one more aspect of the proliferation of sexualities that attended the notion of sexual development. As Phyllis Blanchard, a child psychologist at the Philadelphia Child Guidance Clinic, and her co-author, Carolyn Manasses, recognized, the term transformed into "normal" adolescent sexuality acts "that were once termed perversions"—"mutual masturbation—manipulation of the boy's genitals by the girl while he plays with hers, the sensual contact of nude or nearly nude bodies with external contact of the genitals, even oral manipulations." Blanchard was at pains to make clear that parents who worried that petting was a preliminary to sexual intercourse "did not understand" the nature of adolescent sexuality. However much it might look like foreplay, Blanchard explained, "for many boys and girls petting becomes an end in itself, to some extent a substitute for more advanced sexual activities, bringing about relief of sexual tension in many instances without the need of carrying it over into intercourse."[5]

Blanchard and other mental hygienists writing for a popular audience reinforced this distinction by describing adolescent sexual activity as "sex play." The association with play provided a way of imagining adolescent behavior as being different from that of adults, despite its similar appearance. It also conveyed to parents that such activity did not destroy childhood, as a vision founded on innocence would have it. "Because sex play does not enlist the whole personality," sex educator Frances Bruce Strain explained, "because it is just 'play,' not love-making, children seem not to be in any way harmed by it."[6] It was participation in same-sex acts that harmed adolescents. By contrast, sex play "is far less harmful from a psychological standpoint," psychologist Winifred Richmond advised parents, "since union with the opposite sex is the normal course of events in maturity."[7] Her formulation cast sexual expression, even taken to the extent of sexual intercourse, as a lesser evil, less threatening to a successful transition to adulthood than a deviation in sexual object choice would be. It left only a tenuous boundary between adolescent heterosexuality and adult heterosexuality—and diminished the perception of harm done by heterosexual violence.

Whereas the adoption of the notion of sexual development led legislators and prosecutors to a vision of prepubescent children further at odds with how jurors saw them (that is, in terms of innocence), it had the opposite effect in regard to children in their teens. The sexually developing adolescent was much closer to the potential adult perceived by jurors than was the adolescent envisaged by Hall and child protectors, placing proponents of sexual development in conflict with the law and the New York Society for the Prevention of Cruelty to Children (NYSPCC).

Attitudes toward males charged with statutory rape were also altered by the sexualization of adolescence. Having sexual intercourse did not mark a developing boy as deviant, even when the act was accompanied by violence. Discussing delinquent behavior in her volume of advice on the adolescent boy, Winifred Richmond was careful to note that a boy who committed aggressive acts against girls might not be abnormal. His sexual violence might "be merely a substitute for a strong homosexual tendency against which he is fighting," a means of "assuring himself he is a normal personality." "The line between normal and abnormal is very hard to draw," she warned, "and in dealing with children and adolescents one often has to await the effect of further development toward maturity."[8] If an adolescent male's sexual partner was of a similar age, his sexual activity looked even less aberrant.

The concept of sexual development rested on age segmentation, which was increasing, and becoming institutionalized, in the decades after 1930. More and more Americans, including those from working-class and African American communities, spent their teenage years in high schools, segregated from adults. About 50 percent of working-class students attended high school in 1930; by 1960, the proportion had risen to over 90 percent. Beginning in the early 1940s, the percentage of black students finishing high school jumped dramatically; by the early 1960s, almost as many blacks were completing high school as whites.[9] High school established adolescent males as of a kind with teenage girls, as their peers. Sexual activity within this segment of society, involving as it did only immature individuals, was clearly "play."

By contrast, a man from outside a girl's peer group lacked the immature nature to be her "playmate." As a result, there appeared to be, in the words of the Mayor's Committee on Sex Offenses, "a wide disparity in social damage and individual perversity between sex intercourse or sex play between boys and girls of similar ages and the same acts on the part of mature men and young girls."[10] Nowhere was that perception more evident than in the response to the behavior of adolescent girls during World War II. It was the sight of schoolgirls' picking up servicemen in adult, sexualized places such as Times Square—Bureau of Attendance officers found 240 truant girls there one morning in early 1944—in bars, dance halls, and hotels that ignited fears of sexual delinquency.[11] Hence the significance of Thelma's telling the grand jury that Moore was her "boyfriend." Not used in cases prior to the 1930s, the term reflected a new age consciousness in regard to relationships and characterized Moore as sharing Thelma's immaturity rather than threatening it.

In the 1940s, legislators responded to such characterizations of adolescent males. First, in 1943, the New York State Legislature provided for defendants between the ages of sixteen and nineteen to be treated as "youthful offenders." When it was determined that someone fit this category, his indictment was nullified, his records were sealed, and he received a suspended sentence or a period of probation.[12] In 1950, the legislature amended the rape law to narrow the offense of statutory rape so that it applied to any man over the age of twenty-one who had sexual intercourse with a female under the age of eighteen years. Men under the age of twenty-one who had intercourse with an underage female in circumstances that did not constitute forcible rape committed only a misdemeanor.[13]

Efforts to enforce statutory rape diminished in the face of those new ideas and legal categories. ADAS increasingly encouraged grand juries not to indict a man unless he had employed some form of force, was an adult involved with a virgin, or failed to provide for the pregnancy and child that resulted from his actions. When prosecutors confronted African American and Puerto Rican couples, ideas of race further encouraged that tendency. In the 1930s, cultural interpretations of the sexual behavior of African Americans began to compete with biologically based visions of racial degeneracy.[14] However, the import of both views for statutory rape prosecutions was the same: that sexual activity by nonwhite adolescents was not a sign of abnormality and did not warrant treatment as sexual violence. Sex educator Frances Bruce Strain argued that, for adolescents from cultures uneducated in "American," middle-class ideals, cultures that offered them no "patterns of indirect expression" for their growing sexual feelings, the "direct forms of expression" — the "direct form of release in coitus" — remained the "normal" form of sexuality.[15] That sexual intercourse with girls in their teens was normal behavior in these groups did not make it acceptable to social agencies and legal authorities, but it did recast it as a problem of sexual disorder rather than of sexual violence, the result, as sociologist E. Franklin Frazier formulated it in his influential midcentury study of the black family, of family and community disorganization and the persistence of "rural folkways" in urban environments.[16]

Despite these shifts in attitudes, large numbers of statutory rape cases still appeared in the New York County district attorney's case files in the middle decades of the twentieth century. In part, their presence reflected the attempts of working-class New Yorkers to use the law for their own purposes, as their predecessors had done in earlier decades. Because the NYSPCC retained its role in the legal system, it could continue to promote law enforcement and thereby a vision of extended childhood that encompassed the teenage years. However, the NYSPCC found itself increasingly unable to successfully prosecute cases. Legal records make clear that as older ideas about teenagers drew new strength from the concept of sexual development, community attitudes toward statutory rape changed. Acts with underage girls that did not involve physical force were increasingly regarded not as rape but as simply "normal sexual relations." With the concept of ruin losing its sway in working-class communities, such acts also had fewer consequences that necessitated legal sanction. By the 1950s, despite the incidence of statutory rape in the DA's caseload, the broad definition of sexual violence contained in the statute no longer had much force.

New ideas about adolescence had a similar impact on the treatment of cases of sexual assault on boys. With the recognition of a homosexual stage of development, boys appeared to be capable of desire, and to be less innocent, in their encounters with men. The change in perception brought their treatment into line with that accorded girls, defining them primarily in terms of their age, rather than their gender. As a result, even as mental hygienists painted same-sex activity after early adolescence as more psychologically harmful than heterosexual activity, boys received less protection from homosexual aggression than previously. Whether the victim was male or female, the middle decades of the twentieth century were thus a period in which age lost much of the power to define sexual violence that it had at the turn-of-the-century.

Anacelia Lopez, a thirteen-year-old Puerto Rican schoolgirl, arrived at her home at 255 East 10th Street, on August 25, 1936. With her was her twenty-one-year-old boyfriend, Ronaldo Feliciano, who had been living on Home Relief since arriving in the city from Puerto Rico four years earlier. It was the first time in two days that her mother, Candida, had seen Anacelia. In the meantime, she had reported to the police that her daughter was a missing person. Consequently, when Anacelia returned, Mrs. Lopez summoned Detective Joseph Neary of the Ninth Precinct, who had been assigned to the case. When he questioned the girl, she told him that she had stayed with Feliciano in his furnished room at 140 East 16th Street and had had sexual intercourse with him. The couple had been seeing each other for eighteen months, for the last month in secret, after Mrs. Lopez began to disapprove of their relationship. Feliciano freely admitted having intercourse with Anacelia, professing his affection for her and a desire to marry her—as soon as his divorce was finalized in Puerto Rico. After listening to the couple, Detective Neary arrested Feliciano and took Anacelia to the NYSPCC. An examination by the Society's physician found that Anacelia's hymen was ruptured, confirming her sexual activity, but he saw no sign of disease or pregnancy. Three days later, she was adjudged a delinquent child in the children's court. By then, Feliciano had appeared before a magistrate and been held for action by the grand jury.[17]

It was parents like Candida Lopez, or other family members, who instigated almost all statutory rape cases in the period after 1930, but increasingly it took more than the discovery that a girl had had sexual intercourse to prompt them to turn to the legal system. As had been the case since the late nineteenth century, many of those parents had turned to the authorities for help in finding a missing daughter, not to lodge a charge of rape. Puerto Rican and African American parents were as prepared to turn to authorities for such help as were European immigrants, despite having to deal with a predominantly white police force. But involving the police ensured that if an underage girl was found, she would be turned over to the NYSPCC, as New York law continued to require the police to do. The Society would then investigate her sexual activity and, if a medical examination and questioning revealed that she had had sexual intercourse, seek to identify and prosecute the male involved.

Before the 1930s, it is clear that most parents shared the Society's view that some action needed to be taken in all such cases, even if their first resort might have been to an extralegal remedy such as marriage, rather than to a charge of rape. But after 1930, when not drawn into the legal system by efforts to find a missing girl, an increasing minority of parents opted not to take action, extralegal or legal, unless a girl became pregnant. By the 1940s, more than one in every three statutory rape cases involved a pregnant girl.[18] In part, that statistic reflected the fact that a girl's pregnancy was the one circumstance that often attracted the attention of people outside her family.[19]

In most instances, it was parents who reported cases involving pregnant girls. After 1930, that scenario became common enough for assistant district attorneys (ADAS) to speak somewhat cynically of it as a type: "another case where boy and girl friend had intercourse over a period of time, and when the girl got pregnant her mother made a complaint," as one put it in 1941.[20] One such mother was Diane Brady, an African American housewife living on Eighth Avenue in Harlem. In August 1955, when her fifteen-year-old daughter Mary twice missed her period, she took her to a physician on West 145th Street. The doctor determined that Mary was pregnant. She eventually admitted to her mother that the man responsible for her condition was a twenty-four-year-old African American shipping clerk named Moses Brown. Mrs. Brady then went looking for Brown, and eventually he appeared at her apartment. She later explained to Probation Department investigators that she had contacted Brown "to arrange for possible financial aid for the expected child and to learn if he was desirous of fulfilling his alleged promise to marry her daughter." Mary claimed that Brown had promised to marry her "if anything happened." He initially agreed to fulfill that promise, but by October he had neither done so nor made any contribution to the costs of Mary's pregnancy. Mrs. Brady and Mary appeared prepared to accept Brown's decision not to go through with the marriage, but his failure to provide financial assistance was another matter; and on 10 October they appeared at the 30th Precinct to make a complaint of statutory rape. Responding to notes from the detective assigned to the case, Moses Brown presented himself at the police station, where he admitted having intercourse with Mary. However, he claimed that she had told him she was eighteen years of age and that there were other men who might be the father of Mary's child. He was then arrested.[21]

Charging rape was not the only legal action that Diane Brady and her daughter took against Moses Brown. In an action that distinguished cases in the years after 1930 from those in earlier decades, they also petitioned the paternity part of the court of special sessions to obtain financial support from him for Mary's child. Criminal paternity proceedings, which had not been available to families in the first quarter of the twentieth century, offered a new legal avenue by which they could put pressure on men, one that was often used, as it was by Diane Brady, in conjunction with a charge of rape. Prior to 1925, Poor Law officials handled bastardy cases, prosecuting men only when children were in danger of becoming public charges. But in the second decade of the twentieth century, the Progressive child welfare movement began to urge the reform of bastardy laws. The reform campaign grew out of a recognition of the particular vulnerability of illegitimate children to an early death, ill treatment, and dependency on the state. The campaigns promoted the reform of bastardy laws in lieu of more radical proposals to grant illegitimate children the same rights as legitimate ones. In 1925, the New York State Legislature created criminal paternity proceedings that provided another way for families to secure financial support for an unmarried mother and her child. In New York City, the court of special sessions was empowered to conduct hearings to establish a child's paternity and to make orders that fixed a weekly sum to be paid by the man declared to be a child's father until the child reached sixteen years of age. Families, rather than only Poor Law officials, could initiate legal actions. That power allowed them to use such actions as an additional lever to pressure men into marriage or the payment of support, or to obtain support payments negotiated outside the legal system.[22] Prosecutors supported the coupling of paternity actions and charges of statutory rape, and they allowed the paternity hearing to be held first, while the rape charge hung over the putative father.[23] Given that attitude, it is perhaps unsurprising that very few men contested paternity proceedings in New York City in the middle decades of the twentieth century.[24]

Unlike their counterparts earlier in the century, parents who used the law to put pressure on men were not always seeking marriage. Mrs. Brady was one of a growing minority more concerned with obtaining financial support for a girl than with securing her a husband. One explanation for that shift was the increased presence of African Americans in the DA's caseload. One in every four men charged with having sexual intercourse with a teenage girl after 1930 was black; almost all were involved with a black girl.[25] African American girls were overrepresented among those who were pregnant, constituting 33 percent of the total.[26] Efforts to arrange marriages for them occurred far less often than in the cases involving pregnant immigrant girls in earlier decades.[27] That pattern is consistent with the picture provided by sociologists and social workers, who made much of the acceptance of illegitimacy in African American communities. "If a girl is pregnant, [her parents] feel that she should 'have the baby' and that the father (if they can find him) should contribute to its support," St. Clare Drake and Horace Clayton wrote of lower-class black families in Chicago in 1945. "They seldom insist, however, that he marry the girl to 'give the child a name' or to save their daughter's honor." Drake and Clayton traced that stance to a belief that a girl who had an illegitimate child "has not necessarily 'ruined' herself," since "lower-class men do not necessarily refuse to live with or marry [such a] girl."[28] Diane Brady's life was a testimony to that belief. She was unmarried when she gave birth to Mary, and she never married the seaman who was the child's father. Nevertheless, Diane was still able subsequently to marry another man, a factory worker.

However, the case files reveal that race alone does not explain the increased acceptance of illegitimacy after 1930. Lower-class whites displayed the same reduced concern about whether a pregnant girl was married that African Americans did. Although proportionally fewer white men were charged in cases that involved a pregnant girl, even fewer of those men were involved in discussions of marriage than was the case with African Americans, only one in four compared with one in three.[29] For whites, unlike blacks, such behavior was new; white illegitimacy and premarital pregnancy rates were on the increase in the years after 1930.[30] The notion of ruin was on the wane in working-class neighborhoods even before African Americans arrived. Its decline appeared to be a consequence of Americanization as much as of liberalization, the accommodation of immigrant cultures to the American norm.

Only Puerto Ricans, who appear in the DA's caseload in large numbers for the first time in the 1950s, following a wave of immigration after the end of World War II, showed the concern with ruin and illegitimacy that was evident in the first quarter of the century.[31] Efforts to arrange a marriage not only featured in half of the cases involving a pregnant Puerto Rican girl, but also often when the girl did not become pregnant, as in the case of Anacelia Lopez, the thirteen-year-old schoolgirl whose story opened this section.[32] Those discussions reflected the emphasis on virginity in Latin cultures. Although none of the case files record Puerto Rican parents using the language of ruin, other evidence makes clear that they saw a "good girl" as a virgin until marriage, with a family's reputation, and a father's standing in particular, hinging on protecting a girl's purity. Like the southern European immigrants of the previous generation, Puerto Ricans and other Hispanic immigrants continued to rely on ideas shaped outside the United States, in another context.[33]

Working-class parents' new focus on obtaining financial support also owed something to the fact that marriage was no longer so available to girls and boys in their teens. New obstacles now confronted them, in the form of extended schooling, new legal restrictions, better enforcement of the marriage laws, and less support from a new generation of children's court judges and legal officials. It was the consequences of schooling, rather than acceptance of illegitimacy, that made some African American parents decide not to pursue a marriage. The mothers of seventeen-year-old Arthur Joseph and fourteen-year-old Marie Murray agreed that their children should not marry, despite Marie's pregnancy, because of "their youth and immaturity." But the immaturity that concerned parents like Mrs. Joseph and Mrs. Murray was not the emotional instability, undeveloped personality, and lack of moral standards that worried reformers. It was Arthur's "inability to shoulder any responsibility," to support Marie and the child, as a result of being "a school boy."[34] Arthur's immaturity was, quite literally, a product of the institutionalization of new notions of development. The expansion of schooling to take in increasing numbers of working-class children gave significant weight to new, less fluid, visions of the years around puberty.

Puerto Ricans, however, still displayed a lack of concern about the marriage of girls in their early teens. They came from a culture where marriage occurred at a young age, with brides thirteen or fourteen years of age not uncommon, and seven out of every ten girls married before the age of twenty-one. Given those practices, it is no surprise that Ronaldo Feliciano's offer to marry thirteen-year-old Anacelia Lopez prompted little comment about her age. The experience of schooling notwithstanding, "adolescence did not exist for most Puerto Ricans," as Nathan Glazer and Daniel Patrick Moynihan put it. Instead, they "moved directly from childhood to adult responsibility."[35]

In the aftermath of the campaigns targeting child marriage in the 1920s, parents and couples also encountered stricter enforcement of marriage laws, as well as new legal restrictions on girls younger than sixteen. Previously, clerks had routinely ignored a girl's obvious immaturity, especially if she was pregnant, and had been allowed to accept the word of her parents as to her age.[36] After 1927, clerks could only issue a license to applicants younger than twenty-one years old, and those who looked to be that young, if they produced documentary proof of age.[37] Fourteen- and fifteen-year-old girls also required not only their parents' permission but also that of a children's court judge. Those who had not become pregnant often found themselves denied permission to marry. Children's court judges argued that sparing girls' "disgrace" did not constitute sufficient grounds for relaxing the law.[38]

In the 1950s, a new generation of judges also showed more concern with the nature of a girl's relationship than had their predecessors. In January 1947, a deputy assistant district attorney (DADA) took Ricardo Garcia, a thirty-year-old laborer, before Judge Wallace for a pre-pleading hearing to see if marriage between Garcia and Concetta Martinez, the sixteen-year-old laundry worker he was accused of raping, "would be proper." Concetta claimed that Garcia, whom she had met a week earlier, had dragged her from the street, placing his hand over her mouth, and forced her into a furnished room. Once inside, he had removed her clothing and, after hitting her several times, had sexual intercourse with her. Despite that violence—which he denied—Concetta's family wanted her to marry Garcia, who, for his part, was willing to cooperate with their plan. An earlier generation of judges had endorsed marriage in such circumstances as an appropriate outcome. In this case, "Judge Wallace didn't see it that way," as the DADA dryly put it. What the judge saw was a rape; he suggested that a plea of guilty to felony assault, rather than marriage, would be the proper outcome for the case.[39] Concerns about ruin no longer weighed so heavily on the minds of midcentury judges that they discounted men's behavior.

In addition, social workers, largely without influence in the New York City's criminal courts earlier in the century, began to play a greater role in shaping the outcome of prosecutions. As judges ordered pre-sentence investigations and placed increasing numbers of defendants on probation, more families found themselves dealing with the social workers employed by the probation department of the court of general sessions and their colleagues from the children's court.[40] Probation officers (POS) rejected the notion of ruin and could work against marriages sanctioned by judges and other legal officials. A pre-sentence investigation of Ronaldo Feliciano, the unemployed twenty-one-year-old Puerto Rican who had pled guilty to the statutory rape of thirteen-year-old Anacelia Lopez in 1936, reported that both he and Anacelia were "anxious" to marry. Her mother was worried that she was too young, but was prepared to accept the court's decision. Judge John Freschi decided to suspend Feliciano's sentence, place him on indefinite probation, and order him to marry Anacelia as soon as he was divorced. Earlier in the century, such an outcome would almost certainly have led to the couple's marriage. However, in 1936, the case passed into the hands of a PO, F. O'Brien. In his initial analysis he noted that, given Anacelia's age and "taking into consideration the type of individual the probationer has proved himself to be," it was doubtful whether it was in the girl's interest to marry Feliciano. O'Brien's case supervisor agreed. A "marriage is not desireable," he wrote after reviewing Feliciano's file, "because of the probationer's inability or unwillingness to accept responsibility especially since the girl is not pregnant." Mrs. Anglin, the children's court PO who was "advising" Anacelia, shared her colleagues' opinion that her charge should not marry Feliciano. Ultimately, the social workers prevailed. Four months after Feliciano's sentencing, the couple met for the first time since his court appearance, together with the two POs, in Mrs. Anglin's office. On this occasion, Anacelia "stated very emphatically that she did not care for the probationer and would not marry him." She appeared less emphatic a month later, when Feliciano reported to his PO that Anacelia had told one of his friends that she was anxious to see Feliciano. But by then the POs had conveyed her statement to Judge Freschi and convinced him to rescind his marriage order. In light of that decision, Feliciano told his PO that felt he had "fulfilled his obligation," and he opted to stay away from Anacelia.[41]

Despite the appearance of these obstacles, the extralegal outcome of marriage did not become entirely unavailable to working-class New Yorkers involved in rape cases. When the children's court refused a girl permission to marry, her family often simply waited until her sixteenth birthday, when she would no longer need the court's permission. Social workers' opposition to a marriage could be rendered moot in a similar way, with a couple's marrying once a man was released from probation.[42]

It was also the case that social workers' dismissal of the concept of ruin did not create an absolute barrier to marriage. Thomas Woods, a twenty-year-old African American who worked for a sportswear company, and fifteen-year-old Frances Reed, were anxious to marry, but the judge who placed Woods on probation required only that he support the child Frances was about to have. However, the couple convinced a social worker at Inwood House, the home for unmarried mothers to which the Department of Welfare committed Frances, and another worker from the probation department of the Brooklyn Children's Court that they had "a mature outlook on their situation" and that "the union might prove to be a stable one." The key to that endorsement was the social workers' belief that both Thomas and Frances knew that marriage would "not be easy." It also helped that he had repudiated the African-American community's acceptance of premarital sexual behavior. Previously, Thomas had been "adjusted to a low cultural level," as the report from the court's psychiatric clinic put it, which caused his sexual activity to appear to him to be "natural and accepted." After his experience with the court, his PO reported he had "some appreciation of the true implications of his conduct."[43]

There is evidence that by midcentury broad support existed for such marriages of couples in their teens, unions that promised stability rather than a rapid collapse that would spawn further social problems. When the issue of child marriage reappeared in the media in 1937, the brides were not the teenage girls that had drawn attention in the 1920s, but rather prepubescent girls. That coverage was precipitated by the marriage in rural Tennessee of twenty-two-year-old Charlie Johns and nine-year-old Eunice Winstead—the "youngest native American to be married in the history of marital statistics," according to the *New York Times*.[44] Photographs accompanying these stories illustrate that it was physically immature girls, not psychologically immature ones, whose marriage scandalized middle-class Americans. *Newsweek* pictured Eunice sitting on her husband's knee. The *New York Daily News* achieved a similar effect by posing a twelve-year-old bride from the mountains of Tennessee seated, while her husband stood towering above her.[45] Anxiety about these "baby brides," as *Newsweek* labeled them in 1938, did not carry over into concern about their teenage sisters, as a group of New York legislators found when the scandal failed to provide a vehicle for their proposal to raise the age of marriage for girls from fourteen to sixteen.[46]

By the postwar period, the acceptance of adolescent relationships and teenagers' increased incomes were reflected in their rising rates of marriage. By 1956, the median age of marriage for women in the United States was 20.1 years, a lower average age than in any other Western nation, with eighteen becoming the most popular age for brides, and as many as a million teenage Americans were married.[47] Not surprisingly given this context, grand juries continued to support underage girls and their partners who sought to marry. In one striking example, a grand jury in 1955 heard Luis Arroyo, a twenty-one-year-old night watchman testify that he had twice sought the permission of the children's court to marry fourteen-year-old Juanita Hernandez. On the first occasion, he was refused; on the second, the judge ordered his arrest. After Arroyo, Juanita, and her mother all testified to how in love the couple were, the grand jury dismissed the case and, the DA recorded, "recommended that the Children's Court be advised of this action and allow the defendant and the girl to marry."[48] Feeling sufficiently confident that teenagers could be mature enough to marry, the grand jury not only nullified the law it was meant to enforce, but also contradicted the arm of the legal system specifically responsible for protecting children.

Such talk of being in love distinguished statutory rape cases after 1930 from those earlier in the century, and it undermined a girl's position as a victim of sexual violence. In earlier decades, girls had not mentioned love, a reflection of working-class concepts of marriage that emphasized a man's ability to be a dependable provider and a woman's ability to supply help and domestic services. These attributes contrasted with the emotional intimacy that the middle-class valued as the key to marriage. By the 1920s, a new generation of working-class adolescents who had grown up with *True Love* and other mass circulation "sex adventure" magazines, told sociologists Robert and Helen Lynd that they "demanded love as the only valid basis for marriage."[49] A love story could overcome the obstacles to an underage girl's marriage, but a need for love could also narrow the circumstances in which girls sought to marry men, helping to explain the falling proportion of prosecutions that did not involve pregnancy. By the 1960s, some African American girls reported that not even pregnancy would lead them to marry men they did not love.[50]

Girls who talked of being in love usually went on to express consent and sexual desire, another distinctive feature of case files from the years after 1930. In summarizing a case, ADAs frequently would say something along the lines of "she was in love with the defendant and was willing to have intercourse with him." Behind such dry language often lay more romantic statements. "I felt the same way he did," seventeen-year-old Anna Diaz told a prosecutor in 1941. "He was very passionate and I was with him and I guess I felt the same way. It was mutual on both sides. We both felt the same way. I loved him and he loved me at the time."[51] Adolescents who wrote to Doris Blake, the advice columnist of the *New York Daily News*, offered similar visions of love as "excusing moral lapses, . . . as a talisman against accusations of sexual promiscuity."[52] In the context of a statutory rape prosecution, a girl's declaration of love had the effect of providing her male partner with much the same protection from sanction. Expressions of love and desire could no more be reconciled with the passivity and innocence expected of the childhood that the law sought to protect than could the exchange of sex for money that characterized the behavior of some runaways.[53] As a result, men charged with statutory rape often did not appear to jurors and legal officials as rapists who had exploited the immaturity of a child or had acted on abnormal sexual desires. Nor did most see themselves as sex criminals.

Almost all who were charged with statutory rape admitted to the act of sexual intercourse of which they were accused. Typically, such admissions did not result from confusion or ignorance of the law, as had often been the case earlier in the century, although some Puerto Rican men did echo the claims of European immigrants that sexual intercourse with a girl in her teens was not illegal in their homeland.[54] More often, men displayed an awareness of the law and a willingness to challenge it. Manuel Guerra, one of the many defendants who opted to waive their rights in order to appear before the grand jury in 1946, told the jurors, "I am guilty; what else is there to say?" It is hard not to sense in this twenty-two-year-old counterman's statement a strong note of sarcasm, for he certainly said much more than simply offering that admission. According to the ADA's notes, he "testified that he had used no force on the girl, that she suggested the act, that he believed her to be 19 and that they had intercourse."[55] The circumstances Guerra highlighted, a girl's consent and the belief that she was not underage, were the basis on which most defendants challenged the charge made against them.

A girl's consent had been the basis of challenges to the age of consent ever since the legislature had raised the age to sixteen, but its pairing with a claim that a man had believed her to be of legal age was new. That combination reflected an awareness of age that turn-of-the-century men had often lacked and served to challenge the law's arbitrariness. By the 1930s, documenting a girl's age was no longer difficult, but, as defendants reminded grand juries, discerning her age in everyday encounters was far from easy. Appearances could still be deceptive, perhaps even more so with the increasing use of makeup. By World War II, one newspaper report claimed, thirteen-year-old girls could "make-up with lipstick and rouge to pass for legal age," fooling even veteran bartenders.[56] Thus one defendant made the almost plaintive appeal that "the girl was mature and that her age never entered his head."[57] More often, defendants reported that they had been more circumspect and asked a girl her age, only to have her lie and tell them that she was over sixteen.

While British law formally recognized mistake of age as a defense against statutory rape, New York law did not. Self-interested defendants were not alone in challenging the law's narrow reliance on age without extenuating circumstances. That position had support at the highest level of state government. New York governor Herbert Lehman, in directing the State Law Revision Commission to examine the statutory rape law in 1937, wrote, "I do not think it is sound to predicate the crime arbitrarily and exclusively upon the age. I am sure that there are numerous cases of persons sentenced for the commission of this crime when they didn't know that they were committing a crime or even have the means of ascertaining the age of the girl."[58]

While, in different ways, defendants and girls couched their relationships in terms that diminished the significance of age, prosecutors often described them as "boyfriend and girlfriend," terms that foregrounded that characteristic.[59] However, that approach posed no less of a challenge to the law than did the positions taken by the parties to a case. While DAS accepted the importance of age, they gave it a new meaning derived from concepts of sexual development. Labeling a couple a "boy" and a "girl" not only distinguished them from adults, but also placed them on par with each other, a situation at odds with a view of defendants as adults who had taken advantage of children. The yoking of "boy" and "girl" with "friend" also diminished the relationship. It suggested something less than an adult liaison, founded on an immature form of love. As such, it evoked the notion of sex play, of teenagers' playing at being in an adult relationship. Given that such a game had few psychological consequences for a girl, and no physical ones unless it resulted in pregnancy, a case framed in those terms hardly appeared to warrant punishment as rape. But prosecutors went further: they also distinguished girls from children by giving prominence to their consent and desire, rather than seeking to mask them, as had been done in the past. ADAS did not merely record that a girl consented. To guard against any inclination to see girls as essentially passive and innocent, they also employed adjectives such as "willing" or "voluntary."[60] Ellsworth Lawrence, the district-attorney-elect of Franklin County, expressed the understanding behind that approach when he appeared before the Joint Legislative Committee to Investigate the Administration and Enforcement of the Law in 1937: "A girl 16 years of age knows enough to consent to the act [of sexual intercourse]."[61]

The overall effect of that approach was to highlight the grounds for nullifying the law, rather than those for indicting a man for rape. After noting that nineteen-year-old Richard Stewart admitted to twice having sexual intercourse with his fifteen-year-old "girlfriend," ADA Jack Pace wrote the following remarks in Stewart's case file: "No force was used, the girl consented freely, no money was paid, no promises were made by the deft [sic], the girl isn't pregnant or disturbed about what was done to her, but the [grand jury] would not dismiss."[62] Pace's recounting of the details of the case in negative terms systematically emptied it of the circumstances that constituted sexual violence in the eyes of jurors. The final phrase revealed Pace's expectation that the grand jury would respond by dismissing the charges, something that on this occasion, to his evident frustration, they had refused to do.[63]

New York City prosecutors were not alone in challenging the law in this way. Andrew Ryan, the district attorney of Clinton County, told the Joint Committee in 1937 that statutory rape "is being defeated by the district attorneys and the judges, and if it were not defeated by them, it would be by juries if they attempted to bring those cases to trial."[64] The state's DAs were clear about the reason for the law's defeat. "I don't class rape second degree as a sex crime," William Marlin, the district attorney of Onondaga County declared, in a frequently echoed statement.[65] That position enjoyed the support of psychiatrists, the experts to whom the public increasingly turned during the years of the sex crime panic. "Statutory rape is, after all, normal sexual relations," as it was put by Dr. Walter Bromberg, director of the Psychiatric Clinic of the Court of General Sessions of New York County.[66] Governor Thomas Dewey, himself a former New York County DA, agreed. "Under the present law," he complained in 1950, "adolescents have been stigmatized as rapists even though the crime they committed had no elements of violence and even though neither party to the act realized that a crime was being committed."[67]

The NYSPCC, however, continued to think otherwise. The brief prepared by the Society bore little resemblance to Jack Pace's account of the case against Richard Stewart. After noting that on the evening in question, Stewart and his girlfriend had entered his apartment after talking on the stoop of the Lenox Avenue building, the brief stated that Stewart "induced her to submit while he perpetrated an act of sexual intercourse." In place of Pace's matter-of-fact recounting of the case's departures from the circumstances that constituted sexual violence, the NYSPCC agent attempted to impute sufficient passivity to the girl and coerciveness to Stewart to create a scenario of statutory rape. The discrepancy between those two accounts captures the increasingly marginal position the NYSPCC occupied in the legal system.

With most child protection agencies adopting a social work approach at the turn of the century, the NYSPCC's continued orientation toward law enforcement left it increasingly exposed to criticism that threatened its influence. In 1937, an investigation of the NYSPCC by Paul Blanshard, the New York City commissioner of accounts, attacked the Society for its failure to adopt the methods of social work, asserting that its officers made "no attempt to adjust family situations, administer social treatment, or do case work." Instead, they immediately took cases to court. Blanshard's investigation also found that the Society did not require its staff to have any educational qualifications or experience, and as a result "only [two-tenths of 1 percent] of the work done is remedial in character to even a slight degree, and the remainder is law enforcement."[68] That attack was just one salvo in a broader conflict between the Society and Mayor La Guardia in the late 1930s and 1940s, one that saw the NYSPCC forced to give up responsibility for providing temporary accommodation for children involved with the legal system.[69] Despite such attacks, the NYSPCC was not completely anomalous in holding out against social work. In many maternity homes, for example, evangelical women continued to pursue the redemption of unmarried mothers, rather than their scientific treatment. However, unlike those women, whose work in providing girls with a temporary home was not compromised by changing views of unmarried mothers, the Society found the effectiveness of its law enforcement project seriously compromised by changes in behavior and community attitudes.[70]

A disruption to the routine of the court of general sessions in 1946 strikingly illustrated the situation in which the NYSPCC found itself. Judge Goldstein, going through the formality of asking the parties to a case "the usual questions" required to confirm a plea bargain, asked Theodore Raderick, an NYSPCC agent, whether he recommended acceptance of the plea. Raderick startled the courtroom by answering, "No." Goldstein promptly adjourned the case so that the ADA, Ernest Lappano, could obtain approval from the Society's general manager. Pressed by Lappano as to why he had broken with the usual practice, Raderick explained that "of late Mr. Smithers [the general manager] was complaining about the low pleas being given defendants and he thought it was well to have had this incident so that Smithers may see what he is up against." As was often the situation in statutory rape prosecutions, the girl at the center of the case, fourteen-year-old Anna Polk, bore little likeness to the "helpless little child," in need of protection, that dominated NYSPCC rhetoric. Nor did the defendant, a thirty-seven-year-old bartender named Charles Sawyer, fit the Society's portrait of offenders as men driven by "brutal passions" that would only be kept in check by conviction for a crime. Anna had babysat Sawyer's children for several years. On 4 July 1945, she had visited his home and found him in bed. According to Sawyer, he was "under the influence of liquor." "He asked her if she cared to have sexual intercourse with him," Anna told the ADA, "and she agreed, without any more urging than just the request." Anna compounded that admission of consent with an expression of desire, revealing that "she enjoyed the experience," so much so that she returned on another occasion to have sexual intercourse with Sawyer. Even her mother, who had walked in on the couple having intercourse, did not think that Sawyer should be punished, believing "that her own daughter contributed to the commission of the crime by her willingness."[71] The case evidently allowed Raderick to make his point to the general manager. Lappano reported that Smithers "agreed that the plea [to impairing the morals of a minor] was ok [sic] and told Raderick to recommend it."[72]

As if the increasing frequency with which prosecutors agreed to such outcomes was not enough of a blow to the NYSPCC's efforts at law enforcement, the grand jury ensured that most defendants never faced even minimal punishment. In response to how ADAs presented facts and charges, and to what was said by girls and defendants, grand juries frequently dismissed cases, effectively nullifying the law as it applied to consensual acts with an underage girl. As a result, the proportion of defendants indicted for the rape of a girl in her teens dropped by a third in the 1930s and 1940s; in the 1950s, the proportion fell a further third below that level. In that decade, three out of every four men charged with rape who appeared before the grand jury walked free, even after almost all of them admitted that they were guilty of having sexual intercourse with an underage girl.[73]

That one in four men was indicted on a charge of statutory rape indicates that jurors and prosecutors did not entirely nullify the law. In some of those cases, the girl charged that she had been subject to physical force. In other words, the DA had chosen to prosecute certain first-degree rape cases on a charge of statutory rape, a strategy that allowed prosecutors in New York, and other states, to win convictions without having to provide corroboration of a girl's allegation that she had been coerced.[74] Those indictments relied on definitions of sexual violence centered on force, not on the broader definition reflected in the age of consent.

Until the 1950s, two other sets of circumstances also produced indictments. The first relied on age or, more specifically, a difference in age. "It is my opinion," one ADA wrote, in explanation of a lenient plea-bargain in 1941, "that the purpose of the statute setting forth the crime of rape in the second degree was to protect children and young girls from older men, and was not intended to punish so severely moral deviation when both parties were children of tender age."[75] Despite the expansive language used by this ADA, in practice not every girl in her teens qualified for protection from older men—generally only those who were virgins. That distinction was not born of a concern about ruin; it derived from the significance of virginity as a marker of immaturity. In older, fluid notions of youth, a girl remained a child until she became sexual, usually with marriage. Adult men, by virtue of the earning power and independence that accompanied male maturity, appeared to both legal officials and jurors to be in such a position of power relative to girls that any relationship between them would involve exploitation. Even before the creation of the youthful offender procedures and the offense of misdemeanor rape made it formally possible, prosecutors and judges treated defendants in their teens more leniently than they did older men. Case file after case file from the 1930s records that the prosecutor, the NYSPCC officer, and the judge had agreed to allow a defendant to plead guilty to a misdemeanor "in view of the defendant's youth."[76] Jurors extended such treatment to a larger group that encompassed men in their twenties, apparently relying on an older vision of youth rather than the concept of age peers that lay behind prosecutors' approach.

Jurors and prosecutors also shared the concerns about pregnancy and providing for illegitimate children that brought many working-class families to the legal system. Men who, at the time they appeared before the grand jury, had not provided for the child resulting from their sexual activity, either by arranging to pay for its support or by marrying the mother, found themselves indicted for statutory rape.[77] All the signs pointed to the grand jury's dismissing the charges laid against twenty-one-year-old Jerome Fields in 1941. He was young, had not used force, and had no previous arrests or convictions. But the ADA also noted that Fields's "apparent lack of inclination to marriage impressed GJ [sic]," so much so that the jury indicted him notwithstanding the other circumstances of the case.[78] Grand juries were equally struck by the need to enforce the law when they encountered married men, whose existing obligations compromised their ability to provide for an illegitimate child, and men who had reneged on a promise to marry a girl.[79] After their indictment, some of those defendants changed their minds, submitting to paternity proceedings, arranging support payments, or going through with marriage. When they ameliorated the social problems they had created in this way, men were generally able to plead guilty to a misdemeanor and come away from the legal system with only a suspended sentence.

However, even when unmitigated, acts in those circumstances came to be regarded less seriously than they had been in the early decades of the century, as the pleas accepted by prosecutors and the sentences dispensed by judges make clear. Until 1926, when defendants agreed to a plea bargain, in a majority of cases they pled guilty to a felony. From 1931 to 1946, 77 percent of those indicted for the rape of girls aged eleven to seventeen years pled guilty to a misdemeanor.[80] The proportion in 1951 and 1955 was 69 percent.[81] In 1926, only half of those convicted were sentenced to spend less than a year behind bars or had their sentences suspended. In the years after 1930, an overwhelming majority, 85 percent, of those convicted received such lenient treatment.[82] These outcomes fell far short of the punishments meted out to men found to have committed acts of sexual violence; as a result, girls in their teens were treated not as children in need of protection but as sexual subjects, like adult women.

Prosecutors and judges also extended this new leniency to men who performed sexual acts with boys in their teens, despite the increased hostility toward homosexuals in American culture from the 1930s.[83] Those decisions not only downgraded the protection provided to boys but also erased differences based on gender. Prior to 1930, although evidence that teenage boys had consented to acts of sodomy had produced more lenient sentences than those given to men who assaulted younger boys, those sentences had been far harsher than those given to men convicted of sexual intercourse with girls in their teens. However, while adolescents of both genders now received the same minimal degree of protection, prosecutors and jurors did not see their sexual relations with men in the same way. If statutory rape cases appeared to be "normal sexual relations," same-sex acts were clearly abnormal, on the wrong side of the new heterosexual/homosexual binary that defined sexuality. That distinction ensured that the sodomy law was enforced, rather than nullified. Men charged with sodomy with boys were indicted at more than twice the rate of those charged with rape, with prosecutors working to ensure, rather than prevent, their prosecution. Nonetheless, when jurors and legal officials came to weigh how severely to punish those men, it was their changed attitude toward boys, not their antipathy toward abnormal sexuality, that came to the fore.

After 1930, jurors began to display a suspicion of boys previously directed only at girls. Throughout the twentieth century, they had inferred that physically mature teenage girls had sufficient intelligence and sexual understanding to make it likely that their involvement in sexual acts was the product of consent rather than childish ignorance. Before the 1930s, the physical maturity of teenage boys did not produce a parallel inference that a boy might have consented to a same-sex act. The adult sexuality that jurors suspected that a physically mature teenage boy had attained did not include a desire for sex with another male. New Yorkers' attitudes began to change in the 1930s, with the dissemination of mental hygienists' notions of adolescence in child-rearing advice and the response to the sex crime panic. They encountered the idea that the early years of puberty were a phase in which, as part of their normal growth, both boys and girls developed a sexual attraction to members of the same sex. In cases of sexual violence, that recognition of a homosexual stage caused an adolescent's sexual contacts with a man to become an object of suspicion, regardless of the child's gender. An adolescent boy could now have a sexual interest in a man, raising the possibility that he might consent to an oral or an anal act. That concern paralleled the long-standing anxiety that physically mature adolescent girls had the desire and understanding to consent to sexual intercourse.

As a result, jurors displayed a new unwillingness to see a boy's failure to resist as the product of a lack of understanding, rather than a sign of consent. When Mitchell Stevens, a fourteen-year-old runaway, encountered forty-year-old Alex Walker, an unemployed African American, in the neighborhood of Broadway and 42nd Street in 1941, the older man suggested he come to his room and wash up. At Walker's trial, Stevens testified that after he and Walker got to the room, "we were just sitting around and he asked me if I wanted to have some fun. I didn't know what he was talking about. Then he asked me if I ever was sucked off before, and I told him no, and he said, "Well, I would like to try it," and I told him no, because I never did it before and I would not know what it was. I could say nothing, or yell, because if I did—[at this point the defense attorney objected, and Stevens' statement about being unable to resist was struck out] He said he would show me how, and he got on his knees and took it and put it in his mouth."[84] Claims of a lack of homosexual experience, like that offered by Mitchell, echoed prosecutors' concern about establishing the virginity, and hence immaturity, of a teenage girl. However, a girl's claim to be a virgin was generally grounded in her body, in medical evidence of a recently ruptured hymen. A boy's previous lack of experience of "abnormal" sexuality, by contrast, lacked such a physical referent to give it credibility, and did not have the same power to cast him as a child. When a boy testified that he had gone to a man's room, he provoked questions from members of the grand jury about his claims that he had not realized what the man would do.[85] Judges displayed similar concerns. Although Mitchell Stevens said all the things necessary to establish his immaturity—claiming ignorance, a lack of experience, and circumstances that kept him from resisting—he failed to convince Judge Freschi that he had not consented. Instead, as the judge saw it, "by persuasion, [Walker] induced him, by talking to him . . . the young man submitted voluntarily. He did not resist or refuse. The testimony plainly indicates that he submitted to the proposal of the defendant, and this practice was indulged in."[86] That reasoning relied on the same narrow conception of force as injurious physical violence that judges employed throughout this period in cases that involved teenage girls; it betrayed no sign of the earlier sense that boys were unlikely to consent to sexual acts with men.

In addition, juries began to pay attention to a boy's character, displaying the same unwillingness to treat as victims those with bad traits that they showed in cases involving teenage girls. At the trial of twenty-seven-year-old Oscar Devereaux in 1946, for example, fourteen-year-old Frank Hertz and fifteen-year-old John Weiss testified that on separate occasions Devereaux took them on a shopping trip, to dinner, and then back to his room at the YMCA. Both told similar stories of falling asleep in Devereaux's room and awakening to find him kneeling beside the bed with the boy's penis in his mouth. Hertz and Weiss also admitted to boasting of committing burglaries and other crimes, to being truants and runaways, and, in Weiss's case, to being drunk on many occasions prior to meeting Devereaux and to lying about his age. The principal of the boys' school also testified that their teachers had characterized them as "insolent, indolent, unco-operative, and dirty." In contrast, Devereaux was an air force veteran who claimed "that he had always been interested in youth movements" and "was merely interested in the boys who appeared to be underprivileged." He was also, in the DADA's opinion, "not obviously effeminate in speech or demeanor." Despite the prosecutor's assessment of the man's conduct with the boys as "suspicious," the jury could not agree on a verdict, voting seven to five to acquit Devereaux. "Many of the jurors," the DADA reported with some frustration after interrogating them, "seemed more concerned with what was to be done with the boys than with anything the defendant might have done. All of them expressed a reluctance to convict a veteran with a good record on the unsupported testimony of two boys such as these."

In this case the defense attorney succeeded in presenting the boys' claim to have been victims of sexual violence as another expression of their bad, delinquent character, as a logical extension of their previous criminal behavior. So large did this bad character loom before the jurors that for a majority there was much less reason to be concerned about the suspicious behavior of a man whose residence at the YMCA, and lack of a good reason for his interest in underprivileged boys marked him as gay.[87] Although the concern with a teenage boy's character was akin to how rape cases involving teenage girls were assessed, jurors nevertheless understood bad character in the case of girls in more narrowly sexual terms, as evidenced by previous sexual experience, extensive sexual knowledge, or the exchange of sex for some kind of payment. Bad character in boys, by contrast, while sometimes indicated by "provocative" sexual behavior and homosexual experiences, was more often seen to be based on the sort of nonsexual behaviors displayed by Hertz and Weiss, the petty crime and rejection of authority that remained at the heart of concepts of male juvenile delinquency.

Despite the survival of such traces of gender difference, it was the new heterosexual/homosexual binary that lay at the root of divergences in the treatment of statutory rape and sodomy. Although sodomists received the same lenient treatment that statutory rapists did, more of those who committed same-sex acts were subject to legal sanction than were men who had sexual intercourse with a pubescent girl. Even when they did not involve physical violence, acts between men and boys were abnormal in a way that heterosexual acts were not, involving as they did an "immature" sexual object choice. Acts of sodomy consequently continued to attract punishment.

The same could not be said of acts of sexual intercourse with pubescent girls. By 1955, more of the small group of men indicted for statutory rape had allegedly used physical force, and thus had committed rape as it had been traditionally understood, than had had sexual intercourse with an underage girl in other circumstances.[88] New ideas of adolescence, new populations in New York City, the waning influence of the concept of ruin, pubescent girls' expressions of love and desire, and the growing influence of social work in the courts had all acted to dissolve the concept of extended childhood that had supported the broad definition of sexual violence contained in the statutory rape law. With only traces of the concept remaining by the 1950s, statutory rape was even less associated with sexual violence than was the offense of child molestation that applied to prepubescent children. New meanings had accrued to older understandings of adolescence, but they had done little to change the core concepts. In one area, however, age retained its power to explain sexual violence, and it would do so into the 1960s. The major focus of the sex crime panic was the repeat sex offender, characterized as a sexual psychopath. It was "the study of the emotional development and the stages through which a human being passes until he reaches psycho-sexual maturity," psychologist Bertram Pollens and his colleagues contended, that offered "the key to the solution" to the problem of the psychopath.[89]

The Age of the Psychopath

Separating the Men from the Boys

In the wake of the rash of child sex murders in New York City in 1937, the New York Welfare Council called together a conference of psychiatrists, judges, social workers, and public officials to discuss ways of coping with the problem. Among those in attendance was Richard McGee, the warden of the city's Rikers Island Penitentiary. Writing about the gathering a year later, he described a scene that in the ensuing decades would be repeated in countless public meetings and gatherings of public officials and in the work of fifteen state commissions. "Much of the day," McGee wrote, "was spent in an effort to draw out from the eminent psychiatrists present some advice as to how to treat the ingrained offenders brought to the courts for overt acts of sexual immorality."[1] In looking to psychiatrists, McGee and his colleagues were acknowledging the growing stature of the profession and the practice of having recourse to experts, a trend that had developed in the twentieth century. The attitude of those at the conference was broadly shared. A survey of public opinion in Michigan found that 65 percent of the respondents believed that sex offenders should be treated as mentally ill.[2] A similar proportion of the citizens of Louisville, questioned in a Roper opinion poll, likewise favored sending sex criminals to the hospital rather than to prison, as did three-quarters of the respondents to a comparable survey in the District of Columbia.[3]

Psychiatrists had been promoting the explanations of crime in general expressed in those responses since the early twentieth century, when they moved out of the asylum and sought to develop a "psychiatry of everyday life."[4] But prior to the late 1930s, psychiatric accounts of sex crime did not feature in New York City's courts, in large part because psychiatrists had not offered a specific explanation of sex crime. As men who committed sex offenses did not fit definitions of insanity, they became subjects for psychiatry only after the profession broadened its focus from the insane to the character structure of "normal human beings." Sex offenders then fell within the purview not of mental hygienists but of psychiatrists from the other wing of the profession, those concerned with psychopathy and variations from the normal, rather than with the maintenance of mental health.[5] In the 1910s and 1920s, those psychiatrists established clinics in reformatories, jails, penitentiaries, and urban courts "as part of a new regime of scientific investigation, professional expertise, and 'individualized treatment.'"[6] New York City, however, was slow to provide its criminal courts with such facilities; a clinic was not established for the court of general sessions until 1931.[7] But that delay was not responsible for the absence of a psychiatric explanation of sex crime in the city's courts. Historian Michael Willrich found that even in the Municipal Court of Chicago, which opened its psychiatric clinic in 1914, judges sought a psychiatric diagnosis most often when they had to deal with prostitutes, youth, and participants in domestic disputes, and only rarely when deciding the fate of adults accused of violent crimes or crimes against property.[8] Serious offenders continued to be seen as subjects for retributive punishment.[9] It took the specter of the "ingrained offenders" invoked by Warden McGee, men who continued to offend even after being subject to such punishment, to prompt judges to seek the help of psychiatrists.

When psychiatrists were called on to explain the sex criminal to audiences such as the New York City conference, they presented him as the product of distorted or arrested development, as a "sexually immature individual," in McGee's rendering.[10] In doing so, they drew on the same discourse of sexual development that was transforming understandings of sexual violence and its victims. To talk of sex crime at midcentury was thus to talk not only of child victims but also of childlike offenders and of the childhoods of those men. The story of the sexual psychopath is therefore not just an episode in the history of sexuality and the growth of psychiatric authority; it also forms part of the history of childhood, an echo of the debates about the nature of childhood that took place around victims of sexual violence. Historians have been most struck by the other key trait psychiatrists attributed to the sex criminal, his uncontrollable desires.[11] But it was the concept of sexual development that performed the critical function of explaining why those impulses were directed at children, the victims who attracted the most attention during the sex crime panic.

Psychiatrists described sex offenders' choice of sexual object as the product of the immaturity that such men shared with the young: they were drawn to individuals like them in terms of their development. The concept of psycho-sexual development also allowed psychiatrists to effectively "whitewash" the sexual psychopath, to present him in terms that did not undermine the figure of the bestial black rapist that justified the incarceration or killing of African American offenders. Psychiatrists' explanation of the sex criminal lent itself to a mental hygiene program of prevention. Correct child-rearing practices could avert the childhood experiences that led to sex crime. Parents had to provide their sons with sex education and avoid responding to the boys' sexual problems with severe reprimands or embarrassment. Boys also needed to be free of overprotective mothering and to have instead an adult male with whom they could identify. Finally, parents needed to protect their sons from sexual encounters with adult men.

Politicians and the public wanted a program of treatment to remove the danger that adult sex criminals posed to society, but many psychiatrists were not certain that they knew enough about sex criminals to provide such treatment. Those at the conference attended by Warden McGee made the "frank admission" that "they could offer no practical and effective plan for treating the fully developed sex deviate."[12] However, such disclosures did little to dim the faith of politicians and officials, as well as of the press, that psychiatrists had the answers to the problem of the sex criminal. Under pressure to provide a solution, public officials created, from the explanations offered by psychiatric experts, a type of offender labeled the sexual psychopath, and then made psychiatrists responsible for those offenders. New laws were enacted that provided for psychiatric examinations to identify sexual psychopaths, and for the committal of such men for treatment until psychiatrists determined they no longer posed a threat to society. By 1950, the year the New York State Legislature passed such a law, eleven states and the District of Columbia had already enacted similar statutes; eighteen more states followed in the 1950s and 1960s.

In practice, psychiatrists struggled to identify and treat dangerous sex of-fenders. In New York, as in about two-thirds of the states that enacted laws, only small numbers of offenders were committed to hospitals as sexual psy-chopaths. Where the examining psychiatrists subjected offenders to extensive testing and examination, the number of men found to fall within the scope of the law was particularly small. More tellingly, psychiatrists failed to develop an effective treatment for those offenders they did commit. The lack of treatment undermined the rationale for separate legal procedures for sex offenders, and it left the laws open to challenges that they violated due process and an offender's civil rights. The sex offender laws also failed to provide Americans with the protection from sexual violence that legislators had sought, a situation given immediacy in many states by sensational sex crimes similar to those that had originally prompted the legislation. By the early 1980s, both psychiatrists and their image of the immature sex offender had been discredited. Age, along with the developmental framework that gave it significance, had lost almost all its power to explain sex crime.

Many Americans found Lawrence Marks difficult to understand. It was not just that, in 1937, he admitted committing a horrific crime, a rape and murder. Nor was it that his victim, Paula Magagna, was only eight years of age, a child. What put Marks entirely beyond their understanding was that this crime was not the first sexual assault on a child that he had committed. Twice before he had been jailed for attacks on young girls. On parole after serving time for his second conviction, he had committed another offense and been returned to prison as a parole violator. Marks had been free only two months when he assaulted Paula. Five days after that crime, he was annoying another girl, an act that led to his arrest and, ultimately, to his confession that he had killed Paula.[13] Marks's choice of children as victims and, particularly, the repeated nature of his offending did not fit the widely held belief that white men who committed sex crimes had suffered a momentary loss of control, the result of excessive arousal, or lack of sexual outlets, or the effects of alcohol. Whatever its exact cause, an act of sexual violence was an aberration, not a reflection of an individual's usual sexual behavior.

In the case of Marks, however, the young age of all of his victims, and his repeated transgressions, meant that his crimes could not so easily be dismissed as being incidental to his identity or his sexuality. Nonetheless, Marks was not insane, the only legal identity available before the twentieth century that marked an individual as unlike the rest of society.[14] By 1915, however, psychiatrists had abandoned the sharp distinctions between sanity and insanity in favor of "a language of normalization—of deviations, grades, and scales." In the process they articulated a new identity, the psychopath, which encompassed individuals whose behavior deviated only slightly from normality. Psychopathy was an indeterminate category, "a singularly expansive, malleable, and unstable rubric" that allowed psychiatrists to bring a broad range of defects within the scope of their science.[15] A specifically sexual form of psychopathy, one that could explain men such as Lawrence Marks, was not articulated until the 1950s. The sexual psychopath was the creation, in the first instance, of the press and legislators; the term was, as Benjamin Karpman, chief psychotherapist at St. Elizabeth's Hospital in Washington, D.C., put it, "of popular origin and standing."[16]

As a result of that lack of clinical substance, the enshrinement of sexual psychopathy in popular discussions and in law made it the subject of extensive theoretical debates among psychiatrists and led to new research projects that aimed to clarify its nature. The most important examples of the new psychiatric writing are theoretical works by Benjamin Karpman, Walter Bromberg, Manfred Guttmacher, and Karl Bowman and his collaborators in the California Sexual Deviation Study, and major studies of sex offenders by David Abrahamsen and Bernard Glueck in New York, Albert Ellis and Ralph Brancale in New Jersey, Asher Pacht and his colleagues in Wisconsin, and Harry Kozol and his colleagues in Massachusetts.[17] Elements of these new psychiatric studies found their way into public forums, particularly state and local government investigations of sex crime, and into newspapers, periodicals, and radio broadcasts. Government committees and commissions reported on sex crime in eleven states. The most influential reports were New York City's *Report of the Mayor's Committee for the Study of Sex Offenses*, New Jersey's *The Habitual Sex Offender*, and Michigan's *Report of the Governor's Study Commission on the Deviated Criminal Sex Offender*.[18] Stories on sex crime appeared in periodicals ranging from *Christian Century* to *Collier's* and *Parents' Magazine*. Newspapers also increased their coverage of sex crime in both their news and features sections; even the mainstream *New York Times* had to create a new index heading for the 143 stories it carried in 1937.

Psychiatrists' theorizing, research, and practice produced a variety of different profiles of the men who committed sex crimes. But those profiles generally agreed on only two points: sex offenders suffered from uncontrollable sexual desires, and such offenders lacked emotional and sexual maturity. According to Karpman's theory, the sexual psychopath who was "driven compulsively to seek gratification of an apparently insatiable urge" had "not matured sexually" and "represent[ed] a kind of sex life that at an early period of development [had] detoured into aberrant channels leading to an abortive aim-inhibited sexual activity."[19] Immaturity was given a similar prominence in psychiatrists' diagnosis of sexual psychopaths. When researchers from Alfred Kinsey's Institute of Sex Research conducted a study of men adjudged sexual psychopaths in California, they found that "immature" was the second most frequently applied adjective in the clinical diagnostic report produced by the examining psychiatrists.[20]

Renderings of the sexual psychopath's traits for a popular audience, in books, newspapers and periodicals, likewise coupled immaturity with uncontrolled impulses. Bertram Pollens, senior psychologist at New York's Rikers Island Penitentiary, for example, produced a book on the sex criminal for the general reader that employed folksy metaphors to convey psychiatric thought to lay readers. To elaborate his assertion that "sex perversion in an adult" was "merely a stunting of growth," Pollens explained, "It is as though the individual began to climb up a ladder, but was either prevented by some obstacle from reaching the top, or decided to stay and progress no further when he found a comfortable home on one of the steps." He also presented immaturity as literally making men like children. The sexual deviate, Pollens claimed, "can be best explained by comparing his condition with a child and indicating at what psychosexual stage he has become fixated."[21]

It was the sexual psychopath's immaturity, psychiatrists argued, that produced his uncontrollable sexual desires. As David Abrahamsen of Columbia University saw it, the control of sexual impulses required "emotional understanding and maturity," characteristics lacking in the sex offenders whom he studied at Sing Sing Prison.[22] For Karpman, sex offenders' diminished ability to control their desires was compounded by the strength of those desires. Since their immaturity left them at a stage closer to the instinctual, and their desires had never been subject to the repression that came with maturity, the force of those desires was greater than normal.[23] If Karpman's psychopath was oversexed, the sex offenders studied by another school of psychiatrists appeared undersexed, left "internally inhibited" by their arrested development and immaturity. A man with such a "compulsive neurotic" personality was destined to "abnormally explode, from time to time," Albert Ellis and Ralph Brancale claimed, "because he abnormally holds himself in most of the time."[24] Whatever form it took, the notion of a connection between immaturity and lack of control was apparently uncontentious within psychiatry and self-evident to the broader public. Such an association fitted in neatly with the practice, in popular accounts, of likening the sex offender to a child. Irma Hewlett employed that analogy when she told the readers of *Parents' Magazine* that sex offenders frequently had "no more control over their impulses than the child who wants what he wants when he wants it."[25]

Given the immaturity of the sex offender's desires, it was only logical, in terms of sexual development, that children became the objects of his interest. An offender was drawn to, and could relate to, a child, psychiatrists argued, because they shared the same stage of development and, in that sense, shared the same desires.[26] The most elaborate development of this argument came in the *Final Report of the New York State Research Project for the Study and Treatment of Persons Convicted of Crimes Involving Sexual Aberrations*, a project directed by Bernard Glueck. Published in 1956, this report laid out an elaborate age-based typography that differentiated "pedophiles"—offenders against children—and "hebephiles"—offenders against adolescents—and tied the men's object to their psychosexual development. According to Glueck and his colleagues, heterosexual hebephiles "tend to be fairly well integrated, but on an adolescent, or childish, level of performance." Heterosexual pedophiles, by contrast, showed "an arrest of psychosexual development at a childhood or early adolescent level, and appear to be more comfortable with children than adults." Homosexual hebephiles "show marked disturbances in their psychosexual development" and a "psychosexual age . . . at the early adolescent level." Homosexual pedophiles, who showed the "greatest amount of disturbance of all groups," could only "successfully relate [to] boys, who are sexually non-threatening, and who are on the same level of psychological development as the offender."[27]

Many Americans found something immediately comprehensible about the argument that a man who was essentially a child should seek out a child. It made sense of sex crimes against children that, as sociologist Edwin Sutherland noted in 1950, most found otherwise "incomprehensible." "The ordinary citizen can understand fornication or even forcible rape of a woman," Sutherland argued, "but he concludes that a sex attack on an infant or girl must be the act of a fiend or a maniac."[28] Acts with women were intelligible in terms of uncontrollable desires because, as adults, women were recognized as arousing desire. But most Americans still saw children as sexually innocent, without sexuality, and therefore unable to provoke sexual desire, let alone uncontrollable desire. As an account of one crime published in the *Saturday Evening Post* put it, only to a "twisted mind [could] the child's innocently affectionate prattle and gestures, her wide-eyed interest in her big uncle's prowess, [take] on an aura of flirtation."[29] It was the inexplicability of offenders' choice of child victims evident in that description that opened the way for popular acceptance of psychiatric explanations of their behavior.[30] The commonsense, self-evident logic of the connection between immature desires and immature objects of desire cemented the appeal of psychiatrists' explanation. As Gladys Denny Schultz, a writer for the *Ladies' Home Journal* and author of a popular study of the sex criminal, noted, "It is not hard to understand why a boy or man whose normal sexual development has been halted at some infantile level should be unable to work out life on a mature basis."[31]

Americans found it almost as easy to understand the other types of men identified as sex offenders in terms of their immaturity. The elderly man, an earlier figure, and the sinister homosexual, of more recent appearance, could both be found a place in the ranks of sexual psychopaths. African American sex offenders could also continue to be treated differently, to be subjected to more severe penalty, on the grounds that, as members of an immature race, their behavior was "normal" and not the product of arrested development.

Elderly men had been singled out as responsible for many of the sexual assaults on children since the end of the nineteenth century.[32] Medical writers had explained those assaults as the product of elderly men's diminished potency. According to the authors of treatises on medical jurisprudence, men's "fears of impotence," and of the ridicule at the hands of an adult woman to which that condition exposed them, led them to commit acts with children. Elderly men could complete a sexual act with an ignorant and weak child, or "conceal their deficiency" from such a child, more easily than they could with an adult woman.[33] In the context of the sex crime panic, psychiatrists looked at elderly offenders from "a psychological point of view" and saw them as psychosexually immature, rather than sexually debilitated.[34] By the 1930s, mental deterioration in old age, or senility, had already been cast in developmental terms, as a regression to childhood. Psychiatrists such as James Henninger, director of the Allegheny County Behavior Clinic of the Criminal Court in Pittsburgh, simply extended that vision of a "second childhood" to the psychosexual realm. "It is my contention that associated with this obvious mental regression is a further psychological regression," Henninger argued, "which is, in part at least, responsible for the fact that sex offenses are perpetrated, for the most part, against small children of the age of those who were the recipients of much of the offender's attention — i.e., were love objects — at the period to which he is regressing — his childhood."[35] Since Americans already saw the senile man as intellectually a child, it required little adjustment in their thinking to reconcile their image of the elderly offender with the new picture of the immature psychopath.[36]

Seeing the homosexual offender against children in terms of immaturity required Americans to make more of an adjustment in how they understood sexuality. Although men who sexually assaulted children did appear in the annual reports of child protection agencies like the New York Society for the Prevention of Cruelty to Children, they remained shadowy, ill-defined figures as late as 1925. In that year, in the deluge of press coverage devoted to Nathan Leopold and Richard Loeb's murder of fourteen-year-old Bobby Franks, the unsubstantiated charges that the boy had also been sexually assaulted remained hidden in public discussion by the row of asterisks that newspapers put in place of "the unprintable matter." By 1936, the asterisks had fallen away: *Time* magazine claimed that the "two perverted Chicago youths" had "violated" Bobby Franks before they killed him. *Time*'s retelling of the Leopold and Loeb case reflected the appearance of a new, sinister portrait of the homosexual in culture and politics.[37] By 1950, the media had begun to split homosexual offenders away from pedophiles and to present them as a problem in their own right, a "New Moral Menace to Our Youth," as the title of an article in *Coronet* magazine trumpeted.[38]

The newly emerged homosexual offender fitted easily into the framework of sexual development employed by psychiatrists to explain sex offenders. Once a homosexual phase was recognized as a stage of normal psychosexual development, one that preceded adolescence, then homosexuality appeared to be a particular form of immaturity. Homosexual offenders had failed to achieve the "gradual transference of interest to the opposite sex" that a Children's Bureau publication told parents in 1954 was "one of the main developments due in [adolescence]." Their arrested development also often led homosexuals to focus on older children or young adolescents, those at the same stage of development at which they had become fixated on same-sex objects.[39] That picture of the homosexual offender gained ground in the 1930s, with the decline of the "obvious," effeminate "fairy" as the governing image of the homosexual. With the modern homosexual no longer visibly different from other men, as the fairy had been, with sexuality located increasingly in the psyche, rather than discernible on the surface of the body, Americans had to find another way to identify the homosexual offender. They looked to experts—to psychiatrists—to probe men's minds for their sexual identity.[40]

However much white Americans lost faith in their ability to establish a person's sexuality from his or her appearance, they entertained few doubts that race defined the sexual identity of African Americans and explained their sexual transgressions. Few African American offenders were included in the media accounts of the sexual psychopath and sex crime that drove the midcentury panic. Reports of sex crimes committed by African American men tended to focus on attacks on whites in the South and turned on the issues of lynching and the death penalty.[41] Legislatures in six of the eleven former Confederate states, where African Americans dominated the ranks of sex offenders, continued to view sex crime as a racial issue and saw no need to take action against sexual psychopaths.[42] Even in those states that did legislate provisions for psychopaths, judges less often perceived the behavior of African American men in those terms. In Maryland, judges sent a smaller proportion of African American men for psychiatric examinations than they did white men. Psychiatrists contributed to this "whitewashing" of the sexual psychopath by diagnosing a smaller proportion of African American offenders as sexual psychopaths than they did in the case of white offenders.[43]

Although the psychiatric literature does not shed any direct light on the encounters between white psychiatrists and African American men that produced the differential rates of diagnosis, the concept of psychosexual development that psychiatrists employed was circumscribed by racial ideology. A belief in the immaturity of the African race effectively put black Americans outside the framework of psychosexual development that explained white men's sex crimes. Behaviors that identified white men as immature were regarded as normal for African American males. Images of black men as beasts, creatures consumed by a sexual desire that drove them to rape, survived in twentieth-century justifications for the practice of lynching. Thomas Dixon, in the novel on which D. W. Griffith based the film *The Birth of a Nation*, evoked that image of the bestial black rapist in a description of the African American as "half child, half animal, the sport of impulse, whim and conceit, . . . a being . . . whose passions, once aroused, are as the fury of the tiger."[44] In this racial vision, a black skin signaled a sexuality marked by uncontrolled impulses. The uncivilized, animal nature of blacks gave them strong sexual desires, while their childish character ensured they could not control those desires; they lacked the "moral sense" that came with maturity.[45]

Such a view of African Americans helped prevent psychiatrists from seeing black sex offenders as suffering from abnormal mental conditions. Ellis and Brancale described African Americans convicted of sex crimes as "less emotionally disturbed . . . and less deviational" than their white counterparts, a state they traced to black men's lack of inhibition, a "childlike" trait attributed to them in racial ideology.[46] As a result of black sex offenders' lack of mental disturbance and the racial origins of their behavior, they made poor subjects for psychiatric investigation. Those men lacked the potential to achieve maturity and thus could not be treated or "cured." Only incarceration or death could prevent black sex offenders from committing further crimes.

In the case of white men, however, the psychiatric portrait of the sexual psychopath offered two new means to prevent sex crimes, one directed at boys, the other at men. Historians have been preoccupied with the latter, the institutionalization and treatment authorized by sexual psychopath laws, but efforts to prevent boys from developing the propensity to commit sexual assaults occurred alongside efforts to restrain and rehabilitate men who had already committed sex crimes. Preventive efforts relied on the concept of psychosexual development and amplified the advice that mental hygienists had been offering parents since the 1920s. In arguing that "the creation of a healthful atmosphere for the emotional growth of the child is the surest and cheapest way of reducing the burden which sex deviation annually lays upon society and the tribute it exacts from many unhappy and tormented lives," the Michigan Governor's Study Commission "attached much importance to the instruction in sound mental hygiene principles of the adults who surround a child."[47]

The sexual psychopath originated, mental hygienists argued, in parent-child relationships. In order to prevent the development of a new generation of psychopaths, parents had to recognize that their sons were going through a process of psychosexual development. The parents' role in that process, psychiatrists advised, was to provide a boy with a balanced amount of care and protection; they should avoid the extremes of behavior that could "disturb" their relationship with their son and impair the boy's development.[48] "Cold, hostile, sadistic" parents who provided too little care caused "emotional starvation and a stunting of growth" in their sons.[49] Subjecting a son to "abnormally strong pressures to control their biological needs, especially those needs which will become sexual," Samuel Hartwell warned the parents of Michigan, would produce in him "a particularly dangerous type of anxiety." If a boy's parents succeeded in "greatly inhibit[ing] or entirely prevent[ing him] from gratifying his erotic desires in one of his psychosexual stages, he [might] never be able to go on to the next from a psychological standpoint."[50] A concern about repressing a boy's sexuality also often caused parents to dangerously overreact when they discovered a son's indulgence in sexual behavior necessary for his normal development. When his parents became upset and excited, a boy could experience feelings of confusion and anxiety that might prevent him from reaching maturity.[51] A mother who emotionally overprotected her son—"infantilizing him unduly and too long," demanding his affection and preventing him from forming relationships with other women—left him emotionally immature.[52] As Bertram Pollens put it, in another of the folksy metaphors he favored for conveying psychiatric ideas to a lay audience, the overprotected boy was "like a plant, which, overcast by a large shadow, can't grow because the rays of the sun never reach it."[53]

When disruptions in the relationship between parent and child were compounded by a failure in gender identification or by a homosexual experience with an adult, a boy's immaturity would take the form of homosexuality. A boy became fixated at the homosexual phase of adolescence as a result of his childhood, which "conditioned" him, psychiatrists advised, rather than simply as a result of the events of his teenage years.[54] The key circumstance that produced such conditioning was the lack of "the opportunity for positive identification with the parent of his own sex."[55] Identification provided a pattern for the boy to follow in shaping his gender identity. If prevented from identifying with his father, a boy was led to pattern himself after his mother. That identification led him to desire males rather than females as sexual objects, and sometimes to "act in a feminine, submissive manner toward men in [his] search for acceptance."[56] A father could disrupt gender identification by exhibiting a brutality that repelled his son. Ralph Rabinovitch offered the case of Charles—who proclaimed "I'll never be like my father. I can't grow up like that. I'd rather not grow up at all"—as an example of this pattern: his father's hostility and violence toward his wife drove Charles toward "an ever closer relationship with his mother," until "in his sexual fantasies [he] played the role of a woman, later acting out these fantasies in his homosexual activities."[57]

However, mothers who prevented gender identification were of more concern to psychiatrists and popular writers. A woman's dominance over her husband overshadowed him as a model and pushed a son toward identifying with her instead.[58] Or a mother could directly prevent her son's identification with his father by treating him as a girl. An example of such a case appeared in an article in *Collier's*, a national magazine, in 1947. Emil's mother, who had wanted a daughter, called her son "Emmy," clothed him in dresses until he was three, kept his hair "long and wavy," made him her "chief assistant" in the kitchen, and caused him to feel he was "two-timing" her when he went out with girls. Only when Emil was with boys did he not feel like a "traitor to Mum."[59]

Outside the family, the origin of homosexuality lay not in the separation of men from boys but rather in the failure to separate men from boys. Bertram Pollens argued that if a boy "happens to be seduced by a homosexual . . . and he finds the relationship satisfying, he may become fixated in that direction and it may be next to impossible to change the direction of his sexual drive after that." The language of seduction, typically used in psychiatric writing about relationships between men and boys, marked this experience as different from the "crushes" and friendships that were a normal part of the homosexual phase of early adolescence. A consciously homosexual, sexually knowledgeable adult introduced into his relationship with a boy a clearly sexual aspect missing from "innocent" adolescent "experiments." Pollens, like all psychiatric writers, argued that acts with adults had only a limited role in producing homosexuality, noting that in many cases such "seductions" simply triggered homosexual tendencies produced by family dynamics.[60]

Despite the restricted significance given to such relationships by psychiatrists, the idea that adult homosexuals added to their ranks by seducing boys became prominent in popular accounts. The article in *Coronet* magazine that proclaimed homosexuals to be the "new moral menace to our youth" went on to assert that, "each year, literally thousands of youngsters of high-school and college age are introduced to unnatural practices by inveterate seducers."[61] Accounts of "recruitment" appealed in part because of the Cold War association of homosexuals with Communists, a group that also sought to "poison the minds" of the young.[62] Accounts of recruitment also fed into arguments that persuasively simplified the problem of sex crime, linking the crime and its causes in what one journalist called a "vicious cycle of proselytism": men sexually assaulted boys because as boys they had been victims of sexual assaults by men.[63] Parents could thus prevent sex crime both now and in the future by protecting their sons.

It was not enough for parents to recognize that a boy was going through a process of psychosexual development, to provide an adult male with whom he could identify, and to protect him from adult homosexuals. Mental hygienists also urged parents to provide sex education for their sons. A lack of instruction about sexuality, or a "grotesque sex education," created a "tremendous amount of confusion, distortion, ignorance, and anxiety" in boys, psychiatrists warned, and left them vulnerable to "distorted ideas" and "unwholesome practices." Sex education would help children along the road to normal growth and equip them to deal with possible disruptions.[64]

Ensuring the healthy development of the next generation of American boys did nothing to alleviate the threat posed by the present generation of adult sexual psychopaths. That task required more of psychiatrists than advice. Politicians and ordinary Americans charged psychiatrists with the responsibility of removing the threat posed by sexual psychopaths. Psychiatrists were expected not only to identify psychopaths among the men who committed sex crimes but also to take custody of them until they were no longer dangerous, providing treatment that would make it safe to return them to society. Few, if any, psychiatrists in the 1930s believed that such treatment existed, but some, at least, shared the faith of lay people like Edwin Roemer, president of the Chicago Bar Association, that it would only be a matter of time before that lack of therapeutic efficacy was remedied. "In view of the experience that members of the medical profession have had in [the] field of infections with their antibodies, and particularly in view of the greater stress that is being placed upon the study of psychiatry in medical schools today," Roemer told a meeting of the Chicago Crime Prevention Bureau, "I think sooner or later we may be able to effect a cure even in those cases which perhaps now are considered incurable."[65]

That optimism was sustained by the portrait of the sex offender as immature that psychiatrists developed in the next two decades. As a product of arrested or distorted development, such an offender appeared to be a good candidate for psychotherapy. Psychiatrists could "dislodge from the unconscious repressed material [that] needed to be accepted, experienced, and understood" before an individual could achieve maturity. A patient in psychotherapy also could gain insight into his or her behavior and self-acceptance, enabling him or her to adjust to society.[66] In theory, a variation of that approach could instill in sex offenders the ability to control their impulses and shift the object of their sexual behavior to adults of the opposite sex. However, the theory proved hard to put into practice, with the development of psychotherapeutic approaches rarely getting beyond the experimental stage. As a result, psychiatric treatment failed to deliver the results that politicians and the public expected.

In New York City in August 1937, after the second of the sex murders that began the midcentury panic, Mayor Fiorello La Guardia made the first effort in the state to put sex offenders in the care of psychiatrists. His plan relied not on the concept of sexual psychopathy but on the older category of insanity. All those convicted of impairing the morals of a minor or of "sex crimes involving perversion" were to be placed under medical observation, La Guardia ordered. At the completion of their sentences, those men were to be taken before a magistrate so that they could be committed to Bellevue Hospital for psychiatric examination. Any found to be insane would be committed to an asylum for an indefinite period. The police commissioner and the commissioner of correction endorsed La Guardia's plan, as did an assortment of prosecutors and magistrates. A reporter who had the temerity to suggest that many offenders would fall within the legal definition of sanity was firmly rebuked by the mayor. "If this plan is followed with common sense, it will work," he retorted. "If it is met with legalistic and technical objections, they will defeat it."[67] To help ensure that the new procedure did work, La Guardia himself sat as a magistrate. A week after announcing his plan, he committed a thirty-eight-year-old man, who, after being convicted of impairing the morals of a thirteen-year-old girl, had completed a six-month term at the Rikers Island Penitentiary.[68] The city's magistrates clearly followed his lead.

The staff of the psychiatric unit at Bellevue Hospital reported a sharp rise in the number of sex offenders sent to them for examination, but the task of performing those examinations proved so burdensome that, in 1946, the unit asked to be relieved of the responsibility, which was passed to the New York City Department of Correction's newly appointed psychiatrist.[69]

La Guardia's plan might have kept the psychiatrists employed by the city busy, but it failed to offer the protection against sex offenders that the mayor claimed would ensue.[70] In 1939, when the Citizens Committee on the Control of Crime reported on sex offenses in New York City, it identified scores of offenders "who would be rated as abnormal under almost any other standards than those of *legal* insanity and mental deficiency which govern procedure under present laws."[71] Such offenders were returned to the community notwithstanding the procedure La Guardia had put in place. La Guardia then set up the Mayor's Committee on Sex Offenses, and it is not surprising that its first recommendation related to "abnormal sex offenders," who were, although "neither mentally defective nor insane," possessed of "constitutional penchants for abnormal methods of satisfying sexual passions" that made them "dangerous to be at large." To protect society from such men, the Mayor's Committee proposed a "sexual psychopath law," which would require a psychiatric examination of all convicted sex offenders in order to keep in institutional confinement those who were still dangerous after they had served their time in prison.[72]

The Prison Association of New York took on the task of putting the recommendation of the Mayor's Committee into action. After the state legislature ignored the association's repeated proposal that a sexual psychopath law be enacted, the association took it upon itself to have a bill drafted. It enlisted the aid of Morris Ploscowe, a Brooklyn magistrate and the former chief clerk of the court of special sessions, who had been a consultant to the Mayor's Committee. He drew up a bill that Senator Thomas Desmond introduced into the state senate in 1947.[73] The legislation provided that a person convicted of rape, impairing the morals of a minor, carnal abuse, sodomy, incest, indecent exposure, or the disorderly conduct of soliciting men in a public place could be remanded by the court for a psychiatric examination to determine whether he was a sexual psychopath. If the defendant had a previous conviction for one of those offenses, the court had to order his examination. Those not found to be psychopaths were dealt with according to the criminal statute. Psychopaths, on the other hand, were committed to an institution designated by the Department of Correction, to be held there until they were judged to be cured and to no longer pose a danger to society.[74] The proposal attracted widespread support, with groups ranging from the New York County Lawyers' Association and the Medical Society of the State of New York to the Russell Sage Foundation and the American Social Hygiene Association writing to Governor Thomas Dewey to praise the bill.[75] Not surprisingly, given that support, the bill passed both the state senate and the state assembly.

Ploscowe's bill did have at least one influential opponent, John Lyons, the state commissioner of correction. While accepting that the issue was one of "deep concern," Lyons argued that "this bill is far from being the solution to the problem of the sexual psychopath. It is cumbersome, inadequate, and impractical. It would create many administrative difficulties in the courts, as well as in [the Department of Correction] and the Department of Mental Hygiene." Of particular concern to Lyons was the lack of an effective cure or treatment for sexual psychopathy, which meant that those in charge of institutions would face problems in determining when it was safe to release a sexual psychopath. To enact the legislation would be premature, Lyons contended; what was needed now was "intensive study and research on the part of psychiatrists, with the hope that it would lead to a greater understanding of the problem and more successful treatment."[76] Governor Dewey shared Lyons's misgivings. He also criticized the inclusion in the bill of offenses involving little social harm, such as the soliciting of men in public places, a crime Ploscowe had not included in his draft legislation. Men guilty of such offenses "commit their acts privately and are their own greatest victims," Dewey argued. "Incarceration for life of such persons," he went on, "seems unnecessarily inhuman and least calculated to provide a cure." Ultimately, however, he decided to veto the bill because "we are not justified in engaging upon any program which is not reasonably sound and properly considered, and most certainly, in the process we should not demolish the important safeguards that surround personal liberty in our State."[77]

In the aftermath of that veto, Charles Breitel, the governor's counsel, convened an informal committee to decide on a course of action to combat sex offenders. Its members were John Lyons; Edwin Cass, the general secretary of the Prison Association; Frederick Moran, the parole commissioner; and Dr. Frederick MacCurdy, the commissioner of the Department of Mental Hygiene. After "considerable discussion," the committee agreed not to introduce a revised bill, as the Prison Association had proposed, but instead to set in motion a study of the sexual psychopath, as Lyons had urged, in order to produce "a sounder guide for future action."[78] In March of the next year, on Dewey's recommendation, the state legislature authorized such a study, to be carried out at Sing Sing Prison. The task of conducting the research was given to Dr. David Abrahamsen, of Columbia University, and the New York State Psychiatric Institute.

Abrahamsen's findings changed the nature of New York State's response to the sex offender. He rejected the diagnosis of psychopathy, on the grounds that psychopathy "is difficult to define with scientific precision." In doing so, he abandoned the approach taken in the bill Dewey had vetoed in 1947, which had relied on the concept of the sexual psychopath. Following the direction taken by Lyons, the study classified the 102 offenders it examined "in accordance with their predisposition to violence, their suitability for psychiatric treatment, and their probable adaptability to society." Two categories of offenders were considered untreatable: men predisposed to violence and "those who are chronic alcoholics or too old to be treated or whose personality maladjustments are too deep-seated to indicate the probability of change at the present time." Neither of those groups proved capable of cooperating with a psychiatrist, let alone developing the close personal relationship required for psychotherapy, the treatment method that Abrahamsen and his colleagues employed. The study characterized psychotherapy as "a process of emotional growth induced by a therapist, who practically assumes the role of substitute parent or adviser, enters into a most intimate confidential relationship with the subject, seeking for patterns of conduct and unrealized motivations." The remaining two categories of offenders were both able to benefit from therapy: one group would require intensive therapy before release into the community, and the other comprised those who could be treated as outpatients while on parole.[79]

Abrahamsen's findings suggested that the state had to provide for the continued detention of offenders who could not be treated and that it had to develop a means of ensuring that offenders who could be treated were not released until they had been rehabilitated. The mechanism that the governor's committee proposed, in the report's supplementary recommendations, was an indeterminate sentence of one day to life, available for felony sex crimes. Before imposing such a sentence, the court would have to order the psychiatric examination of an offender. Anyone given an indeterminate sentence would continue to be examined at least once every two years to ascertain if his condition had improved sufficiently for him to be released.[80]

The bill that Dewey signed into law in April 1950 followed those recommendations, backing them up with provisions for the Department of Mental Hygiene to set up and staff psychiatric clinics in prisons and for further research to be conducted. The only element of the report that the law failed to support was a treatment facility separate from the prison system, an omission that would have an impact on how the law worked in practice. The new law differed from the 1947 bill in several crucial respects. It made no mention of the sexual psychopath. It provided a criminal sentence, rather than a civil commitment, ensuring that an offender retained his civil rights, and guaranteed that he would receive regular psychiatric examinations to establish if he was fit for release. Finally, the law applied only to offenders who had committed sex crimes involving violence or the abuse of children, a limitation, Dewey explained, resulting not from a belief that men who committed those offenses could be "scientifically divided from other criminals but because it is impossible to attempt at one step to apply such a change to all prisoners."[81] Which of the men convicted of those crimes should receive an indeterminate sentence was left to the discretion of the sentencing judge. As an analysis of the statute in the *Yale Law Journal* pointed out, "The law does not even suggest psychiatric standards which would make indefinite sentence advisable."[82]

Despite Governor Dewey's claim that the new procedure gave "New York a lead over other states in providing scientific treatment for this type of offender," other state legislatures declined to follow suit, enacting, instead, laws similar to those vetoed by Dewey in 1947.[83] Those laws differed essentially from New York's only in relying on the concept of the sexual psychopath and in providing for indefinite civil commitment to a mental hospital, rather than a criminal sentence. It was precisely those two features that proved to be the most controversial elements of the statutes.[84] Both psychiatrists and lawyers regarded the various legal definitions of the psychopath as too vague and indefinite to meet the standards of due process, and they considered the different treatment of sexual psychopaths as a violation of their right to equal protection. Proponents of the laws defended their lack of procedural protections by insisting that the laws were civil rather than criminal in character, intended to treat not to punish. The United States Supreme Court accepted that argument in a decision in 1940, but when it revisited the issue in 1967, the justices decided that anyone subject to a procedure that could lead to indeterminate institutionalization was nonetheless entitled to protections such as the rights to counsel, to give evidence, and to confront and cross-examine the witnesses against him. The 1960s also saw the laws challenged on the grounds that no treatment was in fact provided to those committed as psychopaths.

Ultimately, the delay in addressing those legal flaws did not matter, according to most analyses of the sexual psychopath statutes, because the laws were not put into practice. Most such claims relied on the findings of Paul Tappan, a sociologist working for the New Jersey Commission on the Habitual Sexual Offender, whose inquiries in 1950 revealed the sexual psychopath statutes of four states to have been completely nullified and those of another six to be almost completely ineffective.[85] Almost as influential, and more dramatic, was the finding of a study sponsored by the American Bar Foundation: that in 1958 only two states, California and Michigan, had operative sexual psychopath laws.[86]

Such a fate did not befall New York's law. It remained in effect until 1967 without attracting a significant challenge to its constitutionality.[87] During that time, courts did impose indeterminate sentences, although only fragmentary evidence survives concerning the law's operation. Two hundred and seventy-two offenders were given indeterminate sentences in the period from 1950 to November 1962, with most, 196, being sentenced in the first seven years of the law's existence.[88] New York's experience was not unusual, contrary to the generally accepted view that prosecutors and judges did not use the sexual psychopath laws. Sixteen other states also had laws that operated on a small scale.[89] What generally distinguished those states from California, Michigan, New Jersey, and Wisconsin, where large numbers of offenders were committed over a period of several decades, was the narrower range of sex crimes to which their laws applied and their lack of separate institutions to house sex offenders. It was not that the laws were inoperative, but rather that the number of men committed under most sexual psychopath laws fell short of public expectations.

The small number of men sentenced under New York's law reflected the fact that relatively few men came within the scope of the statute. Of the ninety-five men convicted in prosecutions for felony sex crimes in my sample years 1951 and 1955, only thirty-six were found guilty of a felony offense.[90] Eighty-nine percent of those convictions came as a result of plea-bargaining.[91] Since prosecutors took the lead in that process, they were involved in determining which offenders would be eligible for an indeterminate sentence. In one case in 1951, the ADA recorded that the defendant had been allowed to plead guilty to attempted carnal abuse because it would make him subject to the new law.[92] That example suggests that the New York County DA did not share the concerns of prosecutors in Illinois that such a sentence would be shorter than the prison term an offender would otherwise have received.[93] Given the relatively short prison terms handed out to most sex offenders convicted of felonies—a typical sentence was imprisonment for a term of between two and a half years and five years—they probably felt that they had little to lose by making it possible for judges to impose an indeterminate sentence. But that openness to the new procedure had little impact on how prosecutors disposed of cases. Almost the same proportion of offenders was convicted of felonies in the years 1951 and 1955 as in the preceding four sample years.[94] There is also little evidence that prosecutors were able to use the threat of an indeterminate sentence to persuade defendants to plead guilty to a misdemeanor, as happened in Indiana.[95]

It was not prosecutors but judges and psychiatrists who were responsible for the limited number of indeterminate sentences handed out in New York City. Only three of the thirty-six eligible offenders in my sample received indeterminate sentences, all in 1951. That low proportion appears to reflect the psychiatrists' recommendations to judges, although, since the report of the psychiatric examination appears in the DA's files in only four cases, that conclusion has to remain tentative. In Manhattan, staff from the Psychiatric Clinic of the New York County Court of General Sessions designated to "inquire into the mental condition" of an offender not only conducted a psychological examination but also held a formal hearing, at which the victim and arresting officer, as well as the offender, gave statements.[96] The head of the clinic, Dr. Emanuel Messinger, and his colleagues, Drs. Albert LaVerne, Helen Rogers, and Vitold Arnett, received no guidance from the statute as to what mental conditions made an offender a fit subject for an indeterminate sentence. Their reports reveal that they saw the law's target as offenders who suffered from "sexual maladjustment," who displayed compulsive behavior, and who possessed the ability to respond to treatment.

The clearest sign of maladjustment, in the psychiatrists' opinion, was sexual activity with children, a position that reflected the examiners' reliance on a developmental framework. Both of the offenders in my sample recommended as suitable for sentencing under the law had assaulted boys; the two men given indeterminate sentences whose psychiatric examinations do not survive had also assaulted boys.[97] Such offenders are equally prominent in a survey of the use of the indeterminate sentence in the state as a whole during the first two and a half years that it was available, constituting at least two out of every three men imprisoned indefinitely.[98] Both men were active homosexuals of long standing, a trait that the psychiatrists not only took as further evidence of the men's maladjustment but also, more crucially, as a sign that they lacked control over their behavior.[99] Messinger and LaVerne classified thirty-year-old Harold Geller, an unemployed white man, as a "Psychopathic Personality Sexual Type with Neurotic Traits." Their examination found "specific evidence of severe psychosexual maladjustment" (Geller, they wrote, "has never demonstrated heterosexual interests") and an "obsessive pattern of repeated anti-social, sexual behavior over which, he, at this time, evidences no control." They based the latter conclusion on Geller's admission that he had engaged in "regular perverse sexual activities since the age of 14," "practically all of [which] have been directed against pre-adolescent boys."[100]

Without such evidence of homosexuality, even sexual activity with a child was not always enough to persuade Messinger and his colleagues of an offender's maladjustment and inability to control his sexual behavior. In 1955, they deemed James Rush, a forty-year-old shipping clerk, who pled guilty after being charged with touching the breasts and genitals of a ten-year-old girl, and had a previous conviction for carnal abuse of a girl, unsuitable for an indeterminate sentence. The fact that Rush had prior arrests had caused the psychiatrists to think "that he might be habituated to perverse practices with minor children." But, ultimately, they concluded that, although he was "very unstable in his emotional field," his compulsion was not to sexually attack minor children but to physically assault "young girls when frustrated by their actions." As a result, although the psychiatrists thought that Rush would "continue to handle young girls in an unsatisfactory manner," they concluded that "we cannot assume that he is sexually dangerous from a sexual-deviant point of view." Messinger and Rogers instead classified him as a "pathological individual, schizoid type."[101]

That finding indicates that psychiatrists were still prepared to dismiss a heterosexual act with a child as aberrant, as not revealing of an offender's sexual identity, even as they regarded acts with a child of the same sex as defining an offender as homosexual and thus as maladjusted and lacking in control. For all the psychiatric theorizing about pedophiles and hebephiles, in practice these cautious practitioners gave the most weight in shaping sexual identity not to the age of the offender's victim but to whether that victim was male or female and to the heterosexual/homosexual binary.

A male offender whose victim was an adult woman had not, in the opinion of Messinger and his colleagues, made a sexual object choice that suggested sexual maladjustment. In such cases, psychiatrists concentrated their attention on the violence an offender employed. In assessing a man's use of force, they were as suspicious as legal officials and jurors were of women who claimed that they had been raped. A focus on violence also brought into play beliefs about the inherently violent nature of nonwhite men. Both those attitudes figure in Messinger and Arnett's decision that Mitchell Gould was not suitable for an indeterminate sentence. In 1955, the forty-four-year-old African American factory worker had been accused of accosting a woman whom he knew on 122nd Street, forcing her into his apartment at knifepoint and beating her in an unsuccessful attempt to rape her. Gould had been arrested on twelve previous occasions for violent crimes, including three times for rape; one of those rape prosecutions had produced a conviction. "While we do not feel that he has any compulsive or socially dangerous sexual tendencies on the whole, and furthermore are disinclined to attach full credence to the complainant's story," Messinger and Arnett wrote, "we cannot rule out entirely the suspicion that he may be episodically prone to aggressive, anti-social sexual behavior." Nonetheless, they concluded, "he is basically a primitive, hostile and aggressive individual, and that he is quite unstable emotionally."[102]

Messinger and Arnett's failure to accept the woman's story was in line with the unwillingness of judges and juries to see a woman who had been assaulted by a man she knew—and had not suffered grievous injuries—as having been raped. It was also in line with the attitude of other examining psychiatrists and judges in New York. Across the state, in the first two and a half years of the law's existence, it was men convicted of rape who were by far the least likely to receive an indeterminate sentence.[103] While the attitude of the New York City psychiatrists was not unusual, it is striking that they did not appear to regard Gould's repeated arrests for rape and other violent crimes as adding weight to his victim's charges. They attributed his aggressive behavior to his being a "primitive personality type," a description that invoked beliefs about the uncivilized character of blacks. More often, psychiatric reports on black and Hispanic offenders used another phrase even more revealing of the implications of racial ideology for psychiatric assessments of sex offenders; they classified a nonwhite man as "an individual who is adjusted to a low cultural level."[104] Such a classification rendered the culture, not the individual, maladjusted. In the final analysis, Messinger and Arnett judged that Gould's pattern of violent sexual behavior, a sign of mental abnormality in a white man, was in his case more likely a reflection of the normal—that is, "low"—standards of African American culture.[105]

Ultimately, the decision concerning an offender's sentence lay with judges, although some confusion existed over the extent of their discretion. The instruction of the court of general sessions to psychiatrists, that they report "whether [the offender] is a proper subject for the imposition of an indeterminate sentence," was more pointed than was the language of the statute, which simply required that the report of the psychiatric examination "include all facts and findings necessary to assist the court in disposing of the case."[106] The wording of the instruction suggests that the judges who sat in the court considered that their discretion came into play only when psychiatrists gave them grounds to impose an indeterminate sentence, rather than allowing them to impose such a sentence even in the absence of psychiatric findings that it was justified. In 1951, in the case of Harold Geller, Judge Jacob Schurman followed the psychiatrists' recommendation and gave Geller an indeterminate sentence, but, in 1955, Judge Edward Breslin ignored the psychiatric report and imprisoned Samuel Thompson for a term between one year and three months and two years and six months. Despite those different sentences, both men had admitted to being homosexuals of long standing—in sixty-six-year-old Thompson's case, to having had "homosexual tendencies for over 40 years"—and had been found by psychiatrists to lack control over their sexual behavior.[107] What distinguished Thompson from Geller was the age of his victims, who were adolescents rather than the preadolescents targeted by Geller. By the mid-1950s, courts did not see boys in their teens as innocent children, but as sexual subjects who might be at the point in their psychosexual development where they felt sexual attraction to members of the same sex. Since his victims were not children, Thompson's acts appeared not to be sexual violence but rather homosexual solicitation, an offense that Governor Dewey had argued involved too little social harm to warrant indefinite incarceration. Breslin's decision showed that judges did draw their own conclusions. Moreover, contrary to charges that the judiciary ignored the law, that decision appeared to follow to the letter its author's intention that the statute should apply only to offenders who had committed sex crimes involving violence or the abuse of children.[108]

A comparison of the procedure in New York County with that in other counties supports the conclusion that it was the rigor with which New York City's psychiatrists and judges applied the law, not their aversion to it, that led to the relatively small proportion of offenders who received indeterminate sentences.[109] Appellate court cases reveal that behind the higher proportion of sentences given out in other counties lay inadequate psychiatric reports and judicial decisions that paid scant regard to the requirements of the sex offender law. Trial judges often failed to order a psychiatric examination after an offender had been convicted, and instead relied on pre-pleading psychiatric reports. Those reports had a different purpose from that required by the sex offender law, namely, to establish the alleged offender's sanity and ability to understand the charge made against him.[110] Even some psychiatric examinations done before sentencing addressed only the issue of an offender's sanity.[111] Other reports made no mention of an offender's sexual problems or whether he was likely to engage in violent sexual conduct. A report submitted in Kings County simply classified its subject as a "sociopathic personality without a favorable prognosis."[112] In 1968, when the New York State Court of Appeals did impose a standard for the psychiatric examinations required by the sex offender law, it was in line with the approach taken in New York County. The judges held that a report "should discuss and analyze the defendant's sexual problem and whether such condition was of a type which would yield to treatment. The report is inadequate if it does not state the risk to society involved in the defendant's immediate release."[113]

New York State's experience of diverse, inconsistent, and often inadequate psychiatric practices and judicial decision-making was hardly unique. The practice in New York County was broadly in line with those in states with elaborate programs. In Wisconsin, for example, a sixty-day period was provided for the diagnostic examination. During that time, a psychiatric social worker compiled a detailed social history, supplemented with material gathered from "interested parties." Each offender was subjected to a battery of psychological tests, a medical examination, and a series of interviews with a psychiatrist. A staff conference then made the decision about whether to recommend his commitment.[114]

In many states, psychiatric practices had more in common with the counties whose procedures were challenged in the appellate courts. A study of committals in Indiana between 1949 and 1956, for example, found that psychiatrists' reports frequently showed no evidence that psychiatrists had "administered psychological tests, projective techniques, neurological tests or any of the factors which would ordinarily be considered in a psychiatric work-up." The examinations they described often consisted of little more than a short interview.[115] In other states, psychiatric reports contained only conclusions and recommendations, with no elaboration of the psychiatrists' reasoning or evidence to support their conclusions.[116]

For all the flaws and inconsistencies in how psychiatrists diagnosed sex offenders, the acceptance of sexual psychopath laws ultimately rested on the profession's ability to treat those who were identified as dangerous. Reflecting that emphasis, once New York's sex offender statute was enacted, the psychiatrists whose study had provided the basis for the law shifted the orientation of their work at Sing Sing from research to therapy. Or, at least, they attempted to. In 1952, as a result of "a general dissatisfaction with the results of the therapeutic efforts," they refocused their efforts on research. Without more information on the "personality patterns" of sex offenders and the "developmental environmental factors" that affected them, the psychiatrists felt that they could not provide "adequate psychiatric therapy."[117] Their therapeutic goal was for offenders to complete their psychosexual development, to achieve maturity.

Three approaches were tried at Sing Sing. Most offenders met with a psychiatrist once or twice a week for two or three months. Not surprisingly, given that very few sex offenders would discuss the acts for which they were imprisoned or even admit their guilt, Glueck and his colleagues concluded that those sessions were "essentially useless, as far as any hope of changing the basic personality patterns is concerned." A small group of fifteen inmates underwent more intense therapy: three sessions a week for up to three years. That approach proved to be very effective in revealing the dynamics of personality functioning, but the psychiatrists were uncertain about its therapeutic results. Three of the fifteen men in the group shifted the orientation of their sexual behavior from boys or adolescents to adult males. "Whether this changing pattern will continue, to an eventual choice of an adult female as the sexual object," the psychiatrists commented, "remains to be seen." They also remained concerned about the obstacles to doing intensive therapy in a prison environment. In response to those difficulties associated with psychotherapeutic approaches, the unit at Sing Sing also experimented with the use of electroconvulsive therapy. In 1956, when the *Final Report* was written, the psychiatrists were still following the forty-four men given that treatment, but they reported that the prisoners "have shown lessened tension and anxiety, are less hostile, and have shown changes in their sexual adjustment, either in the type of fantasies employed, or in dreams, or, in two instances, in their overt sexual behavior in the institution." The *Final Report* concluded that "continued experimentation with treatment techniques is essential if the individuals who are incarcerated for sexual offenses are to be successfully rehabilitated."[118]

However, despite that finding, once the research project was completed in 1956, the unit at Sing Sing was closed down, ending both its therapeutic work and efforts to create an effective program of treatment. As a result, even though all the state's prisons had psychiatric clinics, sex offenders received little treatment.[119] One man incarcerated at Attica had his pedigree taken when he arrived, but he received no other treatment for two years. An attempt was then made at group therapy. Ten men met for an hour a week with a psychiatrist, who merely observed their conversations, which usually concerned "sports, the weather, and the rules and regulations of the prison."[120] Another inmate received only five and a half hours of psychiatric help in eleven years in prison.[121] By the 1960s, the failure to treat men sentenced to indeterminate terms was becoming widely known. In December 1963, the *New York Times* reported on Justice Francis Bergen's criticisms, in *People v. Jackson,* of the treatment of the appellant, who had spent eleven years in prison under an indeterminate sentence without receiving any psychiatric care. "It was not contemplated," Bergen maintained, "that an offender be held for many years without treatment and without some sound professional basis for believing that during all of this period it would be unsafe to release him."[122] The publication of such statements suggests that Gladys Denny Schultz was right to claim that the failure of imprisoned sex offenders to receive treatment underlay judges' less frequent use of indeterminate sentences after the late 1950s.[123]

The frustration that the staff of the Sing Sing clinic experienced in their search for an effective treatment was shared by psychiatrists who worked in other large sex offender programs. While psychiatrists' research and experimentation could obscure their inability to offer offenders treatment, the results were no different from the more obvious failures of their colleagues in states without programs, units, or institutions dedicated to the sex offender. Harry Kozol, director of the Center for the Diagnosis and Treatment of Dangerous Persons in Massachusetts, described the treatment carried out by his staff as being, "out of necessity and ignorance," "experimental." "We have no firm answers and we doubt that others have," he continued, "but we do have some emerging hypotheses which we are currently testing." However, those hypotheses remained largely unproven, given that "the ultimate test" only came when the offenders were returned to the community. As had their colleagues at Sing Sing, the Massachusetts psychiatrists settled on "a combination of individual and group therapy" as the treatment that offered "the greatest promise for the largest number."[124] In states where no separate provision was made for sex offenders, treatment fell far short of even that standard. In Iowa, for example, the superintendent of the Mt. Pleasant Mental Health Institution reported that his staff employed occupational therapy and music therapy to treat sexual psychopaths, "not particularly with therapy in mind but as merely something to occupy their time."[125]

When New York's Temporary Commission on Revision of the Penal Law and Criminal Code began work in 1963, it was well aware of the lack of treatment for sex offenders in the state's prisons and in psychiatric institutions in other states. When no one who appeared at the public hearings held by the commission brought up the sex offender law, the commission recalled the general secretary of the Prison Association, now renamed the Correctional Association, to discuss the indeterminate sentence. The issue that concerned the commissioners, the general secretary reported to the association, was "the fact that many sex offenders are not amenable to psychiatric treatment."[126] Compounding that problem was the state's failure to pursue study of the sex offender, or to create a definite program of treatment, after the closure of the clinic at Sing Sing.[127] By the mid-1960s, where treatment was not effective or even available, courts in New York and other states had begun to take the position that there was no rationale for a different sentence for some sex offenders.[128] Cases revealing the flawed procedures being employed in many New York counties were also beginning to make their way through the state's higher courts, although the New York Court of Appeals would not set a standard for psychiatric examinations until the late 1960s. Thus, although no concerted attack had been made on the sex offender law, the commissioners clearly saw the writing on the wall. Consequently, they omitted the indeterminate sentence from the new codes. In 1967, New York's sex offender law simply disappeared from the statute book.

Most states with sexual psychopath laws took similar action in the mid-1970s, either modifying their laws to make treatment voluntary or repealing them entirely. In doing so, they were impelled not only by court decisions on due process and treatment but also by a popular sentiment that the laws, and the psychiatric treatment that they provided for, had failed to stop sex crime. Sensational crimes, like those that had galvanized public support for the sexual psychopath laws, provoked calls for those laws' repeal. In California, the catalyst was the case of Theodore Frank. Committed as a mentally disordered sex offender in 1974, after assaulting a six-year-old girl, Frank admitted that he had assaulted more than 100 children. The hospital staff had considered him a model patient, who responded well to various forms of treatment, and granted him early release in January 1978. Within six weeks, he assaulted and killed a two-year-old girl; four months later, he was arrested after abducting and assaulting an eight-year-old girl. A week after Frank was sentenced to death in February 1980, a grass-roots organization, S.L.A.M. (Concerned Citizens for Stronger Legislation against Child Molesters), was formed to urge replacement of the "ineffective" sex offender law with one providing for lengthy imprisonment.[129]

In a sense, psychiatrists had run out of time. No evidence existed that their experimental approach to treatment had delivered the cure that commentators in the 1930s and 1940s had expected. In fact, allowing psychiatrists to experiment with treatment seemed not to have protected Americans, but rather to have exposed them to danger. In the view of Irving Prager, one of the leaders of the movement to abolish California's law, "The harm done by freed molesters is much too high a price to pay" in order to assess the merits of an "experiment with psychiatric criminology."[130]

In rejecting the notion that sex offenders could be treated by psychotherapy, Americans also abandoned the picture of the sex offender as immature, as suffering an arrested or distorted development that could be remedied by a psychiatrist. Prager, a former California DA, attacked psychiatrists who supported the law for "overlooking the inescapable conclusion that it must be eminently less difficult to talk a burglar, robber or check forger out of his way of life than to convince a man to forego action impelled, at least in part, by one of the strongest impulses known—the instinctual urge for sexual relations."[131] As Prager understood the sex offender, he was a creature of uncontrollable and unalterable impulses. For second wave feminists, the offender was an ordinary man acting on impulses shaped and stimulated by the sexist and misogynist culture of a patriarchal society. In neither characterization did the sex offender's stage of development have the power to explain his behavior.

Nor did the concept of psychosexual development any longer provide the basis for understandings of what constituted sexual violence. By the mid-1970s, age did not feature prominently in the characteristics used to identify victims of sexual violence. The children most in need of protection were identified instead by their social situation, their membership in a family. The threat faced by children was not rape or molestation by a stranger outside their home, but an assault by a male relative within it, a mode of behavior that had attracted almost no attention from the press or the courts earlier in the twentieth century. Incest, or child sexual abuse as it was often labeled, came to the forefront of the discussion of sexual violence in the wake of feminist critiques of the patriarchal family and physicians' "discovery" of the widespread physical abuse of children in families. The harm children suffered from incestuous assaults was neither the physical injury and social ruin that had concerned working-class New Yorkers nor the disruption to a child's psychosexual development that mental hygienists had described. Instead, it was a modern hybrid of both frameworks. At the core of late-twentieth-century notions of harm was the concept of long-term injury associated with the older concept of ruin, but the damage was now presented as broadly psychological, rather than physical, social, or sexual. The experience of sexual assault in childhood was seen as something that would define its victims, or "survivors," as they came to be called, for the rest of their lives.[132] For all that such an understanding owed to the developmental framework, it marked a move away from the reliance on age to define sexual violence that had marked the first half of the twentieth century.

That the explanatory power of age had become diluted by the last quarter of the twentieth century does not take away from one of the central insights offered by this book: that the imperative to see sexuality through the prism of age was a central part of twentieth-century concepts of sexuality. New ideas did not simply sexualize childhood and adolescence; they endowed those stages of life with a variety of different sexualities. To determine an individual's sexuality, to identify an appropriate sexual partner, to understand the meaning of an individual's sexual behavior, or, in the case of those skeptical of modern ideas, to understand the legal consequences of sexual activity with an individual, it was necessary to know his or her age. New understandings of sexual violence were only one facet of the spectrum of new meanings that attached to sexuality when it was refracted through the concept of psychosexual development. Regardless of the extent to which they embraced those new ideas, twentieth-century Americans paid attention to age when they thought about sexuality. Their concern with children and adolescents was not simply a response to the unprecedented threats that appeared to assail the young in a modern society and culture; it was a reaction to new ideas about childhood and sexuality.

The story told here of how age shaped the ways that Americans saw sexual violence does not represent the extent of the significance accorded to age in modern culture. That such a claim needs to be made is a consequence of the tendency of historians who study age-specific groups to give little or no attention to the meanings of age as such and to rely, instead, on unexamined concepts of the child, the adolescent, and the adult. In doing so, they fail to treat age as a category of analysis. And yet that is exactly how age needs to be regarded. Against the tendency to restrict the concern with age to the history of childhood, we have to be alert to its broader resonance. Ideas about age were not only located in the legal system examined in this book; they flowed to that site from medicine, psychology, education, and popular culture, fields that had been permeated by a consciousness of age. Such ideas also found institutional expression in many other facets of American life. Whereas many nineteenth-century Americans were ignorant of the precise date of their birth, which reflected its limited salience in their daily lives, Americans in the twentieth century needed to know their chronological age. By the 1920s, New Yorkers who went to the City Bureau of Vital Statistics in search of their birth records were pursuing a wide variety of goals: they required proof of age to enroll a child in school, to obtain a passport, to take civil service examinations, to get a chauffeur's license, to receive an allowance from the Child Welfare Board, to vote, to enlist in the military, and to apply for work in public utility companies and commercial houses.[1] All those areas of life saw conflicts, similar to those that occurred in regard to sexual violence, about how old was old enough.

In the late 1980s, Howard Chudacoff argued that, in the twentieth century, age not only came to represent a chronological, biological phenomenon but also "acquired social meaning, affecting attitudes, behavior, and the ways in which individuals relate to each other." "Throughout American society," he concluded, "age has been adopted as an organizing principle."[2] Historians have been slow to engage with that conclusion, perhaps because Chudacoff's brief book was necessarily a schematic cultural history focused on the urban, white middle-class. By offering a social history focused on southern and eastern European, African American, and Puerto Rican workers, my study amplifies Chudacoff's argument. This book demonstrates that when we study the twentieth century, the litany of categories that guides the analysis of American history—race, class, and gender—must be extended to include age.

If one of the central insights that this book offers into the culture of the twentieth-century United States is that age came to matter, another is that the law continued to matter. This was particularly true for working-class Americans, for whom the criminal courts remained a resource to use on their own terms, often in the service of efforts to achieve outcomes other than those prescribed by the law. The legal system was, as middle-class reformers had intended it to be, a site for the dissemination of modern ideas. But working-class New Yorkers' encounters with new ideas about childhood and sexuality in and around the city's courtrooms did not result in their passive acceptance of those concepts. Instead, while working-class people were influenced by legal categories and practices, they also rejected elements of the law or put them to use in ways other than those envisioned by legislators. Those responses forced changes in legal practices and categories, and they ultimately influenced the nature of the broader ideas of childhood and sexuality from which the law was derived. In the first half of the twentieth century, then, the law was not simply supplanted by science as a site for the production of meaning any more than older ideas simply gave way to modern understandings.

The law thus retained a constitutive role in twentieth century culture, shaping the way that people understood the world by "giving particular sense to particular things in particular places (things that happen, that fail to, things that might)."[3] However, it was not constitutive in the straightforward sense that a change in the law led to a change in cultural attitudes and understandings. Instead, legal change initiated debates and negotiations at the level of practice; it was those contests and shifting relationships that shaped Americans' understanding of their world. Reformers learned that lesson by the early twentieth century. The editor of the *Philanthropist*, responding to a critic in 1896, noted that "any code . . . whatever its provisions, must, of course, depend largely upon the prevalent public opinion — the opinions of men, who are the jurors and judges — for its vitality and practical value."[4]

Yet much analysis of the law, particularly by legal historians and policy makers, looks elsewhere to understand the law and its constitutive cultural role. It is no longer the case that those analyses look exclusively to legislatures and appellate courts. Much recent scholarship has sought to recover the cases that formed the basis of appellate court decisions or has sought to examine the work of lower courts. Nonetheless, analyses of the law continue to give too much power to the formal law and to position it as a closed system beyond the reach of the ordinary Americans who appeared in criminal and juvenile courts. In the New York City courts examined in this book, however, legislatures and appellate court judges exerted little more, if not less, influence on the legal process and the meanings produced in the legal system than did ordinary citizens.

The everyday legal practice that shaped the meaning of the law took place at a distance from the legislators who had enacted it. In theory, prosecutors, entrusted with the task of enforcing the law, did represent their position. In practice, however, twentieth-century prosecutors, both the amateurs who worked in tandem with NYSPCC agents and the better-trained lawyers who succeeded them in the 1930s, displayed considerable pragmatism in fulfilling that charge. Their primary commitment was to winning convictions, which often led them to opt not to prosecute cases that had a firm legal basis but were not within the realm of what jurors understood to be criminal. Even appellate court judges had only a limited ability to influence the meanings given to the law in practice. Decisions about the meaning of statutes were frequently not applied or followed in New York City's criminal courts, and only in the small proportion of cases that were appealed were appellate court judges able to bring the verdicts of those courts into line with their opinions.

It is not surprising that analyses of legislation, appellate court decisions, and the attitudes of prosecutors are so difficult to mesh with accounts of the workings of lower courts. Nor is it hard to explain why such analyses have offered only partial explanations for the limited results of the rape law reform movement of the 1970s and 1980s.[5] The insights contained in this book suggest that understanding both the constitutive role of the criminal law and how legislation should be shaped to achieve particular ends requires a shift in focus to analysis of the law in practice.

While young victims no longer predominate in American courtrooms to the marked extent that they did in the period covered by this book, and though understandings of sexual violence are no longer as significantly shaped by issues of age, the concern about children described here remains with us. So too do the tensions that ran through that concern in the first half of the twentieth century. Americans still cannot agree on the nature of childhood, on how to answer the question, "Who is a child?" In particular, concepts of childhood innocence and of puberty as a time of sexual sublimation still compete with concepts of child sexuality and of adolescence as a stage of development that requires sexual expression. As part of the response to sexual violence, we do now ask victims, "How old are you?" But so long as there is no agreement on the significance of the answer to that question, we are handicapped in our efforts to offer children the protection that, for over a hundred years, we have known they require. The continued presence of children at the forefront of discussions of sexual violence is a haunting reminder of that failure.

appendix: tables 1 – 10

TABLE 1. Age Distribution of Complainants, 1886–1955

Year	Age 10 and Younger (%)	Ages 11 to 17 (%)	Age 18 and Older (%)
1886	26	48	26
1891	35	57	8
1896	13	82	5
1901	10	83	7
1906	13	74	13
1911	13	71	16
1916	7	82	11
1921	6	79	15
1926	6	77	17
1931	11	77	12
1936	10	75	15
1941	18	71	11
1946	9	71	20
1951	10	63	27
1955	11	72	17

Sources: Court of General Sessions Case Files, 1886, 1891; District Attorney's Closed Case Files, 1896, 1901, 1906, 1911, 1916, 1921, 1926, 1931, 1936, 1941, 1946, 1951, 1955.

TABLE 2. Age of Complainants, 1886–1955

Year	Age 10 and Younger	Ages 11 to 17	Age 18 and Older
1886	10	18	10
1891	21	35	5
1896	5	32	2
1901	7	58	5
1906	12	68	12
1911	20	113	25
1916	13	160	21
1921	9	117	22
1926	13	159	36
1931	24	175	29
1936	23	178	35
1941	34	137	22
1946	18	143	41
1951	11	66	28
1955	16	104	24

Sources: Court of General Sessions Case Files, 1886, 1891; District Attorney's Closed Case Files, 1896, 1901, 1906, 1911, 1916, 1921, 1926, 1931, 1936, 1941, 1946, 1951, 1955.

TABLE 3. Distribution of Cases by Offense, 1886–1955

Year	Rape	Rape 1	Rape 2	Attempted Rape 1	Attempted Rape 2	Abduction	Seduction	Incest	Carnal Sodomy	Abuse
1886		18		6		16	1		1	
1891		29		5		16	2		10	
1896		21		1		7			11	
1901		11	42	1		8	4		9	
1906	8	13	39	3	1	12	5		13	
1911	18	21	75	8	1	19	14	1	14	
1916	46	23	102	12	3	15	11	2	10	
1921	33	26	76		1	9	4		6	
1926	48	40	97	7	2	9	9		12	
1931	148	8	25	2		6	6	1	26	17
1936	67	25	96	16		3	9	1	27	12
1941	127	18	50	4	3	3	1	3	19	28
1946	70	45	63	7	6		1	5	30	11
1951	28	23	50	5		4	2	2	23	10
1955	85	13	54	5			1	3	37	10

Sources: Court of General Sessions Case Files, 1886, 1891; District Attorney's Closed Case Files, 1896, 1901, 1906, 1911, 1916, 1921, 1926, 1931, 1936, 1941, 1946, 1951, 1955.

Note: This table includes all the cases that I identified in the docket books. The totals are greater than those in the other tables because not all the case files could be found and not all contained information on the age of the complainant or the outcome of the case. "Rape 1" is first-degree rape; "Rape 2" is second-degree rape, also known as statutory rape.

TABLE 4. Outcomes of Sexual Violence Prosecutions, 1886–1901

Outcome	Age 10 and Younger				Ages 11 to 17					Age 18 and Older		
	Sodomy		Rape	Attempted Rape	Sodomy		Rape	Attempted Rape	Abduction	Rape	Attempted Rape	Seduction
	Boys	Girls			Boys	Girls						
Number indicted	9	3	23	6	13	4	67	4	41	11	3	4
Number tried	2	0	11	2	4	0	34	3	14	4	2	1
Number of tried convicted	2		5	1	2		20	2	8	1	1	1
% of total tried convicted	100		45	50	50		59	66	57	25	50	100
Total convictions	8	1	14	5	11	3	46	3	24	7	1	1
% of total number	89	33	61	83	85	75	69	75	59	64	33	25

Sources: Court of General Sessions Case Files, 1886, 1891; District Attorney's Closed Case Files, 1896, 1901.

Note: This table includes the sample years for which there are no records of cases dismissed by the grand jury. "Rape" includes both first-degree rape and second-degree rape.

TABLE 5. Outcomes of Sexual Violence Prosecutions, 1906–1926

	Age 10 and Younger				Ages 11 to 17				Age 18 and Older		
	Sodomy		Rape	Attempted Rape	Sodomy		Rape	Attempted Rape	Rape	Attempted Rape	Seduction
Outcome	Boys	Girls			Boys	Girls					
Total number	18	5	27	11	12	6	514	12	65	13	31
Number indicted	17	5	26	10	9	5	345	9	34	9	21
% of total number	94	100	98	91	75	83	67	75	52	69	68
Number tried	4	1	11	3	0	1	66	3	7	2	6
Number of tried convicted	0	0	6	2		1	23	1	4	1	3
% of total tried convicted	0	0	54	66		100	35	33	57	50	50
Total convictions	12	3	16*	8	9	4	257	6	19	3	5
% of total number	67	60	60	73	75	67	50	50	29	23	16

Source: District Attorney's Closed Case Files, 1906, 1911, 1916, 1921, 1926.

Note: "Rape" includes cases of both first-degree rape and second-degree rape.

*One defendant was also committed as a mental defective

TABLE 6. Cases That Involved Extralegal Investigations or Efforts to Arrange a Marriage or a Financial Settlement, 1896–1955

	1896	1901	1906	1911	1916	1921	1926	Total 1896–1926	1931	1936*	1941*	1946	1951	Total 1931–1951	1955	Total 1951–1955	Total
Cases involving women who did not become pregnant	15	31	7	54	37	43	73	260	75	25	16	57	43	173	73	116	549
Number of cases involving extralegal efforts	2	5	2	20	13	14	12	68	21	3	5	7	8	36	15	23	127
As a proportion of the cases involving women who did not become pregnant	13%	16%	28%	37%	35%	32%	16%	26%	28%	12%	31%	12%	19%	21%	20%	20%	23%
Cases involving pregnant women	1	2	4	8	12	3	10	40	27	34	21	49	23	131	31	54	224
Number of cases involving extralegal efforts	0	1	1	6	8	1	5	22	10	6	7	20	12	43	10	22	87
As a proportion of the cases involving pregnant women	50%		25%	75%	66%	33%	50%	55%	37%	18%	33%	41%	52%	33%	32%	41%	39%

Sources: District Attorney's Closed Case Files, 1896, 1901, 1906, 1911, 1916, 1921, 1926, 1931, 1936, 1941, 1946, 1951, 1955; Probation Department Case Files, 1926, 1936, 1946, 1955.

Note: The totals include only those case files that contained sufficient details to reveal extralegal efforts. This table is a revised version of the one published in Robertson, "Making Right a Girl's Ruin," 208. The changes reflect the results of additional research, particularly material contained in a sample of Probation Department case files. Because I did not examine all the Probation Department case files relating to cases in my sample, the totals likely still underrepresent the extent of working-class extralegal activity.

*The totals for 1936 and 1941 are aberrantly low because assistant district attorneys or their clerks appear to have stopped the practice of recording that a grand jury had dismissed a case after the couple had married. In 1936 there were twelve cases and in 1941 a further six cases in which a grand jury dismissed the charges against a man who admitted impregnating a girl. Usually such a dismissal meant that the couple married—in my nine other sample years there are only four such cases that did not involve a marriage—but these files in-

TABLE 7. Prosecutions Involving Female Complainants, Ages 11 to 17, 1886–1955

Year	Abduction	Attempted Rape 1 & Rape 1	Attempted Rape 2 & Rape 2	Rape	Carnal Abuse	Incest	Seduction
1886	14	5					
1891	13	19					1
1896	7	15					
1901	7	6	38				
1906	12	4	38	8			1
1911	16	4	69	18			1
1916	16	10	94	34			2
1921	8		74	33			
1926	7	7	94	46			
1931	6	6	89	55		1	
1936	3	2	95	64			
1941	2	5	43	83		3	
1946		11	59	52		4	
1951	1	15	47		1	2	
1955		12	53	34	2	3	

Sources: Court of General Sessions Case Files, 1886, 1891; District Attorney's Closed Case Files, 1896, 1901, 1906, 1911, 1916, 1921, 1926, 1931, 1936, 1941, 1946, 1951, 1955.

Note: Not included are prosecutions on charges of sodomy. "Rape 1" refers to first-degree rape; "Rape 2" refers to second-degree rape, also known as statutory rape.

TABLE 8. Outcomes of Sexual Violence Prosecutions, 1931–1946.

Outcome	Age 10 and Younger						Ages 11 to 17				Age 18 and Older		
	Sodomy		Rape	Attempted Rape	Carnal Abuse		Sodomy		Rape	Attempted Rape	Rape	Attempted Rape	Seduction
	Boys	Girls			Boys	Girls	Boys	Girls					
Total number	17	4	4	6	8	59	46	8	551	14	81	23	14
Number transferred	1	1	2	3	2	12	6	1	13	3	3	1	0
Number indicted	13	2	2	2	6	33	33	6	245	6	31	12	4
% of total number	76	50	50	33	75	56	72	75	44	43	38	52	29
Number tried	3	0	0	0	0	9	7	2	26	1	7	3	0
Number of tried convicted	3					7	5	1	13	1	3	1	
% of tried convicted	100					78	71	50	50	100	43	33	
Total convictions	13	2	2	2	6	27	31	5	195	5	18	8	2
% of total number	76	50	50	33	75	46	67	62	35	36	22	35	14

Source: District Attorney's Closed Case Files, 1931, 1936, 1941, 1946.

Note: "Rape" includes both first-degree rape and second-degree rape. "Number transferred" refers to cases that the grand jury transferred to the court of special sessions.

TABLE 9. Outcomes of Sexual Violence Prosecutions, 1951 and 1955

	Age 10 and Younger						Ages 11 to 17				Age 18 and Older		
	Sodomy		Rape	Attempted Rape	Carnal Abuse		Sodomy		Rape	Attempted Rape	Rape	Attempted Rape	Seduction
Outcome	Boys	Girls			Boys	Girls	Boys	Girls					
Total number	6	4	1	2	2	12	22	10	155	6	30	15	2
Number transferred	2	2	0	1	0	5	5	3	23	0	2	1	0
Number indicted	4	1	0	1	2	7	16	6	44	2	10	9	0
% of total number	66	25		50	100	58	73	60	28	33	33	60	
Number tried	0	0	0	0	1	0	0	1	2	0	0	2	0
Number of tried convicted					1			1	1			2	
% of total tried convicted					100			100	50			100	
Total convictions	4	1	0	1	2	6	16	6	38	2	10	9	0
% of total number	66	25		50	100	50	73	60	24	33	33	60	

Source: District Attorney's Closed Case Files, 1951, 1955.

Note: "Rape" includes cases of both first-degree rape and second-degree rape.

TABLE 10. Men Committed under Sexual Psychopath Laws, 1937–1980

State	1940s	1950s	1960s	1970s
California	In regular use	2,081 1953–58[1]	7,200–7,650 1955–72[2]	
Colorado[3]		62 1957–64		
District of Columbia[4]		161 1949–64		
Illinois	94 1940–58[5]		111 1959–64[6]	
Indiana[7]		637 1949–68		
Iowa[8]		33 1955		
Maryland		86 1955–60[9]		
Massachusetts		226 1959–71?[10]		In regular use[11]
Michigan[12]		1,111 1937–64		
Minnesota[13]	141	85	32	18
Missouri	50 1949–58[14]		74 1959–64[15]	
Nebraska	41 1949–56[16]		In regular use[17]	
New Hampshire[18]		12 1958–60		
New Jersey		1,138 1949–65[19]		In regular use[20]
Ohio[21]		596 1943–64		
Oregon		139 1956–57[22]	107 1963–72[23]	In regular use[24]
Pennsylvania[25]		126 1952–63		
Virginia[26]		11 1956		
Washington		46 1955–57[27]	207 1961–65[28]	In regular use[29]
Wisconsin		632 1951–60[30]	In regular use[31]	

1. Lindman and McIntyre, *The Mentally Disabled*, 303.
2. "Throughout the period 1955 through 1972, the number of commitments remained stable at 400 to 425 per year" (Dix, "Differential Processing," 234).
3. Vuocolo, *The Repetitive Sex Offender*, 120–21.
4. Ibid., 122.
5. Bowman and Engle, "Certain Aspects," 695.
6. Vuocolo, *The Repetitive Sex Offender*, 127.
7. Granucci and Granucci, "Indiana's Sexual Psychopath Act," 561–62, 568.
8. Fahr, "Iowa's New Sexual Psychopath Law," 545.
9. Vuocolo, *The Repetitive Sex Offender*, 131.
10. Kozol, Boucher, and Garofalo, "The Diagnosis and Treatment of Dangerousness," 378. This article reports on admissions over a ten-year period, but it does not say what dates that period covers.
11. Brakel, Perry, and Weiner, *The Mentally Disabled and the Law*, 740 n. 557.
12. Vuocolo, *The Repetitive Sex Offender*, 134. Lindman and McIntyre report 478 committals in the period 1953 to 1958 (Lindman and McIntyre, *The Mentally Disabled and the Law*, 303).
13. Janus, "Sex Offender Commitments," 96 n. 128, 97 n. 131.
14. Bowman and Engle, "Certain Aspects," 694.
15. Vuocolo, *The Repetitive Sex Offender*, 137.
16. Caporale and Hamann, "Sexual Psychopathology," 325.
17. Brakel, Perry, and Weiner, *The Mentally Disabled and the Law*, 740 n. 557.
18. Niswander, "Some Aspects of 'Sexual Psychopath' Examinations," 67, 73.
19. Vuocolo, *The Repetitive Sex Offender*, 63.
20. Brakel, Perry, and Weiner, *The Mentally Disabled and the Law*, 740 n. 557.
21. Vuocolo, *The Repetitive Sex Offender*, 143.
22. Bowman and Engle, "Certain Aspects," 695.
23. Bradley and Margolin, "The Oregon Sexually Dangerous Persons Act," 374–75.
24. Brakel, Perry, and Weiner, *The Mentally Disabled and the Law*, 740 n. 557.
25. Vuocolo, *The Repetitive Sex Offender*, 145.
26. Bowman and Engle, "Certain Aspects," 695.
27. Ibid.
28. Vuocolo, *The Repetitive Sex Offender*, 150.
29. Brakel, Perry, and Weiner, *The Mentally Disabled and the Law*, 740 n. 557.
30. Pacht, Halleck, and Ehrmann, "Diagnosis and Treatment of the Sexual Offender," 807.
31. Ransley, "Repeal," 946.

notes

Abbreviations

ARNYSPCC	*Annual Report of the New York Society for the Prevention of Cruelty to Children*
ARPANY	*Annual Report of the Prison Association of New York*
CGSCF	Court of General Sessions Case Files, Municipal Archives, New York City
DACCF	District Attorney's Closed Case Files, Municipal Archives, New York City
DAS	District Attorney's Scrapbooks, Municipal Archives, New York City
NYDN	*New York Daily News*
NYT	*New York Times*
PANY	Prison Association of New York
PDCF	Court of General Sessions, Probation Department Case File, Municipal Archives, New York City
TTC	Trial Transcript Collection, Special Collections, John Jay College of Criminal Justice, New York City

Introduction

1. Draper, *A Textbook of Legal Medicine*, 123. Draper had taught at Harvard for twenty-six years. Prior to that he had been one of the principal leaders of the medical examiners movement and president of its professional organization, the Massachusetts Medico-Legal Society. See Mohr, *Doctors and the Law*, 244. Brouardel held the chair in legal medicine at the University of Paris from 1879 until his death in 1906. He had previously been the assistant of Ambroise Tardieu, his predecessor in the chair. For a discussion of Brouardel and the tradition of French legal medicine of which he was part, see Masson, *The Assault on Truth*, 14–54. For an analysis of physicians' struggle to accommodate themselves to legal authority and to legal practices in

regard to rape, as well as to the cases that they encountered, see Robertson, "Signs, Marks, and Private Parts," 345–88.

2. From 1820 to 1829, girls under nineteen years made up 76 percent of the total. See Gilfoyle, *City of Eros*, 349–50. Other studies reveal that anywhere between one-fifth and one-third of cases of rape in the years before 1880 involved an alleged assault on a young girl. Cornelia Dayton found two of the twelve rape complainants in Connecticut in the years 1639 to 1699 were younger than ten years of age, and three others were between eleven and seventeen years old. Five of the eighteen rape complainants in Connecticut in the eighteenth century were under ten years of age, and three others under eighteen years of age. See Dayton, *Women before the Bar*, 236–37, 244–45. Sharon Block's study of coerced sex in British North America in the period 1700 to 1820 found thirty-eight cases that involved girls under the age of ten (6 percent of the total), and an additional twenty-six cases that involved girls aged ten to thirteen years, making a total of 10 percent younger than fourteen years old. See Block, "Coerced Sex in British North America," 196. Research on Britain shows similar patterns. See Bashar, "Rape in England between 1550 and 1700," 37; Simpson, "Vulnerability and the Age of Female Consent," 188, 191–92; Clark, *Women's Silence, Men's Violence*, 98.

3. For studies that note the increased concern with children, see Parker, "To Protect the Chastity of Children under Sixteen," 49 (discussing Ingham County, Mich.); Odem, "Delinquent Daughters," 134 (discussing Alameda and Los Angeles Counties, Calif.); Wood, "Schoolgirls and the Dark Curriculum of Vice" (discussing Scott County, Iowa); Freedman, "'Uncontrolled Desires,'" 211–13. A new concern with children as victims of sexual violence in this period has also been noted in other national contexts: see L. Jackson, *Child Sexual Abuse*, 18–22; Lambertz, "Feminists and the Politics of Wife-Beating," 33; Engelstein, *The Keys to Happiness*; Bavin-Mizzi, *Ravished*.

4. N = 1,415 of 1,656. See tables 1 and 2 in the appendix. The sample includes every case of rape in every fifth year from 1886 to 1951, together with all those in 1955 (the docket books for 1956 were incomplete, forcing an examination of 1955). Until 1906, the case file collection included only those men indicted by the grand jury. After 1906, the files included all those men held for the grand jury, including those who were not indicted. Only men accused of a felony, the offenders dealt with by the court of general sessions, appear in the DA's records. For a brief overview of the New York City court system, see K. Jackson, *The Encyclopedia of New York City*, 290–95. The New York City legal system is discussed further in chapter 1.

5. N = 1,799 of 2,115. See tables 1 and 2 in the appendix.

6. Forbath, Hartog, and Minnow, "Introduction," 764–65; Tomlins, "Subordination, Authority, Law," 66–67. For a critical overview of the concept of legal culture, see R. Ross, "The Legal Past of Early New England," 32–39.

7. P. Jenkins, *Moral Panic*.

8. Halperin, "How to Do the History of Male Homosexuality," 91; Sedgwick, *The Epistemology of the Closet*, 45, 47. I quote Sedgwick here because her insightful argument has been crucial in helping me develop my understanding of cultural change in the twentieth century.

9. Their occupations provide a relatively clear indication of their class identity, one confirmed by the details of the cases. Of the fifty occupations reported by defendants in 1901, the most common were barber, laborer, and painter. The defendants in subsequent years came from similar groups. In 1936, an even greater proportion were laborers, with the other most common occupations being porter, chauffeur (taxi-driver), dishwasher, and painter. There were also clerks, janitors, bellboys, shoemakers, carpenters, salesmen, hairdressers, packers, laundrymen, and seamen.

10. In 1901, for example, after the one-third of defendants who were American-born, the next largest groups were Italians, who constituted nearly one in every five defendants, Russians, and Germans (N = 69). Twenty-three defendants were American-born; thirteen were born in Italy, nine in Russia, and eight in Germany. The remainder included several Englishmen, a West Indian, a Canadian, a Norwegian, a Frenchman, and an Austrian. After 1930, approximately one in every five defendants in the DA's caseload was African American. At the same time, small numbers of Puerto Ricans also appeared, and by the 1950s they made up one-third of the caseload.

11. That conclusion must be couched somewhat generally because the legal records do not allow a fine-grained analysis of different groups. The forms used by the DA's office recorded only birthplace, providing evidence of ethnicity only when most working-class New Yorkers were first-generation immigrants, in the years before 1930. An individual's name obviously provides some guide to his or her ethnicity, but names are not sufficiently reliable evidence to support a fine-grained analysis of differences between ethnic groups. Moreover, there was no section on the forms that required clerks to record any information about an individual's race. As a result, African Americans can only be identified when their racial identity is mentioned in documents contained in a file, or when a clerk or prosecutor added a scrawled note to the file. But not every African American who appeared before a grand jury had such a notation in his file. Only the Probation Department files invariably provided information on race, but records for the period before the 1920s have not survived, and since the 1920s only records for some of the small group of men who were convicted are extant. More significant, however, is the fact that only in regard to a narrow range of issues do the details of the cases themselves offer any evidence of differences within the working class.

12. In Chicago, the Juvenile Protection Association operated in a similar manner. See Willrich, *City of Courts*, 126.

13. For the period up to 1906, files only survive for those cases where the grand jury voted in favor of an indictment.

14. By the turn of the century, each case file took the form of a legal-size cardboard envelope. On the outside was the file number, the defendant's name and address, annotations, and, later, stamps, recording the disposition of the case. Most of the file envelopes relating to cases of sexual violence that I found in the docket books are thin. When that was the case, their contents were generally limited to a copy of the charge made by the complainant in the magistrates' court, and, unless the grand jury dismissed the case, the indictment. The latter is simply a form; the former, recorded by a clerk, usually echoes the language of the statute, describing the particular

circumstances of a case in a few words, or at most a few sentences. By the 1940s, a thin case file also contained a one-page form on which a prosecutor recorded the basic circumstances of a case, through answers to a series of questions and some additional remarks, generally amounting to a short paragraph. About one-third of the file envelopes, generally those for cases in which the defendant was indicted, are thicker. Most often these envelopes contained a brief prepared by the NYSPCC, which summarized the statements of the prosecution witnesses, and was occasionally accompanied by the NYSPCC officer's notes and the Society's case file. ADAs themselves also took statements from witnesses, the transcripts of which are present in some files. Less often there are transcripts of the defendant's arraignment in the magistrates' court, and the hearing before the grand jury. Most rare of all are trial transcripts, although I did locate transcripts for thirty-five cases in my sample in a collection of transcripts from the period 1896 to 1921 held at the John Jay College of Criminal Justice in New York City. This collection includes cases in which defendants appealed their convictions, or for which a judge requested the transcript. Some file envelopes also yield items such as correspondence from lawyers or interested social agencies, reports of psychiatric and medical examinations, and items of evidence, such as letters, address books, and photographs. For the years before 1920, the court records are also available; generally the only material they contain that is not also in the DA's files are transcripts of sentencing hearings. At the very end of my research, the records of the probation department of the court of general sessions became available. I looked at a sample of 120 of the records for cases that I had found in the DA's records, from the years 1926, 1936, 1946, and 1955. These records contain the department's pre-sentencing report to the judge, a form that describes the offense, and a discussion of mitigating and aggravating circumstances, and offers a detailed portrait of the convicted man, describing his education and early life, family and neighborhood, work history, and personality. Filed with that report are the results of a psychiatric examination and correspondence from any social agency with which he or his family had been involved. If he was placed on probation, the files also include his probation officer's notes on their regular meetings.

15. That cultural process went hand in hand with changes in economic, occupational, and family structures. Industrial capitalism required a skilled, educated workforce, diminishing the productive value of children. The nineteenth century also saw an increasing separation of economic production and the home, weakening the instrumental ties that had bound families together, and increasing the saliency of emotional ties. At the same time, the domestication of middle-class women led them to invest children with further value. See Zelizer, *Pricing the Priceless Child*.

16. Wiebe, *The Search for Order*, 169, 171.

Chapter One

1. *NYT*, 17 December 1874, reproduced in Bremner, *Children and Youth in America*, 1:190.

2. For the NYSPCC, see Pleck, *Domestic Tyranny*, particularly 69–87; Costin, Karger, and Stoesz, *The Politics of Child Abuse in America*. For an example of the NYSPCC's in-

fluence on child protection agencies in other countries, see Behlmer, *Child Abuse and Moral Reform in England*. The lack of women in leadership positions in the NYSPCC is in contrast to the prominent role of women in both the Massachusetts Society for the Prevention of Cruelty to Children and the Pennsylvania Society to Protect Children from Cruelty; see Gordon, *Heroes of Their Own Lives*, 34–76; Broder, *Tramps, Unfit Mothers, and Neglected Children*, 208–9 n. 6. The quote is from Pleck, *Domestic Tyranny*, 73.

3. Gordon, *Heroes of Their Own Lives*, 60–61, 65, 72, 326 n. 18. For the law enforcement activities of the Pennsylvania Society to Protect Children from Cruelty, see Broder, *Tramps, Unfit Mothers, and Neglected Children*.

4. For Gerry's response to the press attacks on the Society, see Elbridge Gerry, "Children of the Stage," *North American Review*, July 1890, reprinted in *The Sixteenth ARNYSPCC*, 123–24.

5. For a discussion of the debate about child performers and the way that it divided even child labor reformers, see Zelizer, *Pricing the Priceless Child*, 85–96.

6. Such concerns determined the actions of the Massachusetts Society for the Prevention of Cruelty to Children. In 1882, the MSPCC voted against trying to enforce the state's law restricting performances by children in the case of a popular singer and actress whom the NYSPCC had prevented from performing in New York City. Taking action would, in the words of one director, "injure our reputation with the public [and] lessen our chance of subscriptions" (Gordon, *Heroes of Their Own Lives*, 41).

7. *The Sixth ARNYSPCC*, 7.

8. Gerry, "Children of the Stage," 120. For another extended defense of his views on child performers, see Gerry's letter to the secretary of the Cleveland Humane Society, excerpted in *The Fifth ARNYSPCC*, 79–81.

9. *The Sixth ARNYSPCC*, 6–7.

10. H. Jenkins, "Introduction," 13.

11. J.-J. Rousseau, *Emile*, 5, 54. For particularly insightful accounts of this widely discussed transformation in understandings of childhood, see Cunningham, *Children and Childhood in Western Society since 1500*; Heininger, "Children, Childhood, and Change in America"; Green, "Scientific Thought and the Nature of Children in America"; Hendrick, *Child Welfare*; Sommerville, *The Rise and Fall of Childhood*.

12. Hendrick, *Child Welfare*, 24–32; Stansell, *City of Women*, 202–3, 208–14.

13. Steedman, *Strange Dislocations*, 7–8; Kett, *Rites of Passage*, 11–14.

14. Kincaid, *Child Loving*, 4–5, 72–73, 77–78, 91–93, 159. For the importance of a clear break between childhood and adulthood, see also H. Jenkins, "Introduction," 14.

15. On the persistence of beliefs in the child's innate depravity, see Hendrick, *Child Welfare*, 23–33; Cunningham, *Children and Childhood in Western Society since 1500*, 70–71; Green, "Scientific Thought and the Nature of Children in America." On the child of nature, see Kincaid, *Child Loving*, 74–75; Lears, *No Place of Grace*, 145–46.

16. This contrast, and the fascination with children it produced in the Victorian period, is captured by this passage from Proust: "It comes so soon, the moment when there is nothing left to wait for, when the body is fixed in an immobility which

holds no fresh surprises in store . . . it is so short, that radiant morning time that one comes only to like the very youngest girls, those in whom the flesh, like a precious leaven is still at work" (cited in Ovenden and Melville, *Victorian Children*, n.p.). See also Steedman, *Strange Dislocations*; Kincaid, *Child Loving*. For romantic descriptions of childhood, see Heininger, "Children, Childhood, and Change in America," 12–15. For a discussion of paintings of children, see Higonnet, *Pictures of Innocence*, 15–49.

17. Cited in Halperin, *American Pediatrics*, 52. See also Chudacoff, *How Old are You?* 44–45.

18. Chudacoff, *How Old are You?* 44–45; Halperin, *American Pediatrics*, 88–89; Stern, " 'Beauty Is Not Always Better' "; Stern, "Making Better Babies." The quote is from Heininger, "Children, Childhood, and Change in America," 1.

19. White and White, *Stylin'*, 182–84, 195–97.

20. Jones, *Taming the Troublesome Child*, 16–24. See also Macleod, *The Age of the Child*, 27, 51.

21. Kett, *Rites of Passage*, 133–37; Kincaid, *Child Loving*, 116–25.

22. *Laws of New York, 1881*, chap. 130, 114.

23. Rothman, *The Discovery of the Asylum*, 207–9. See also Gordon, *Heroes of Their Own Lives*, 55.

24. He went on to affirm, "The universal testimony of the medical profession concurs in endorsing as wise the age so fixed." See *The Fifth ARNYSPCC*, 79–80.

25. "Letter from Hon. Elbridge Gerry," *Philanthropist* 10, 6 (June 1895): 5.

26. Brumberg, *The Body Project*, 3–25.

27. Macleod, *The Age of the Child*, 140.

28. For New York's school attendance and child labor laws, see Felt, *Hostages of Fortune*. Zelizer notes that it was not until the 1860s that age began to play a significant part in determining what constituted legitimate work for children, and its use as such continued to meet with considerable resistance well into the twentieth century. Only in the 1920s did child labor reformers attempt to raise the age limit from fourteen years to sixteen years (Zelizer, *Pricing the Priceless Child*, 75–76).

29. *The First ARNYSPCC*, 5. For other examples of appeals to humanitarian sentiment, see *The Seventh ARNYSPCC*, 5; *The Twenty-seventh ARNYSPCC*, 9. For the spread of humanitarianism in the United States, see Turner, *Reckoning with the Beast*.

30. *The Forty-first ARNYSPCC*, 15.

31. Here I disagree with Elizabeth Pleck's argument that the NYSPCC always had a broad agenda and focused on cruelty merely as a strategy for building support (Pleck, *Domestic Tyranny*, 83–84). My view is in line with Linda Gordon's picture of how the MSPCC developed its work (Gordon, *Heroes of Their Own Lives*, 37–42).

32. For an example, see *The Tenth ARNYSPCC*, 5–6.

33. Stansell, *City of Women*, 213; *The Nineteenth ARNYSPCC*, 8; *The Tenth ARNYSPCC*, 5.

34. *The Second ARNYSPCC*, 40–41; *The Twenty-seventh ARNYSPCC*, 9; *The Twelfth ARNYSPCC*, 6–7; *The Fifteenth ARNYSPCC*, 4–5.

35. "Decennial Address of the President," *The Tenth ARNYSPCC*, 5.

36. *The Sixteenth ARNYSPCC*, 44–45.

37. *The Eighth ARNYSPCC*, 56.

38. *The Eleventh ARNYSPCC*, 5 – 7; *The Thirty-ninth ARNYSPCC*, 15.

39. Stansell, *City of Women*, 200. For an expression of that sense of threat, see Brace, *The Dangerous Classes of New York*, 30.

40. Bederman, *Manliness and Civilization*, esp. 23 – 31 (quotes from 23 and 27); Broder, *Tramps, Unfit Mothers, and Neglected Children*, 61.

41. Rothman, *The Discovery of the Asylum*, 207 – 9; Stansell, *City of Women*, 210.

42. *The Tenth ARNYSPCC*, 6 – 7.

43. *Thirty-first Annual Report of the American Humane Association, 1907*, cited in Roswell McCrea, *The Humane Movement: A Descriptive Survey* (New York, 1910), in Bremner, *Children and Youth in America*, 2:214.

44. For a summary of the child protection statutes in place by 1922, see W. Schultz, *The Humane Movement in the United States*, 265 – 91. For newsgirls, see *The Thirteenth ARNYSPCC*, 31. Gerry also sought the power to regulate child factory work but failed—in 1882 and again in 1884—to get laws enacted that would have given the Society the power to inspect factories. When the New York State Legislature did pass a child labor law in 1886, they did not give the NYSPCC inspection powers. See Felt, *Hostages of Fortune*, 8, 19.

45. For the police department procedure, see New York Police Department, General Order No. 13, 15 March 1910, cited in NYSPCC, *Instructions for Officers and Staff*, 4.

46. Until 1880 the NYSPCC made arrangements with the matron at police head-quarters to care for these children. When it secured permanent quarters for itself, the Society housed children there. See W. Schultz, *The Humane Movement in the United States*, 164. In the early twentieth century, the NYSPCC also supervised the parole and probation of children convicted in the City of New York Children's Court. The city took over this work in 1912. See ibid., 165; *The Twenty-seventh ARNYSPCC*, 19 – 21; Fishman, "New York's Criminal Justice System," 272 – 75.

47. *The Nineteenth ARNYSPCC*, 7; *The Twenty-third ARNYSPCC*, 6 – 8; *The Twenty-seventh ARNYSPCC*, 19.

48. *The Seventh ARNYSPCC*, 7 – 8.

49. Cited in Pleck, *Domestic Tyranny*, 80.

50. *The Ninth ARNYSPCC*, 8 – 9.

51. Ginzberg, *Women and the Work of Benevolence*, 206.

52. Bederman, *Manliness and Civilization*, 29.

53. *The Fifth ARNYSPCC*, 12.

54. Address to First International Humane Conference, 1910, cited in W. Schultz, *The Humane Movement in the United States*, 202; *The Nineteenth ARNYSPCC*, 7; *The Twenty-first ARNYSPCC*, 7.

55. *The First ARNYSPCC*, 5 – 7.

56. *The Nineteenth ARNYSPCC*, 7; *The Twenty-third ARNYSPCC*, 6 – 8.

57. *The Twenty-fourth ARNYSPCC*, 10 – 11; *The Thirty-third ARNYSPCC*, 10. The court of appeals endorsed this view of the Society's work in a decision in 1900. The court ruled that the NYSPCC did not do charitable work, which would have made it liable to the inspection and supervision of the New York State Board of Charities;

rather, it did "work that would otherwise devolve upon the Police Department" (cited in W. Schultz, *The Humane Movement in the United States*, 201).

58. *Laws of New York, 1881*, chap. 130, 114. See also *The Twenty-seventh ARNYSPCC*, 8. For a discussion of the NYSPCC's legal origins, see Pleck, *Domestic Tyranny*, 80. Not all child protection agencies had the same powers. Agents of the Pennsylvania Society for the Prevention of Cruelty to Children made arrests, but their powers were contingent on permission from magistrates or the help of police (Broder, *Tramps, Unfit Mothers, and Neglected Children*, 209 n. 6). Agents of the MSPCC were never given police powers, nor did the MSPCC ever take public funds, as the NYSPCC did (Gordon, *Heroes of Their Own Lives*, 52).

59. *The Second ARNYSPCC*, 62.

60. For discussions of the state's delegation of its authority in this period, see Reagan, *When Abortion Was a Crime*, 3; Willrich, *City of Courts*, 126.

61. Russell Sage Foundation, *Boyhood and Lawlessness*, 89.

62. The superintendent commented in 1897 that "[anonymous] complaints in the great majority of cases come from people who live in the poorer sections, in the tenements, and among the very brutes against whom they complain, and from whom they themselves would have reason to fear personal violence, should their names become known as complainants" (*The Twenty-second ARNYSPCC*, 25). See also *The Thirtieth ARNYSPCC*, 39.

63. *The Forty-first ARNYSPCC*, 40.

64. M. R. Smith, "The Social Aspect of New York Police Courts," 152.

65. Ibid., 145–46. On the conditions in magistrates' courts, see also Fishman, "New York's Criminal Justice System," 68–69.

66. *The Twenty-third ARNYSPCC*, 6–8; *The Twenty-seventh ARNYSPCC*, 19–21.

67. *The Twenty-third ARNYSPCC*, 6–8.

68. Fishman, "New York's Criminal Justice System," 33, 59, 224. This situation also led to what Mary Roberts Smith described as "extraordinary contrasts in the manner, tone, and general behavior of the magistrates." She complained that two magistrates she observed "listened to each prisoner with the ironical, indifferent air of one who had heard all that before and who knew the man lied; neither took the least pains to get from the prisoner what he really had to say in his own behalf, or to give it reasonable consideration." See M. R. Smith, "The Social Aspect of New York Police Courts," 150–51.

69. Fishman, "New York's Criminal Justice System," 49–54.

70. Cited in W. Schultz, *The Humane Movement in the United States*, 208.

71. *The Forty-seventh ARNYSPCC*, 19.

72. *Laws of New York, 1909*, chap. 35.

73. Fishman, "New York's Criminal Justice System," 115–21; Train, *The Prisoner at the Bar*, 222.

74. Train, *The Prisoner at the Bar*, 266, 269; Fishman, "New York's Criminal Justice System," 333–38.

75. N = 67 of 227. See tables 5, 6, and 9 in the appendix. The case files for the years from 1886 to 1901 include only cases in which the grand jury voted an indictment.

76. Fishman, "New York's Criminal Justice System," 89, 156.

77. The statute defined rape as

an act of sexual intercourse with a female not the wife of the perpetrator, committed against her will or without her consent. A person who perpetrates such an act,

1. When the female is under the age of ten years, or

2. When through idiocy, imbecility or any unsoundness of mind, either temporary or permanent, she is incapable of giving consent; or,

3. When her resistance is forcibly overcome; or,

4. When her resistance is prevented by fear of immediate and great bodily harm, which she has reasonable cause to believe will be inflicted upon her; or,

5. When her resistance is prevented by stupor, or weakness of mind produced by an intoxicating narcotic, or anesthetic agent administered by, or with the privity of, the defendant; or,

6. When she is, at the time, unconscious of the nature of the act, and this is known to the defendant.

. . . Any penetration, however slight, is sufficient to complete the crime. (Penal Code of the State of New York, title X, chap. 2, secs. 278 and 280, in *Laws of New York, 1881,* vol. 3, chap. 676, 66–67)

78. *Boddie v. State,* 52 Ala. 395, 398 (1875), cited in Wigmore, *A Treatise on the System of Evidence,* 2:2757–58.

79. Ibid., 2758. Only New York and Iowa required corroboration in rape cases. By 1940 Oklahoma had adopted a statute that required corroboration in rape cases (Hawaii and Washington introduced and then repealed such laws in this period); seven other states had adopted statutes that required corroboration in rape cases that involved girls under the age of consent; and eleven more states adopted statutes that applied to seduction. See ibid., 2759–60; Wigmore, *A Treatise on the System of Evidence,* 3rd ed., 7:350–54. Appellate court decisions in several other states did impose corroboration requirements in the absence of legislative action. In the District of Columbia, Nebraska, and Georgia, judicial decisions required full corroboration in rape cases. By the mid-twentieth century, judicial decisions in ten other states required either limited corroboration or corroboration in certain circumstances. See Note, "The Rape Corroboration Requirement," 1366–68; and Pratt, "The Demise of the Corroboration Requirement," 805–39.

80. Goldman, "'A Most Detestable Crime,'" 197.

81. *People v. Grauer,* 12 App. Div. 468 (1896).

82. New York State Law Revision Commission, *Communication and Study Relating to Sexual Crimes,* 77.

83. Those who argue that the corroboration requirement prevented successful prosecutions for rape usually rely on the evidence of an almost complete absence of rape convictions in New York State in the 1970s.

84. For an overview of appellate court decisions, see Estrich, *Real Rape.*

85. For example, nineteen-year-old Susan Nicholas spent a week in the hospital

after being assaulted by Jonathon Reynolds following a party at the Decker Record Company, where they both worked. She received two stitches in lacerations to her mouth and was treated for bruises on the throat, injuries and lacerations of her nose, and swelling of both of her eyes. See DACCF 3715 (1946). For other examples, see DACCF 35385 (1901); DACCF 167338 (1926); DACCF 186006 (1931); DACCF 211275 (1936); DACCF 229384 (1941); DACCF 364 (1946); DACCF 1931 (1946); DACCF 1976 (1946); DACCF 3052 (1946).

86. For comments concerning a woman's lack of injuries, see DACCF 187321 (1931); DACCF 2550 (1946); DACCF 3489 (1946); DACCF 1719 (1946); DACCF 2270 (1946); DACCF 3333 (1946); DACCF 3489 (1946).

87. DACCF 207491 (1936); DACCF 207587 (1936); DACCF 228867 (1941); DACCF 3215 (1946); DACCF 3203 (1946). Courts throughout the United States took similar positions. See Estrich, *Real Rape*, 29–36.

88. *Laws of New York, 1848*, chap. 111. For the laws in other states, see Feinsinger, "Legislative Attack on 'Heart Balm,'" 988 n. 58. Those laws were still in place in 1951. The thirteen states without seduction laws were Delaware, Florida, Idaho, Kansas, Louisiana, Maine, Maryland, Nevada, New Hampshire, Tennessee, Utah, Vermont, and West Virginia. See Bensing, "A Comparative Study of American Sex Statutes," 66–67.

89. N = 51. In the same period, there were 265 other cases of sexual violence involving women aged eighteen years or older. See table 4, 5, 8, and 9 in the appendix. Women described being subject to physical force in 39 percent (N = 31) of the files that contain details of the circumstances of the case, or 24 percent (N = 51) of my total sample of seduction cases. The only other study of criminal seduction cases, Karen Dubinsky's work on Ontario, found that 20 percent of the cases involved violence. However, the Canadian law applied only to promises of marriage made to females under twenty-one years of age; it also covered sexual intercourse with girls aged between fourteen and sixteen years and sexual intercourse with a female ward or employee under twenty-one years of age. See Dubinsky, *Improper Advances*, 66–79.

90. N = 8 of 51 ended in conviction. A further eight cases were dismissed after the couples involved married. See DACCF 35443 (1901); DACCF 139808 (1921); DACCF 136956 (1921); DACCF 165886 (1926); DACCF 165137 (1926); DACCF 188658 (1931).

91. Haag, *Consent*, 3. See also VanderVelde, "The Legal Ways of Seduction," 862–64.

92. Bana was refused a room at the Astor. New York City law prohibited letting rooms to couples without luggage. The Astor Hotel house detective looked at Clara, who appeared to him to be drugged or drunk, and told the clerk to send Bana away. Bana then hailed a taxi, rode to a druggist and bought a tonic to revive Clara, and continued to ride around until she seemed better. Then he took Clara to the Hotel Werner, where the clerk saw nothing out of the ordinary and gave Bana a room.

93. DACCF 85409 (1911); TTC, case 1440, roll 187 (1911).

94. TTC, case 1440, roll 187 (1911), 255–61. Clara's father disputed the judge's interpretation of the case, creating what a reporter for the *New York Tribune* described as "a scene." For her part, Clara ran up the courtroom aisle to the bar "waving her

arms frantically" and screaming. Court attendants had to forcibly remove her to an anteroom. See "Girl Denounces Judge," *New York Tribune*, 30 November 1911, DAS.

95. For a particularly disturbing example, see DACCF 1816 (1946).

Chapter Two

1. Brief for the People, DACCF 85723 (1911). From her description, the police recognized Bailey as a repeat offender who they knew lived in the neighborhood. Both Jane and another girl then picked Bailey out of a lineup.

2. Brief for the People, CGSCF, *People v. C.P.* (September 1886). While I have altered the names of the participants in all the cases I discuss, in my citations of the court of general sessions case files I use the defendants' actual initials since these records are filed alphabetically by defendant's name and by date.

3. Of the forty cases for which I have information on the location of the offense, eighteen took place on the street and twenty-two in locations around the child's home.

4. For cases that involve strangers, see CGSCF, *People v. J.S.* (March 1886); CGSCF, *People v. G.S.* (June 1891); CGSCF, *People v. L.G.* (March 1891); DACCF 167450 (1926).

For cases that involved men the girls knew, see DACCF 36934 (1901) [boarder]; DACCF 35362 (1901) [employee of parents]; DACCF 57571 (1906) [ex-employee of parents]; DACCF 81821 (1911) [uncle]; DACCF 109904 (1916) [employee of parents]; DACCF 109212 (1916) [neighbor]; DACCF 139218 (1921) [neighbor]; DACCF 163380 (1926) [uncle]; DACCF 167639 (1926) [friend of family]; DACCF 167283 (1926) [friend of family].

5. CGSCF, *People v. P.C.* (September 1886); CGSCF, *People v. P.L.* (July 1891); DACCF 85141 (1911); DACCF 82997 (1911); DACCF 82082 (1911); DACCF 82728 (1911); DACCF 113049 (1916); DACCF 139570 (1921); DACCF 167450 (1926).

6. CGSCF, *People v. B.M.* (June 1886) [money]; CGSCF, *People v. J.M.* (February 1891) [money]; DACCF 37259 (1896) [wood]; DACCF 83699 (1911) [candy and a doll]; DACCF 111344 (1916) [shoeshine]; DACCF 112009 (1916) [nuts].

7. Only the abduction statute treated all girls younger than sixteen years in the same terms—it actually applied to "any unmarried female of previous chaste character, under the age of twenty-five years." See *Laws of New York, 1848*, chap. 105, 118. That law punished any person who abducted a girl for the purposes of prostitution, although courts ruled it applied only in circumstances involving persuasion, not coercion. A second statute, which punished anyone who coerced a female into prostitution or marriage, applied only to those "under the age of fourteen years." See 2 Rev. Stat. (1829), sec. 26, 553, cited in New York State Law Revision Commission, *Communication and Study Relating to Sexual Crimes*, 59. For further discussion of these laws, see chapter 4 below.

8. *Laws of New York, 1892*, chap. 325, 681. The label for the law comes from the Supplement to the *Philanthropist* 6, 3 (March 1891): 9–10. For analysis of this law, see New York State Law Revision Commission, *Communication and Study Relating to Sexual Crimes*, 89. New York was one of a group of states that at some point in the early twentieth century divided rape into two degrees and included consensual acts

with very young girls in the definition of first-degree rape. The Model Penal Code also included intercourse with a girl younger than ten years old in its definition of first-degree rape. See American Law Institute, *Model Penal Code: Tentative Drafts Nos. 1, 2, 3, and 4*, 88, 242, 250–52.

9. *People v. Harriden*, 1 Parker Cr. R., 344 (1852). New York's incest law stated, "When persons within the degrees of consanguinity, within which marriages are declared by law to be incestuous and void, intermarry or commit adultery or fornication with each other, each of them is punishable by imprisonment for not more than ten years" (The Penal Code of the State of New York, sec. 302, in *Laws of New York, 1881*, vol. 3, chap. 676, 73). There are four incest cases among the sixty-seven cases involving girls aged ten years or younger discussed in this chapter.

10. In this context, mental weakness referred to ignorance, not to mental deficiency or insanity, which were dealt with by other sections of the rape statute.

11. *Morning Journal* (New York), 22 June 1891; unidentified newspaper [the *Press?*], 22 June 1891 (both in DAS).

12. For other examples, see *New York Journal*, 10 December 1896; *New York Press*, 28 March 1901; *World* (New York), 29 March 1901; *Sun* (New York), 29 March 1901; *Sun*, 20 December 1901 (all in DAS).

13. *New York Journal*, 10 December 1896; *World*, 28 March 1901 (both in DAS).

14. *Morning Journal*, 22 June 1891 (DAS).

15. Five years before Bailey assaulted Jane Gardner, however, he was attacked by a crowd that had been attracted by the screams of a fourteen-year-old girl whom Bailey tried to drag into a building. See *World*, 20 February 1906 (DAS).

16. Zelizer, *Pricing the Priceless Child*, 22–23, 36–39.

17. A woman janitor, investigating a noise in the hallway, looked over the banister of the stairs to find a man, his trousers unbuttoned, holding a young girl, with her clothes pulled up, close to his body. The woman immediately screamed, grabbed at the man, and, when he broke free of her, pursued him out of the building (DACCF 113049 [1916]). For other examples, see DACCF 86003 (1911); DACCF 83699 (1911); DACCF 113049 (1916).

18. Transcript of Court of General Sessions Trial, 5–6, in CGSCF, *People v. F.V.* (May 1911). The brief is in DACCF 82728 (1911).

19. Arnold, "'The Life of a Citizen in the Hands of a Woman,'" 43–44.

20. Stansell, *City of Women*, 182–83.

21. N = 4 of 30.

22. N = 8 of 30.

23. Four examples in my sample: DACCF 7259 (1896); DACCF 109212 (1916); DACCF 111344 (1916); DACCF 138762 (1921).

24. For examples, see CGSCF, *People v. F.P.* (September 1886); DACCF 82728 (1911); DACCF 82082 (1911); DACCF 109904 (1916). The questioning of a mother in a case from 1901 suggests that prosecutors expected that New Yorkers would interpret bleeding in this way, that it was "common knowledge." See DACCF 36934 (1901).

25. DACCF 84774 (1911). For other examples, see CGSCF, *People v. C.P.* (September 1886); DACCF 139570 (1921).

26. Williams, "Rape in Children and Young Girls: Part One," 262. For examples,

see CGSCF, *People v. G.S.* (June 1891); CGSCF, *People v. P.L.* (July 1891); DACCF 35362 (1901); DACCF 112009 (1916).

27. During a trial in 1916, for example, a father testified about a previous occasion on which he had chosen not to report an assault after a doctor found his daughter's hymen still intact. See TTC, case 2232, roll 280 (1916).

28. Gibb, "Indecent Assaults upon Children," 656. Doctors' ability to identify other signs of rape on the bodies of young girls—inflammation of the vaginal entrance, swelling of the labia majora, bleeding—made little difference in the reporting of cases because parents felt confident about interpreting such signs themselves.

29. Wharton and Stillé, *A Treatise on Medical Jurisprudence*, 330. This was the most widely used medical jurisprudence text in nineteenth-century America. See also the testimony of Dr. Wycoff in TTC, case 3093, roll 370 (1921), 47–48.

30. For examples, see Clifton-Edgar and Johnston, "Rape," 684; Webster, *Legal Medicine and Toxicology*, 265. For further discussion of this issue, and additional examples, see Robertson, "Signs, Marks, and Private Parts."

31. Sacco, "Sanitized for Your Protection."

32. DACCF 109904 (1916).

33. CGSCF, *People v. C.P.* (September 1886).

34. DACCF 85723 (1911).

35. Ibid.

36. *The Third ARNYSPCC*, 29–30.

37. Transcript of Court of General Sessions Trial, 21, in CGSCF, *People v. F.V.* (May 1911).

38. Transcript of Court of General Sessions Trial, 3–4, in CGSCF, *People v. P.L.* (July 1891).

39. For discussions of the importance attached to the language used by children testifying in rape cases, see Walker, "Reports, Part One," 280, "Reports, Part Two," 329; Williams, "Rape in Children and Young Girls: Part One," 252, 256–57.

40. A girl's language was also studied as a guide to the truthfulness of her testimony. When ten-year-old Patricia Hay used "connection" (meaning "sexual intercourse") among a variety of other terms in her testimony in 1901, but could not say what it meant, the defense attorney asked in his summation, "Who put that word into that little girl's mouth? Did that little, ignorant ten-year-old child ever, of her own notion, out of her own mind, supply this word 'connection' as applicable to a case of this kind?" (TTC, case 250, roll 46, [1901], 131). Defense attorneys seized on a girl's use of language such as "sexual intercourse" or "connection" as evidence that she had been tutored or influenced, that, as the state appellate court put it in a decision in 1913, her testimony was, "to a considerable extent, the thoughts of others—thoughts developed after repeated conversations and much pressure" (*People v. Shaw*, 142 N.Y.S. 782, 158 App. Div. 147 [1913]). The defense attorney cross-examining Patricia Hay pointed the finger at the NYSPCC. Medical jurists blamed mothers. Two physicians employed by the NYSPCC, for example, claimed that mothers taught their daughters to lie in order to blackmail or gain revenge on men; or, after noticing a vaginal discharge, they would "storm, threaten and torment" them into accusing an innocent man. See Clifton-Edgar and Johnston, "Rape," 711.

41. *Sun*, 21 December 1891 (DAS).

42. *Philanthropist* 22, 7 (July 1907): 3. For a similar statement, see *The Fifth ARNYSPCC*, 38–39.

43. For an expression of that expectation, see *Morning Journal*, 22 June 1891 (DAS). I cannot be certain how far the language expected of children reflected the way they spoke outside the courtroom. However, it does not matter for my argument if the language children used in court was the language they actually used outside the court. What is important is whether a girl's language fitted the jurors' conception of childhood and children's language.

44. Williams, "Rape in Children and Young Girls: Part One," 252. For discussions of occasions on which girls had difficulty making clear what happened to them, see *Morning Journal*, 22 June 1891 (DAS); *The Thirty-eighth ARNYSPCC*, 27. I found only one instance in which a case broke down because of the vagueness of a child's language. See Transcript of Court of General Sessions Trial, 20–31, in CGSCF, *People v. F.V.* (May 1901).

45. TTC, case 2157 (1916), roll 273, 9–10, 102.

46. For example, see TTC, case 250 (1901), roll 46, 131; TTC, case 611 (1906), roll 98, 22. For other evidence of how such language was interpreted, see *People v. Shaw*, 142 N.Y.S. 782, 158 App. Div. 147 (1913); Woods and Kennedy, *Young Working Girls*, 89; Strong, "Ideas of the Early Sex Education Movement," 148; Battan, "'The Word Made Flesh,'" 223–26.

47. Addams, *The Spirit of Youth*, 46. For similar arguments by other middle-class reformers, see True, *The Neglected Girl*, 77, 87, 93; Woods and Kennedy, *Young Working Girls*, 42, 88–89.

48. Brewer, "Age of Reason?" 293–316. See also Wigmore, *A Treatise on the System of Evidence*, vol. 1, sec. 505–9, 638–41.

49. New York Code of Criminal Procedure, sec. 392. See also *People v. Baldwin*, 124 N.Y.S. 433, 139 App. Div. 404 (1910).

50. For an example of a five-year-old, see DACCF 82728 (1911). Only in two cases, involving a three-year-old and a one-year-old, did the girls not testify. See DACCF 36934 (1901); CGSCF, *People v. G.S.* (February 1891). For the seven-year-old who gave sworn testimony, see DACCF 167450 (1926).

51. *Laws of New York, 1886*, chap. 663, 953.

52. *Noonan v. The State*, 55 Wis. 260 (1882). See also *People v. Schultz*, 260 Ill. 40 (1913); *People v. O'Connor*, 295 Ill. 203 (1920); *People v. Ardelean*, 368 Ill. 278 (1938).

53. For a trial in which two doctors tried to offer different opinions, see Transcript of Court of General Sessions trial, CGSCF, *People v. V.O.* (May 1886).

54. See, for example, Dr. Samuel Brown's certificate in DACCF 83905 (1911). NYSPCC doctors also routinely noted whether the penetration was recent. NYSPCC doctors' development of a formula that accommodated legal rules reflected their experience and specialization. By the 1890s, the variety of doctors who conducted examinations for the NYSPCC in 1886 had dwindled to a small group of two or three, who performed large numbers of examinations over the course of the subsequent decades. William Travis Gibb, for example, examined more than 2,500 girls in the twenty-five years up to 1916.

55. For examples, see TTC, case 2239, roll 281 (1916), 34–35; TTC, case 74, roll 19 (1896); TTC, case 268, roll 49 (1901).

56. For further discussion of medical evidence in rape cases, see Robertson, "Signs, Marks, and Private Parts."

57. N = 23 of 43. This total excludes seven cases for which I do not have this information.

58. For decisions regarding evidence of opportunity, see *People v. Plath*, 100 N.Y. 590 (1885); *People v. Cole*, 134 App. Div. 759 (1909); *People v. Brehm*, 218 N.Y.S. 469, 218 App. Div. 266 (1926); and the discussion in New York State Law Revision Commission, *Communication and Study Relating to Sexual Crimes*, 77.

59. *People v. Terwilliger*, 74 Hun 316, 26 N.Y.S. 674 (1893). Decisions relating to the less rigorous corroboration requirement applied to the testimony of accomplices would have given credibility to the decision to accept evidence of opportunity as corroborative.

60. *People v. Kingsley* 166 App. Div. 322, N.Y. Supp. 980 (1915).

61. *People v. Shaw*, 158 App. Div. 146, 142 N.Y.S. 782 (1913). See also *People v. Brehm*, 218 N.Y.S. 468, 218 App. Div. 266 (1926).

62. *The Thirty-eighth ARNYSPCC*, 10–11. The Society's *Annual Report* does include one reference to another response to a lack of corroborative evidence—the prosecution of men for the lesser offenses of attempted rape and misdemeanor assault, to which the requirement did not apply. See *The Twenty-sixth ARNYSPCC*, 35–36. Although that practice would become relatively common in the second half of the twentieth century, in all eight attempted rape cases in my sample a completed assault did not take place.

63. For the case in which prosecutors had no corroboration of the girl's identification, see CGSCF, *People v. J.M.* (July 1891). The other three defendants, one of whom was Walter Bailey, faced evidence of venereal disease. See CGSCF, *People v. C.L.* (September 1891); DACCF 81821 (1911); DACCF 85723 (1911).

64. N = 46. In two cases, prosecutors had no corroboration of the girl's identification; see CGSCF, *People v. H.W.* (March 1886); DACCF 11230 (1896). In the third case, a medical examination showed that the defendant did not have the venereal disease that afflicted the girls; see DACCF 111344 (1916). The total excludes two additional cases where there are no details of the grounds for discharge (DACCF 36895 [1901] and DACCF 56736 [1906]), a case in which a rape indictment was discharged because the defendant pled guilty to sodomy under another indictment (DACCF 84811 [1911]), and a case where the defendant skipped bail (DACCF 139218 [1921]). In cases involving adult women, ADAs prosecuted 77 percent of the men indicted (N = 31 of 40). That total excludes five cases in which the district attorney discharged the defendant because the woman did not appear.

65. *People v. Page*, 162 N.Y. 277 (1900).

66. The only corroborative evidence presented in that case was evidence of opportunity; see DACCF 137270 (1921). It is possible that the judge acted as he did because this was a case of incest, but the handling of the other three incest cases in my sample do not reveal a clear pattern. There are no details of the one incest case that produced a conviction, in the form of a plea of guilty to second-degree rape (DACCF

139953 [1921]). In both of the remaining cases, the prosecution had no evidence to corroborate the girl's identification of her assailant. In one, the ADA discharged the defendant, who was the victim's brother (DACCF 11230 [1896]). In the other, the case went to trial, and the jury acquitted the defendant, the girl's father (CGSCF, *People v. F.P.* (September [1886]).

67. *People v. Cullen*, 5 N.Y. Supp. 887 (1889).

68. See CGSCF, *People v. F.P.* (September 1886); DACCF 85141 (1911); DACCF 112009 (1916); DACCF 111970 (1916).

69. For the convictions, see CGSCF, *People v. C.P.* (September 1886); CGSCF, *People v. P.L.* (July 1891). In DACCF 7796 (1896), the jury disagreed, and the DA discharged the defendant. For the acquittals, see CGSCF, *People v. J.C.* (August 1891); DACCF 37259 (1896).

70. DACCF 36934 (1901); DACCF 82082 (1911). Race is an additional element in the later case, as I discuss below. Venereal disease is also the key evidence in one conviction for attempted rape; see DACCF 35362 (1901).

71. Starr, *The Social Transformation of American Medicine*, 4–5; see also 17–21, 134–44. For a more detailed discussion of this point, see Robertson, "Signs, Marks, and Private Parts."

72. In eleven of the fourteen cases that relied on evidence that a girl suffered from venereal disease to provide corroboration, the defendant did not submit to an examination. This view of venereal disease could also undermine prosecutions. In a case in 1916, when the defendant did submit to a medical examination, it showed that he did not suffer from the venereal disease afflicting his alleged victims. Despite the testimony of several girls who witnessed his acts with other girls, the DA discharged him. See DACCF 111344 (1916).

73. CGSCF, *People v. L.G.* (March 1891).

74. *The Thirty-seventh ARNYSPCC*, 26. The case referred to is DACCF 82082 (1911).

75. See table 4 in the appendix.

76. In six out of nine cases concerning an assault on a young girl, the jury convicted the defendant of rape, compared to two of five cases involving an adult victim.

77. N = 5 of 14.

Chapter Three

1. DACCF 57807 (1906).

2. The adjectives and phrases are from American appellate court decisions, as cited in Murphy, "Defining the Crime against Nature," 52–55. For New York's law, see The Penal Code of the State of New York, title X, chap. V, sec. 303, in *Laws of New York, 1881*, chap. 676, 74–75.

3. DACCF 36478 (1901). All of the small group of cases of anal acts with girls also involved intercourse or attempted intercourse. See CGSCF, *People v. F.S.* (May 1891); DACCF 82750 (1911); DACCF 113129 (1916).

4. See, for example, CGSCF, *People v. C.S.* (May 1891); DACCF 84154 (1911).

5. Throughout the period of this study, most sodomy cases involved children under sixteen years of age and were instigated by the NYSPCC. George Chauncey's

research on sodomy prosecutions confirms this pattern. He found that consensual same-sex behavior by adult men was prosecuted as disorderly conduct rather than sodomy. See Chauncey, *Gay New York*, 140–41, 147, 171–73, 407–8.

6. For New York's law, see The Penal Code of the State of New York, title X, chap. V, sec. 303, in *Laws of New York, 1881*, chap. 676, 74–75.

7. The annual reports of the New York Police Department reveal that a small number of women were arrested for sodomy in this period; see Eskridge, "*Hardwick* and Historiography," 655. The failure of any of these women to appear in my sample suggests that few, if any, of the arrests led to prosecutions, an outcome that indicates that they did not involve acts with children. There was at least one woman indicted for sodomy in this period, the African American author Zora Neale Hurston, who was accused by two boys of performing fellatio on them in 1948. The boys later recanted, and the DA dismissed the indictment against Hurston. See Boyd, *Wrapped in Rainbows*, 387–401. Thanks to Shane White for bringing this case to my attention.

8. N = 52 of 70. See tables 4 and 5 in the appendix.

9. Gold, *Jews without Money*, 58–60.

10. See, for example, DACCF 164262 (1926).

11. Trial Brief, CGSCF, *People v. J.C.* (December 1891). For another example, see DACCF 84767 (1911).

12. On seeing three boys with a man who appeared to be "suspicious and a degenerate," two Park police officers followed the group to a cave in Central Park. When they went inside, one officer followed, posing as a man who had lost a dog, and then waited outside to arrest the man as he exited the cave; see DACCF 33633 (1901). For another example, see DACCF 58063 (1906). I found probation records for two further cases: PDCF 2795 (1926) and PDCF 4505 (1926).

13. CGSCF, *People v. T.K.* (March 1891); CGSCF, *People v. D.S.* (February 1891); DACCF 81251 (1911).

14. See tables 4 and 5 in the appendix.

15. Trial Brief, DACCF 85614 (1911). The only other similar case, in which a mother saw semen on a daughter's face, is DACCF 109415 (1916).

16. Trial Brief, DACCF 112678 (1916).

17. One mother did show considerable uncertainty about what had happened to her nine-year-old son, even after hearing what he had told a ten-year-old playmate. "I remember Sunday, Dec. 3, 1916, when my little boy came home, and could hardly walk, and I didn't know what was the matter with him. Monday night [the mother of my son's friend] came to my house and told me what had happened to the boy. I went right away to the drug store and told the man there what had happened to the boy. While there Dr. Henry Sherman came in, and he went to my house with me and examined the child, and told me right away what had happened to him" (Trial Brief, DACCF 113274 [1916]).

18. Trial Brief, DACCF 36318 (1901). Gender also had a role in the officer's willingness to examine the boy, whereas attitudes toward the female body would likely have prevented any male stranger other than a physician from examining a girl.

19. For example, see *The Twenty-second ARNYSPCC*, 21; *The Twenty-seventh ARNYSPCC*, 46. The only sodomy case from my sample involving a girl that ap-

pears in the *Annual Report* is labeled "a most heinous crime" and described in terms that do not distinguish it from other sexual assaults on girls. See *The Thirty-seventh ARNYSPCC*, 29–30.

20. For a discussion of the reticence of the press about discussing boys as victims of sexual violence in the 1920s, see Fass, "Making and Remaking an Event." For an exception, a scandal in Portland in 1912 that involved boys as well as adult members of the city's gay culture, see Gustav-Wrathall, *Take the Young Stranger by the Hand*, 161–65; Boag, "Sex and Politics in Progressive-Era Portland and Eugene."

21. The same discourse of gender difference was at work within the discourse of juvenile delinquency, with female delinquency conceived largely in terms of sexual behavior and male delinquency in terms of petty crime and public disorder. See, for example, Odem, *Delinquent Daughters.*

22. This is also true of Mike Gold's autobiography, which opens with an account of the prostitutes in his Lower East Side neighborhood and features them prominently. See Gold, *Jews without Money*, esp. 13–19, 25–35. The best discussion of reformers' treatment of the sexual dangers faced by boys is DiGirolamo, "Crying the News," 349–88.

23. *The Tenth ARNYSPCC*, 46; *The Seventeenth ARNYSPCC*, 23; *The Twentieth ARNYSPCC*, 43; *The Twenty-seventh ARNYSPCC*, 47; *The Thirty-first ARNYSPCC*, 39; *The Thirty-second ARNYSPCC*, 35, 50; *The Thirty-fourth ARNYSPCC*, 30; *The Thirty-fifth ARNYSPCC*, 25; *The Thirty-seventh ARNYSPCC*, 30. On occasion, the superintendent's descriptions read like cryptic crossword clues. In the first account of a sodomy case included in the *Annual Report*, he referred to the offender as having been arrested "while in the commission of a heinous crime, the penalty for which is provided in Section 303 of the Penal Code" (*The Tenth ARNYSPCC*, 46).

24. Cited in DiGirolamo, "Crying the News," 373.

25. Russell Sage Foundation, *Boyhood and Lawlessness*, 155.

26. DACCF 57807 (1906).

27. Other officers took a balder approach to the force employed by a man, making liberal use of the adverb "forcibly" in their summaries. See CGSCF, *People v. T.K.* (March 1891); CGSCF, *People v. G.W.* (indicted May 1891); DACCF 7269 (1896); DACCF 10988 (1896); DACCF 85614 (1911); DACCF 137778 (1921).

28. I have not included Wisconsin in this group. A law enacted in 1897 did punish masturbation involving boys and girls, but as part of the definition of sodomy rather than as a distinct offense (*Laws of Wisconsin, 1897*, chap. 198, 359–60). As such, it is more properly considered part of the move by turn-of-the-century legislatures and courts to specify what acts constituted the crime against nature, discussed below, rather than an age-based definition of sexual violence. Wisconsin did define acts other than intercourse with children as a crime, in 1953, as part of the wave of legislative action discussed in part 3 of this book.

29. Oppenheimer and Eckman, *Laws Relating to Sex Offenses against Children*, 21 [Arizona, enacted 1913], 23 [California], 33 [Illinois, enacted 1907], 35 [Iowa, enacted 1907], 47 [Montana, enacted 1913]. The original dates of enactment were checked using William Eskridge's research as a starting point; see Eskridge, *Gaylaw*, appendix A3, 342–51 (which mistakenly records Arizona as passing its law in 1939). An earlier

Illinois statute, enacted in 1905, was struck down by the Illinois Supreme Court in 1906, on the grounds that its title was unconstitutionally vague (*Milne v. The People*, 224 Ill. 125 [1906]). The California statute was also adopted in Puerto Rico in 1911 (Oppenheimer and Eckman, *Laws Relating to Sex Offenses against Children*, 61).

30. Oppenheimer and Eckman, *Laws Relating to Sex Offenses against Children*, 25 [Colorado, enacted 1905], 38 [Louisiana, enacted 1912], 39 [Maine, enacted 1913]. For dates of enactment, see Eskridge, *Gaylaw*, 342–51.

31. See *Milne v. The People*, 224 Ill. 125 (1906); *State v. Comeaux*, 131 La. 930 (1913). For a decision rejecting a claim that Colorado's law was too vague, see *Dekelt v. The People*, 44 Colo. 525 (1908).

32. For the crime against nature statute, see The Penal Code of the State of New York, title X, chap. V, sec. 303, in *Laws of New York, 1881*, chap. 676, 74–75. For judicial interpretation of that law, see *Lambertson v. The People*, 5 Parker's C.R. 200 (1861). For the amendments, see *Laws of New York, 1886*, chap. 31, 41; *Laws of New York, 1892*, chap. 325, 682. Both statutes are connected to the NYSPCC by their adoption as part of packages of laws dealing with children, including, in the case of the 1886 law, amendments to the abduction law discussed in the next chapter and, in the case of the 1892 law, the division of rape into two degrees discussed in the previous chapter.

33. Pennsylvania was the first state to specify the acts encompassed by the crime against nature, including oral acts, in legislation in 1879. Most of the states where change came through judicial decision were in the South. See Eskridge, "*Hardwick* and Historiography," 655–59; Eskridge, *Gaylaw*, 24–26, 158–59; Murphy, "Defining the Crime against Nature," 52–62.

34. Here the legislature was enacting a position articulated by the higher courts of a number of states in the course of the nineteenth century. See Eskridge, "*Hardwick* and Historiography," 647–48.

35. *People v. Deschessere*, 74 N.Y.S. 761 (1902). See also the copy of the decision in CGSCF, *People v. Deschessere* (April 1901).

36. DACCF 113366 (1916).

37. For a discussion of turn-of-the-century perceptions of boys, see Rotundo, *American Manhood*, 31–55.

38. Trial Brief, CGSCF, *People v. F.S.* (May 1891). For other examples, see CGSCF, *People v. C.S.* (May 1891); DACCF 82750 (1911).

39. Trial Brief, DACCF 167251 (1926). For another example, see DACCF 83950 (1911).

40. DACCF 33633 (1901); DACCF 57807 (1906); DACCF 164262 (1926).

41. DACCF 163576 (1926).

42. Chauncey, *Gay New York*, 66. No boys referred to as effeminate appear in my sample of cases.

43. DACCF 163576 (1926). For other examples, see DACCF 33633 (1901); DACCF 53835 (1906); DACCF 164262 (1926).

44. The cases dismissed by the grand jury are DACCF 58063 (1906); DACCF 53709 (1906); DACCF 54299 (1906); DACCF 84159 (1911); DACCF 113172 (1916).

45. For cases in which physicians did use the phrase "penetration by a blunt object," see CGSCF, *People v. T.K.* (March 1891); DACCF 82750 (1906).

46. DACCF 54195 (1906).

47. For examples, see DACCF 11267 (1916); DACCF 137778 (1921); DACCF 140163 (1921). In earlier years in my sample, Gibb on two occasions presented his evidence in the form used by Brown. See DACCF 34104 (1901); DACCF 36478 (1901).

48. For examples, see Abbe, *Wharton and Stillé's Medical Jurisprudence*, 3:166–67; Webster, *Legal Medicine and Toxicology*, 273–74. Charles Chaddock did comment on the equivocal nature of some signs of sodomy, but not those that NYSPCC doctors described in their evidence. See Chaddock, "Unnatural Sexual Offenses," 1050–51.

49. N = 4 of 18 compared to N = 26 of 48 (49 percent).

50. For discussions of this problem, see *The Twenty-seventh ARNYSPCC*, 47; *The Thirty-second ARNYSPCC*, 35.

51. In the case of girls, N = 4 of 17. In the case of boys, N = 3 of 48.

52. DACCF 83950 (1911); DACCF 82750 (1911).

53. The cases that produced convictions were DACCF 8039 (1896), DACCF 8911 (1896), and DACCF 11669 (1896). The one acquittal before 1902 came in DACCF 34104 (1901). The two later acquittals came in DACCF 82750 (1911); DACCF 113274 (1916).

54. DACCF 132956 (1921); DACCF 167458 (1926).

55. Of the nine men convicted in sodomy prosecutions, eight were sentenced to at least five years in prison. Of the 193 men convicted in rape prosecutions, 46 percent received suspended sentences or terms of no more than one year in prison. Only 14 percent received a prison term of at least five years.

56. For older boys, N = 7 of 15. For younger boys, N = 4 of 19.

Chapter Four

1. NYSPCC Case File 25324 (1886).

2. Of the two rape prosecutions, one involved an invalid, deaf-mute girl, whose disability overshadowed her age and brought her within the rape law; see CGSCF, *People v. T.M.* (April 1886). The other, revealingly, was a mistake. Both the arraignment and the indictment took place without the involvement of the NYSPCC. When the Society did become involved, Gerry reported that the case was not one where he would have brought a charge of rape, given the lack of sufficient evidence and a victim whose truthfulness could not be relied on; see CGSCF, *People v. J.F.* (May 1886).

3. CGSCF, *People v. J.S.* (April 1886).

4. CGSCF, *People v. E.H. and S.C.* (August 1886); CGSCF, *People v. J.M.* (June 1886); CGSCF, *People v. F.S.* (August 1886); CGSCF, *People v. F.H.* (May 1886).

5. Brumberg, "Zenanas and Girless Villages," 365–66; Brumberg, "'Ruined' Girls," 249–50.

6. *The Fifteenth ARNYSPCC*, 58–59. For similar comments by the superintendent regarding brothels, see *New York Herald*, 6 September 1886 (DAS).

7. *The Ninth ARNYSPCC*, 9–10; *The Sixteenth ARNYSPCC*, 44–45; *The Nineteenth ARNYSPCC*, 8; *New York Herald*, 6 September 1886 (DAS).

8. CGSCF, *People v. J.D.* (September 1886). For another example, see CGSCF, *People v. A.T.* (November 1886).

9. *NYT,* 27 August 1886 (DAS).

10. *Morning Journal* (New York), 27 August 1886 (DAS).

11. *NYT,* 27 August 1886 (DAS); *Morning Journal,* 27 August 1886 (DAS). For other reports of this case, see *Sun,* 27 August 1886; *Morning Journal,* 28 August 1886; *NYT,* 28 August 1886 (all in DAS). For reports of other cases involving the surveillance of brothels and assignation houses, see *Sun,* 22 October 1886; *Morning Journal,* 13 November 1886; *Sun,* 13 November 1886 (all in DAS).

12. CGSCF, *People v. F.K.* (September 1886).

13. Affidavit, 4 September 1886, 1–2, ibid.

14. 2 Rev. Stat. (1829), sec. 26, 553, cited in New York State Law Revision Commission, *Communication and Study Relating to Sexual Crimes,* 59.

15. Ibid., citing *People v. Parshall,* 6 Parker Cr. Rep. 129 (1864).

16. Ibid., 60, citing *Carpenter v. People,* 8 Barb. 603 (1850).

17. For the 1848 law, see *Laws of New York, 1848,* chap. 105, 118. This law had been adopted at the same time as New York's celebrated seduction law, and it included a chaste character provision, a corroboration requirement, and a two-year time frame in which charges could be brought, which were all features of the seduction statute.

18. The Penal Code of the State of New York, title X, chap. V, sec. 282, in *Laws of New York, 1881,* chap. 676, 68–69. The Law Revision Commission could find no explanation for the increased age; see New York State Law Revision Commission, *Communication and Study Relating to Sexual Crimes,* 62 n. 187. A study of law enforcement by the Committee of Fourteen, New York City's leading anti-prostitution organization, attributed the increased age to the efforts of the NYSPCC; see Committee of Fourteen, *The Social Evil in New York City,* 12. The amended law also had an increased penalty of up to five years in prison.

19. The revised statute provided that a person who "1. Takes a female under the age of sixteen years for the purpose of prostitution or sexual intercourse, or without the consent of her father, mother, guardian or other person having legal charge of her person, for the purpose of marriage, or . . . 4. Being parent, guardian or other person having legal charge of the person of a female under the age of sixteen years, consents to her taking or detaining by any person for the purpose of prostitution or sexual intercourse; is guilty of abduction" (*Laws of New York, 1884,* chap. 46, 44).

20. *People v. Plath,* 100 N.Y. 596 (1885).

21. *Laws of New York, 1886,* chap. 31, 39.

22. New York State Law Revision Commission, *Communication and Study Relating to Sexual Crimes,* 64; *People v. Stott,* N.Y. Crim. Rep. 308 (1886). For press reports identifying Gerry as the law's author, see *New York Herald,* 19 January 1886, 7; *NYT,* 21 January 1886, 4; *Star* (New York), 20 May 1886; *World* (New York), 22 May 1886 (all in DAS).

23. *Sun* (New York), 6 September 1886; *Morning Journal* (New York), 6 September 1886 (both in DAS).

24. *Morning Journal,* 16 July 1886 (DAS). For another example, see *Morning Journal,* 22 May 1886 (DAS).

25. The transcripts contained in abduction case files are those of the police court hearing, not of the trial, and, with one exception, include only the defense attorney's

cross-examination, not the girl's testimony. What she said appears to have been recorded only as an affidavit. As a result, the case files provide no evidence of how ADAs went about presenting a girl's testimony.

26. Transcript of Hearing in Fifth District Police Court, 7 September 1886, 44–45, in CGSCF, *People v. F.K.* (September 1886).

27. Ibid., 39.

28. For other examples of the language understood by girls in abduction cases, see Transcript of Hearing in Second District Police Court, [?] June 1886, 19, in CGSCF, *People v. J.M.* (June 1886); Transcript of Hearing in Second District Police Court, 17 November 1886, 1–3, 5, in CGSCF, *People v. A.T.* (November 1886); Transcript of Court of General Sessions Trial, 19 May 1886, 6, in CGSCF, *People v. F.H.* (May 1886); Transcript of Police Court Hearing, 6 July 1886, 3, 5, 15, in CGSCF, *People v. E.H. and S.C.* (August 1886).

29. *Star*, 9 September 1886; *Morning Journal*, 9 November 1886 (both in DAS).

30. *Sun*, 6 September 1886; *World*, 8 September 1886 (both in DAS).

31. *Morning Journal*, 6 September 1886 (DAS).

32. Not surprisingly, his statement reduced Ruth to tears, and she had to be excused from the witness stand. Neither this offer nor Ruth's subsequently breaking into tears, and being excused, is recorded in the transcript. The report in the *Morning Journal* (8 September 1886) mentions the superintendent's offer and Ruth's tears; the *Sun*'s report mentions only Ruth's breaking into tears (8 September 1886) (both in DAS).

33. Transcript of Hearing in Fifth District Police Court, 37–39, 41, 60–62, in CGSCF, *People v. F.K.* (September 1886). For other examples of attorneys taking this approach, see CGSCF, *People v. E.H. and S.C.* (August 1886); CGSCF, *People v. J.M.* (June 1886).

34. Transcript of Hearing in Fifth District Police Court, 90–96, in CGSCF, *People v. F.K.* (September 1886). For another example of vague testimony about age, see *People v. Marks* 146 App. Div. 11 (1911). In another case in 1886, involving a French girl, her birth certificate and the family Bible had been lost, but her father was able to produce a passport. See CGSCF, *People v. J.M.* (June 1886).

35. The justices did not rule on that issue, but held that it was an error to admit the Bible without establishing that the author of the entry, the girl's father, could not be found to testify to her age. He had deserted her five years earlier, immediately after her mother's death, leaving her to live with an aunt and uncle. See "Report," 1, in CGSCF, *People v. F.S.* (indicted August 1886); *People v. Sheppard*, 44 Hun 565 (1887).

36. See *People v. Lammes* 203 N.Y.S. 740 (1924).

37. *Laws of New York, 1884*, chap. 46, 44 (amending sec. 19 of the penal code).

38. *People v. Justices of Special Sessions*, 10 Hun 226 (1877).

39. N = 5 of 14. Five of the remaining nine girls were fourteen years of age. In 1891, fifteen-year-old girls made up more than half of the complainants in abduction cases (N = 7 of 13).

40. *People v. Lammes* 203 N.Y.S. 740 (1924) (J. Davis dissenting). The girl in that case was only sixteen days short of being of legal age when the act was perpetrated, and she was fourteen days past her birthday when the trial began.

41. Court of General Sessions Trial Transcript, 21–24, in CGSCF, *People v. A.F.* (July 1901).

42. "Report," 2, in CGSCF, *People v. F.S.* (indicted August 1886); *People v. Sheppard*, 44 Hun 565 (1886); *The Twentieth ARNYSPCC*, 43–44. For another appeal involving similar charges against the NYSPCC, see *People v. Ragone*, 67 N.Y.S. 24 (1900). On clothing, see Paoletti, "Clothing and Gender in America."

43. "Report," 2–3, in CGSCF, *People v. F.S.* (indicted August 1886).

44. *Morning Journal*, 27 October 1886 (DAS).

45. The Society claimed it agreed to this outcome in order to avoid a trial, which would "bring out evidence of a revolting nature, tending to injure the character of girls of respectable parentage, and ought to be averted if possible" (*Sun*, 6 November 1886 [DAS]). See also *Morning Journal*, 6 November 1886 (DAS), for criticism of the light sentence. A sentence to the reformatory lasted a minimum of one year, after which the prisoner could be released whenever the authorities considered him reformed or when he had served the maximum sentence for the offense for which he had been convicted. The *Morning Journal* noted that it took very good behavior to be released in less than two years. Fletcher was still in the reformatory in October 1887, when he wrote to Gerry that he now saw he was wrong, expressed his admiration of the Society's work, offered to help apprehend the companions who had led him astray, and asked that the past be forgotten; see NYSPCC Case File 25324 (1886). The case record in the NYSPCC file also suggests that, its public comments notwithstanding, the Society had not been able to convince any of the other girls involved with Fletcher to bring charges against him.

46. There was just one sodomy prosecution in 1886, so no meaningful comparison can be made with that offense. On the surface, the conviction rate for abduction prosecutions appears marginally lower, 50 percent (N = 14) as compared to 55 percent (N = 9), but that gap is produced by circumstances not replicated in child rape and sodomy prosecutions. DADAs discharged four of the fourteen defendants, a rate as high as in rape cases involving adult women and four times that in child rape cases and sodomy cases involving boys. One man had his indictment dismissed because he had married the complainant, a resolution not available in child rape or sodomy cases involving boys. Another who was discharged had not been accused of having intercourse with a girl; he was alleged to have received and harbored her while she worked as a prostitute, a behavior that did not fall within the scope of the rape or sodomy statutes. And George Baker was discharged after a court ruled that sufficient evidence of Lizzie Silver's age had not been provided, evidence not required for child rape or sodomy convictions. If those three cases are put to one side, the conviction rate for abduction is higher than that for child rape, 64 percent (N = 7 of 11) compared to 55 percent.

47. See CGSCF, *People v. J.M.* (June 1886); CGSCF, *People v. J.D.* (September 1886); CGSCF, *People v. F.D.* (November 1886); CGSCF, *People v. M.M.* (September 1886). It may be that the corroboration requirement loomed larger in the outcome of abduction cases than it did in rape prosecutions. Both grand juries and DADAs appear to have paid more attention to evidentiary requirements in abduction cases than they did in rape and sodomy prosecutions. Only two cases in my sample lacked corrobora-

tive evidence, and in both cases the DADA discharged the defendant. In less often disregarding the requirement when faced with men charged with abduction, they revealed less concern for older girls than for their younger sisters.

48. N = 13 of 33.

49. *Morning Journal*, 22 May 1886; *Sun*, 5 June 1886 (DAS).

50. Editorial Notes, *Arena*, February 1891, 383.

51. Marks, "The Age of Consent."

52. Pivar, *Purity Crusade.*

53. Adam Powell, "Editorial," *Philanthropist* 1, 1 (January 1886): 4–5.

54. For other writings by purity reformers that linked the age of consent to rape, see Marks, "The Age of Consent," 4; and the comments of WCTU president Frances Willard in the *Philanthropist* 2, 2 (February 1887), 3.

55. Blackwell, "Age of Consent Legislation," 1.

56. For another example of purity reformers linking the age of consent to the age of majority, see *Philanthropist* 1, 3 (March 1886): 8.

57. Ibid.

58. "Report of the WCTU State Superintendent of Legislation and Petition [Nebraska]," in Gardener, "A Battle for Sound Morality, Part II," 21, 27. For the arguments of opponents of the age of consent campaigns, see also Gardener, "A Battle for Sound Morality, Part III"; "The Age of Consent," *Union Signal*, 10 June 1886, 2; the discussions in Larson, "'Even a Worm Will Turn at Last,'" 36, 53–55, 58–59, 61; Dunlap, "The Reform of Rape Law and the Problem of White Men," 359–60.

59. For the five statutes, see Oppenheimer and Eckman, *Laws Relating to Sex Offenses Against Children*, 29 [Florida], 34 [Indiana], 37 [Kentucky], 42 [Michigan], 68 [Washington]. Laws to protect boys involved in acts of sexual intercourse that explicitly relied on a framework of prostitution rather than of sexual violence, and hence treated them in terms different from those employed in the case of girls, were also enacted by another small group of states. Under a Colorado law, for example, a female of any age who had sexual intercourse with a male under eighteen years of age and of "good moral character" was guilty of rape in the third degree when the act was "had at [her] solicitation, inducement, importuning or connivance," or when, at the time of the offense, she was "a free, common, public or clandestine prostitute" (ibid., 24). Delaware and Nebraska had similar laws; ibid., 26–27, 48. Massachusetts and Oregon had laws that, although less detailed, also employed the language of "enticing" rather than of sexual assault; ibid., 41, 58–59.

60. "The Amended Penal Code—First Successful Case of Prosecution," *Philanthropist* 3, 2 (February 1888): 3.

61. Editorial, *Philanthropist* 6, 3 (March 1891): 4.

62. Ibid.; "Memorial," Supplement to the *Philanthropist* 6, 3 (March 1891): 9–10.

63. "Memorial." The amendments also removed a conflict in the law by bringing the penalty for abduction into line with that for second-degree rape.

64. "Legal Protection for Girlhood," *Philanthropist* 10, 6 (June 1895): 4; Committee of Fourteen, *The Social Evil in New York City*, 121; Gardener, "A Battle for Sound Morality, Part I," 357–60.

65. Editorial, *Philanthropist* 7, 9 (September 1892): 4.

66. "Legal Protection for Girlhood," *Philanthropist* 11, 2 (February 1896): 10; "Letter from Hon. Elbridge T. Gerry," *Philanthropist* 10, 6 (June 1895): 5. See also Committee of Fourteen, *The Social Evil in New York City*, 123–25.

67. "Age of Consent Discussion," *Vigilance* (May 1913): 20–22.

Chapter Five

1. DACCF 84167 (1911).

2. A charge of abduction had a similar scope, but it was only after the age of consent was raised that it had the same weight as a threat. Until then, it carried a relatively light punishment.

3. I have analyzed statutory rape prosecutions in these terms in Robertson, "Making Right a Girl's Ruin." Here I take a different approach to this material, giving more attention to the implications of working-class New Yorkers' use of the law for understandings of childhood and sexual violence.

4. DACCF 188405 (1931).

5. In the second half of the nineteenth century, other states raised the minimum age from the common law marks of twelve years for girls and fourteen years for boys. An effort to set the ages in New York at fourteen and seventeen in 1830 was reconsidered and repealed. See Grossberg, *Governing the Hearth*, 107. The state legislature increased the ages for marriage without parental consent to sixteen and eighteen years in 1887 (*Laws of New York, 1887*, chap. 24, 5) and to eighteen and twenty-one in 1896 (*Laws of New York, 1896*, chap. 272, 216).

6. For accounts that highlight how judges were at odds with reformers and teenage girls, see Alexander, *The Girl Problem*; Odem, *Delinquent Daughters*; Ullman, *Sex Seen*, 28–44.

7. Hartog, *Man and Wife in America*, 4.

8. N = 90 of 300. See table 6 in the appendix. This total includes only those cases where the file contains sufficient material to reveal such efforts. It likely underrepresents how often efforts to arrange marriage or financial settlements figured in the response to premarital sexuality. What became part of the legal record were those instances in which confrontation and negotiation did not make right a girl's ruin before somebody charged the man with rape or before law enforcement officials discovered the situation. The absence of a section in which to note extralegal outcomes on the forms used in the case files also meant that the record of extralegal efforts depended on the practices of clerks, particularly in cases that did not go far enough in the legal process to generate witness statements and trial records. This incidence is greater than that found in Alameda County, California, the only other locale of which a comparable analysis has been conducted, but the disparity appears to be largely a product of the sources, which are far richer for New York. Mary Odem found a small number of instances in which families in Alameda County tried to use a charge of rape to prompt men to agree to such marriages, but those families' attempts left too few traces in the court records to command more than passing attention in her analysis. The court records that she studied encompassed only those cases prosecuted in the criminal court and not those resolved earlier in the legal process, as were many

of those that ended in marriage (Odem, *Delinquent Daughters*, 51–52, 191–92). Efforts to force marriage on men who had sexual intercourse with single women or made them pregnant are also largely absent from records of such institutions as the reformatories studied by Ruth Alexander and the maternity homes investigated by Regina Kunzel, because only girls who could not pursue informal means—those rejected by their families or unable to find the men who had impregnated them—were drawn to institutions. See Alexander, *The Girl Problem*; Kunzel, *Fallen Women, Problem Girls*, 67–68.

9. True, *The Neglected Girl*, 19. For the concept of "ruin," see Towne, "Young Girl Marriages in Criminal and Juvenile Courts," 292; Brumberg, "'Ruined' Girls," 250; D'Emilio and Freedman, *Intimate Matters*, 77.

10. For evidence of the practices of cohabitation and serial monogamy in African American communities, see Du Bois, *The Philadelphia Negro*, 67, 72, 166, 192–93; Frazier, *The Negro Family in the United States*, 89–101, 209–24, 256–67, 271–76; Gutman, *The Black Family in Slavery and Freedom*, 61–75, 449; Johnson, *Shadow of the Plantation*, 49, 67. For evidence that reveals more concern with virginity, respectability, and marriage among some working-class African Americans, see Du Bois, *The Philadelphia Negro*, 193–94; Davis and Dollard, *Children of Bondage*, 51, 55; Johnson, *Growing Up in the Black Belt*, 224–29, 232, 239–41; and the various studies discussed in Franklin, *Ensuring Inequality*, 132–36.

11. Blackwell, "Age of Consent Legislation," 2. In her article, Blackwell explained the impossibility of this approach to critics who questioned why girls, shielded as they were by "good home environments," needed the additional protection of the age of consent.

12. Odem, *Delinquent Daughters*, 21–23; Kessler-Harris, *Out to Work*, 122; Addams, *The Spirit of Youth*, 5.

13. Josephine Roche, "The Italian Girl," in True, *The Neglected Girl*, 111–12. For other discussions of Italian girls escaping from parental surveillance, see Ware, *Greenwich Village*, 182–83, 186–87; Peiss, *Cheap Amusements*, 69–70. For a contrary argument that Italian girls lacked the opportunities and time to escape strict supervision, see M. Cohen, *From Workshop to Office*, 59–64.

14. True, *The Neglected Girl*, 79.

15. See, for example, Towne, "Young Girl Marriages in Criminal and Juvenile Courts," 290–91.

16. True, *The Neglected Girl*, 73–74.

17. Josephine Roche, "The Italian Girl," ibid., 114–15.

18. See table 6 in the appendix. For an example of a girl's pregnancy clearly altering how her parents sought to deal with her ruin, see DACCF 112943 (1916).

19. N = 90.

20. DACCF 86286 (1911). For other studies that argue that violence was an unexceptional part of working-class sexual culture, see Lunbeck, *The Psychiatric Persuasion*, 219; K. White, *The First Sexual Revolution*, 80–105, esp. 89–92.

21. This is so in ten cases, or 11 percent of those that involved extralegal efforts.

22. It is not always possible to determine who initiated efforts to resolve a case through marriage. A significant number of less documented case files simply record

that a man offered to marry a girl or that a marriage had taken place; they do not make clear whether the girl, or her family, had been seeking a marriage.

23. Ware, *Greenwich Village*, 111.

24. See the studies cited in n. 10 of this chapter.

25. Whyte, "A Slum Sex Code," 26, 28.

26. For a good example, see DACCF 113284 (1916).

27. For the African American family, see PDCF 2850 (1926) and DACCF 165356 (1926). For cases in which families rejected a man's offer because, in their eyes, he had a bad character, see DACCF 85730 (1911); DACCF 86225 (1911). For cases where ethnic differences led parents to refuse a man's offer, see DACCF 9258 (1896); DACCF 111304 (1916).

28. Additional Statement of Antonio Napolitano, DACCF 113408 (1916).

29. True, *The Neglected Girl*, 73; Ware, *Greenwich Village*, 181.

30. Abstract of Court of General Sessions Trial (December 29 1896), CGSCF, *People v. W.S.* (December 1896); DACCF 11881 (1896).

31. DACCF 84789 (1911). For other examples, see DACCF 11387 (1896); DACCF 35751 (1901); DACCF 83905 (1911); DACCF 86356 (1911); DACCF 109457 (1916); DACCF 108927 (1916); DACCF 110642 (1916).

32. Transcript of Arraignment in Magistrates' Court (18 April 1901), 4, in DACCF 34760 (1901).

33. Brief, DACCF 83640 (1911).

34. Dayton, *Women before the Bar*, 160–61, 195, 203–4, 221–23; Godbeer, *Sexual Revolution in Early America*, 228, 255.

35. Steinberg, *The Transformation of Criminal Justice*, 13–91.

36. Edwards, *Gendered Strife and Confusion*, 211–13.

37. Dayton, *Women before the Bar*, 12–13, 208, 215, 227, 305–7, 327.

38. For private networks, the WCTU, and private maternity homes, see Brumberg, "'Ruined' Girls." For private reformatories, to which families could send girls without recourse to the courts, see Alexander, *The Girl Problem*, 172 n. 44.

39. DACCF 109115 (1916).

40. Claghorn, *The Immigrant's Day in Court*, 223. Lower East Side Jews had similar experiences, finding American courts "uncongenial" not only because they were conducted in English but also because the judges were Gentiles, and the legal process was expensive and slow. See Goldstein, *Jewish Justice and Conciliation*, 87–91.

41. The Jewish Conciliation Board was one such institution; see Goldstein, *Jewish Justice and Conciliation*, 87–252.

42. For examples of men who made an offer of marriage at their arraignment, see DACCF 81568 (1911); DACCF 163661 (1926). For the case of Michael Lione and Donna Gallo, see TTC, case 619, roll 100 (1906), 10, 21, 39, 64, 90, 146–91, 240–42.

43. Friedman, *Crime and Punishment in American History*; Steinberg, *The Transformation of Criminal Justice*.

44. Schlossman and Wallach, "The Crime of Precocious Sexuality"; Alexander, *The Girl Problem*; Odem, *Delinquent Daughters*; Edwards, *Gendered Strife and Confusion*.

45. ADA's notes on trial testimony, 2, in DACCF 209984 (1936).

46. DACCF 111246 (1916).

47. Ibid.

48. "Wed When Jerome's Aide Threatened Jail," *New York American*, 4 May 1906 (DAS).

49. Transcript of grand jury hearing (3 April 1916), 3, 5–7, 9, 11, in DACCF 109238 (1916).

50. Towne, "Young Girl Marriages in Criminal and Juvenile Courts," 293–94; Pollens, *The Sex Criminal*, 159–63.

51. In the 1940s, for example, Paul Tappan found that most judges in New York City's wayward minor court, a court that had jurisdiction over girls aged between sixteen and twenty-one years, preferred to institutionalize girls rather than allow them to marry. But even in this court, there was one judge who saw marriage as the most desirable outcome. See Tappan, *Delinquent Girls in Court*, 156–57, 161.

52. Much of the evidence for the following argument is provided by the comments of children's court judges, rather than by what magistrates who sat in the criminal courts might have said. Children's court judges, who in 1926 gained the power to decide whether fourteen- and fifteen-year-old girls could marry, were more influenced by modern ideas about childhood, which formed the premise for their courts, than their criminal court colleagues were. As a result, they less consistently showed sympathy for efforts to arrange marriages. But when they did support marriages, they expressed beliefs more strongly held by criminal court judges.

53. *Proceedings of the Seventh Annual Conference of the New York State Association of Judges of County Children's Courts*, 22.

54. Ibid.

55. Towne, "Young Girl Marriages in Criminal and Juvenile Courts," 293.

56. TTC, case 619, roll 100 (1906), 240–42.

57. Towne, "Young Girl Marriages in Criminal and Juvenile Courts," 290–91.

58. "The Child Marriage Law in Operation," *Proceedings of the Eighth Annual Conference of the New York State Association of Judges of County Children's Courts*, 74–75.

59. *Proceedings of the Seventh Annual Conference of the New York State Association of Judges of County Children's Courts*, 20.

60. Alexander, *The Girl Problem*, 64–66.

61. PDCF 4542 (1926) and DACCF 166753 (1926).

62. Towne, "Young Girl Marriages in Criminal and Juvenile Courts," 291, 294. For an overview of reformers' arguments for child marriage laws, see M. Richmond and Hall, *Child Marriages*.

63. For the new law, see *Laws of New York, 1926*, chap. 590, 1056–57. The campaigns against "child marriage" are discussed in more detail in chapter 9 of this book.

Chapter Six

1. DACCF 109033 (1916).

2. DACCF 112943 (1916).

3. DACCF 112559 (1916).

4. See table 7 in the appendix.

5. *People v. Harriden*, 1 Parker Cr. R., 344 (1852). For a discussion of rulings on this point in other states, see D. R. N. Blackburn, "Incest." New York's incest statute stated that "when persons within the degrees of consanguinity, within which marriages are declared by law to be incestuous and void, intermarry or commit adultery or fornication with each other, each of them is punishable by imprisonment for not more than ten years" (The Penal Code of the State of New York, sec. 302, in *Laws of New York, 1881*, vol. 3, chap. 676, 73). New York's marriage law prohibited intermarriage of "ancestors and descendants of every degree," including brothers and sisters related by whole or half blood. See Vernier, *American Family Laws*, 1:179. Incest featured in only 2 percent (N = 12 of 514) of the statutory rape cases in my sample years, 1906 to 1926.

6. Train, *The Prisoner at the Bar*, 266.

7. This development fits with the broad trend to redefine incest as a sex crime, a trend discussed by Leigh Bienen, who does not consider, however, the role of the age of consent in that transformation. See Bienen, "Defining Incest." In the case of adult women, incest continued to be defined as an inappropriate relationship, not a form of sexual violence, an act for which the law held both parties equally responsible.

8. Statement of Rosa Colletti, "taken by Officer F., in [NYSPCC's] rooms, January 20th, 1916"; NYSPCC Report of Investigation; and Brief, all in DACCF 109033 (1916).

9. DACCF 112943 (1916).

10. DACCF 35249 (1901).

11. See TTC, case 2232, roll 280 (1916), 171; Rosen, *The Lost Sisterhood*, 48.

12. TTC, case 2157, roll 273 (1916), 2–16.

13. TTC, case 2250, roll 282 (1916), 9–10. T. J. Sullivan, Buchanan's attorney, did try to disrupt this characterization of Catherine. In his cross-examination, he asked her to specify when she "first [learned] what an act of sexual intercourse was"; having established that it was when a doctor examined her, Sullivan questioned her about why, when she understood what had happened to her, she still did not tell her mother. Sullivan also challenged Catherine about how she could testify to having felt Buchanan's "privates" against her legs during the assault, for if she knew nothing about sexual intercourse, she should have known nothing about a man's privates (ibid., 12–13, 15–16).

14. TTC, case 264, roll 49 (1901), 152, 165–66.

15. Addams, *A New Conscience*, 166.

16. TTC, case 619, roll 100 (1906), 9–10. Occasionally, a defense attorney complained about the failure of other judges to act as Judge Rosalsky did, protesting, as one did in appealing for a mistrial in 1911, that "it would be beyond human experience that this jury could fairly and impartially render a verdict that only related to a question of intercourse, and leaving out all the disgusting details of force that has [*sic*] been injected into the case" (TTC, case 1412, roll 183 [1911], 10, 100–101, 105).

17. For examples, see DACCF 83671 (1911); DACCF 81034 (1911).

18. Arraignment for Sentencing, 2–3, in CGSCF, *People v. M.D.* (March 1901). For a similar statement by a defense attorney, see DACCF 163418 (1926).

19. Report of Mental Examination, 8 January 1927, PDCF 2849 (1926). For similar

statements in case files, see DACCF 84042 (1906); DACCF 134861 (1921); DACCF 165794 (1926).

20. The corroboration requirement did not apply to the offense of incest. However, since, as in sodomy, the statute punished both parties, a girl was treated as an accomplice, which required her testimony to be corroborated. It took less evidence to satisfy that requirement than was needed to meet the corroboration requirement that applied to rape. In terms of the law, winning a conviction for rape was thus more difficult than winning one for incest. On at least one occasion, when prosecutors presented insufficient evidence to win a conviction for rape, the judge, jury, and appellate court found that the evidence did warrant a verdict of guilty of incest. See DACCF 57558 (1906); TTC, case 612, roll 98 (1916); *People v. Block*, 105 N.Y.S. 175 (1907). Whether men could in fact be indicted for both rape and incest in this way, given the different rules of evidence for the two offenses, remained in question until the New York State Supreme Court approved it in 1954. See *People v. Wilson*, 135 N.Y.S. 2d 893 (1954).

21. N = 131 of 187. Not all the case files provide information on corroborative evidence. The totals by year are 2 of 6 in 1906; 26 of 35 in 1911; 22 of 39 in 1916; 35 of 47 in 1921; 46 of 60 in 1926. Admissions played a role in half of the incest cases included in the sample (N = 5 of 10).

22. NYSPCC, *Instructions for Officers and Staff of the NYSPCC*, 9.

23. TTC, case 619, roll 100 (1906), 53–54. For another case in which the court interpreter's translation was challenged, see DACCF 81514 (1911). For more on the problems caused by interpreters, see Gordon, *Heroes of Their Own Lives*, 14, 224.

24. TTC, case 619, roll 100 (1906), 72–76, 79, 83. As we saw in the previous chapter, the jury ultimately did not have to make that determination. Lione pled guilty to second-degree assault at the end of the defense case.

25. See, for example, DACCF 83661 (1911).

26. *People v. Page* 162 N.Y. 272 (1900); *People v. Downs*, 140 N.E. 708 (1923). For another decision literally interpreting sexual language, see *People v. Talesnik*, 225 N.Y. 495 (1919). For decisions that interpreted ambiguous statements as admissions of guilt, see *People v. Elston*, 186 App. Div. 229 (1919); *People v. Brehm*, 218 N.Y.S. 469, 218 App. Div. 266 (1926).

27. DACCF 133233 (1921). For another example, see DACCF 84482 (1911).

28. NYSPCC case file 525369 (1936). For other examples where police officers used colloquial language to make sure defendants understood their questions, see TTC, case 2208, roll 278 (1916), 44–45 ["screwed"]; DACCF 84167 (1911) ["fucked"].

Two defendants claimed they had made their statements under duress. See TTC, case 2208, roll 278 (1916), 96; TTC, case 2960, roll 356 (1921).

In light of the legal culture discussed in the previous chapter, it is likely that many men offered admissions because they expected to resolve a case through marriage, and did not expect to be punished as a consequence of their statements.

29. For child rape, N = 21 of 46. For rape cases involving girls in their teens, N = 60 of 346. The figures for child rape are for the sample years 1886 to 1926; the figures for the rape of girls in their teens are for the years 1906 to 1926.

30. N = 3 of 10.

31. N = 35 of 60. In my sample years, 1916 to 1926, prosecutors discharged a significantly smaller proportion of the men indicted by grand juries than in earlier years: 7 percent (N = 82) in 1916, 6 percent (N = 63) in 1921, and 7 percent (N = 97) in 1926, down from 12 percent (N = 34) in 1906 and 20 percent (N = 70) in 1911. That drop reflects, at least in part, the fact that, thanks to the actions of grand juries, prosecutors less often faced the decision to discharge. Grand juries dismissed an increasing proportion of cases, 37 percent (N = 132) in 1916 and 41 percent (N = 106) in 1921, compared to only 21 percent in 1906 (N = 43) and 1911 (N = 89). See table 5 in the appendix.

32. N = 3 of 17.

33. DACCF 139958 (1921); DACCF 109745 (1916).

34. For cases involving girls in their teens, N = 10 of 15; for cases involving younger girls, N = 7 of 13.

35. For cases involving girls in their teens, N = 10 of 25; for cases involving younger girls, N = 1 of 14.

36. For the cases involving police officers, see TTC, case 2232, roll 280 (1916); DACCF 108864 (1916) and the trial transcript for that case, TTC, case 2156, roll 270 (1916). One conviction was subsequently overturned on appeal. For the cases involving foremen, see DACCF 34932 (1901) and the trial transcript for that case, TTC, case 264, roll 49 (1901); and CGSCF, *People v. A.F.* (July 1901). The later case, *People v. A.F.*, was also overturned on appeal. For the case involving the Chinese defendant, see DACCF 135342 (1921).

37. TTC, case 4, roll 1 (1890), n.p. [prior to the beginning of the transcript]. See also *Morning Journal* (New York), 13 June 1891; *Press* (New York), 16 June 1891 (DAS).

38. True, *The Neglected Girl*, 77, 87, 93. See also Woods and Kennedy, *Young Working Girls*, 42, 88–89.

39. The Research Committee of the Committee of Fourteen, New York City's leading anti-prostitution organization, reported in 1910 that the reluctance to convict defendants was "based on the loose way in which the present law relating to rape is drawn, since the whole effect of the law is weakened by the omission of the words 'of previous chaste character'" (Committee of Fourteen, *The Social Evil in New York City*, 124). In 1926, in a sign of what was to come in the 1930s and 1940s, grand juries dismissed the charges against nine men who had each admitted to having sexual intercourse with an underage girl. Those men represented 20 percent of the total number who offered an admission.

40. Transcript of Grand Jury Hearing, 15 December 1916, 5, 7, 8, 10–11, 17–19, DACCF 113348 (1916). For another example, see DACCF 166690 (1926).

41. DACCF 35023 (1901). For other cases where juries failed to convict men who had intercourse with bad girls, see DACCF 56108 (1906); DACCF 81426 (1911); DACCF 86357 (1911) and TTC, case 1487, roll 193 (1911); DACCF 110210 (1916) and TTC, case 2208, roll 287 (1916).

42. See table 5 in the appendix. Only incest cases—in which blood ties and abuse of familial authority aggravated, if not overshadowed, the factor of the victim's age—stood outside this pattern. Two out of every three prosecutions (N = 8 of

12) resulted in a conviction, the highest rate for any sex crime. Of the four men not convicted, two were discharged by the DA, one was acquitted at the direction of the trial judge, and one was acquitted by a jury.

43. See table 7 in the appendix.

44. In 1901, prosecutors agreed to plea bargains with only 35 percent (N = 37) of the defendants held for trial by the grand jury. The proportion increased steadily in the first two decades of the twentieth century, more than doubling by 1921. In that year prosecutors agreed to plea bargains with 73 percent (N = 66) of the defendants held for trial. For more on plea bargaining, see Alschuler, "Plea Bargaining and Its History"; K. Hall, *The Magic Mirror*, 183–84; Friedman, *Crime and Punishment in American History*, 252–53, 390–91.

45. In the years 1906 to 1921, men who pled guilty to a misdemeanor made up only 6 percent (N = 9 of 154) of those who made plea bargains.

46. Here are the figures by year: 1906, N = 11 of 17; 1911, N = 18 of 31; 1916, N = 15 of 53; 1921, N = 7 of 43. Cases involving incest also followed this trend. Until 1921, the plea accepted was one of guilty of second-degree rape. In 1921, two of the three men who entered guilty pleas pled to lesser offenses, one to a misdemeanor. In 1926, one man pled guilty to second-degree assault, the other to a misdemeanor.

47. N = 56 of 75. Eighteen men pled guilty to second-degree assault.

48. For a uniquely well-documented account of the negotiations between the defense attorney, the DADA, the NYSPCC officer, and the judge, see DACCF 112205 (1916).

49. TTC, case 1494, roll 194 (1911), 39, 98. For another example, see TTC, case 268, roll 49 (1901), 2–3.

50. Transcript of arraignment for sentencing, 23 February 1916, 8 March 1916, CGSCF, *People v. W.H.* (January 1916). For another example of an attack on a girl's character at a sentencing hearing, see CGSCF, *People v. J.S.* (May 1916). For further discussion of judges' concern with a girl's character, see Committee of Fourteen, *The Social Evil in New York City*, 124.

51. PDCF 2781 (1926); PDCF 4605 (1926).

52. In 1916, two-thirds of the men (N = 42 of 63) received such sentences. In 1921, the proportion was one-half (N = 20 of 40).

53. N = 24 of 52.

54. Bell, *Fighting the Traffic in Young Girls*, 14, 16.

55. Addams, *A New Conscience*, 21, 150.

56. D. Ross, *G. Stanley Hall*, 305.

57. Ibid., 326; G. S. Hall, *Adolescence*, 1:371. See also G. S. Hall, *Adolescence*, 1:127–28, 308, 406–7, 2:71–72, 88–91, 108, 120–21; Moran, *Teaching Sex*, 17, 21. For an insightful discussion of the development of child study, see Riley, *War in the Nursery*, 42–59.

58. Lindsey and Evans, *The Revolt of Modern Youth*, 81–82. For similar statements by other reformers, see True, *The Neglected Girl*, 58; Woods and Kennedy, *Young Working Girls*, 8–9; Addams, *A New Conscience*, 101.

59. For preventive reforms, see Alexander, *The Girl Problem*, 42–52; Moran, *Teaching Sex*, 23–67; Addams, *A New Conscience*, 100. Further evidence of the shift in the

strategies pursued by reformers can be found in the pages of *Vigilance*: by the 1910s, discussions of sex education had taken the space in the periodical earlier occupied by discussions of the age of consent.

60. DACCF 185489 (1931).

Chapter Seven

1. *NYT*, 21 March 1937, 24. For Ossido's trial, conviction, and death sentence, see *NYT*, 22 March 1937, 40; *NYT*, 24 March 1937, 11; *NYT*, 13 April 1937, 52; *NYT*, 20 April 1937, 52; *NYT*, 21 April 1937, 17; *NYT*, 24 April 1937, 36; and *NYT*, 12 May 1937, 48.

2. *NYT*, 1 August 1937, 23; and *NYT*, 9 August 1937, 1. For Marks's trial, conviction, and death sentence, see *NYT*, 29 October 1937, 13; *NYT*, 30 October 1937, 11; and *NYT*, 10 November 1937, 5.

3. *NYT*, 14 August 1937, 30; *NYT*, 15 August 1937, 1. For Elmore's trial, conviction, and death sentence, see *NYT*, 23 November 1937, 48; *NYT*, 24 November 1937, 3; *NYT*, 25 November 1937, 4.

4. Freedman, "'Uncontrolled Desires'"; Chauncey, "The Postwar Sex Crime Panic"; P. Jenkins, *Moral Panic*, 49–93.

5. Freedman does note this point, but it warrants only a short paragraph in her article. See Freedman, "'Uncontrolled Desires,'" 211–12.

6. May, *Homeward Bound*, 136.

7. Bender and Blau, "The Reaction of Children to Sexual Relations with Adults," 513–14.

8. *NYDN*, 21 March 1937, 1, 5; *NYT*, 21 March 1937, 24. Crowds also gathered at the police station where Ossido was held, and large crowds assembled outside the tenement where Lawrence Marks killed Paula Magagna. See *NYDN*, 1 August 1937, 3.

9. *NYT*, 27 August 1937, 10; *New York Herald Tribune*, 27 August 1937, 3. A magistrate discharged the man in one such case after the girls said he had neither touched nor talked to them. See *NYDN*, 3 September 1937, 24; MacCormick, "New York's Present Problem," 4.

10. "Pedophilia," *Time*, 28 August 1937. See also Wile, "Society and Sex Offenders"; Palmer, "Crimes against Children."

11. For the committee's stated objective, see Senator McNaboe's opening statement, "Public Hearings," New York State Legislature, *Report of the Joint Legislative Committee*, 335. On 24 March, in the aftermath of the first murder, Senator McNaboe had introduced a resolution in the New York State Legislature calling for this committee; the legislature passed his resolution on 7 May, but the governor vetoed the appropriation. Normally, that veto would have spelled the end of the committee, but the second and third murders helped McNaboe convince legislative leaders to make funds available for the investigation. See *NYT*, 24 March 1937, 27; *NYT*, 14 August 1937, 30; *NYT*, 18 August 1937, 42; *NYT*, 26 August 1937, 22; *NYT*, 4 September 1937, 32.

12. New York State Legislature, *Report of the Joint Legislative Committee*, 343.

13. Testimony of Henry Hirschberg, district attorney of Orange County, in New

York State Legislature, *Report of the Joint Legislative Committee*, 679. For similar testimony by other DAs, see New York State Legislature, *Report of the Joint Legislative Committee*, 687, 688, 750.

14. Ibid., 404, 805. For similar testimony by other DAs, see ibid., 749–50, 768, 815.

15. Staff of the Citizens Committee on the Control of Crime, *The Problem of Sex Offenses in New York City*, 9. In providing figures on the age of the victims of sex crime, the report emphasized their young age and noted that "of all the aspects of this problem of sex offenses there is none that can stir the observer more deeply than the age of the victims" (ibid.).

16. Ibid., 19–20. La Guardia had abandoned plans for such a committee in 1937, having decided that it would overlap with the Joint Legislative Committee. See La Guardia to Board of Estimate and Apportionment, 16 September 1937, Papers of Mayor La Guardia, Subject Files, "Sex Crime," roll 223, Municipal Archives, City of New York.

17. The committee was made up of seven judges, three magistrates, five probation and parole officials, three corrections officials, a district attorney, the police commissioner, and five psychiatrists. The witnesses that appeared before the committee overwhelmingly mirrored its membership. Other than the superintendent of the Brooklyn SPCC and a doctor from the Commission on Marriage and the Home of the Federal Council of the Churches of Christ, the witnesses were all judges, magistrates, parole officials, district attorneys, and psychiatrists. See *Report of the Mayor's Committee for the Study of Sex Offenses*, 3, 7.

18. Ibid., 6. The committee had laid out an ambitious program of six separate studies, dealing with the existing literature on sex crime, statistics related to arrests and convictions, the existing law, the role of socioeconomic factors in sex crime, the psychiatric study of individual offenders, and the parole and correctional treatment of offenders. See Mayor's Committee for the Study of Sex Offenses, *Program* (1940); Minutes of the "Meeting of the Planning Committee of the Mayor's Committee for the Study of Sex Offenses, June 21, 1939," and "Tentative Draft of Research Project to Be Sponsored by the Mayor's Committee on Sex Offenses" (December 1939), Papers of Mayor La Guardia, Subject Files, "Sex Crime," roll 223. The *Report* made no mention of the broader program or the reasons why it had not been carried out.

19. "Tentative Draft of Research Project to Be Sponsored by the Mayor's Committee on Sex Offenses"; Mayor's Committee for the Study of Sex Offenses, *Program*, 1.

20. *Report of the Mayor's Committee for the Study of Sex Offenses*, 9–10, 35.

21. Ibid., 34.

22. Ibid., 35. The lone dissenting voice came from Robert Lane, the executive director of the Welfare Council. A footnote appended to the committee's recommendations about law reform recorded his position that "many persons concerned with the protection of children against sexual abuse think the age limit [of ten years in the carnal abuse statute] is set too low" (ibid., 9 n. 2).

23. Bender and Blau, "The Reaction of Children to Sexual Relations with Adults."

24. Whitman, "The City That *Does* Something about Sex Crime," 20.

25. This account of the press coverage in Detroit is taken from Chauncey, "The Postwar Sex Crime Panic," 163–64. For more on these murders, see *Newsweek*, 28 November 1949, 19; Bowling, "The Sex Offender and Law Enforcement," 11. For more on the media reaction to sex crime generally, see Sutherland, "The Diffusion of Sexual Psychopath Laws," 144.

26. Hoover, "How Safe Is Your Daughter?" 32–33, 102–4. For other examples of magazine coverage of sex crime that focused on children, see Harris, "Sex Crimes"; Waldrop, "Murder as a Sex Practice"; Wittels, "What Can We Do about Sex Crimes?" For further examples of illustrations that portrayed victims of sex crime as children, see ibid.; *Newsweek*, 28 November 1949, 19.

27. Whitman, "The City That *Does* Something about Sex Crime," 20. For another example, see Harris, "Sex Crimes," 4.

28. Whitman, "The City That *Does* Something about Sex Crime," 64. For another example of public action in the wake of a child sex murder, in Miami in 1954, see Fejes, "Murder, Perversion, and Moral Panic," 325–26, 343–44.

29. Freedman, "Uncontrolled Desires," 209–10.

30. Brakel and Rock, *The Mentally Disabled and the Law*, 341. Brakel and Rock omit the New York law on the grounds that it was essentially an indeterminate sentence statute. However, the act was passed in response to the sex crime panic, and it was frequently categorized by contemporary commentators, if not more recent authors, as a sexual psychopath statute. For further discussion of these laws, see chapter 10 of this book.

31. Freedman, "Uncontrolled Desires," 210. For further discussion of the sex offender studies, see chapter 10.

32. For the Bradley case, see *Chicago Daily News*, 31 July 1947, 1; ibid., 1 August 1947, 1, 6, 7, 30; *Chicago Sun*, 1 August 1947, 1, 2. For the Counter case, see *Detroit Free Press*, 22 April 1949, 1, 2, 3. For the Levin case, see *Evening Bulletin* (Philadelphia), 10 January 1949, 1, 3, 31; ibid., 11 January 1949, 1, 3, 44. Thanks to Craig Robertson for gathering this material. For an insightful discussion of crimes against boys as part of the midcentury sex crime panic, see Chauncey, "The Postwar Sex Crime Panic."

33. Whitman, "The City That *Does* Something about Sex Crime," 64.

34. Hoover, "How Safe Is Your Daughter?"; Hoover, "How *Safe* Is Your Youngster?", 101. For other examples of the new attention to boys, see Harris, "Sex Crimes"; Whitman, "The City That *Does* Something about Sex Crime," 64; Report of Thomas Soble, Chairman, County Affairs Committee, Third Ward Republican Association of New Rochelle, New York, in re: *Proposed Legislation on Sex Crimes*, 9, Papers of Governor Lehman, series 13682–53, "Sex Crimes," reel 86, New York State Archives, Albany, N.Y.

35. May, *Homeward Bound*, 147; Mintz and Kellogg, *Domestic Revolutions*, 189–90; Griswold, *Fatherhood in America*, 207–10.

36. The tabloid press did report the physical injuries of murdered girls in some detail. For example, whereas the *New York Times* simply described Joan Morvan as having been beaten, the *Daily News* quoted the medical examiner's statement that "I could not count the numerous bruises on the child's body. There are long, ugly-

looking scrapes on her legs and back, as well as bruises on her legs, chest, back, abdomen, head and neck" (3 March 1937, 3). For another example, the treatment of Joan Kuleba, see *NYDN*, 14 August 1937, 6.

37. Whitman, "The City That *Does* Something about Sex Crime," 20. For other examples, see Major, "New Moral Menace to Our Youth"; Hoover, "How Safe Is Your Daughter?" 102; "Study Mental Effects of Sex Crime Attacks," *Science News Letter*, 13 November 1937, 313.

38. *Report of the Mayor's Committee for the Study of Sex Offenses*, 67.

39. Ladd-Taylor, *Raising a Baby the Government Way*; N. P. Weiss, "Mother, the Invention of Necessity."

40. Cited in Halpern, *American Pediatrics*, 89; see also ibid., 90, 96–97, 106–8; Grant, *Raising Baby by the Book*, 10.

41. C. Floyd Haviland, "Undernourished Minds," in *The Doctor Looks at Child Labor* (1929), 21, cited in Novkov, "Historicizing the Figure of the Child in Legal Discourse," 396–97.

42. Rose, *Governing the Soul*, 141–50. See also Riley, *War in the Nursery*, 42–59; Horn, *Before It's Too Late*, 136–39; Richardson, *The Century of the Child*, 152–54.

43. My understanding of the mental hygiene movement draws on Jones, *Taming the Troublesome Child*; Horn, *Before It's Too Late*; Riley, *War in the Nursery*, 62–64; Richardson, *The Century of the Child*. Only Jones gives any attention to the place of sexuality in mental hygiene thought and practice.

44. W. A. White, "Childhood."

45. Jones, *Taming the Troublesome Child*, 91–119; Horn, *Before It's Too Late*, 42–50.

46. William Healy, the most influential psychologist of 1910s and 1920s, and a major influence on the juvenile justice system, encapsulates that distinction. He engaged with Freudian thought but rejected the vision of the prepubescent child as a sexual being. See Healy, *The Individual Delinquent*; and the discussion in Robertson, "Sexuality through the Prism of Age," 239–44.

47. W. A. White, *The Mental Hygiene of Childhood*, 113–14, 121.

48. Groves and Groves, *Sex in Childhood*, 22–23, 28–29, 41, 109, 140, 153. For other examples of popular texts that describe a variety of child sexualities, see W. Richmond, *The Adolescent Girl*, 43–45; W. Richmond, *The Adolescent Boy*, 44–60; Strain, *The Normal Sex Interests of Children*, 12–27.

49. Groves and Groves, *Sex in Childhood*, 222–23.

50. W. A. White, *The Mental Hygiene of Childhood*, 121; W. Richmond, *The Adolescent Girl*, 44; W. Richmond, *The Adolescent Boy*, 50–51, 117, 137–38, 182.

51. Hartwell, *A Citizens' Handbook*, 47–48. For other accounts of homosexuals as fixated and immature, see Henry, *Sex Variants*, 1023; Karpman, *The Sexual Offender and His Offenses*, 148–51; Pollens, *The Sex Criminal*, 51; G. D. Schultz, *How Many More Victims?* 308.

52. Childers, "Some Notes on Sex Mores among Negro Children"; Williams, "Rape in Children and Young Girls: Part One," 246. The work of Lauretta Bender offers one exception to this pattern. In an article published in 1939, she presented evidence that contradicted Childers, and argued that the sexual experiences and responses

of African Americans were "in no way dissimilar to those of white children." See Bender, "Behavior Problems in Negro Children," 224–25.

53. Russett, *Sexual Science*, 53; Bederman, *Manliness and Civilization*, 93. G. Stanley Hall's description is cited in Gould, *Ontogeny and Phylogeny*, 129.

54. W. A. White, *The Mental Hygiene of Childhood*, 125.

55. Groves and Groves, *Sex in Childhood*, vii.

56. Ibid., 23.

57. Ibid., 213.

58. Thom, *Everyday Problems of the Everyday Child*, 266, 275–76, 277–78, 288.

59. Melanie Klein mentioned sexual contact with adults only in a footnote to her discussion of the place of sexual relations with other children in the sexual development of the girl. There she notes that when "a child has been seduced or raped by a grown-up person[,] [s]uch an experience, as is well known, can have very serious effects upon the child's mind." See Klein, *The Psychoanalysis of Children*, 306. Helene Deutsch's later psychoanalytic study of women noted that "premature [heterosexual] experiences produce disturbances in the development of [a girl's] whole personality," but made no specific mention of sexual contact with adults. See H. Deutsch, *The Psychology of Women*, 1:17.

60. Bender and Blau, "The Reaction of Children to Sexual Relations with Adults," 510.

61. Bender and Grugett, "A Follow-up Report on Children Who Had Atypical Sexual Experience," 836–37.

62. Bender and Blau, "The Reaction of Children to Sexual Relations with Adults," 516.

63. Bender and Grugett, "A Follow-up Report on Children Who Had Atypical Sexual Experience," 825–29, 836–37. To some extent, psychiatrists' concern to reject countervisions of children as innocent led them to minimize the degree to which children had been affected. Bender and Blau glossed over the damage they noted had been caused to the personality development of some of the children in their study, including loss of the latent stage, mental retardation, thwarted school accomplishments, and premature development of the rebellion against authority associated with adolescence. In the follow-up study, Bender and Grugett paid little attention to psychological conditions other than mental illness that was sufficiently intense to warrant institutionalization. In regard to those who had troubled lives, they argued that the children's sexual experiences with adults were "not focal, but symptomatic," one aspect of a broader psychosis not "predisposing to a psychotic adjustment," which had "limit[ed] their potential and frustrate[d] normal development" (ibid., 829).

64. Rogers, Weiss, Darwin, and Dutton, "Study of Sex Crimes against Children," 83; Bender and Blau, "The Reaction of Children to Sexual Relations with Adults," 511. Alfred Kinsey dismissed the emotional upset and fright reported by his female subjects who had sexual encounters with adults in their childhoods as at the "level that children will show when they see insects, spiders, or other objects against which they have been adversely conditioned." He blamed the disturbance they experienced on "cultural conditioning," on the "emotional reactions" of the adults who dis-

covered the child's experience. See Kinsey, Pomeroy, Martin, and Gebhard, *Sexual Behavior in the Human Female*, 117–22.

65. As evidence for that claim, they pointed to the children's lengthy relationships with those men and their "emotional placidity" and failure to act as injured parties, which the psychiatrists saw as indicating that the children "derived some fundamental satisfaction from the relationship." See Bender and Blau, "The Reaction of Children to Sexual Relations with Adults," 513–14.

66. Weiss, Rogers, Darwin, and Dutton, "A Study of Girl Sex Victims," 1–3.

67. Rogers and Weiss, "Introduction and Conclusions," in Rogers, Weiss, Darwin, and Dutton, "Study of Sex Crimes Against Children," 48, 51.

68. The first example of such a perspective that I found, an article by John Gagnon, was published in *Social Problems* in 1965. Gagnon argued that the behavior psychiatrists categorized as participation was often generated by the adult man's appeal to a child's particular, distinctive nature. See Gagnon, "Female Child Victims of Sex Offenses," 185. See also Charles, "Child Victims of Sexual Offenses," 52–56.

69. "Study Mental Effects of Sex Crime Attacks," 313; Bender and Blau, "The Reaction of Children to Sexual Relations with Adults," 513–14.

70. For photographs of the girls, see *NYDN*, 1 August 1937, 1; ibid., 2 August 1937, 3; ibid., 14 August 1937, 1; ibid., 15 August 1937, 1. For accounts of funerals for the girls, see *NYT*, 24 March 1937, 11; *NYDN*, 24 March 1937, 10; *NYT*, 4 August 1937, 42; ibid., 17 March 1937, 40; *NYDN*, 17 March 1937, 3. For photographs of the boys, see *Chicago Sun*, 1 August 1949, 1; *Evening Bulletin* (Philadelphia), 11 January 1949, 3. For accounts of funerals for the boys, see *Chicago Daily News*, 4 August 1947, 6, 32; *Chicago Sun*, 5 August 1949, 2; *Chicago Daily Tribune*, 5 August 1949, 6; *Detroit Free Press*, 24 April 1949, 3.

71. *NYT*, 15 August 1937, 20.

72. *NYDN*, 14 August 1937, 10.

73. [Unsigned] to La Guardia, 16 August 1937, Papers of Mayor La Guardia, Subject Files, "Sex Crime," roll 223. See also Linton Collier to La Guardia, 19 August 1937, Papers of Mayor La Guardia, Subject Files, "Sex Crime," roll 223.

74. "Sex Crimes," *Newsweek*, 21 August 1937, 22; Whitman, "The City That *Does* Something about Sex Crime," 64; Chauncey, "The Postwar Sex Crime Panic," 173–74. See also Harris, "A New Report on Sex Crimes," 7; Hoover, "How Safe Is Your Daughter?" 104; Mangus, "Society and Sexual Deviation," 91–92.

75. Mangus, "Society and Sexual Deviation," 92. See also MacCormick, "New York's Present Problem," 9–10; *NYT*, 6 June 1950, 33.

76. Testimony of Martin Littleton, district attorney of Nassau County, in New York State Legislature, *Report of the Joint Committee*, 722–23.

77. For testimony by other DAs supporting this proposal, see New York State Legislature, *Report of the Joint Committee*, 670–71, 736, 742, 779–80, 808, 814. The Westchester Committee also endorsed private trials; see ibid., 819, 827.

78. For testimony by DAs supporting this proposal, see ibid., 722–23, 780, 814. Other witnesses noted that newspapers in Broome and Westchester counties already withheld the name of complainants. See ibid., 760, 818. For Hoover's position, see Hoover, "How Safe Is Your Daughter?" 32. For similar statements by other public

officials, see Harris, "A New Report on Sex Crimes," 5; Whitman, "The City That *Does* Something about Sex Crime," 64.

79. For proposals to reform the corroboration requirement, see Testimony of Thomas Soble, Chairman, Westchester County Legislation Committee, in New York State Legislature, *Report of the Joint Committee*, 821; "Report of Westchester County Legislation Committee Regarding Sex Crimes against Children," in New York State Legislature, *Report of the Joint Committee*, 832; *NYDN*, 22 March 1937, 6; *NYDN*, 23 March 1937, 4; *NYT*, 10 August 1937, 7; and *Newsweek*, 21 August 1937, 22. For opposition to that proposal, see Testimony of Lewis Valentine, Commissioner of Police, New York City, in New York State Legislature, *Report of the Joint Committee*, 536; the testimony of several DAs, ibid., 645, 668, 742, 808; Staff of the Citizens Committee on the Control of Crime, *The Problem of Sex Offenses in New York City*, 4–5, 9; and *Report of the Mayor's Committee*, 32–36.

80. *NYT*, 28 March 1937, 2.

81. Brown, *Legal Psychology*, 133, 139. See also Burtt, *Legal Psychology*, 104–9, 121, 141. For an overview of the American psychological literature on child witnesses, see Goodman, "Children's Testimony in Historical Perspective." On the turn-of-the-century French literature on child witnesses, see Matsuda, *The Memory of the Modern*, 101–19.

82. For accounts of children's unreliability that employ psychoanalytic language, see *Report of the Mayor's Committee*, 32; Groves and Groves, *Sex in Childhood*, 221.

83. Major, "New Moral Menace to Our Youth," 103.

84. Pollens, *The Sex Criminal*, 50–51. For other examples of this argument see Strain, *The Normal Sex Interests of Children*, 179–80; Crow and Crow, *Adolescent Development and Adjustment*, 247; De River, *The Sexual Criminal*, xii, 89, 91; Reinhardt, *Sex Perversions and Sex Crimes*, 21, 43.

85. Major, "New Moral Menace to Our Youth," 105.

86. Chauncey, *Gay New York*, 124. See also Terry, *An American Obsession*, 58–60.

Chapter Eight

1. The quoted passage actually comes from a letter supporting the 1929 amendment to the statute, but the letters written in support of that bill clearly indicate that the NYSPCC was responsible for this legislation. See Ernest Coulter, General Manager of the NYSPCC to Governor Franklin Roosevelt, 1 April 1929; N. J. Walker, Secretary, Convention of Societies for the Prevention of Cruelty to Children and Animals in New York State, to Governor Franklin Roosevelt, 5 April 1929; Charles Golnick, Superintendent, Nassau County SPCC, to Governor Franklin Roosevelt, 3 April 1929, all in Senate Bill No. 1779, Int. 1488 (1929), Bill Jacket Collection, New York Public Library, New York, N.Y. Beginning in the early 1930s, the NYSPCC's *Annual Reports* singled out crimes against young children for special mention. In 1934, for example, the general manager made a special point of noting that one-third of the victims of sex crime dealt with by the Society were younger than six years of age. See *The Sixtieth ARNYSPCC*, 5. See also *The Fifty-seventh ARNYSPCC*, 5; *The Seventy-fifth ARNYSPCC*, 9.

2. *Laws of New York, 1927*, chap. 383, 873.

3. *People v. Belcher*, 299 N.Y. 324, 87 N.E. 2d 279 (1949). This decision looked to rulings in other states to establish the meaning of New York law. See *State v. Hummer*, 73 N.J.L. 714 (1906); *State v. MacLean*, 135 N.J.L. 491 (1947).

4. Previously, such acts would have fallen within the scope of the misdemeanor offense of "impairing the morals of a minor," a catchall, broadly defined in terms of morality. That statute punished a person who "willfully causes or permits the life and limb of any child actually or apparently under the age of sixteen years to be endangered, or its health to be injured, or its morals to become depraved." In the 1930s, only half of those charged with impairing the morals of a minor were found guilty. Appellate court decisions noted the "practical difficulties" ADAs faced in finding the "evidence of actual depravity resulting in the child" that was required to make out a case. For the statute, see *Laws of New York, 1881*, chap. 676, 70; *Laws of New York, 1909*, chap. 88. For the conviction rate for prosecutions, see *The Report of the Mayor's Committee*, 53. For appellate court decisions regarding the crime of impairing the morals of a minor, see *People v. Hopkins*, 208 App. Div. 442 (1924); *People v. Belcher*, 299 N.Y. 324, 87 N.E. 2d 279 (1949).

5. *Report of the Governor's Study Commission*, 135.

6. *People v. Gibson*, 232 N.Y. 458 (1922).

7. *Laws of New York, 1929*, chap. 684, 1621–22. However, if the offender had previously been convicted of a similar crime, or of rape, abduction, incest, or sodomy, then the offense became a felony, punished by up to ten years in prison. Ernest Coulter, general manager of the NYSPCC, promoted that clause by explaining that "we have found in our experience here that the degenerates in this class are almost invariably repeaters." See Ernest Coulter, General Manager of the NYSPCC to Governor Franklin Roosevelt, 1 April 1929, Senate Bill No. 1779, Int. 1488 (1929), Bill Jacket Collection.

8. *Laws of New York, 1933*, chap. 423, 964–65.

9. Until 1937, the concept of sexual development contained in the carnal abuse law had a further dimension. Only acts by adults, those over eighteen years of age, were punished. Acts by younger individuals, by a child's age peers, were implicitly not seen as causing the same harm. The reference to the offender's age was removed from the law in 1937; see *Laws of New York, 1937*, chap. 691, 1583.

10. A decade-long hiatus separates this wave of legislative action from the smaller one earlier in the century, the last of which occurred in 1913, in Arizona, Maine, and Montana. After 1958, this legislative action became absorbed into the response to the Model Penal Code. For the statutes, see *Laws of North Dakota, 1923*, chap. 167, 175; *Laws of Nevada, 1925*, chap. 11, 17; *Session Laws of Minnesota, 1927*, chap. 394, 546; *Acts of Vermont, 1937*, no. 211; *Acts of the General Assembly of the Commonwealth of Kentucky, 1948*, chap. 36, 84; *Laws of New Mexico, 1949*, chap. 140, 329; *Laws of Delaware, 1949*, chap. 81; *Laws of Missouri, 1949*, 249; *Laws of Idaho, 1949*, chap. 214; *Acts of Texas, 1950*, chap. 12, 52–53; *Acts of Georgia, 1950*, no. 790, 387–88; *Laws of Florida, 1951*, chap. 26580, 234; *Acts of Oklahoma, 1951*, chap. 45, 60–61; *Public Acts of Michigan, 1952*, no. 73, 81; *Acts of Arkansas, 1953*, no. 94, 281–83; *Page's Ohio Revised Code, Annotated, Title 29* (1954), chap. 2903.01, 42 (enacted 1953); *Laws of South Carolina, 1953*, chap. 48, 346; *Laws of Wisconsin,*

1953, cited in American Law Institute, *Model Penal Code: Tentative Draft No. 4*, 300; *Laws of North Carolina, 1955*, chap. 764; *Acts of Alabama, 1955*, no. 397, 932–33; *Laws of South Dakota, 1955*, chap. 127, 48; *Laws of Massachusetts, 1955*, chap. 763, sec. 4, 802; *Laws of Washington, 1955*, chap. 127; *Laws of Kansas, 1955*, chap. 196, 399; and *Acts of the General Assembly of Virginia, 1958*, chap. 163, 216–17. I have relied primarily on William Eskridge's invaluable tabulation to identify these laws; it does however contain some minor errors and mistakenly includes several statutes that are of a different nature. I have omitted statutes he included from New Jersey, Oregon, and Wyoming, which employ the broad terms associated with juvenile delinquency and do not clearly refer to sexual violence. I have also excluded the law he identified from Nebraska, which deals with intercourse in the context of prostitution. See Eskridge, *Gaylaw*, 342–51.

11. The states that joined New York were Kentucky, Michigan, Minnesota, North Dakota, Ohio, Washington, and Wisconsin. The states that employed "lewd and lascivious" were Delaware, Idaho, Massachusetts, Nevada, South Carolina, South Dakota, and Vermont. The states that used both were Alabama, Florida, Georgia, Kansas, Missouri, North Carolina, and Oklahoma.

12. *Acts of Texas, 1950*, chap. 12, 52–53. The other states were Arkansas, New Mexico, and Virginia. In 1955, the Model Penal Code took yet another approach. It labeled the offense "sexual assault," and the act "sexual contact," defined as "contact, other than intercourse[,] . . . for the purpose of arousing or gratifying sexual desire of the actor or the victim," but not including "acts commonly expressive of familial or friendly affection" (American Law Institute, *Model Penal Code: Tentative Draft No. 4*, 93–95, 292–302).

13. For 1931 to 1946, N = 67 of 99. For 1951 and 1955, N = 15 of 29. See tables 8 and 9 in the appendix.

14. For 1931 to 1946, N = 8 of 26. For 1951 and 1955, N = 2 of 9. See tables 8 and 9 in the appendix.

15. *Report of the Governor's Study Commission*, 135.

16. Transcript of Grand Jury Hearing, 25 September 1941, 5, in DACCF 229121 (1941).

17. DACCF 229121 (1941).

18. N = 4 of 20 sodomy cases in which details survive.

19. See, for example, DACCF 189017 (1931).

20. Recommendation, Defense Motion, and Statement of Special Officer Cordillo, NYSPCC, 20 January 1932, DACCF 189562 (1931). Mrs. Marcus might have acted out of a desire to protect her daughter from the ordeal of testifying in court, but there is no reference to such concerns in the case file.

21. This total excludes one case from 1951 that was prosecuted as carnal abuse but was reported as sodomy by the boy's mother, who walked in on the defendant in the act of performing fellatio on her son. See DACCF 736 (1951).

22. DACCF 230248 (1941).

23. DACCF 230136 (1941). Among this evidence of a persistence of older ideas are scattered signs that, by 1946, new ideas were making some inroads into working-class communities. Among the six cases involving girls that provide details of how the

offense came to be reported are two—one involving touching, the other a genital act—that were set in motion by parents despite the absence of any physical injury to the child. In one case, a mother first took her daughter to the hospital; but when the examination found no evidence of penetration, she still went from the hospital to the police. In 1951, all three cases involving men who touched a girl's genitals were reported by parents, although in one the girl had suffered physical injury, and in a second the accused man was her father, a circumstance that likely overshadowed the nature of the act he committed. Details survive for only one of the cases in 1955, which was reported by a witness.

24. See tables 8 and 9 in the appendix.

25. The most distinct from the acts prosecuted as child rape are a handful of cases that involved men who deliberately avoided penetrating girls, restricting themselves to placing their penises between a girl's legs. See DACCF 185579 (1931); DACCF 187594 (1931); DACCF 210984 (1936).

26. DACCF 230042 (1941). For other examples, see DACCF 230215 (1941); DACCF 3713 (1946); DACCF 781 (1946); DACCF 1159 (1955).

27. DACCF 227419 (1941); DACCF 2528 (1951).

28. Clifton-Edgar and Johnston, "Rape," 708. In their study of cases examined by NYSPCC doctors between 1884 and approximately 1894, Clifton-Edgar and Johnston found sixty-nine cases that involved girls under the age of twelve years. In only twenty-one cases, or less than one-third of the total, did the examinations find ruptured hymens (ibid., 723).

29. PDCF 29768 (1936). That file pertains to DACCF 210794 (1936).

30. See tables 8 and 9 in the appendix. The disappearance of rape and attempted rape prosecutions was even more dramatic than the numbers suggest. Only two rape cases in my sample made it past the grand jury in the years 1931 to 1955. One of those involved a ten-year-old girl, whose age put her outside the scope of the carnal abuse statute; see DACCF 228148 (1941). The other cases were either transferred to the court of special sessions or dismissed, outcomes that essentially rejected their classification as cases of rape, by NYSPCC agents and magistrates, earlier in the legal process. Only three prosecutions for attempted rape got past the grand jury. Two of those cases involved ten-year-old girls and could not have been prosecuted as carnal abuse, leaving only one prosecution for attempted rape, in 1951; see DACCF 1561 (1951). A charge of attempted rape was typically included in indictments in which carnal abuse was the lead charge, but in the cases in my sample that charge never came into play.

31. One case did include evidence of penetration; see DACCF 208414 (1936). It was originally treated as a sodomy case. There are few details in the case file, but it appears that there was no evidence to corroborate the claims made by the seven-year-old victim. That situation could have precluded a sodomy charge, which led the prosecutor to turn to carnal abuse as a safer bet.

32. In the 1930s, only 8.6 percent of the male victims in sodomy cases were eighteen years of age or older. See *The Report of the Mayor's Committee*, 66.

33. The two exceptions are DACCF 189579 (1931); DACCF 227419 (1941).

34. N = 15 of 20. That total includes only those cases for which details survive.

35. DACCF 227208 (1941).

36. Transcript of Hearing before the First, March 1941, Grand Jury, 1 April 1941, 3 – 5, ibid.

37. DACCF 188135 (1931).

38. ADA's handwritten notes, DACCF 230042 (1941). For another girl who used "privates," see DACCF 2482 (1951). For girls who used the word "thing," see DACCF 188821 (1931); DACCF 189579 (1931); DACCF 188282 (1931); DACCF 210860 (1936); DACCF 781 (1946); DACCF 2764 (1955).

39. For examples of girls who used "wee wee," see DACCF 187415 (1931); DACCF 1793 (1951). For examples of girls using "pee pee," see DACCF 1159 (1955). For "number one," see DACCF 229121 (1941); DACCF 227208 (1941). For "wetter," see DACCF 2528 (1951). In many cases, it is not possible to identify the language that girls used because NYSPCC agents chose instead to employ the "scientific" terms "penis" and "vagina" in their briefs, to make clear the act that the defendant had committed.

40. DACCF 2490 (1955). For other examples, see DACCF 210227 (1936); DACCF 211002 (1936); DACCF 898 (1946); DACCF 2285 (1946); DACCF 2464 (1951); DACCF 2938 (1955). For cases still presented to emphasize force, see DACCF 186128 (1931); DACCF 211435 (1936).

41. Boys' language did not change to the same extent as that used by girls, although there are some instances in which boys used the phrases "number one" and "wee wee." See DACCF 210227 (1936); DACCF 736 (1951); DACCF 1504 (1955).

42. *Laws of New York, 1950*, chap. 525, 1278 – 79. Both boys and girls still lacked protection from sexual assaults by females other than acts of sodomy.

43. For the reference to the New York law in the Model Penal Code Commentary, see *Tentative Draft No. 4*, 279. It is not clear why New York acted so much earlier than any other state.

44. See, for example, Eskridge, *Gaylaw*, 106 – 8. Legislatures in Arkansas, Georgia, Nevada, and New Jersey did reduce the minimum penalty for sodomy to one year in the mid-1950s, but they continued to classify the crime as a felony, punishable by long prison sentences up to life.

45. New York State, *Public Papers of Thomas E. Dewey, 1950*, 412.

46. By omitting any mention of "voluntary submission" and not including sodomy in the corroboration requirement that applied to other sex offenses, the 1950 law allowed a conviction on the basis of a victim's testimony alone, a change that distinguished sodomy from rape. Although the statute applied to both male and female victims, that provision perhaps recognized jurors' greater willingness to believe the testimony of boys. Whatever the reasoning of those who drafted the new law, the state's court of appeals quickly reinstated the corroboration requirement. For the appellate court ruling concerning the twelve-year-old boy, see *People v. Doyle*, 304 N.Y. 120 (1952). See also W. Nelson, *The Legalist Reformation*, 202 – 5.

47. N = 28 of 81.

48. DACCF 188424 (1931); DACCF 210860 (1936). The case from 1936 was anomalous in other ways. A medical examination revealed a ruptured hymen, evidence of

penetration that should have resulted in a charge of rape. Initially, the defendant pled guilty to misdemeanor carnal abuse, but, for reasons not recorded in the file, he withdrew that plea. Although the case then went to trial, it ended, on the motion of the ADA, in an acquittal.

49. DACCF 210227 (1941).

50. DACCF 188821 (1931); DACCF 189562 (1931).

51. N = 14 of 31, or 14 of 19 men indicted for sodomy. Witnesses reported only four of twenty sodomy cases involving young boys for which there are details, and two of seven involving young girls.

52. See tables 8 and 9 in the appendix. At first glance, it appears that an older emphasis on the gender of the victim continued to assert itself in carnal abuse prosecutions: in the years 1931 to 1946, the conviction rate for cases that involved girls was only two-thirds of that for cases that involved boys (see table 8). A closer examination reveals that the low conviction rate in cases involving girls resulted from the age of the victims and the nature of the acts encompassed by the new law: cases involving boys were not handled differently than cases involving girls; rather, they involved different circumstances and evidence. As a result, the handful of carnal abuse prosecutions that involved boys more often produced convictions. In six of the eleven cases prosecuted from 1936 to 1955, the defendant admitted the charge, mitigating the need for sworn testimony. In one of the remaining cases, the eight- and nine-year-old boys involved were judged able to give sworn testimony; in another, there was an adult eyewitness to the crime. The grand jury transferred the remaining three cases to the court of special sessions, to be prosecuted, in 1946 and 1951, as misdemeanors. For the cases involving admissions, see DACCF 209186 (1936); DACCF 230136 (1941); DACCF 230248 (1941); DACCF 227103 (1941); DACCF 228576 (1941); DACCF 1441 (1955). For the case in which the boys were sworn, see DACCF 228686 (1941). For the case involving the eyewitness, see DACCF 736 (1951). For the cases that were transferred, see DACCF 2435 (1946); DACCF 1330 (1946); DACCF 2499 (1951).

53. N = 16 of 33. The proportion is similar in sodomy cases: N = 6 of 11.

54. For examples, see DACCF 229226 (1941); DACCF 228913 (1941); DACCF 230088 (1941); DACCF 885 (1951).

55. New York State Legislature, *Report of the Joint Committee*, 668.

56. Transcript of Magistrates' Courts Hearing, 9 December 1946, 26, in DACCF 3713 (1946).

57. The ADA's notes on the trial include a list of jurors that records their occupations and how many children they had; most had adult children. The six female jurors were a physician, a radio scriptwriter, an RT conductor, a secretary, a woman who worked in furniture, and one whose occupation is not legible in the ADA's notes. The 1937 law made jury service voluntary for women. Not until 1975 did it become mandatory. See Perry, "Rhetoric, Strategy, and Politics in the New York Campaign for Women's Jury Service."

58. ADA's notes, DACCF 229121 (1941).

59. From 1886 to 1926, the proportion was 20 percent (N = 25); from 1931 to 1955, it was 85 percent (N = 20).

60. Krush and Dorner, "Ten-Point Protection against Molesters," 7. For more

on the discourse of child molestation, see P. Jenkins, *Moral Panic*, 72, 98–106; Fejes, "Murder, Perversion, and Moral Panic," 325–26.

61. P. Jenkins, *Moral Panic*, 98–106.

Chapter Nine

1. DACCF 1934 (1946).

2. In 1930, the African American population of New York City numbered 327,706. By 1940, it had jumped to about 450,000, or 6 percent of the population. Further migration from the South saw it increase still more in subsequent decades, reaching 1,668,115 in 1970, or 20 percent of the population. See Binder and Reimers, *All the Nations under Heaven*, 158, 214. The major period of Puerto Rican migration began in the mid-1940s, lifting the population in New York City from 61,463 in 1940 to 187,420 by 1950, and 429,710 by 1960. See Fitzpatrick, *Puerto Rican Americans*, 11.

3. The only sustained discussions of the transformed understanding of adolescence are Alexander, *The Girl Problem*, and Jones, *Taming the Troublesome Child*.

4. Staff of the Child Study Association of America, "Sex Education Today," 237.

5. Blanchard and Manasses, *New Girls for Old*, 60–61, 69. For more on this point, see Palladino, *Teenagers*, 28–29, 167–68.

6. Strain, *The Normal Sex Interests of Children*, 138. Strain was the widow of a Congregational minister; she had studied at the University of Colorado and conducted research on sex education at the University of Minnesota. By 1948, she had spent a decade conducting classes in high schools and giving lectures at universities.

7. W. Richmond, *The Adolescent Girl*, 54. Richmond was a psychologist at St. Elizabeth's Hospital in Washington, D.C.

8. W. Richmond, *The Adolescent Boy*, 127.

9. Gilbert, *Cycle of Outrage*, 18–19.

10. See *Report of the Mayor's Committee*, 35. For other examples of New York state public officials making this argument, see Moran, *The Sex Criminal on Parole*, 23; Ploscowe, *Sex and the Law*, 178–84, 193.

11. For a discussion of the reaction to adolescent girls during World War II, see Robertson, "Sexuality through the Prism of Age," 377–84.

12. *Laws of New York, 1943*, chap. 549, 1128–30; *Laws of New York, 1944*, chap. 632, 1301–4. Those under sixteen years of age were already dealt with separately from adults, in the Children's Court. The procedure made defendants not indicted for an offense punishable by death or life imprisonment and not previously convicted of a felony eligible to be examined and investigated to determine if they should be adjudged youthful offenders. If, on the basis of the report prepared by the Probation Department, the judge determined a defendant was a youthful offender, the indictment was nullified. The judge could then commit the defendant, give him a suspended sentence, or place him on probation for up to three years. Being judged a youthful offender did not represent a conviction; the proceedings took place in private, and all the records relating to the case were sealed. See *Young People in the Courts of New York State* (Legislative Document 55, 1942). This document is the fifth and last in a series produced by the Children's Court Jurisdiction and Juvenile Delinquency

Committee, a joint legislative committee created in 1937 to examine whether minors aged sixteen to eighteen years of age needed to be dealt with differently from adult offenders.

13. *Laws of New York, 1950*, chap. 525, 1280. Other states with similar statutory rape laws by 1949 included South Carolina, Vermont, West Virginia, and Wisconsin; see Sherwin, *Sex and the Statutory Law*, 75. New Jersey, Connecticut, Maryland, Massachusetts, and Wyoming included age disparity as one of the elements that needed to be present in a sex crime to bring it within the scope of the state's sexual psychopath statute; see Vuocolo, *The Repetitive Sex Offender*, 38, 121, 130, 132, 153.

14. Kunzel, *Fallen Women, Problem Girls*, 157.

15. Strain, *The Normal Sex Interests of Children*, 138.

16. Frazier, *The Negro Family in the United States*, 256–67. For Frazier's influence on social workers, see Kunzel, *Fallen Women, Problem Girls*, 156–65.

17. PDCF 29344 (1936) and DACCF 210212 (1936).

18. See table 6 in the appendix.

19. School authorities, for example, reported pregnant girls to the NYSPCC. For examples, see PDCF 51296 (1946) and DACCF 3327 (1946); DACCF 187082 (1931); DACCF 1934 (1946); DACCF 3575 (1946); DACCF 3755 (1946); DACCF 1041 (1951); DACCF 1859 (1951); DACCF 3619 (1955); and DACCF 1609 (1955).

20. DACCF 228615 (1941).

21. DACCF 3216 (1955) and PDCF 71014 (1955).

22. For an analysis of bastardy law and its reform in the nineteenth century, see Grossberg, *Governing the Hearth*, 196–233. For the emergence of illegitimacy as a problem that concerned Progressive reformers, and their decision to address that problem through a focus on paternity and maintenance, see Tiffin, *In Whose Best Interest?* 166–86. For the New York law, which was added to the domestic relations law, see *Laws of New York, 1925*, chap. 255, 508–14. For a discussion of paternity proceedings in the late 1940s and early 1950s, see Association of the Bar of the City of New York and Gellhorn, *Children and Families in the Courts of New York City*, 192–216; Schatkin, *Disputed Paternity Proceedings*, 357–89.

23. For example, in explaining his decision to recommend that Jacob Buchwald be allowed to plead guilty to a misdemeanor in 1936, an ADA noted that "paternity proceedings were instituted in the Court of Special Sessions and the defendant admitted to being the father of the said child. An order of affiliation was filed in the said court directing the defendant to pay $3 a week for support of the child. . . . In view of this fact, and the immaturity of both of the parties concerned, . . . nothing further could be gained by presenting the above facts to a petit jury, as the sentence in this case, under the above plea, can be commensurate with the nature of the crime committed" (DACCF 209817 [1936]). For another example, see DACCF 229064 (1941).

24. In 1951, for example, men admitted paternity in 837 of the 917 cases decided; see Association of the Bar of the City of New and Gellhorn, *Children and Families in the Courts of New York City*, 198.

25. African American men constituted 24 percent of the defendants in cases involving girls aged eleven to seventeen years (excluding sodomy cases) (N = 178 of

754). In the 1940s, the proportion reached over 40 percent (N = 62 of 137 in 1941; N = 51 of 126 in 1946).

26. N = 61 of 185.

27. Efforts to arrange a marriage took place in 36 percent of the cases (N = 22 of 61), compared to an average of 45 percent of cases in the earlier period (see table 6 in the appendix).

28. Drake and Clayton, *Black Metropolis*, 592, 594. See also E. Smith, *A Study of Twenty-five Adolescent Unmarried Mothers in New York City*; and the studies discussed in Franklin, *Ensuring Inequality*, 132–36.

29. N = 22 of 95.

30. D'Emilio and Freedman, *Intimate Matters*, 300.

31. Of the sixty-six men charged with the rape of an eleven- to seventeen-year-old girl in 1951, twenty-three were Puerto Rican. Of the 104 charged in 1955, forty-five were Puerto Rican.

32. In the years 1951 and 1955, marriage was discussed in nine of the eighteen cases involving a pregnant Puerto Rican girl, in only two of the eleven cases involving a pregnant African-American girl, and in six of the twenty-five cases involving a pregnant white girl.

33. Fitzpatrick, *Puerto Rican Americans*, 81, 96–97; Glazer and Moynihan, *Beyond the Melting Pot*, 89, 125.

34. PDCF 51296 (1946) and DACCF 3460 (1946).

35. Glazer and Moynihan, *Beyond the Melting Pot*, 89–90.

36. M. Richmond and Hall, *Child Marriages*, 72–73, 75, 79–80, 102, 107–8; "Finds 15-Year-Olds Permitted to Wed," *NYT*, 6 March 1925, 11.

37. See, for example, DACCF 187293 (1931).

38. "The Child Marriage Law in Operation," *Proceedings of the Eighth Annual Conference of the New York State Association of Judges of County Children's Courts*, 71. For examples of cases in which the Children's Court refused to permit a marriage, see DACCF 3375 (1946); DACCF 3916 (1946); DACCF 370 (1951); DACCF 2276 (1951); and DACCF 1139 (1955).

39. DACCF 3916 (1946).

40. Only one in four men convicted received suspended sentences in my two sample years in the 1930s (N = 34 of 132). The proportion jumped to one in every two in 1941 (N = 20 of 37), and then again to two in every three in 1946 (N = 22 of 33), before dropping back to just under half of those convicted in the 1950s (N = 16 of 34).

41. PDCF 29344 (1936) and DACCF 210212 (1936).

42. See PDCF 51296 (1946), in which a marriage that took place after the man had been released from two years of probation came to light only because he was placed on probation again five years later.

43. DACCF 448 (1946) and PDCF 49507 (1946).

44. "Child Bride Happy in Play with Doll," *NYT*, 31 January 1937, sec. 2, 2; "Child Marriages Not Rare in Nation," *NYT*, 7 February 1937, sec. 2, 2; "What God Hath Joined," *Time*, 15 February 1937, 41–2.

45. *Newsweek*, 13 February 1937, 15; *NYDN*, 21 April 1937, 1.

46. *Newsweek*, 14 November 1938, 14; *NYT*, 5 February 1937, 2; *NYT*, 23 March 1937, 10.

47. Gilbert, *Cycle of Outrage*, 20–1; Palladino, *Teenagers*, 169; Modell, *Into One's Own*, 243–53.

48. DACCF 1139 (1955).

49. Lynd and Lynd, *Middletown*, 114, 241. Frazier noted that African American girls also read, and were influenced by, those magazines; see Frazier, *The Negro Family in the United States*, 264. See also Hollingshead, *Elmtown's Youth*, 427.

50. For examples of girls who talked of being "in love," see DACCF 188025 (1931); DACCF 209984 (1936); DACCF 229277 (1941); DACCF 2297 (1946); DACCF 203 (1951); DACCF 1238 (1955); DACCF 3826 (1955). On ideas about the nature of marriage, see D'Emilio and Freedman, *Intimate Matters*, 73–78. On the attitude of African American girls in the 1960s, see Solinger, *Wake Up Little Susie*, 78–79.

51. DACCF 229507 (1941). For another example, see DACCF 208318 (1936). Kunzel notes that few unmarried mothers were prepared to express such desire to social workers; see Kunzel, *Fallen Women, Problem Girls*, 111.

52. Haag, "In Search of the 'Real Thing,'" 555. See also Fass, *The Damned and the Beautiful*, 272–76; D'Emilio and Freedman, *Intimate Matters*, 261.

53. See Robertson, "Sexuality through the Prism of Age," 405–10, for a discussion of runaways.

54. In 1925, the age of consent in Puerto Rico was fourteen. See Oppenheimer and Eckman, *Laws Relating to Sex Offenses against Children*, 61.

55. DACCF 3168 (1946).

56. Robert Conway, "Cagey Delinquents Shun 'Great Vice Way,'" *NYDN*, 27 February 1944, 38 (in "Juvenile Delinquency," Subject Files, roll 110, Papers of Mayor La Guardia, Municipal Archives, City of New York).

57. DACCF 2967 (1946).

58. New York State Law Revision Commission, *Communication and Study Relating to Sexual Crimes*, 7.

59. This language does not appear in case files in 1931; "keeping company" is used in its place. See DACCF 189572 (1931); DACCF 187470 (1931); DACCF 186800 (1931). In the 1951 cases, twenty-nine of the sixty-six defendants are identified as boyfriends.

60. DACCF 229304 (1941).

61. New York State Legislature, *Report of the Joint Legislative Committee*, 749.

62. DACCF 227716 (1941).

63. The decision is perhaps less inexplicable if we note that Stewart was an African American.

64. New York State Legislature, *Report of the Joint Committee*, 750.

65. Ibid., 768.

66. Ibid., 404. For other examples, see Robertson, "Separating the Men from the Boys," 33.

67. *Papers of Governor Dewey, 1950*, 412.

68. For the child protection movement's adoption of a social work approach,

see Gordon, *Heroes of Their Own Lives*, 34, 52, 60–81. For the investigation of the NYSPCC, see *New York Herald Tribune*, 5 August 1937 (Scrapbooks, roll 33, La Guardia Papers), and the summary of the investigation prepared by E. S. Epstein, an administrative assistant to Mayor La Guardia, in Departmental Correspondence, Mayor's Office, Epstein, SPCC (1937), roll 521, 1718–56, La Guardia Papers.

69. That conflict reached a head early in 1944, with the release of a report highly critical of the NYSPCC. For examples of the extensive coverage it attracted, see "2 Probes Condemn Shelter for 'Oliver Twist' Methods," *New York Post*, 22 January 1944; "Conditions at SPCC Found 'Wretched,'" *NYT*, 23 January 1944. On the NYSPCC's defiant response, see "Assails SPCC 'Misstatements,'" *New York Post*, 27 January 1944; "S.P.C.C. Charges Are Rebutted by Herlands Office," *New York Herald Tribune*, 27 January 1944. On La Guardia's establishment of alternative arrangements, see "City Moving Children from SPCC Shelter," *New York Post*, 7 February 1944; "New Group to Supervise Care of Children Committed to Shelters," *NYT*, 7 February 1944 (all in Scrapbooks, vol. 262, rolls 3 and 4, La Guardia Papers).

70. See Kunzel, *Fallen Women, Problem Girls*, particularly 115–43, for a perceptive analysis of the struggle between evangelical women and social workers.

71. The incident had only come to light, a year after it occurred, because Anna had left home, and her mother had mistakenly assumed that she was with Sawyer, who coincidentally was out "carousing with some friends" that night.

72. DACCF 3074 (1946).

73. See tables 8 and 9 in the appendix. By the 1950s, men under twenty-one years of age accused of sexual intercourse with an underage girl, the age group least likely to be indicted, did not even face the grand jury. They instead faced trial for third-degree rape in the Court of Special Sessions. Their absence likely kept the proportion of men indicted from being even lower. Of those not indicted in 1951, almost three-quarters (N = 30 of 41) had made an admission (no details of the evidence survive in six cases). Of those not indicted in 1955, nine out of every ten (N = 57 of 64) had admitted their guilt.

74. See *Report of the Governor's Study Commission*, 71; Ellis and Brancale, *The Psychology of Sex Offenders*, 15; Vuocolo, *The Repetitive Sex Offender*, 62.

75. DACCF 229064 (1941).

76. DACCF 210461 (1936). For other examples, see DACCF 208013 (1936); DACCF 209055 (1936); DACCF 209817 (1936); DACCF 210142 (1936); DACCF 211409 (1936).

77. For examples of cases in which men were indicted because no arrangements had been made for a child's support, see DACCF 229064 (1941); DACCF 227747 (1941); DACCF 487 (1946); DACCF 685 (1946).

78. DACCF 226753 (1941).

79. For examples of cases in which married men were indicted, see DACCF 186831 (1931); DACCF 229260 (1941); DACCF 1843 (1951); DACCF 2448 (1951); DACCF 2439 (1955); DACCF 2210 (1955); DACCF 3619 (1955). In the 1950s, almost all the married men who escaped indictment had initiated divorce proceedings to allow them to marry the girl with whom they had had sexual intercourse. See DACCF 690 (1951); DACCF 1650 (1951); DACCF 3826 (1955); DACCF 3269 (1955). For examples of cases

in which men had reneged on promises, see DACCF 209518 (1936); DACCF 210074 (1936); DACCF 229277 (1941); DACCF 229304 (1941); DACCF 448 (1946); DACCF 2785 (1946); DACCF 3355 (1946); DACCF 607 (1951).

80. N = 186.

81. N = 42.

82. N = 223.

83. From 1931 to 1946, 88 percent (N = 26) of those indicted for sodomy with boys aged eleven to seventeen years pled guilty to misdemeanors, compared to 77 percent (N = 186) of those indicted for the rape of girls aged eleven to seventeen years. The proportions in 1951 to 1955 were 73 percent (N = 11) for sodomy and 69 percent (N = 42) for rape. In sodomy cases, 76 percent (N = 38) of those convicted were sentenced to spend no more than a year behind bars, or had their sentences suspended, in the years 1931 to 1955; in rape cases, the proportion was 85 percent (N = 223).

84. Court of General Sessions Trial Transcript, 17 October 1941, 15, DACCF 228808 (1941).

85. See, for example, Transcript, Grand Jury, 2 February 1955, DACCF 278 (1955).

86. Ibid., 20–21. The testimony of other boys about more dramatic reactions after acts of sodomy—vomiting and hysteria—likewise failed to convince prosecutors that they had not submitted. See DACCF 1333 (1946); DACCF 3535 (1946).

87. DACCF 429 (1946).

88. N = 14 of 24 with details.

89. Pollens, *The Sex Criminal*, 28.

Chapter Ten

1. Foreword to Pollens, *The Sex Criminal*, 12.

2. *Report of the Governor's Study Commission*, 235–37.

3. Bowman and Engle, "A Psychiatric Evaluation of Laws of Homosexuality," 311–12.

4. For an insightful account of the articulation of the "psychiatry of everyday life," see Lunbeck, *The Psychiatric Persuasion*.

5. Here I follow Elizabeth Lunbeck, who argues that the focus on the normal represented a different project from mental hygiene. That distinction is captured in Herman Adler's statement that "the term psychopathic lays the emphasis on variation from the normality, whereas the term mental hygiene emphasizes the maintenance of mental health." See ibid., 327–28 n. 4.

6. Willrich, "The Two Percent Solution," 8.

7. For the clinic in the Court of General Sessions, see Department of Hospitals, *Annual Report of the Psychiatric Clinic*, 24–25; Bromberg, *Psychiatry between the Wars*, 109–19.

8. Willrich, "The Two Percent Solution," 96.

9. T. A. Green, "Freedom and Criminal Responsibility in the Age of Pound," 1942.

10. Pollens, *The Sex Criminal*, 12.

11. Freedman, "'Uncontrolled Desires'"; Chauncey, "The Postwar Sex Crime Panic"; P. Jenkins, *Moral Panic*, 49–93.

12. Pollens, *The Sex Criminal*, 12.

13. See chapter 7; Pollens, *The Sex Criminal*, 18.

14. The lawyer for Salvatore Ossido, one of the other child murderers arrested in 1937, did enter a plea of insanity. However, the commission of psychiatrists appointed to examine Ossido declared, by a vote of two to one, that he was sane. Three other doctors who testified for the defense at his trial disagreed. Family members also testified that Ossido had changed after contracting syphilis as a teenager. Nonetheless, the jury convicted him. See the sources cited in n. 1 of chapter 7.

15. See Lunbeck, *The Psychiatric Persuasion*, especially 65–71.

16. Karpman, *The Sexual Offender*, 490.

17. Ibid.; Bromberg, *Crime and the Mind*; Guttmacher, *Sex Offenses*; Mangus, "Society and Sexual Deviation"; Abrahamsen, *Report on Study of 102 Sex Offenders*; New York State [Glueck], *Final Report*; Ellis and Brancale, *The Psychology of Sex Offenders*; Pacht, Halleck, and Ehrmann, "Diagnosis and Treatment of the Sexual Offender," 802–8; Kozol, Boucher, and Garofalo, "The Diagnosis and Treatment of Dangerousness."

18. *Report of the Mayor's Committee*; Tappan, *The Habitual Sex Offender*; *Report of the Governor's Study Commission*.

19. Karpman, *The Sexual Offender*, 478–79. For other examples, see Guttmacher, *Sex Offenses*, 43, 69, 77; Leppmann, "Essential Differences between Sex Offenders," 368–69; Roche, "Sexual Deviations," 4. Researchers who attempted to bring the nature of the sexual psychopath into focus also emphasized his immaturity. See Halleck and Pacht, "The Current State of the Wisconsin State Sex Crime Law," 21; Pacht, Halleck, and Ehrmann, "Diagnosis and Treatment of the Sexual Offender," 808; Abrahamsen, *Report on Study of 102 Sex Offenders*, 5–6, 22; Ellis and Brancale, *The Psychology of Sex Offenders*, 56–60; New York State [Glueck], *Final Report*, 23–24, 85–87; Apfelberg, Sugar, and Pfeffer, "A Psychiatric Study of 250 Sex Offenders," 769; Kozol, Boucher, and Garofalo, "The Diagnosis and Treatment of Dangerousness," 379.

20. Gebhard, Gagnon, Pomeroy, and Christenson, *Sex Offenders*, 850. Clinicians used "immature" in 38 percent of the cases the study examined; only "neurotic" was used more often, in 45 percent of cases.

21. Pollens, *The Sex Criminal*, 11, 39. For similar arguments in other popular writing by psychologists and psychiatrists, see Hartwell, *A Citizens' Handbook*, 36; Piker, "A Psychiatrist Looks at Sex Offenses," 394. (Piker's paper was presented as part of a panel at an observance of National Social Hygiene Day.) Newspapers and periodicals gave a similar prominence to immaturity in their reporting of psychiatric accounts of the sex offender, but they favored the parallel with childishness at the expense of other metaphors. See Hewlett, "What Shall We Do about Sex Offenders?" 38; Shoenfield, *The Sex Criminal*, 34, 37–38, 42; Whitman, "The Biggest Taboo," 38; G. D. Schultz, *How Many More Victims?* 157, 159, 315, 317, 325.

22. Abrahamsen, *Report on Study of 102 Sex Offenders*, 5.

23. Karpman, *The Sexual Offender*, 479.

24. Ellis and Brancale, *The Psychology of Sex Offenders*, 43. For other examples of ar-

guments that immaturity was a source of the sexual psychopath's lack of control, see Kozol, Boucher, and Garofalo, "The Diagnosis and Treatment of Dangerousness," 379; Pacht, Halleck, and Ehrmann, "Diagnosis and Treatment of the Sexual Offender," 804–5.

25. Hewlett, "What Shall We Do about Sex Offenders?" 38. For another example, see Tappan, "The Sexual Psychopath," 356.

26. See Bromberg, *Crime and the Mind*, 88–89; Karpman, *The Sexual Offender*, 45; Guttmacher, *Sex Offenses*, 86.

27. New York State [Glueck], *Final Report*, 86–87. A variation of this argument asserted that the sex offender's emotional immaturity manifested itself in feelings of inferiority and anxiety about potency, which, as Manfred Guttmacher put it, caused them to "lack the courage to attempt to make sexual contact with contemporaries, or fear the obligation of performing satisfactorily for a sexually experienced, and possibly critical, female" (Guttmacher, *Sex Offenses*, 43). For other examples of this argument, see Bromberg, *Crime and the Mind*, 88; Abrahamsen, *Report on Study of 102 Sex Offenders*, 6; Ellis and Brancale, *The Psychology of Sex Offenders*, 58.

28. Sutherland, "The Diffusion of Sexual Psychopath Laws," 143. For similar conclusions, see Wile, "Sex Offenses against Young Children," 39.

29. Wittels, "What Can We Do about Sex Crimes?" 52.

30. See Staff of the Citizens Committee, *The Problem of Sex Offenses in New York City*, 9; *Report of the Mayor's Committee*, 35; Ploscowe, *Sex and the Law*, 181, 184.

31. G. D. Schultz, *How Many More Victims?* 131. For another example, see Hewlett, "What Shall We Do about Sex Offenders?" 69.

32. For a discussion of child protection discourse about elderly men, see Gordon, *Heroes of Their Own Lives*, 222–26.

33. See, for example, Chaddock, "Sexual Crimes," 543–44; Emerson, *Legal Medicine and Toxicology*, 115; Williams, "Rape in Children and in Young Girls: Part One," 246.

34. Henninger, "The Senile Sex Offender," 438. For other examples, see Guttmacher, *Sex Offenses*, 43–44, 95–97; Hartwell, *A Citizen's Handbook*, 15; De River, *The Sexual Criminal*, 75; Frosch and Bromberg, "The Sex Offender," 765; Apfelberg, Sugar, and Pfeffer, "A Psychiatric Study of 250 Sex Offenders," 766.

35. Henninger, "The Senile Sex Offender," 438–39.

36. For nonscholarly discussions of senile offenders, see Palmer, "Crimes against Children," 15; G. D. Schultz, *How Many More Victims?* 130; *Report of the Mayor's Committee*, 35.

37. For Leopold and Loeb, see Fass, "Making and Remaking an Event," 940–42. For the growing hostility toward homosexuals in the 1930s and the new sinister portrait of the homosexual, see Chauncey, *Gay New York*, 301–61; D'Emilio, "The Homosexual Menace," 226–40.

38. Major, "New Moral Menace," 101–8.

39. Faegre, *The Adolescent in Your Family*, 50. For accounts of homosexuals as fixated and immature, see Henry, *Sex Variants*, 1023; Karpman, *The Sexual Offender*, 148–51; Leppmann, "Essential Differences between Sex Offenders," 369; Pollens, *The*

Sex Criminal, 51; G. D. Schultz, *How Many More Victims?* 308; P. Jenkins, *Moral Panic*, 62.

40. Chauncey, *Gay New York*.

41. P. Jenkins, *Moral Panic*, 95–98.

42. Ibid., 90, 96.

43. For judges' referrals of black men for examination, see Guttmacher, *Sex Offenses*, 59. For diagnoses, see Vuocolo, *The Repetitive Sex Offender*, 79; Mangus, "Society and Sexual Deviation," 139; P. Jenkins, *Moral Panic*, 88–89.

44. Cited in Frederickson, *The Black Image*, 280–81. For the power of the image of the African American man as a bestial rapist in the North, see D'Emilio and Freedman, *Intimate Matters*, 297–98. Even southern and northern moderates who did not accept that image and minimized the bestial, criminal tendencies of African Americans continued to play up their childishness and picture them as "helpless wards" and "harmless children"; see Frederickson, *The Black Image*, 285–88.

45. For example, see Childers, "Some Notes on Sex Mores among Negro Children," 442–48.

46. Ellis and Brancale, *The Psychology of Sex Offenders*, 105. Psychiatrists also brought racial ideas to their subjective assessments of offenders, as is starkly evident in Manfred Guttmacher's explanation for the lack of African American exhibitionists and pedophiles:

> Both the exhibitionists and the pedophiles have a high percentage of passive-dependent individuals, with marked feelings of general and penile inferiority. The common belief, fully confirmed by Kinsey's actual measurements, that the Negro's penis is considerably longer than that of the white man's, may be the basis for their low incidence among the exhibitionists and pedophiles. The low frequency of sexual exhibitionism among Negroes may in part be due to the free rein that many males at certain socio-economic levels give to exhibitionism in other ways—with their gaudy-colored zoot suits and their flashy automobiles (Guttmacher, *Sex Offenses*, 66–67).

47. *Report of the Governor's Study Commission*, 6.

48. Deutsch, "Sober Facts," 64; Hewlett, "What Shall We Do about Sex Offenders?" 68; Piker, "A Psychiatrist Looks at Sex Offenses," 395–96; Shoenfield, *The Sex Criminal*, 47; G. D. Schultz, *How Many More Victims?* 138–55.

49. Pollens, *The Sex Criminal*, 183; Hewlett, "What Shall We Do about Sex Offenders?" 38, 67–68. For other examples, see Karpman, *The Sexual Offender*, 81–84; Rabinovitch, "A Study of Sexually Disturbed Children," 44–45; De River, *The Sexual Criminal*, 19; Deutsch, "Sober Facts," 64; G. D. Schultz, *How Many More Victims?* 138–39.

50. Hartwell, *A Citizen's Handbook*, 15, 36. For other examples, see *Report of the Governor's Study Commission*, 31; Rabinovitch, "A Study of Sexually Disturbed Children," 48–49; New York State [Glueck], *Final Report*, 23–24.

51. Hartwell, *A Citizen's Handbook*, 44; Piker, "A Psychiatrist Looks at Sex Offenses," 396; Wittels, "What Can We Do about Sex Crimes?" 63.

52. Ellis and Brancale, *The Psychology of Sex Offenders*, 56–57, 60. For other examples, see Rabinovitch, "A Study of Sexually Disturbed Children," 48–49; Guttmacher, *Sex Offenses*, 150; Karpman, *The Sexual Offender*, 84–85; *Report of the Governor's Study Commission*, 107; G. D. Schultz, *How Many More Victims?* 139–40, 143–48, 153–45.

53. Pollens, *The Sex Criminal*, 183.

54. Hartwell, *A Citizen's Handbook*, 11. For other examples, see the studies cited in Karpman, *The Sexual Offender*, 151–54.

55. Rabinovitch, "A Study of Sexually Disturbed Children," 49–50. For similar arguments, see Guttmacher, *Sex Offenses*, 149; A. R. Mangus, "Society and Sexual Deviation," in *Final Report of the California Sexual Deviation Research*, 71–73; Hewlett, "What Shall We Do about Sex Offenders?" 69; Shoenfield, *The Sex Criminal*, 61.

56. Charles Dutton, "Psychological Data," in Rogers, Weiss, Darwin, and Dutton, "Study of Sex Crimes against Children," *California Sexual Deviation Research, Third Annual Report, January 1953*, 78. For other examples, see Bender and Paster, "Homosexual Trends in Children"; Karpman, *The Sexual Offender*, 303–4.

57. Rabinovitch, "A Study of Sexually Disturbed Children," 49–50. For other examples, see Hewlett, "What Shall We Do about Sex Offenders?" 69; case of Thomas B., in Henry, *Sex Variants*, 5, 99–107.

58. *Report of the Governor's Study Commission*, 106; New York State [Glueck], *Final Report*, 86–87; Hewlett, "What Shall We Do about Sex Offenders?" 69; G. D. Schultz, *How Many More Victims?* 309; cases of Michael D., Eric D., Louis E., Archibald T., and Gabriel T., in Henry, *Sex Variants*, 5–9, 127–59, 184–206, 291–303, 314–29.

59. Whitman, "The Biggest Taboo," 24. For other examples, see East, "Sexual Offenders," 546; cases of Theodore S., Gene S., Dennis C., Daniel O'L., and Percival G., in Henry, *Sex Variants*, 7–9, 12–13, 231–58, 303–33, 425–38, 477–87.

60. Pollens, *The Sex Criminal*, 50–51 (all four of the case studies of homosexuality offered by Pollens involve seduction by adults). For other examples of arguments that seduction caused homosexuality, see East, "Sexual Offenders," 546; De River, *The Sexual Criminal*, xii, 89, 91; New York State [Glueck], *Final Report*, 87; case of Antonio L., in Henry, *Sex Variants*, 11–12, 414–25; Reinhardt, *Sex Perversions and Sex Crimes*, 21, 43. For other examples of arguments that seduction by adults was merely a trigger, see Hartwell, *A Citizen's Handbook*, 11; cases of Paul A., James D., Archibald T., and Gene S., in Henry, *Sex Variants*, 7–9, 219–30, 242–68, 291–303. Both Rabinovitch and Glueck cautioned that a single, isolated experience was not enough to redirect a boy's development; see Rabinovitch, "A Study of Sexually Disturbed Children," 46; New York State [Glueck], *Final Report*, 23.

61. Major, "New Moral Menace," 102. For other examples, see Ploscowe, *Sex and the Law*, 211, 213–14; and the coverage of a scandal about crimes against boys in Boise, Idaho, discussed in Gerassi, *Boys of Boise*.

62. D'Emilio, "The Homosexual Menace," 232.

63. Whitman, cited in P. Jenkins, *Moral Panic*, 63; Major, "New Moral Menace," 104. Accounts of such cycles rarely appeared in writings by psychiatrists.

64. Pollens, *The Sex Criminal*, 191–97; New York State [Glueck], *Final Report*, 88; Whitman, "The Biggest Taboo," 40. For other examples, see Ellis and Brancale, *The Psychology of Sex Offenders*, 91–92; Guttmacher, *Sex Offenses*, 149, 151; Henry, *Sex*

Variants, 1025–26; Hartwell, *A Citizen's Handbook*, 49; *Report of the Governor's Study Commission*, 181–82.

65. Chicago Crime Prevention Bureau, *Meeting*, 12.

66. See, for example, Glover, "Control of the Sex Deviate"; Sarafian, "Treatment of the Criminally Dangerous Sex Offender."

67. *NYT*, 10 August 1937, 1, 7 (quote on 7); *NYDN*, 10 August 1937, 3; *NYT*, 11 August 1937, 42.

68. *NYT*, 18 August 1937, 42.

69. Shaskan, "One Hundred Sex Offenders," 565; John Mayer, Chairmen, Parole Commission, to Mayor William O'Dwyer, 28 August 1946; Peter Amoroso, Commissioner of Correction, to Thomas Corcoran, Deputy Mayor, 9 September 1946; Edward Bernecker, Commissioner of Hospitals, to Thomas Corcoran, Deputy Mayor, 9 September 1946; Peter Amoroso, Commissioner of Correction, to Thomas Corcoran, Deputy Mayor, 19 September 1946, all correspondence in Subject Files, Crime, 1946, box 136, folder 327, Papers of Mayor William O'Dwyer, Municipal Archives, City of New York.

70. Austin MacCormick, the city's commissioner of correction, reported to a symposium at the annual meeting of the National Committee for Mental Hygiene in November 1937 that, "as we all expected, after a period of observation it is necessary to release most of them, as they cannot usually be declared insane and committed to a state hospital." See MacCormick, "New York's Present Problem," 8.

71. Staff of the Citizens Committee, *The Problem of Sex Offenses*, 10. Among the many examples presented in the report was that of a seventy-year-old defendant determined to be sane, but whose psychiatric report showed him to be mentally defective, senile, and "exhibiting regressive and infantile sexual impulses" (13).

72. *Report of the Mayor's Committee*, 9.

73. *102nd ARPANY, 1946*, 20–21, 120–23; *103rd ARPANY, 1947*, 39–40.

74. The bill also provided for men already imprisoned to be adjudged sexual psychopaths, transferred to a special institution, and held after their sentences had expired. The bill was Senate Int. 1432, Pr. 2790. It is reproduced in *102nd ARPANY, 1946*, 120–23.

75. Veto Jacket Collection, Senate Int. 1432, Pr. 2790 (1947). Editorial writers at the *NYT* and the *NYDN* added their endorsement, albeit in very different language. Whereas the *NYT* extolled the legislation as "not sentimental" but rather a "scientific" and "sensible" means of taking the psychopath "out of circulation," the *NYDN* lauded the bill as an important addition to society's arsenal of weapons "of self-protection against people who are dangerously off beam in the sex department." See *NYT*, 1 March 1947, 14; *NYDN*, 6 March 1947, 14.

76. John Lyons to Charles Breitel, Counsel to the Governor, 26 March 1947, Veto Jacket Collection, Senate Int. 1432, Pr. 2790 (1947). Senator Desmond got wind of Lyons's objections, and wrote to the governor urging that enacting the bill did not conflict with the commissioner's desire for further investigation. He also warned Dewey that "the rape or assault of some child by a sex pervert in the interim between the appointment of a study committee and effectuation of its recommendations would call attention in a very tragic way to the urgency for signing this bill." See Thomas

Desmond to Charles Breitel, Counsel to the Governor, 26 March 1947, Veto Jacket, Senate Int. 1432, Pr. 2790 (1947).

77. *Public Papers of Thomas E. Dewey, 1947*, 254–56. Ploscowe himself wrote to the governor, criticizing the inclusion of disorderly conduct in the bill. "This section is used primarily to deal with persons guilty of homosexual behavior in subway and theatre toilets," Ploscowe noted. "I doubt whether the behavior involved is sufficiently dangerous or anti-social to warrant the use of the procedure provided for in the law." See Morris Ploscowe to Charles Breitel, Counsel to the Governor, 31 March 1947, Veto Jacket Collection, Senate Int. 1432, Pr. 2790 (1947). In his memorandum on the bill, Dewey also expressed fears about giving the power to commit offenders for life to lower courts and justices of the peace.

78. Minutes of the Meeting of the Executive Committee of the PANY, 16 October 1947, 3–4.

79. Abrahamsen, *Report on Study of 102 Sex Offenders*, 5, 15, 17–21.

80. *Recommendations Supplementing Report on Study of 102 Sex Offenders*, 5–6.

81. *Public Papers of Thomas E. Dewey, 1950*, 412. The offenses to which the law applied were first-degree rape, first-degree sodomy, carnal abuse, the attempt to commit one of those crimes, or any felony, other than first-degree murder, that involved sexual abuse of a child or sexual abuse of an adult involving grievous bodily harm. See *Laws of New York, 1950*, chap. 525, 1271–84.

82. Note, "New York's New Indeterminate Sentence Law," 349 n. 18.

83. *NYT*, 12 April 1950, 20. The law enjoyed wide support in New York. See Bill Jacket Collection, Chapter 525, No. 3372, Int. 2830 (1950); *NYT*, 25 March 1950, 12. It did come under attack from Dr. Perry Lichtenstein, who oversaw legal medicine and psychiatric examination for the New York County DA. He told an audience at a conference organized by the Welfare Council that the law was a "sop to public opinion motivated by political considerations." See *NYT*, 18 May 1950, 58. In fact, because it provided for a criminal sentence, not for a civil commitment, New York's law is commonly omitted from accounts of sexual psychopath statutes.

84. Four criteria typically identified sexual psychopaths in those laws: the commission of a sexual offense or conviction of a specified sexual crime; the presence of a mental disorder or of mental illness, but not insanity or mental deficiency; a "propensity to commit sexual offenses" or "habitual course of conduct in sexual matters [that shows] an utter lack of power to control his sexual impulses"; and a risk of future danger. In order to identify those offenders, the statutes provided for the same medical examinations as the New York law, either after a man had been charged or, more often, after he had been convicted. Any found to be sexual psychopaths could be committed to a mental hospital for an indefinite period of time. Just as in the case of the New York law, only when psychiatrists found an offender had been cured, could he be released, or, in some states, returned to the courts for the disposition of the original criminal charge against him. See Lindman and McIntyre, *The Mentally Disabled and the Law*, 314–18.

85. Tappan, *The Habitual Sex Offender*, 34–35.

86. See Lindman and McIntyre, *The Mentally Disabled and the Law*, 303.

87. For a constitutional challenge to the law as cruel and unusual punishment and as a violation of due process, see *People ex rel. Wilson v. Denno* 145 N.Y.S. 2d 175, 1955 N.Y. Misc LEXIS 3302. That case also raised a challenge to the law on the grounds that an offender could be sent to a state prison after being sentenced to an indeterminate term that could be as short as one day; this was in violation of the state penal law's stipulation that no one sentenced to a term of less than one year could be sent to a state prison. For another decision on that issue, see *People ex rel. Schaap v. Martin* 189 N.Y.S.2d 884 1959 N.Y. LEXIS 1159.

88. The total is provided by Gladys Shultz (Schultz, *How Many More Victims?* 170). Official figures, which were published in the annual report of the New York State Department of Mental Hygiene only for the first four years of the law's existence, reveal that 120 of those men were sentenced in the years 1951 to 1954. The numbers by year are as follows: 1951, nineteen; 1952, fifty; 1953, nineteen; 1954, thirty-two (*Annual Report of the Department of Mental Hygiene* [NYSL Document 82, 1953], 73; [NYSL Document 95, 1954], 81; [NYSL Document 90, 1955], 74). Bowman and Engle report a further seventy-six sex offenders given indeterminate sentences in the next three years, for a total of 196 in the first seven years of the law's operation. See Bowman and Engle, "Certain Aspects of Sex Psychopath Laws," 693, 695.

89. See table 10 in the appendix.

90. Those figures are calculated in line with the inconsistency in the statute, whereby neither second-degree rape nor second-degree sodomy fell within the law, but second-degree assault, the attempt to commit those crimes, did.

91. N = 32 of 36. See table 9 of the appendix.

92. DACCF 1793 (1951).

93. Chicago Crime Prevention Bureau, *Meeting*, 8.

94. For the outcome of carnal abuse and sodomy cases, see chapters 8 and 9. Men convicted in rape prosecutions involving adult women were convicted of felonies in 26 percent of cases (N = 6 of 23) in the years 1931 to 1946 and in 28 percent of cases (N = 6 of 21) in the years 1951 and 1955. Only one case departs from the pattern of the earlier years, a carnal abuse case involving touching, not penetration, in which the defendant pled guilty to attempted second-degree assault; all eleven men convicted of committing such an act in the preceding decades had pled guilty to a misdemeanor. See DACCF 524 (1955).

95. Granucci and Granucci, "Indiana's Sexual Psychopath Act," 564.

96. The quoted phrase is from the sworn declaration required of psychiatrists undertaking examinations for the Court of General Sessions. A copy can be found in DACCF 647 (1955). In one case, the offender's lawyer was also present at the hearing. See DACCF 524 (1955). In another case, Dr. Perry Lichtenstein, who oversaw legal medicine and psychiatric examination for the New York County DA, and had been an outspoken critic of the sex offender law, was also in attendance. See DACCF 2909 (1951).

For reasons I have not been able to establish, the figures provided by the psychiatric clinic for the number of examinations conducted there under the sex offender law do not match the number of eligible cases in my sample. The clinic's *Annual Report* recorded four examinations in 1951; five in 1952; eleven in 1953; one in 1954; nine in 1955; none in 1956; one in 1957; no information in 1958; one in 1959; one in 1960; one in 1961; none in 1962; one in 1963; one in 1964; none in 1965; none in 1966; and one in 1967.

97. The two cases for which no psychiatric examinations survive are DACCF 526 (1951) and DACCF 1150 (1951). No file at all survives for the later case; the only information I have is what was recorded in the DA's docket book.

98. At least forty-nine of the seventy-two cases involved children: thirty-two carnal abuse cases and seventeen sodomy cases. In addition, there were nineteen second-degree assault cases, many of which were likely to have involved children. See *108th ARPANY, 1952*, 33–34.

99. For two decades before 1950, the staff of the psychiatric clinic had been identifying homosexual offenders as maladjusted and as psychopathic. A twenty-nine-year-old African American man, convicted of impairing the morals of a minor after being found with several teenage boys in his room in 1946, and considered to be "effeminate and manneristic," was classified by Leo Orenstein as a person of a "constitutional psychopathic state, pathological sexuality." See PDCF 50048 (1946). For other examples, see PDCF 29793 (1936); PDCF 29917 (1936); PDCF 29369 (1936); PDCF 51455 (1946); PDCF 51311 (1946); PDCF 51346 (1946); PDCF 51410 (1946).

100. DACCF 2909 (1951).

101. DACCF 524 (1955).

102. DACCF 647 (1955).

103. Indeterminate sentences were handed down to only four of 147 men convicted of rape. See *108th ARPANY, 1952*, 33.

104. Messinger used the phrase in his report on twenty-four-year-old Moses Brown, a black shipping clerk whose case is discussed in chapter 9. See PDCF 71014 (1955).

105. DACCF 647 (1955).

106. For the court's instruction, see the declaration signed by psychiatrists who conducted examinations, in DACCF 647 (1955). For the language of the statute, see *Laws of New York, 1950*, chap. 525, 1282.

107. Thompson, who had two previous convictions for indecent assault, admitted performing fellatio on three teenage boys, a runaway who had stayed with him and his twenty-two-year-old roommate, and friends who had visited the apartment. Although Thompson told the examining psychiatrists that "he tries to control himself, but does not succeed," they could find "no evidence of a desire to control his homosexual activities." Their report thus concluded that "there is nothing to show he will not continue to annoy young boys for the rest of his life." See DACCF 137 (1955).

108. Senator Desmond accused the state's judges of ignoring the law, of being obstinate, of having an aversion to indeterminate sentences, and of showing reluctance to follow the judgment of psychiatrists. See *108th ARPANY, 1952*, 33–34.

109. According to the figures that the Department of Correction provided Senator Desmond, in New York City only one in ten sex criminals was sentenced under the law, half the proportion in the rest of the state. See *108th ARPANY, 1952*, 33.

110. *People ex rel. Lawson v. Denno* 9 N.Y. 2d 181, 1961 N.Y. LEXIS 1489; *People ex rel. Pealo v. La Vallee* 249 N.Y.S. 2d 534, 1964 N.Y. Misc LEXIS 1760; *People v. Kinney*

19 A.D. 2d 576, 1963 N.Y. App. Div. LEXIS 3758; *People ex rel. Kaganovitch v. Wilkins* 23 A.D. 2d 178, 1965 N.Y. App. Div. LEXIS 4190.

111. *People v. Drake* 30 A.D. 2d 616, 1968 N.Y. App. Div. LEXIS 3874.

112. *People v. Bailey* 21 N.Y. 2d 588, 1968 N.Y. LEXIS 1472.

113. Ibid. The court also held that the U.S. Supreme Court's recent decision in *Specht v. Patterson* did apply to the New York sex offender law, requiring a hearing separate from the finding of guilt before an indeterminate sentence could be imposed. Again, the practice in New York County was already in conformity with that ruling. The decision of the court of appeals led to the re-sentencing of many of the 155 men serving indeterminate sentences at the time that it was handed down. But even one of the psychiatric reports completed at that time still failed to comply with the court's requirements. See *People v. Sickler* 33 A.D. 2d 1050, 1970 N.Y. App. Div. LEXIS 5439.

114. Pacht, Halleck, and Ehrmann, "Diagnosis and Treatment of the Sexual Offender," 803. A similarly elaborate procedure was followed in Massachusetts. Kozol and his colleagues reported that "each diagnostic study is based on clinical examinations, psychological tests, and a meticulous reconstruction of the life history elicited from multiple sources." The clinical examinations were conducted by two psychiatrists, two psychologists, and a social worker. See Kozol, Boucher, and Garofalo, "The Diagnosis and Treatment of Dangerousness," 383–84. The most elaborate practices were those in New Jersey, where an institution was devoted entirely to the diagnosis of sex offenders. See Vuocolo, *The Repetitive Sex Offender.*

115. E. Cohen, "Administration of the Criminal Sexual Psychopath Statute in Indiana," 460–61. A study of psychiatric reports submitted in California in the 1970s failed to find any significant reliance on clinical observations of a defendant's characteristics or behavior derived from an interview. Instead, the psychiatrist would base the diagnosis on the social history obtained by the probation officer. Dix, "Differential Processing of Abnormal Sex Offenders," 236.

116. Brakel and Rock, *The Mentally Disabled and the Law,* 355; Caporale and Hamann, "Sexual Psychopathology," 336–37.

117. New York State [Glueck], *Final Report,* iv.

118. Ibid., 82–83, 89.

119. G. D. Schultz, *How Many More Victims?* 170.

120. *People v. Higgins* 175 N.Y.S. 2d 217; 1958 N.Y. Misc LEXIS 3728. For another example of a man imprisoned in Attica who received no treatment, see *People ex rel. Kaganovitch v. Wilkins* 23 A.D. 2d 178, 1965 N.Y. App. Div. LEXIS 4190.

121. *People v. Copp* 35 A.D. 2d 1065, 1970 N.Y. App. Div. LEXIS 3320.

122. *NYT,* 29 December 1963, 48, cited in Vuocolo, *The Repetitive Sex Offender,* 13–14; *People v. Jackson* 21 A.D. 2d 843 (1963).

123. G. D. Schultz, *How Many More Victims?* 170.

124. Kozol, Boucher, and Garofalo, "The Diagnosis and Treatment of Dangerousness," 386. The Wisconsin program, California's Atascadero State Hospital, and the New Jersey program likewise settled on group therapy as their treatment of choice. See Pacht, Halleck, and Ehrmann, "Diagnosis and Treatment of the Sexual Offender," 806; Glover, "Control of the Sex Deviate," 38–43; Lieberman and Siegel,

"A Program for 'Sexual Psychopaths,'" 805–6; Prager, "'Sexual Psychopathology' and the Child Molesters," 69; Cole, "From the Sexual Psychopath Statute to 'Megan's Law,'" 299–300.

125. Fahr, "Iowa's New Sexual Psychopath Law," 545–46. See also Caporale and Hamann, "Sexual Psychopathology," 341–42.

126. *121st ARCANY, 1965*, 43.

127. Minutes, Executive Committee of the PANY, 24 March 1955, 5; Minutes, Executive Committee of the PANY, 10 October 1957, 6.

128. *People v. Jackson* 20 A.D. 2d 170 (1963).

129. Prager, "'Sexual Psychopathology' and the Child Molesters," 55–59. Similar cases were catalysts to action in Wisconsin and New Jersey. See Ransley, "Repeal of the Wisconsin Sex Crimes Act," 953–55; Cole, "From the Sexual Psychopath Statute to 'Megan's Law,'" 300–301.

130. Prager, "'Sexual Psychopathology' and the Child Molesters," 77.

131. Ibid., 68.

132. For a thorough, if somewhat dismissive, overview of this shift, see P. Jenkins, *Moral Panic*, 118–44.

Conclusion

1. M. Richmond and Hall, *Child Marriages*, 129–30.
2. Chudacoff, *How Old Are You?* 4–5.
3. Geertz, *Local Knowledge*, 232.
4. *Philanthropist* 11, 3 (March 1896): 10.
5. See Spohn and Horney, *Rape Law Reform*.

bibliography

Manuscript Collections

Albany, N.Y.
New York State Archives
Papers of Governor Thomas Dewey
Papers of Governor Lehman
New York, N.Y.
City of New York
Municipal Archives, Department of Records and Information Services
Court of General Sessions Case Files
Court of General Sessions, Probation Department, Case Files
District Attorney's Closed Case Files
District Attorney's Docket Books
District Attorney's Scrapbooks
Papers of Mayor La Guardia
Papers of Mayor William O'Dwyer
John Jay College of Criminal Justice
Special Collections
Trial Transcript Collection
New York Public Library
Bill Jacket Collection
Veto Jacket Collection
Minutes of the Meetings of the Correctional Association of New York

Cases

People v. Ardelean, 368 Ill. 278 (1938)
People v. Bailey, 21 N.Y. 2d 588, 1968 N.Y. LEXIS 1472
People v. Baldwin, 124 N.Y. 433, 130 App. Div. 404 (1910)

Barton v. Bee Line, 265 N.Y.S. 284 (1933)

People v. Belcher, 299 N.Y. 323, 87 N.E. 2d 279 (1949)

Boyles v. Blankenhorn, 153 N.Y.S. 467 (1915)

People v. Block, 105 N.Y.S. 175 (1907)

People v. Brehm, 218 N.Y.S. 469, 218 App. Div. 266 (1926)

People v. Cole, 134 App. Div. 759 (1909)

State v. Comeaux, 131 La. 930 (1913)

People v. Copp, 35 A.D. 2d 1065, 1970 N.Y. App. Div. LEXIS 3320

People v. Crocker, 74 N.Y.S. 2d 593 (1947)

People v. Cullen, 5 N.Y. Supp. 887 (1889)

Dawkins v. The State, 58 Ala. 376 (1877)

Dekelt v. The People, 44 Colo. 525 (1908)

People v. De Salvo, 294 N.Y.S. 87 (1937)

People v. Deschessere, 74 N.Y.S. 761 (1902)

People v. Donohue, 100 N.Y.S. 204 (1906)

People v. Downs, 140 N.E. 708 (1923)

People v. Doyle, 304 N.Y. 120 (1952)

People v. Drake, 30 A.D. 2d 616, 1968 N.Y. App. Div. LEXIS 3874

Dusenbury v. State, 42 N.Y.S. 2d 731 (1943)

People v. Elston, 186 App. Div. 229 (1919)

People v. Gibson, 134 N.E. 532 (1922)

People v. Grauer, 42 N.Y.S. 721, 12 App. Div. 468 (N.Y., 1896)

People v. Harriden, 1 Parker Cr. R., 344 (1852)

People v. Higgins, 175 N.Y.S. 2d 217; 1958 N.Y. Misc LEXIS 3728

People v. Hopkins, 208 App. Div. 438 (1924)

State v. Houx, 109 Mo. 654 (1891)

State v. Hummer, 73 N.J.L. 714 (1906)

Hutto v. The State, 169 Ala. 19 (1910)

People v. Jackson, 21 A.D. 2d 843 (1963)

People v. Justices of Special Sessions, 10 Hun 226 (1877)

People ex rel. Kaganovitch v. Wilkins, 23 A.D. 2d 178, 1965 N.Y. App. Div. LEXIS 4190

People v. Kingsley, 166 App. Div., N.Y. Supp. 980

People v. Kinney 19 A.D. 2d 576, 1963 N.Y. App. Div. LEXIS 3758

Lambertson v. The People, 5 Parker's C.R. 200 (1861)

People v. Lammes, 203 N.Y.S. 741 (1924)

People ex rel. Lawson v. Denno, 9 N.Y. 2d 181, 1961 N.Y. LEXIS 1489

State v. MacLean, 135 N.J.L. 491 (1947)

People v. Marks, 146 App. Div. 13 (1911)

People v. Miller, 96 Mich. 119 (1893)

Milne v. The People, 224 Ill. 125 (1906)

Noonan v. The State, 55 Wis. 260 (1882)

Koenig v. Nott, 2 Hilt. (N.Y.) 323 (1859)

People v. O'Connor, 295 Ill. 203 (1920)

People v. Page, 56 N.E. 750, 162 N.Y. 272, 14 N.Y. Cr. R. 513 (1900)

People ex rel. Pealo v. La Vallee, 249 N.Y.S. 2d 534, 1964 N.Y. Misc LEXIS 1760

People v. Petrucci, 67 N.Y.S. 2d 611 (1947)

People v. Plath, 100 N.Y. 590 (1885)

People v. Rabens, 87 N.Y.S. 2d 183, 275 App. Div. 717 (1949)

People v. Ragone, 67 N.Y.S. 24 (1900)

Dean v. Raplee, 145 N.Y.R. 323–324, 326–327 (1895)

People ex rel. Schaap v. Martin, 189 N.Y.S. 2d 884, 1959 N.Y. LEXIS 1159

People v. Schultz, 260 Ill. 40 (1913)

People v. Shaw, 142 N.Y.S. 782, 158 App. Div. 146 (1913)

People v. Sheppard, 44 Hun 565 (1886)

People v. Sickler, 33 A.D. 2d 1050, 1970 N.Y. App. Div. LEXIS 5439

People v. Sileo, 202 App. Div. 760 (1922)

Sims v. The State, 146 Ala. 109 (1906)

People v. Stott, N.Y. Crim. Rep. 308 (1886)

People v. Talesnik, 225 N.Y. 495 (1919)

People v. Terwilliger, 74 Hun 310, 26 N.Y.S. 674 (1893)

People ex rel. Wilson v. Denno, 145 N.Y.S. 2d 175, 1955 N.Y. Misc LEXIS 3302

People v. Wilson, 135 N.Y.S. 2d 893 (1954)

State v. Wright, 25 Neb. 38 (1888)

Published Primary Sources

Abbe, Truman. *Wharton and Stillé's Medical Jurisprudence*. Vol. 3. 5th ed. Rochester, N.Y., 1905.

Abrahamsen, David. *Report on Study of 102 Sex Offenders at Sing Sing Prison*. Albany, 1950.

Addams, Jane. *A New Conscience and an Ancient Evil*. New York, 1912.

———. *The Spirit of Youth and the City Streets*. New York, 1912.

Apfelberg, Benjamin, Carl Sugar, and Arnold Pfeffer. "A Psychiatric Study of 250 Sex Offenders." *American Journal of Psychiatry* (May 1944): 762–70.

American Law Institute. *Model Penal Code: Tentative Drafts Nos. 1, 2, 3, and 4*. Philadelphia, 1955.

Association of the Bar of the City of New York and Walter Gellhorn. *Children and Families in the Courts of New York City*. New York, 1954.

Beck, Theodoric. *Elements of Medical Jurisprudence*. Vol. 1. Albany, 1823.

Bell, Ernest E. *Fighting the Traffic in Young Girls*. Chicago, 1911.

Bender, Lauretta. "Behavior Problems in Negro Children." *Psychiatry* 2, 2 (May 1939): 213–28.

Bender, Lauretta, and Abram Blau. "The Reaction of Children to Sexual Relations with Adults." *American Journal of Orthopsychiatry* 7 (1937): 500–18.

Bender, Lauretta, and Alvin Grugett. "A Follow-up Report on Children Who Had Atypical Sexual Experience." *American Journal of Orthopsychiatry* 22 (1952): 825–37.

Bender, Lauretta, and Samuel Paster. "Homosexual Trends in Children." *American Journal of Orthopsychiatry* 11 (1941): 730–43.

Bensing, Robert. "A Comparative Study of American Sex Statutes." *Journal of Criminal Law, Criminology, and Police Science* 42 (1951): 57–72.

Blackburn, D. R. N. "Incest." *Criminal Law Magazine and Reporter* 17, 4 (July 1895): 389–99.

Blackwell, Emily. "Age of Consent Legislation." *The Philanthropist* 10, 2 (February 1895): 1–2.

Blanchard, Phyllis, and Carolyn Manasses. *New Girls for Old.* New York, 1930.

Bowling, R. W. "The Sex Offender and Law Enforcement." *Federal Probation* 14 (September 1950): 11–16.

Bowman, Karl, and Beatrice Engle. "A Psychiatric Evaluation of Laws of Homosexuality." *Temple Law Quarterly* 29 (1956): 273–326.

———. "Certain Aspects of Sex Psychopath Laws." *American Journal of Psychiatry* (February 1958): 690–97.

Brace, Charles Loring. *The Dangerous Classes of New York and Twenty Years Work among Them.* New York, 1872.

Bradley, Raymond, and Phillip Margolin. "The Oregon Sexually Dangerous Persons Act." *Willamette Law Journal* 8 (1972): 341–95.

Bromberg, Walter. *Crime and the Mind: An Outline of Psychiatric Criminology.* Philadelphia, 1948.

Brown, M. Ralph. *Legal Psychology: Psychology Applied to the Trial of Cases, to Crime and Its Treatment, and to Mental States and Processes.* Indianapolis, 1926.

Burtt, Harold. *Legal Psychology.* New York, 1931.

Caporale, Domenico, and Deryl Hamann. "Sexual Psychopathology—A Legal Labyrinth of Medicine, Morals and Mythology." *Nebraska Law Review* 36 (March 1957): 320–53.

Chaddock, Charles. "Sexual Crimes." In *A System of Legal Medicine*, vol. 2, edited by Allan Hamilton and Lawrence Godkin. New York, 1894.

———. "Unnatural Sexual Offenses." In *Legal Medicine and Toxicology*, edited by Frederick Peterson, Walter Haines, and Ralph Webster. Philadelphia, 1923.

Charles, Sol. "Child Victims of Sexual Offenses." *Federal Probation* 31 (June 1967): 52–56.

Chicago Crime Prevention Bureau. *Meeting of the Crime Prevention Bureau on Sexual Offenders.* Chicago, 1949.

Childers, A. T. "Some Notes on Sex Mores among Negro Children." *American Journal of Orthopsychiatry* 6 (1936): 442–48.

Claghorn, Kate Holladay. *The Immigrant's Day in Court.* New York, 1923.

Clifton-Edgar, J., and J. Johnston. "Rape." In *Medical Jurisprudence, Forensic Medicine and Toxicology*, edited by R. A. Witthaus and Tracy Becker. New York, 1894.

Cohen, Elias. "Administration of the Criminal Sexual Psychopath Statute in Indiana." *Indiana Law Journal* 32 (1957): 450–76.

Committee of Fourteen. *The Social Evil in New York City: A Study of Law Enforcement by the Research Committee of the Committee of Fourteen.* New York, 1910.

Crow, Lester, and Alice Crow. *Adolescent Development and Adjustment.* New York, 1956.

Davis, Alison, and John Dollard. *Children of Bondage: The Personality Development of Negro Youth in the Urban South.* New York, 1940.

De River, Paul. *The Sexual Criminal: A Psychoanalytical Study.* Springfield, 1949.

Deutsch, Albert. "Sober Facts about Sex Crimes." *Collier's*, 25 November 1950, 15–16, 63–64.

Deutsch, Helene. *The Psychology of Women*. Vol. 1. New York, 1944.

Dix, George. "Differential Processing of Abnormal Sex Offenders: Utilization of California's Mentally Disordered Sex Offender Program." *Journal of Criminal Law and Criminology* 67, 2 (1976): 233–43.

Drake, St. Clare, and Horace Clayton. *Black Metropolis: A Study of Negro Life in a Northern City*. New York, 1945.

Draper, Frank. *A Textbook of Legal Medicine*. Philadelphia, 1905.

Du Bois, W. E. B. *The Philadelphia Negro: A Social Study*. New York, 1899.

East, Norwood. "Sexual Offenders—A British View." *Yale Law Journal* 55 (1946): 527–57.

Ellis, Albert, and Ralph Brancale. *The Psychology of Sex Offenders*. Springfield, Ill., 1956.

Emerson, Robert Leonard. *Legal Medicine and Toxicology*. New York, 1909.

Faegre, Marion. *The Adolescent in Your Family*. Children's Bureau Publication No. 347. Washington, D.C., 1954.

Fahr, Samuel. "Iowa's New Sexual Psychopath Law—An Experiment Noble in Purpose?" *Iowa Law Review* 41 (1956): 523–57.

Feinsinger, Nathan. "Legislative Attack on 'Heart Balm.'" *Michigan Law Review* 33, 7 (May 1935): 979–1009.

Frazier, E. Franklin. *The Negro Family in the United States*. Rev. and abridged ed. New York, 1951.

Frosch, Jack, and Walter Bromberg. "The Sex Offender—A Psychiatric Study." *American Journal of Orthopsychiatry* 9 (1939): 761–76.

Gagnon, John. "Female Child Victims of Sex Offenses." *Social Problems* 13, 2 (1965): 176–92.

Gardener, Helen. "A Battle for Sound Morality, or The History of Recent Age-of-Consent Legislation in the United States, Part I." *The Arena* 13 (August 1895): 353–64.

———. "A Battle for Sound Morality, or The History of Recent Age-of-Consent Legislation in the United States, Part II." *The Arena* 14 (September 1895): 1–32.

———. "A Battle for Sound Morality, or The History of Recent Age-of-Consent Legislation in the United States, Part III." 14 *The Arena* (October 1895): 205–20.

Gebhard, Paul, John Gagnon, Wardell Pomeroy, and Cornelia Christenson. *Sex Offenders: An Analysis of Types*. New York, 1965.

Gibb, W. T. "Indecent Assaults upon Children." In *A System of Legal Medicine*, vol. 1, edited by Allan McLane Hamilton and Lawrence Godkin. New York, 1894.

Glover, Benjamin. "Control of the Sex Deviate." *Federal Probation* 24 (September 1960): 38–43.

Gold, Mike. *Jews without Money*. New York, 1930.

Granucci, Anthony, and Susan Granucci. "Indiana's Sexual Psychopath Act in Operation." *Indiana Law Journal* 44 (Summer 1969): 555–94.

Groves, Ernest, and Gladys Hoagland Groves. *Sex in Childhood*. New York, 1933.

Guttmacher, Manfred. *Sex Offenses: The Problem, Causes and Prevention*. New York, 1951.

Haines, William, Harry Hoffman, and Robert Esser. "Commitments under the Criminal Sexual Psychopath Law in the Criminal Court of Cook County, Illinois." *American Journal of Psychiatry* 105 (December 1948): 420–25.

Hall, G. Stanley. *Adolescence: Its Psychology and Its Relations to Physiology, Anthropology, Sociology, Sex, Crime, Religion and Education.* 2 vols. New York, 1905.

Halleck, Seymour, and Asher Pacht. "The Current State of the Wisconsin State Sex Crime Law." *Wisconsin Bar Bulletin* (December 1960): 17–26.

Harris, Charles. "Sex Crimes: Their Cause and Cure." *Coronet*, August 1946, 3–9.

———. "A New Report on Sex Crimes." *Coronet*, October 1947, 3–9.

Hartwell, Samuel. *A Citizens' Handbook of Sexual Abnormalities and the Mental Hygiene Approach to Their Prevention.* Lansing, Mich., 1950.

Healy, William. *The Individual Delinquent: A Text-Book of Diagnosis and Prognosis for All Concerned in Understanding Offenders.* Boston, 1915.

Hennessy, Maurice. "Homosexual Charges against Children." *Journal of Criminal Psychopathology* 2, 4 (1941): 524–32.

Henninger, James. "The Senile Sex Offender." *Mental Hygiene* 23 (1939): 436–44.

Henry, George. *Sex Variants: A Study of Homosexual Patterns.* New York, 1941.

Hewlett, Irma. "What Shall We Do about Sex Offenders?" *Parents' Magazine*, August 1950, 36–38, 67–71.

Hollingshead, A. B. *Elmtown's Youth.* New York, 1961.

Hoover, J. Edgar. "How Safe Is Your Daughter?" *American Magazine*, July 1947, 32–33, 102–4.

———. "How *Safe* Is Your Youngster?" *American Magazine*, March 1955, 9, 99–103.

Johnson, Charles. *Shadow of the Plantation.* Chicago, 1934.

———. *Growing Up in the Black Belt: Negro Youth in the Rural South.* New York, 1941.

Josselyn, Irene M. "Growing to Adulthood." In *Our Children Today: A Guide to Their Needs from Infancy through Adolescence*, edited by Sidonie Matsner Gruenberg and the Staff of the Child Study Association of America. New York, 1952.

Karpman, Benjamin. *The Sexual Offender and His Offenses.* New York, 1954.

Kinsey, Alfred, Wardell Pomeroy, and Clyde Martin. *Sexual Behavior in the Human Male.* Philadelphia, 1951.

Kinsey, Alfred, Wardell Pomeroy, Clyde Martin, and Paul Gebhard. *Sexual Behavior in the Human Female.* Philadelphia, 1953.

Klein, Melanie. *The Psychoanalysis of Children.* London, 1932 (1963).

Kozol, Harry, Richard Boucher, and Ralph Garofalo. "The Diagnosis and Treatment of Dangerousness." *Crime and Delinquency* 17 (October 1972): 371–92.

Krush, Thaddeus, and Nancy Dorner. "Ten-Point Protection against Molesters." *National Parent-Teacher*, October 1957, 7–10.

Leppmann, Friedrich. "Essential Differences between Sex Offenders." *Journal of Criminal Law and Criminology* 32 (1941): 366–80.

Lieberman, Daniel, and Benjamin Siegel. "A Program for 'Sexual Psychopaths' in a State Hospital." *American Journal of Psychiatry* 114 (March 1957): 801–7.

Lindsey, Ben, and Wainwright Evans. *The Revolt of Modern Youth.* Garden City, N.Y., 1925.

Lynd, Robert, and Helen Merrell Lynd. *Middletown: A Study in Modern American Culture.* New York, 1955 (1929).

MacCormick, Austin. "New York's Present Problem." *Mental Hygiene* 22 (January 1938): 4–10.

Major, Ralph. "New Moral Menace to Our Youth." *Coronet,* September 1950, 101–8.

Mangus, A. R. "Society and Sexual Deviation: A Fact-Finding Report of the California Sexual Deviation Research Program." In California Department of Mental Hygiene and the Langley Porter Clinic, *Final Report on California Sexual Deviation Research, March 1954.* Sacramento, 1954.

Marks, Georgina. "The Age of Consent." *Union Signal,* 3 December 1885, 4.

Meyer, Adolf. "The Meaning of Maturity." In *Our Children: A Handbook for Parents,* edited by Dorothy Canfield Fisher and Sidonie Matsner Gruenberg. New York, 1932.

Moran, Frederick A., *The Sex Criminal on Parole.* Albany, 194[?].

"New York's Child Marriage Law." *Journal of Social Hygiene* 5, 7 (October 1929): 427–28.

New York Society for the Prevention of Cruelty to Children. *Annual Report of the New York Society for the Prevention of Cruelty to Children.* New York, 1876–1950.
———. *Instructions for Officers and Staff of the New York Society for the Prevention of Cruelty to Children.* New York, 1931.

New York State. *Annual Conference of the Children's Court Judges of New York State.* Albany, 1927–31.
———. *Annual Report of the Department of Mental Hygiene.* Albany, 1951–54.
———. *Final Report of the New York State Research Project for the Study and Treatment of Persons Convicted of Crimes Involving Sexual Aberrations.* Albany, 1956.
———. *Laws of New York.* Albany, 1829–1955.
———. *Public Papers of Thomas E. Dewey, Fifty-first Governor of the State of New York.* Albany, 1947, 1950.

New York State Law Revision Commission. *Communication and Study Relating to Sexual Crimes.* Legislative Document 65(O), 1937. Albany, 1937.

New York State Legislature. Joint Legislative Committee to Investigate the Administration and Enforcement of the Law. *Report of the Joint Legislative Committee to Investigate the Administration and Enforcement of the Law.* Legislative Document 98, 1939. Albany, 1939.
———. *Young People in the Courts of New York State.* Legislative Document 55, 1942. Albany, 1942.

Niswander, Donald. "Some Aspects of 'Sexual Psychopath' Examinations in New Hampshire." *New Hampshire Bar Journal* (January 1962): 66–75.

Note. "New York's New Indeterminate Sentence Law for Sex Offenders." *Yale Law Journal* 60 (1951): 346–56.

Note. "The Rape Corroboration Requirement: Repeal Not Reform." *Yale Law Journal* 81 (1972): 1366–68.

Oppenheimer, Reuben, and Lulu Eckman. *Laws Relating to Sex Offenses against Children.* Children's Bureau Publication No. 145. Washington, D.C., 1925.

Pacht, Asher, Seymour Halleck, and John Ehrmann. "Diagnosis and Treatment of the Sexual Offender: A Nine-Year Study." *American Journal of Psychiatry* 119 (1962): 802–8.

Palmer, Gretta. "Crimes against Children." *The Digest*, 2 October 1937, 14–16.

Piker, Phillip. "A Psychiatrist Looks at Sex Offenses." *Journal of Social Hygiene* 33 (1947): 394–97.

Ploscowe, Morris. *Sex and the Law*. New York, 1951.

Pollens, Bertram. *The Sex Criminal*. New York, 1938.

Prager, Irving. "'Sexual Psychopathology' and the Child Molesters: The Experiment Fails." *Journal of Juvenile Law* 6 (1982): 49–79.

Prison Association of New York. *Annual Report of the Prison Association of New York*. Albany, 1937–66.

Psychiatric Clinic of the Court of General Sessions. *Annual Report*. New York, 1951–67.

Rabinovitch, Ralph. "A Study of Sexually-Disturbed Children: Notes from a Child Psychiatrist's Case-book." In *Report of the Governor's Study Commission on the Deviated Criminal Sex Offender*. Lansing, Mich., 1951.

Reese, John. *A Textbook of Medical Jurisprudence and Toxicology*. Philadelphia, 1895.

Reinhardt, James. *Sex Perversions and Sex Crimes*. Springfield, 1957.

Report of the Governor's Study Commission on the Deviated Criminal Sex Offender. Lansing, Mich., 1951.

Report of the Mayor's Committee for the Study of Sex Offenses. New York, 1943.

Richmond, Mary, and Fred Hall. *Child Marriages*. New York, 1925.

———. *Marriage and the State*. New York, 1929.

Richmond, Winifred. *The Adolescent Girl: A Book for Parents and Teachers*. New York, 1925.

———. *The Adolescent Boy: A Book for Parents and Teachers*. New York, 1933.

Robinson, William. *America's Sex, Marriage, and Divorce Problems*. New York, 1934.

Roche, Philip. "Sexual Deviations." *Federal Probation* 14, 3 (1950): 3–11.

Rogers, E. R., Joseph Weiss, Mirian Darwin, and Charles Dutton. "Study of Sex Crimes against Children." In California Department of Mental Hygiene and the Langley Porter Clinic, *California Sexual Deviation Research, Third Annual Report, January 1953*. Sacramento, 1953.

Rousseau, Jean-Jacques. *Emile* Translated by Barbara Foxley. London, 1974 (1911).

Russell Sage Foundation. *Boyhood and Lawlessness*. New York, 1914.

Sarafian, Robert. "Treatment of the Criminally Dangerous Sex Offender." *Federal Probation* 27 (March 1963): 52–59.

Schultz, Gladys Denny. *How Many More Victims? Society and the Sex Criminal*. Philadelphia, 1965.

Schultz, William. *The Humane Movement in the United States, 1910–1922*. New York, 1924.

Shaskan, Donald. "One Hundred Sex Offenders." *American Journal of Orthopsychiatry* 9 (1939): 565–69.

Shatkin, Sidney. *Disputed Paternity Proceedings*. 3rd ed. New York, 1953.

Sherwin, Robert V. *Sex and the Statutory Law in All 48 States: A Comparative Study and Survey of the legal and Legislative Treatment of Sex Problems*. New York, 1949.

Shoenfield, Allen. *The Sex Criminal*. Detroit, 1950.

Smith, Enid. *A Study of Twenty-five Adolescent Unmarried Mothers in New York City*. New York, 1935.

Smith, Mary Roberts. "The Social Aspect of New York Police Courts." *American Journal of Sociology* 5, 2 (1899): 145–54.

Staff of the Child Study Association of America. "Sex Education Today." In *Our Children Today: A Guide to Their Needs from Infancy through Adolescence*, edited by Sidonie Matsner Gruenberg. New York, 1952.

Staff of the Citizens Committee on the Control of Crime in New York, Inc. *The Problem of Sex Offenses in New York City*. New York, 1939.

Strain, Frances Bruce. *The Normal Sex Interests of Children*. New York, 1948.

Strecker, Edward. "The Challenge of Sex Offenders: Introduction." *Mental Hygiene* 22 (January 1938): 1–3.

Sutherland, Edwin. "The Diffusion of Sexual Psychopath Laws." *American Journal of Sociology* 56, 2 (1950): 142–48.

Tappan, Paul. *Delinquent Girls in Court: A Study of the Wayward Minor Court of New York*. Montclair, N.J., 1969 (1947).

———. "The Sexual Psychopath—A Civic-Social Responsibility." *Journal of Social Hygiene* 35, 8 (November 1949): 354–73.

———. *The Habitual Sex Offender*. Trenton, N.J., 1950.

Thom, Douglas. *Everyday Problems of the Everyday Child*. New York, 1928.

———. *Guiding the Adolescent*. Children's Bureau Publication No. 225. Washington, D.C., 1933.

Thomas, William. *The Unadjusted Girl*. New York, 1923.

Tidy, Charles. *Legal Medicine*. New York, 1884.

Towne, Arthur. "Young Girl Marriages in Criminal and Juvenile Courts." *Journal of Social Hygiene* 8, 3 (July 1922): 287–305.

Train, Arthur. *The Prisoner at the Bar: Sidelights on the Administration of Criminal Justice*. New York, 1926.

True, Ruth. *The Neglected Girl*. West Side Studies. New York, 1914.

Vernier, Chester G. *American Family Laws: A Comparative Study of the Family Law of the Forty-eight American States, Alaska, the District of Columbia, and Hawaii (to Jan. 1, 1931)*. 5 vols. Stanford, 1931–38.

Vuocolo, Alfred. *The Repetitive Sex Offender: An Analysis of the Administration of the New Jersey Sex Offender Program from 1949 to 1965*. Menlo Park, N.J., 1969.

Waldrop, Frank. "Murder as a Sex Practice." *American Mercury*, February 1948, 144–50.

Walker, Jerome. "Reports with Comments, of Twenty-one Cases of Indecent Assault and Rape upon Children: Part One." *Archives of Pediatrics* 3, 5 (1886): 269–86.

———. "Reports with Comments, of Twenty-one Cases of Indecent Assault and Rape upon Children: Part Two." *Archives of Pediatrics* 3, 6 (1886): 321–41.

Ware, Caroline. *Greenwich Village, 1920–1930: A Comment on American Civilization in the Post-war Years*. New York, 1935.

Webster, Ralph. *Legal Medicine and Toxicology*. Philadelphia, 1930.

Weiss, Joseph, Estelle Rogers, Miriam Darwin, and Charles Dutton. "A Study of Girl Sex Victims." *Psychiatric Quarterly* 29, 1 (January 1955): 1–27.

Wharton, Francis, and Moreton Stillé. *A Treatise on Medical Jurisprudence.* Philadelphia, 1855.

White, William A. "Childhood: The Golden Period for Mental Hygiene." *Mental Hygiene* 4 (April 1920): 257–67.

———. *The Mental Hygiene of Childhood.* Boston, 1925.

Whitman, Howard. "The Biggest Taboo." *Collier's,* 15 February 1947, 24, 38–40.

———. "The City That *Does* Something about Sex Crime." *Collier's,* 21 January 1950, 20–21, 64–65.

Whyte, William. "A Slum Sex Code." *American Journal of Sociology* 49, 1 (July 1943): 24–31.

Wigmore, John. *A Treatise on the System of Evidence in Trials at Common Law.* 4 vols. Boston, 1904.

Wile, Ira. "Society and Sex Offenders." *Survey Graphic,* November 1937, 569–72.

———. "Sex Offenses against Young Children: What Shall Be Done about Them?" *Journal of Social Hygiene* 25, 1 (January 1939): 33–44.

Williams, Gurney. "Rape in Children and in Young Girls: Part One." *International Clinics* 2, 23rd series (1913): 245–67.

———. "Rape in Children and in Young Girls: Part Two." *International Clinics* 3, 23rd series (1913): 245–67.

Wittels, David. "What Can We Do about Sex Crimes?" *Saturday Evening Post,* December 11, 1948, 30–31, 47, 49–52, 55, 58, 62–63, 65–66, 68–69.

Woods, Robert A., and Albert J. Kennedy, eds. *Young Working Girls: A Summary of Evidence from Two Thousand Social Workers.* Boston, 1913.

Worthington, George. "Stepping Stones to an Improved Law for Children Born Out of Wedlock." *Journal of Social Hygiene* 10, 3 (March 1924): 164–76.

Wortis, Joseph. "Sex Taboos, Sex Offenders, and the Law." *American Journal of Orthopsychiatry* 9 (1939): 554–64.

Secondary Sources

Alexander, Ruth. *The Girl Problem: Female Sexual Delinquency in New York, 1900–1930.* Ithaca, 1995.

Alschuler, Albert. "Plea Bargaining and Its History." *Columbia Law Review* 79, 1 (1979): 1–43.

Antler, Joyce, and Stephen Antler. "From Child Rescue to Family Protection: The Evolution of the Child Protective Movement in the United States." *Children and Youth Services Review* 1 (1979): 177–204.

Arnold, Marybeth Hamilton. "'The Life of a Citizen in the Hands of a Woman': Sexual Assault in New York City, 1790 to 1820." In *Passion and Power: Sexuality in History,* edited by Kathy Peiss and Christina Simmons. Philadelphia, 1989.

Bashar, Nazife. "Rape in England between 1550 and 1700." In *The Sexual Dynamics of History,* edited by the London Feminist History Group. London, 1983.

Battan, Jesse. "'The Word Made Flesh': Language, Authority, and Sexual Desire in

Late Nineteenth Century America." *Journal of the History of Sexuality* 3, 2 (October 1992): 223–44.

Bavin-Mizzi, Jill. *Ravished: Sexual Violence in Victorian Australia.* Sydney, 1995.

Bederman, Gail. *Manliness and Civilization: A Cultural History of Gender and Race in the United States, 1880–1917.* Chicago, 1995.

Behlmer, George. *Child Abuse and Moral Reform in England, 1870–1908.* Stanford, Calif., 1982.

Bessmer, Sue. *The Laws of Rape.* New York, 1984.

Bienen, Leigh. "Defining Incest." *Northwestern University Law Review* 92, 4 (Summer 1998): 1501–640.

Binder, Frederick, and David Reimers. *All the Nations under Heaven: An Ethnic and Racial History of New York City.* New York, 1995.

Block, Sharon. "Coerced Sex in British North America, 1700–1820." Ph.D. diss., Princeton University, 1995.

Boag, Peter. "Sex and Politics in Progressive-Era Portland and Eugene: The 1912 Same-Sex Vice Scandal." *Oregon Historical Quarterly* 100, 2 (1999): 158–81.

Boyd, Valerie. *Wrapped in Rainbows: The Life of Zora Neale Hurston.* New York, 2003.

Brakel, Samuel, John Perry, and Barbara Weiner, eds. *The Mentally Disabled and the Law.* 3rd ed. Chicago, 1985.

Brakel, Samuel, and Ronald Rock, eds. *The Mentally Disabled and the Law.* Rev. ed. Chicago, 1971.

Bremner, Robert H. *Children and Youth in America: A Documentary History.* 3 vols. Cambridge, Mass., 1971.

Brewer, Holly. "Age of Reason? Children, Testimony, and Consent in Early America." In *The Many Legalities of Early America*, edited by Christopher Tomlins and Bruce Mann. Chapel Hill, 2001.

Broder, Sherri. *Tramps, Unfit Mothers, and Neglected Children: Negotiating the Family in Nineteenth-Century Philadelphia.* Philadelphia, 2002.

Brumberg, Joan Jacobs. "Zenanas and Girless Villages: The Ethnology of American Evangelical Women." *Journal of American History* 69, 2 (1982): 347–71.

———. "'Ruined' Girls: Changing Community Responses to Illegitimacy in Upstate New York, 1890–1920." *Journal of Social History* 18 (1984): 247–72.

———. *The Body Project: An Intimate History of American Girls.* New York, 1997.

Chauncey, George. "The Postwar Sex Crime Panic." In *True Stories from the American Past*, edited by William Graebner. New York, 1993.

———. *Gay New York: Gender, Urban Culture, and the Making of the Gay Male World.* New York, 1994.

Chudacoff, Howard. *How Old Are You? Age Consciousness in American Culture.* Princeton, 1989.

Clark, Anna. *Women's Silence, Men's Violence: Sexual Assault in England, 1770–1845.* London, 1987.

Cohen, Miriam. *From Workshop to Office: Two Generations of Italian Women in New York City, 1900–1950.* Ithaca, 1992.

Cole, Simon. "From the Sexual Psychopath Statute to 'Megan's Law': Psychiatric Knowledge in the Diagnosis, Treatment, and Adjudication of Sex Criminals in

New Jersey, 1949–1999." *Journal of the History of Medicine and Allied Sciences* 55 (July 2000): 292–314.

Costin, Lela, Howard Jacob Karger, and David Stoesz. *The Politics of Child Abuse in America.* New York, 1996.

Cunningham, Hugh. *Children and Childhood in Western Society since 1500.* London, 1995.

Dayton, Cornelia. *Women before the Bar: Gender, Law, and Society in Connecticut, 1639–1789.* Chapel Hill, 1995.

D'Emilio, John. "The Homosexual Menace: The Politics of Sexuality in Cold War America." In *Passion and Power: Sexuality in History,* edited by Kathy Peiss and Christina Simmons. Philadelphia, 1989.

D'Emilio, John, and Estelle Freedman. *Intimate Matters: A History of Sexuality in America.* New York, 1988.

DiGirolamo, Vincent. "Crying the News: Children, Street Work, and the American Press." Ph.D. diss., Princeton University, 1997.

Dubinsky, Karen. *Improper Advances: Rape and Heterosexual Conflict in Ontario, 1880–1929.* Chicago, 1993.

Dunlap, Leslie. "The Reform of Rape Law and the Problem of White Men: Age-of-Consent Campaigns in the South, 1885–1910." In *Sex, Love, Race: Crossing Boundaries in North American History,* edited by Martha Hodes. New York, 1999.

Edwards, Laura. *Gendered Strife and Confusion: The Political Culture of Reconstruction.* Urbana, Ill., 1997.

Engelstein, Laura. *The Keys to Happiness: Sex and the Search for Modernity in Fin-de-Siècle Russia.* Princeton, N.J., 1992.

Eskridge, William. "*Hardwick* and Historiography." *University of Illinois Law Review* (1999): 631–702.

———. *Gaylaw: Challenging the Apartheid of the Closet.* Cambridge, Mass., 1999.

Estrich, Susan. *Real Rape: How the Legal System Victimizes Women Who Say No.* Cambridge, Mass., 1987.

Fass, Paula. *The Damned and the Beautiful: American Youth in the 1920s.* New York, 1977.

———. "Making and Remaking an Event: The Leopold and Loeb Case in American Culture." *Journal of American History* 80, 3 (December 1993): 919–51.

Fejes, Fred. "Murder, Perversion, and Moral Panic: The 1954 Media Campaign against Miami's Homosexuals and the Discourse of Civic Betterment." *Journal of the History of Sexuality* 9, 3 (July 2000): 305–47.

Felt, Jeremy. *Hostages of Fortune: Child Labor Reform in New York State.* Syracuse, N.Y., 1965.

Fishman, Eric. "New York's Criminal Justice System, 1895–1932." Ph.D. diss., Columbia University, 1980.

Fitzpatrick, Joseph. *Puerto Rican Americans: The Meaning of Migration to the Mainland.* Englewood Cliffs, N.J., 1971.

Forbath, William, Hendrick Hartog, and Martha Minnow. "Introduction: Legal Histories from Below." *Wisconsin Law Review* (1985): 759–66.

Franklin, Donna. *Ensuring Inequality: The Structural Transformation of the African-American Family.* New York, 1997.

Frederickson, George M. *The Black Image in the White Mind: The Debate on Afro-American Character and Destiny, 1817–1914.* New York, 1971.

Freedman, Estelle. "'Uncontrolled Desires': The Response to the Sexual Psycho-path, 1920–1960." In *Passion and Power: Sexuality in History,* edited by Kathy Peiss and Christina Simmons. Philadelphia, 1989.

Friedman, Lawrence. *Crime and Punishment in American History.* New York, 1993.

Geertz, Clifford. *Local Knowledge.* New York, 1983.

Gerassi, John. *The Boys of Boise.* New York, 1966.

Gilbert, James. *Cycle of Outrage: America's Reaction to the Juvenile Delinquent in the 1950s.* New York, 1986.

Gilfoyle, Timothy. *City of Eros: New York City, Prostitution, and the Commercialization of Sex, 1790–1920.* New York, 1992.

Ginzberg, Lori. *Women and the Work of Benevolence: Morality, Politics, and Class in the Nineteenth-Century United States.* New Haven, 1990.

Glazer, Nathan, and Daniel Patrick Moynihan. *Beyond the Melting Pot: The Negroes, Puerto Ricans, Jews, Italians, and Irish of New York City.* Cambridge, Mass., 1963.

Godbeer, Richard. *Sexual Revolution in Early America.* Baltimore, 2002.

Goldman, Hal. "'A Most Detestable Crime': Character, Consent, and Corrobora-tion in Vermont's Rape Law, 1850–1920." In *Sex without Consent: Rape and Sexual Coercion in America,* edited by Merril Smith. New York, 2001.

Goldstein, Israel. *Jewish Justice and Conciliation.* New York, 1981.

Goodman, Gail. "Children's Testimony in Historical Perspective." *Journal of Social Issues* 40, 2 (1984): 9–31.

Gordon, Linda. *Heroes of Their Own Lives: The Politics and History of Family Violence.* London, 1989.

Gould, Stephen Jay. *Ontogeny and Phylogeny.* Cambridge, Mass., 1977.

Grant, Julia. *Raising Baby by the Book: The Education of American Mothers.* New Haven, 1998.

Green, Harvey. "Scientific Thought and the Nature of Children in America, 1820–1920." In *A Century of Childhood, 1820–1920,* edited by Mary Lynn Stevens Heininger et al. Rochester, N.Y., 1984.

Green, Thomas A. "Freedom and Criminal Responsibility in the Age of Pound: An Essay on Criminal Justice." *Michigan Law Review* 93 (June 1995): 1915–2053.

Griswold, Robert. *Fatherhood in America: A History.* New York, 1993.

Grossberg, Michael. *Governing the Hearth: Law and Family in Nineteenth-Century America.* Chapel Hill, 1985.

Gustav-Wrathall, John Donald. *Take the Young Stranger by the Hand: Same-Sex Relations and the YMCA.* Chicago, 1998.

Gutman, Herbert. *The Black Family in Slavery and Freedom, 1750–1925.* New York, 1976.

Haag, Pamela. "In Search of the 'Real Thing': Ideologies of Love, Modern Ro-mance, and Women's Sexual Subjectivity in the United States, 1920–1940." *Journal of the History of Sexuality* 2, 4 (1992): 547–77.

———. *Consent: Sexual Rights and the Transformation of American Liberalism.* Ithaca, 1999.

Hall, Kermit. *The Magic Mirror: Law in American History*. New York, 1989.

Halperin, David. "How to Do The History of Male Homosexuality." *GLQ* 6, 1 (2000): 87–124.

Halpern, Sydney. *American Pediatrics: The Social Dynamics of Professionalism*. Berkeley, 1988.

Hartog, Hendrick. *Man and Wife in America: A History*. Cambridge, Mass., 2000.

Heininger, Mary Lynn Stevens. "Children, Childhood, and Change in America, 1820–1920." In *A Century of Childhood, 1820–1920*, edited by Mary Lynn Stevens Heininger et al. Rochester, N.Y., 1984.

Hendrick, Harry. *Child Welfare: England, 1872–1989*. London, 1994.

Higonnet, Anne. *Pictures of Innocence: The History and Crisis of Ideal Childhood*. London, 1998.

Horn, Margo. *Before It's Too Late: The Child Guidance Movement in the United States, 1922–1945*. Philadelphia, 1989.

Jackson, Kenneth T., ed. *The Encyclopedia of New York City*. New Haven, 1995.

Jackson, Louise. *Child Sexual Abuse in Victorian England*. London, 2000.

Janus, Eric. "Sex Offender Commitments: Debunking the Official Narrative and Revealing the Rules-in-Use." *Stanford Law and Policy Review* 8, 2 (1997): 71–102.

Jenkins, Henry. "Introduction: Childhood Innocence and Other Modern Myths." In *The Children's Culture Reader*, edited by Henry Jenkins. New York, 1999.

Jenkins, Philip. *Moral Panic: Changing Concepts of the Child Molester in Modern America*. New Haven, 1998.

Jones, Kathleen. *Taming the Troublesome Child: American Families, Child Guidance, and the Limits of Psychiatric Authority*. Cambridge, Mass., 1999.

Kessler-Harris, Alice. *Out to Work: A History of Wage-Earning Women in the United States*. New York, 1982.

Kett, Joseph. *Rites of Passage: Adolescence in America, 1790 to the Present*. New York, 1977.

Kincaid, James. *Child Loving: The Erotic Child in Victorian Culture*. New York, 1992.

Kunzel, Regina. *Fallen Women, Problem Girls: Unmarried Mothers and the Professionalization of Social Work, 1890–1945*. New Haven, 1993.

Ladd-Taylor, Molly, ed. *Raising a Baby the Government Way*. New Brunswick, N.J., 1986.

Lambertz, Jan. "Feminists and the Politics of Wife-Beating." In *British Feminism in the Twentieth Century*, edited by Harold Smith. Aldershot, U.K., 1990.

Langum, David J. *Crossing over the Line: Legislating Morality and the Mann Act*. Chicago, 1994.

Larson, Jane. "'Even a Worm Will Turn at Last': Rape Reform in Late-Nineteenth-Century America." *Yale Journal of Law and the Humanities* 9, 1 (1997): 1–71.

Lears, T. J. Jackson. *No Place of Grace: Antimodernism and the Transformation of American Culture*. New York, 1981.

Lindman, Frank, and Donald McIntyre, eds. *The Mentally Disabled and the Law: The Report on the Rights of the Mentally Ill*. Chicago, 1961.

Lunbeck, Elizabeth. *The Psychiatric Persuasion: Knowledge, Gender, and Power in Modern America*. Princeton, 1994.

MacLean, Nancy. "The Leo Frank Case Reconsidered: Gender and Sexual Politics in the Making of Reactionary Populism." *Journal of American History* 78, 3 (December 1991): 917–48.

Macleod, David. *The Age of the Child: Children in America, 1890–1920.* New York, 1998.

Masson, Jeffrey Moussaieff. *The Assault on Truth: Freud's Suppression of the Seduction Theory.* New York, 1984.

Matsuda, Matt K. *The Memory of the Modern.* New York, 1996.

May, Elaine Tyler. *Homeward Bound: American Families in the Cold War Era.* New York, 1988.

Mintz, Steven, and Susan Kellogg. *Domestic Revolutions: A Social History of American Family Life.* New York, 1988.

Modell, John. *Into One's Own: From Youth to Adulthood in the United States, 1920–1975.* Berkeley, 1989.

Mohr, James. *Doctors and the Law: Medical Jurisprudence in Nineteenth-Century America.* New York, 1993.

Moran, Jeffrey. *Teaching Sex: The Shaping of Adolescence in the 20th Century.* Cambridge, Mass., 2000.

Morantz, Regina Markell. "The Scientist as Sex Crusader: Alfred C. Kinsey and American Culture." *American Quarterly* 29 (Winter 1979): 563–96.

Murphy, Lawrence. "Defining the Crime against Nature: Sodomy in the United States Appeals Court, 1810–1940." *Journal of Homosexuality* 19, 1 (1990): 49–66.

Nelson, Barbara. *Making an Issue of Child Abuse: Political Agenda Setting for Social Problems.* Chicago, 1984.

Nelson, William. *The Legalist Reformation: Law, Politics, and Ideology in New York, 1920–1980.* Chapel Hill, 2001.

Novkov, Julie. "Historicizing the Figure of the Child in Legal Discourse: The Battle over the Regulation of Child Labor." *American Journal of Legal History* 44 (2000): 369–404.

Odem, Mary. "Delinquent Daughters: The Sexual Regulation of Female Minors in the United States, 1880–1920." Ph.D. diss., University of California, Berkeley, 1989.

———. *Delinquent Daughters: Protecting and Policing Adolescent Female Sexuality in the United States, 1885–1920.* Chapel Hill, 1995.

Ovenden, Graham, and Robert Melville. *Victorian Children.* London, 1972.

Palladino, Grace. *Teenagers: An American History.* New York, 1996.

Paoletti, Jo. "Clothing and Gender in America: Children's Fashions, 1890–1920." *Signs* 13, 1 (1987): 136–43.

Parker, Kathleen. "'To Protect the Chastity of Children under Sixteen': Statutory Rape Prosecutions in a Midwest County Circuit Court, 1850–1950." *Michigan Historical Review* 20, 1 (1994): 49–79.

Peiss, Kathy. *Cheap Amusements: Working Women and Leisure in Turn-of-the-Century New York.* Philadelphia, 1986.

Perry, Elisabeth Israels. "Rhetoric, Strategy, and Politics in the New York Campaign for Women's Jury Service, 1917–1975." *New York History* 82, 1 (Winter 2001): 53–78.

Pivar, David. *Purity Crusade: Sexual Morality and Social Control, 1868–1900.* Westport, Conn., 1973.

Pleck, Elizabeth. *Domestic Tyranny: The Making of Social Policy against Family Violence from Colonial Times to the Present.* New York, 1987.

Pratt, Janette. "The Demise of the Corroboration Requirement—Its History in Georgia Rape Law." *Emory Law Journal* 26 (Fall 1977): 805–39.

Ransley, Marie. "Repeal of the Wisconsin Sex Crimes Act." *Wisconsin Law Review* (1980): 941–75.

Reagan, Leslie. *When Abortion Was a Crime: Women, Medicine, and the Law in the United States, 1867–1973.* Berkeley, 1997.

Richardson, Theresa. *The Century of the Child: The Mental Hygiene Movement and Social Policy in the United States and Canada.* Albany, N.Y., 1989.

Riley, Denise. *War in the Nursery: Theories of the Child and Mother.* London, 1983.

Robertson, Stephen. "Signs, Marks, and Private Parts: Doctors, Legal Discourses, and Evidence of Rape in the United States, 1823–1930." *Journal of the History of Sexuality* 8, 3 (1998): 345–88.

———. "Sexuality through the Prism of Age: Modern Culture and Sexual Violence in New York City, 1880–1950." Ph.D. diss., Rutgers University, 1998.

———. "Separating the Men from the Boys: Masculinity, Psycho-sexual Development, and Sex Crime in the United States, 1930s–1960s." *Journal of the History of Medicine and Allied Sciences* 56, 1 (January 2001): 3–35.

———. "Making Right a Girl's Ruin: Working-Class Legal Cultures and Forced Marriage in New York City, 1890–1950." *Journal of American Studies* 36, 2 (2002): 199–230.

Rose, Nikolas. *Governing the Soul: The Shaping of the Private Self.* London, 1990.

Rosen, Ruth. *The Lost Sisterhood: Prostitution in America, 1900–1918.* Baltimore, 1982.

Ross, Dorothy. *G. Stanley Hall: The Psychologist as Prophet.* Chicago, 1972.

Ross, Richard. "The Legal Past of Early New England: Notes for the Study of Law, Legal Culture, and Intellectual History." *William and Mary Quarterly* 50, 1 (1993): 28–41.

Rothman, David. *The Discovery of the Asylum: Social Order and Disorder in the New Republic.* Boston, 1971.

Rotundo, Anthony. *American Manhood: Transformations in Masculinity from the Revolution to the Modern Era.* New York, 1993.

Russett, Cynthia Eagle. *Sexual Science: The Victorian Construction of Womanhood.* Cambridge, Mass., 1989.

Sacco, Lynn. "Sanitized for Your Protection: Medical Discourse and the Denial of Incest in the United States, 1890–1940." *Journal of Women's History* 14, 3 (Autumn 2002): 80–104.

Sarat, Austin. "Redirecting Legal Scholarship in Law Schools." *Yale Journal of Law and the Humanities* 12, 1 (2000): 129–50.

Schlossman, Steven, and Stephanie Wallach. "The Crime of Precocious Sexuality: Female Juvenile Delinquency in the Progressive Era." *Harvard Educational Review* 48, 1 (1978): 65–95.

Sedgwick, Eve. *The Epistemology of the Closet.* Berkeley, 1990.

Sommerville, C. John. *The Rise and Fall of Childhood*. Beverley Hills, Calif., 1982.

Simmons, Christina. "Modern Sexuality and the Myth of Victorian Repression." In *Passion and Power: Sexuality in History*, edited by Kathy Peiss and Christina Simmons. Philadelphia, 1989.

Simpson, Anthony. "Vulnerability and the Age of Female Consent: Legal Innovation and Its Effect on Prosecutions for Rape in Eighteenth-Century London." In *Sexual Underworlds of the Enlightenment*, edited by G. S. Rousseau and Roy Porter. Chapel Hill, 1988.

Solinger, Rickie. *Wake Up Little Susie: Single Pregnancy and Race before* Roe v. Wade. New York, 1992.

Spohn, Cassia, and Julie Horney. *Rape Law Reform: A Grassroots Revolution and Its Impact*. New York, 1992.

Stansell, Christine. *City of Women: Sex and Class in New York, 1789–1860*. Urbana, Ill., 1987.

Starr, Paul. *The Social Transformation of American Medicine*. New York, 1982.

Steinberg, Allen. *The Transformation of Criminal Justice: Philadelphia, 1800–1880*. Chapel Hill, 1989.

Steedman, Carolyn. *Strange Dislocations: Childhood and the Idea of Human Interiority, 1780–1930*. Cambridge, Mass., 1995.

Stern, Alexandra Minna. "'Beauty Is Not Always Better': Perfect Babies and the Tyranny of Pediatric Norms." *Patterns of Prejudice* 36, 1 (2002): 68–78.

———. "Making Better Babies: Public Health and Race Betterment in Indiana, 1920–1935." *American Journal of Public Health* 92, 5 (May 2002): 742–52.

Strong, Bryan. "Ideas of the Early Sex Education Movement, 1890–1920." *History of Education Quarterly* 12, 2 (Summer 1972): 129–62.

Sulloway, Frank. *Freud, Biologist of the Mind*. New York, 1979.

Terry, Jennifer. *An American Obsession: Science, Medicine, and Homosexuality in Modern Society*. Chicago, 1999.

Tiffin, Susan. *In Whose Best Interest? Child Welfare Reform in the Progressive Era*. Westport, Conn., 1982.

Tomlins, Christopher. "Subordination, Authority, Law: Subjects in Labor History." *International Labor and Working-Class History* 47 (1995): 56–90.

Turner, James. *Reckoning with the Beast: Animals, Pain, and Humanity in the Victorian Mind*. Baltimore, 1980.

Ullman, Sharon. *Sex Seen: The Emergence of Modern Sexuality in America*. Berkeley, 1997.

VanderVelde, Lea. "The Legal Ways of Seduction." *Stanford Law Review* 48 (April 1996): 817–901.

Weiss, Nancy Pottishman. "Mother, the Invention of Necessity: Dr Benjamin Spock's *Baby and Child Care*." *American Quarterly* 29 (Winter 1977): 519–46.

White, Kevin. *The First Sexual Revolution: The Emergence of Male Heterosexuality in Modern America*. New York, 1993.

White, Shane, and Graham White. *Stylin': African American Expressive Culture, from Its Beginnings to the Zoot Suit*. Ithaca, 1998.

Wiebe, Robert. *The Search for Order, 1877–1920*. New York, 1967.

Willrich, Michael. "The Two Percent Solution: Eugenic Jurisprudence and the Socialization of American Law, 1900–1930." *Law and History Review* 16 (1998): 66–111.

———.*City of Courts: Socializing Justice in Progressive Era Chicago.* New York, 2003.

Wood, Sharon. "Schoolgirls and the Dark Curriculum of Vice": Sexual Knowledge and the Age of Consent, 1889–1900." Paper presented at the Organization of American Historians Annual Meeting, 29 March 1996.

Zelizer, Viviana. *Pricing the Priceless Child: The Changing Social Value of Children.* Princeton, 1994.

index

Abduction, 73–87; in New York law, 75, 80–81, 87, 259 (n. 7), 269 (nn. 17–19), 272 (n. 63); location of, 77–78; press accounts of, 78–79, 98; emphasis on victim's passivity, 79–80, 82, 120, 121; lack of concern with innocence of victims, 80, 82; victims' testimony in court, 82–84, 122, 123; and evidence of age, 84–86; outcome of prosecutions for, 86–87, 240–41, 244–45, 271 (n. 46); and corroboration, 86, 128, 271–72 (n. 47); and age of consent, 87, 273 (n. 2)

Abrahamsen, David, 209, 210, 221

Addams, Jane, 48–49, 100, 124, 133

Adolescence: concept of, 8, 132–43, 180, 198, 199–200, 202, 215–16, 236; and race, 151, 183, 188; boundary of, 181, 194

Adolescents. *See* Teenage boys; Teenage girls

Adult victims, 32; conviction rates in cases involving, 32, 241–42, 244–45, 305 (n. 94); and race, 34; suspicion of judges toward, 35; and physical signs of rape, 42; and resistance, 45, 130; and plea bargains, 51, 54; suspicion of psychiatrists toward, 225–26. *See also* Rape; Seduction

African Americans, 28, 164, 180, 234, 251 (n. 11); and baby contests, 20; white images of, 24–25, 27, 53, 214, 225–26, 284–85 (n. 52), 301 (nn. 44, 46); as defendants, 53, 179–80, 186, 187, 190–91, 200, 213–14, 225–26, 294–95 (n. 25); and concept of ruin, 99–100, 103, 185, 187, 190–91; attitude toward West Indians, 104; and psychosexual development, 151, 213–14; and statutory rape, 179–80, 183, 185–86, 187, 190–91; and high schools, 182, 188; attitude toward marriage, 187, 190–91, 192; and sodomy, 200; numbers of, 251 (n. 10); 293 (n. 2). *See also* Sex offenders: and race

Age, 4, 5, 9, 233–34; and definition of childhood, 15, 20, 21, 35, 233; and puberty, 22; as basis of sex crime laws, 62–63, 82, 84, 90–91, 144, 161–62, 169, 173, 177, 182–83, 193–94, 288–89 (nn. 9–10); and relationship with gender, 64, 69–70, 89, 141, 147–48, 158, 162, 172–73, 178, 184, 199–200, 272 (n. 59); evidence of, 84–86, 193, 234, 270 (nn. 34–35), 292 (n. 52); of marriage, 98, 104, 115, 188, 191, 273 (n. 5); as basis of statutory rape prosecutions, 119, 193–94, 194–95, 197–98, 243; in working-class sexual rela-

tions, 134–35, 193–94; significance
of differences in, 144, 182, 197–98,
288 (n. 9); declining significance of,
184, 208, 232, 233; as explanation of
sexual violence, 202, 231–32; as category of analysis, 233–34; Americans'
awareness of, 234. *See also* Working
class: understanding of age

Age of consent, 75, 92, 119, 197; in New
York law, 39, 90–91; and child rape,
44–45; campaign to increase, 76,
87–89, 91–92; problems enforcing,
89–90; and legal age of marriage, 98;
and sodomy, 173; applied to boys, 272
(n. 59); in Puerto Rico, 296 (n. 54)

Anal acts, 58, 63, 200; physical signs of,
61, 67–68, 168; and children's language, 65–66. *See also* Oral acts; Sexual acts; Sodomy

Assistant district attorneys (ADAs): in
magistrates' courts, 30; qualifications
of, 30, 140–41, 235; and trial briefs,
43–44; and presentation of victims
of child rape, 46–49; and children's
testimony, 69; and presentation of
victims of abduction, 82–84, 122,
123; role in marriage of ruined girls,
109–10, 189; and presentation of victims of statutory rape, 123–25, 130,
179–80, 183, 194–95; and presentation of victims of carnal abuse, 171–
73; and use of sexual psychopath law,
223. *See also* District attorneys; Plea
bargains

Bastardy actions, 106, 186. *See also* Paternity proceedings; Pregnancy

Bender, Lauretta, 141, 144, 152–53, 154,
284–85 (nn. 52, 63)

Blackwell, Emily, 88, 100

Blanchard, Phyllis, 180–81

Bowman, Karl, 209

Boys: as victims of sexual violence, 23,
54–55, 57, 59, 68, 70–71, 89, 141,
145–48, 155–56, 158, 162, 165, 172–

73, 184, 199–202, 207, 212–13, 216–
17, 224–25, 227, 292 (n. 52); injuries
from sexual assault, 23, 158, 161–62,
166, 173, 184, 199; gender identity of,
64–65, 147, 199–200, 215–16; innocence of, 65–66, 155–56, 199–200,
216; language used by, 65–66, 200,
291 (n. 41); and concept of adolescence, 134, 184, 199–200; changed
presentation of, 172–73, 184, 199–
202; as sex offenders, 207, 214–17

Bromberg, Walter, 195, 209

Brouardel, Paul, 1, 249 (n. 1)

California Sexual Deviation Research
Project, 156, 209

Carnal abuse, 5, 143, 144, 159, 161–72,
174–77; similar laws in other states,
62–63, 162–63, 289 (n. 12); in New
York law, 161, 287 (n. 1), 288 (nn. 4,
7); appellate court interpretations of,
161; and sexual acts, 161–62, 175,
289–90 (nn. 23, 25); boys as victims
of, 162, 163, 166–67, 172–73, 292
(n. 52); relationship to child rape,
163, 167–68, 290 (n. 30); relationship
to sodomy, 163, 168–69; reactions to,
164–65, 289–90 (n. 23); witnesses
to, 164–65, 166; location of, 165; and
physical injury, 166–67, 169–71;
and reinterpretation of penetration,
167–68, 290 (n. 28); as lesser offense,
169, 175–77; and emphasis on girls'
passivity, 169–71; outcomes of prosecutions for, 175–77, 241–42, 244–
45, 292 (n. 52); as part of sexual psychopath law, 219; and impairing the
morals of a minor, 288 (n. 4)

Case files: as sources, 5, 43, 59, 242,
250 (n. 4), 251 (n. 11), 251–52 (n. 14),
269–70 (n. 25), 273–74 (n. 8)

Childhood: definition of, 2, 6, 22, 178,
188, 233, 236; sentimental meaning
of, 6; and reform campaigns, 6, 17;
boundary of, 6, 18, 20, 98, 194; New

York Society for the Prevention of Cruelty to Children's understanding of, 14, 16, 21, 38, 71, 74, 91; and original sin, 17; as distinct from adulthood, 17, 188; romantic conception of, 17–18, 19; and middle-class domesticity, 18, 19, 77; jurors' understanding of, 39, 82, 92, 119, 129, 132, 192–93; fragmentation of, 76, 90–91, 119; and appearance, 84–85; purity reformers' idea of, 89, 91, 92. *See also* Childhood innocence; Physiological development; Psychological development; Psychosexual development

Childhood innocence, 4, 6, 7, 9, 16, 35, 176, 236; and middle-class domesticity, 18, 23; loss of, 18–19; and physiological development, 20–21; language as a sign of, 44, 47–49; and venereal disease, 52–53; and sodomy, 59, 64–66, 199–200; and teenage girls, 74–75, 77, 80, 82, 98, 133, 134, 192–93; in press accounts, 78–79, 155; and appearance, 82, 155; purity reformers' idea of, 89; and psychology, 141, 152–53; psychiatrists' attacks on, 149–50, 153–54, 156, 285–86 (nn. 63–64); and sex crime panic, 154–57, 176, 211; and reporting of sex crimes, 156–57; and nonpenetrative acts, 161–62, 178

Child labor, 22, 23, 25, 148

Child molestation, 177–78, 202. *See also* Sexual acts: nonpenetrative acts as

Child performers, 16–17, 23, 26, 253 (n. 6)

Child prostitution, 46, 77–78, 87

Child protection movement, 13, 14, 15, 195–96

Child psychology, 148–49, 157–58, 176

Child rape, 37–55; location of, 38, 165; in New York law, 39, 90–91; mob violence as reaction to, 40–41; witnesses to, 41; nineteenth-century understanding of, 41–42; physical signs of, 42–43, 167–68; and medical examinations, 43, 290 (n. 28); victims presented as passive, 44–46, 121; victims' testimony in court, 46–49, 156–58; and corroboration requirement, 49–54; and race, 53; outcomes of prosecutions for, 54, 175, 241–42, 244–45, 290 (n. 30); and reinterpretation of penetration, 167–68; disappearance of, 168, 290 (n. 30); and child molestation, 178

Children: concern about, 6–7, 9, 236; bodies of, 19, 167–68; physical abuse of, 22; on streets, 23, 100; as focus of sex crime panic, 140; as focus of postwar culture, 140. *See also* Child labor; Child performers; Child prostitution; Teenage boys; Teenage girls

Children's court, 190–91; attitude of judges in, 111–13, 276 (n. 52); and oversight of marriage, 191–92

Child sexuality, 141, 149–52. *See also* Psychosexual development

Child Study Association, 180

Child study movement, 92

Child victims: numbers of, 2, 236, 237, 238, 250 (n. 2); testimony of, 29, 30, 49, 68–69, 157–58, 174, 176, 261 (n. 40), 292 (n. 52); psychiatric study of, 144, 152–54, 285 (n. 63); images of, 145, 155–56; as participants, 153–54; and reporting of sex crime, 156–57, 289 (n. 20); private trials for, 157, publication of names of, 157. *See also* Boys: as victims of sexual violence; Girls

Chinese, 77, 128

Citizens Committee on the Control of Crime, 143–44, 219

Claghorn, Kate, 107–8

Colombians, 170–71

Conviction rates: in rape cases involving adult victims, 32, 241–42, 244–45; in seduction cases, 34, 241–42,

244–45; in sodomy cases, 69–71, 199, 241–42, 244–45; in statutory rape cases, 128, 197, 241–42, 244–45

Correctional Association of New York. *See* Prison Association of New York

Corroboration requirement: in New York's rape law, 32; in rape laws of other states, 32, 257 (n. 79); as interpreted by New York's higher courts, 32–33, 50–51, 174; in child rape cases, 49–54, 271–72 (n. 47); in sodomy cases, 64, 67–69, 174–75, 271–72 (n. 47); in abduction cases, 86, 271–72 (n. 47); in statutory rape cases, 125, 126, 128, 130, 197, 278 (n. 20); reform of, 157–58

Court of general sessions, 31, 195, 196, 224. *See also* Judges; Jurors; Psychiatric Clinic of the New York County Court of General Sessions

Criminal courts: as site for production of social meaning, 2, 15, 234–35; as social control, 4, 5; and immigrants, 107–8. *See also* Court of general sessions; Legal culture: of working class; Legal culture: of middle class; Magistrates' courts

Cubans, 166

Darwinian revolution, 19

Defense attorneys, 123, 128–29, 131, 171–72, 176, 201, 261 (n. 40), 277 (nn. 13, 16)

Deputy assistant district attorneys (DADAs). *See* Assistant district attorneys

Dewey, Thomas, 140, 173, 195, 220, 221–22

District attorneys (DAs): and professionalization, 140–41, 235; and reporting of crimes against children, 156–57; and publication of victims' names, 157; as sponsors of legislation, 161; and children's testimony, 176; attitude toward statutory rape

of, 194, 195. *See also* Assistant district attorneys; Case files: as sources

District court. *See* Magistrates' courts

Doctors. *See* Physicians

Draper, Frank Winthrop, 1, 249 (n. 1)

Ellis, Albert, 209, 210

Frank, Theodore, 231

Frazier, E. Franklin, 183

Gender-neutral laws, 62–63, 162–63, 178, 288–89 (n. 10). *See also* Carnal abuse; Sodomy

Germans: attitude toward marriage, 100–101

Gerry, Elbridge, 13, 15, 16–17, 21, 23–24, 25, 27, 51, 81, 87, 89–90, 90–91, 125

Gesell, Arnold, 148

Gibb, William Travis, 43, 68, 262 (n. 54)

Girls: as victims of rape, 1–2, 89, 155, 156, 199–200; injuries from sexual assault, 23, 147–48, 152, 154, 158, 161–62, 166; as victims of sodomy, 59, 64–65

Glueck, Bernard, 209, 211, 228–29

Governor's Study Commission on the Deviated Sex Offender (Michigan), 162, 163, 209, 215

Grand jury, 6, 31, 86, 171; and child rape, 54, 290 (n. 30); and children's testimony, 68–69, 174; and marriage of ruined girls, 110, 191–92, 198; and questioning of teenage girls, 129–30; and sodomy, 174, 200; transferring cases, 175–76, 290 (n. 30), 292 (n. 52); and nullification of statutory rape law, 180, 183, 192, 197, 279 (n. 31); appearance of defendants before, 180, 193; and child support, 198. *See also* Jurors

Groves, Ernest, 150, 151–52

Groves, Gladys. *See* Groves, Ernest

Guttmacher, Manfred, 209, 300 (n. 27), 301 (n. 46)

Hall, G. Stanley, 92, 119, 132–34, 148, 151, 180, 181
Hartwell, Samuel, 150, 215
Henninger, James, 212
Homosexuality: concepts of, 66, 150, 158, 213, 216–17; and effects of sexual violence, 158, 184; and adolescence, 181–82, 184, 213, 215–16, 227. *See also* Sex offenders: homosexuals as; Sexual psychopaths: homosexuals diagnosed as
Hoover, J. Edgar, 145, 147, 157
Hymen, 43, 50, 102, 106, 157, 166, 167–68, 184, 290 (n. 28)

Illegitimacy: as stigma, 99, 103–4
Impairing the morals of a minor, 143, 144, 177, 197, 219; in New York law, 288 (n. 4)
Incest, 43, 219, 232, 239, 277 (n. 7); in New York law, 39, 260 (n. 9), 277 (n. 5), 278 (n. 20); and statutory rape, 119, 278 (n. 20); and corroboration, 128, 263–64 (n. 66), 278 (n. 20); outcomes of prosecutions for, 279–80 (n. 42)
Indians, 174
Innocence. *See* Childhood innocence
Irish: attitude toward marriage, 100–101; and concept of ruin, 103
Italians: supervision of daughters, 100, 106; attitude toward marriage, 100–101, 113–14; and concept of ruin, 103, 104, 109; in magistrates' courts, 107–8; and interpreters, 107, 126–27; judges' attitude toward, 111–12; and statutory rape, 130, 132; numbers of, 251 (n. 10)

Jacobi, Abraham, 19
Jailbait, 135
Jews: attitudes toward Irish and Italians, 104
Joint Legislative Committee to Investigate the Administration and Enforcement of the Law, 143, 156–57, 176, 194, 195, 281 (n. 11)
Judges: hostility toward adult victims, 35; and sworn testimony of child victims, 49, 68–69, 157; and medical evidence, 50, 52; and corroboration in child rape cases, 51–52; support of marriage of teenage girls, 98–99, 108–9, 111–13, 189, 276 (nn. 51–52); attitude toward Italians, 111–12; view of force in statutory rape cases, 125; and corroboration in statutory rape cases, 128; and character of teenage girls, 131; suspicion of teenage boys, 200–201, 227; application of sexual psychopath laws by, 226–28. *See also* Magistrates; Sentences
Jurors: and nullification of law, 5, 129, 180, 192; influence on prosecutions, 14, 30, 235; eligibility for jury service, 31; class identity of, 31, 292 (n. 57); attitude toward law, 31–32, 119, 180, 235; understanding of rape, 32, 33, 89; hostility toward adult victims, 35; understanding of childhood, 39, 82, 92, 119, 129, 132, 192–93; focus on child victim's language, 44, 46–48, 65–66, 82–83, 123, 171–72; and corroboration in child rape cases, 52–53; attitude toward venereal disease, 52–53; understanding of sodomy, 65, 67; concern with appearance of teenage girls, 82, 91, 122–23, 128; and character of teenage girls, 129–30, 201; attitude toward nonpenetrative acts, 175–77; women as, 176, 292 (n. 57); and character of teenage boys, 200–201. *See also* Grand jury

Karpman, Benjamin, 209, 210
Kinsey, Alfred, 178, 209–10, 285–86 (n. 64)
Kozol, Harry, 209

La Guardia, Fiorello, 143–44, 196, 218–19, 282 (n. 16)

Law: as constitutive, 92, 135, 235, 236; as fabric, 98; shadow of the, 105, 106–7

Legal culture: definition, 2–3; of working class, 4, 96, 105–8, 180, 183, 193, 234–35; of middle class, 4, 107

Legal process, 6, 29–30, 105, 196

Legal records. *See* Case files: as sources

Lehman, Herbert, 193–94

Lichtenstein, Perry, 304 (n. 83), 305 (n. 96)

Lindsey, Ben, 134, 151

Locke, John, 17

Lyons, John, 220

MacCormick, Austin, 142, 303 (n. 70)

Magistrates, 6, 29–30, 86, 108–9, 176, 184, 256 (n. 68); support for marriage of ruined girls, 111. *See also* Judges

Magistrates' courts, 29, 73–74, 75–76, 96, 107–8, 166, 171

Marks, Lawrence, 139, 142, 208–9

Marriage: of teenage girls, 92, 98, 101–3, 104, 191, 192; as a response to sexual activity outside marriage, 96–98, 100–101, 102–3, 104, 106–8, 114–15, 117, 186–91, 198, 242, 273–74 (n. 8); in New York law, 98, 115, 188–89, 191, 273 (n. 5); legal officials' support for, 108–14, 189–92, 276 (nn. 51–52); campaign to raise age of, 114, 191; men's promises of, 118, 185–86, 198; African American attitude toward, 187, 190–91, 192; and love, 192–93. *See also* Rape: marriage as response to

Mayor's Committee on Sex Offenses, 144, 146, 148, 182, 209, 219, 282 (nn. 16–18, 22)

McNaboe, John J., 143, 281 (n. 11)

Medical examinations: of child victims, 43, 53, 167–68, 261 (n. 28), 265 (nn. 17–18), 290 (n. 28); as corroboration in child rape cases, 50, 262

(n. 54); as corroboration in sodomy cases, 67, 174; as evidence of age, 85; as corroboration in statutory rape cases, 126; in carnal abuse cases, 167–68

Mental hygiene movement, 141, 149, 298 (n. 5); and study of child victims, 144, 152–54; and child sexuality, 149–52; and African Americans, 151; popular reactions to, 154; and adolescence, 180–81, 184, 199, 215–16; and prevention of sex offending, 207, 215–17

Messinger, Emanuel, 224–26

Mexicans, 34–35

Middle class: and modern culture, 8, 158; attitude toward working class, 24; and the state, 28; attitude toward working-class children, 48–49, 129; opposition to marriage of teenage girls, 101, 102–3, 192. *See also* Childhood: and middle-class domesticity; Legal culture: of middle class

Mob violence: by working class, 40, 60; during sex crime panic, 142

Model Penal Code, 173

Modern culture: emergence of, 3, 7, 8, 141, 178; and persistence of older ideas, 3, 8, 113, 141, 178, 289–90 (n. 23)

Moral panic, 3

New York Committee for the Prevention of the State Regulation of Vice, 88

New York County Court of General Sessions. *See* Court of general sessions

New York Society for the Prevention of Cruelty to Children (NYSPCC): as part of legal system, 5, 14, 26–31, 73, 97, 109, 140–41, 183, 184, 185, 195–97, 255 (n. 46), 256 (n. 58); founding of, 13; and law enforcement, 13, 14, 15, 27, 54, 109, 195–96, 256 (n. 58);

and prosecutions, 14, 30–31, 43–44, 51, 183; ideas of childhood, 14, 16, 21, 38, 71, 91; and presentation of victims in court, 15, 85–86; and definition of childhood, 21, 74; compared to nineteenth-century reformers, 21, 25; and physical abuse, 22; and sexual abuse, 22–23; attitude toward working-class parents, 23–24, 25, 41, 166; as sponsor of legislation, 25–26, 63, 75, 80–81, 89, 90–91, 161, 255 (n. 44), 267 (n. 32), 269 (n. 18), 287 (n. 1); illustrations of children, 26; and custody of children before courts, 26, 196; legislative act incorporating, 27–28; work in magistrates' courts, 29–30, 73–74, 75–76; and physicians, 42, 43, 262 (n. 54); and race, 53; and discussion of sodomy, 61; role in marriage of ruined girls, 109; and admissions by offenders, 126, 127; declining influence of, 140, 183, 194–97. *See also* Child protection movement; Trial briefs

Oral acts, 58, 129; and physical signs, 61, 67, 173; sodomy law extended to cover, 63; and children's language, 66. *See also* Sexual acts; Sodomy
Ossido, Salvatore, 139, 142, 157, 299 (n. 14)

Pacht, Asher, 209
Paternity proceedings, 123, 186, 198, 294 (n. 23). *See also* Bastardy actions; Pregnancy
Petting, 180–81
Philanthropist, 47, 88, 89, 91, 235
Physicians: understanding of rape, 1; definition of childhood, 21; working for NYSPCC, 42, 43, 67–68, 184, 262 (n. 54); and failure to report child rape, 43; working-class attitudes toward, 43, 105–6, 166, 265 (n. 17); constrained by legal system, 50, 67–

68, 262 (n. 54); understanding of anal acts, 67–68. *See also* Medical examinations
Physiological development, 7, 15, 17, 19–20, 35; and Darwinian revolution, 19; and pediatrics, 19–20; norms of, 20; and childhood innocence, 20–21; and teenage girls, 75, 91, 98, 114, 133–34
Plea bargains: in child rape cases, 51, 54, 128, 132; in adult rape cases, 51, 54; in sodomy cases, 69; in abduction cases, 86, 131, 271 (n. 45); in statutory rape cases, 128, 130–31, 132, 196–97, 197–99, 280 (n. 44); in carnal abuse cases, 177; in incest cases, 280 (n. 46)
Ploscowe, Morris, 219–20, 304 (n. 77)
Police, 4–5, 26, 28, 29, 61, 108, 117, 164, 179, 184, 186; as sex offenders, 128
Pollens, Bertram, 111, 158, 202, 210, 215, 216–17
Powell, Adam, 88, 90, 91
Praeger, Irving, 231–32
Pregnancy, 99, 106, 118, 179–80, 183, 184; and efforts to arrange marriage, 102, 107, 110, 185–91, 198, 242. *See also* Bastardy actions; Paternity proceedings
Prepubescent girls. *See* Child victims; Girls; Teenage girls: as different from prepubescent girls
Prison Association of New York, 219, 230
Probation Department, 185; and marriage of ruined girls, 113–14, 189–91; and character of teenage girls, 131–32
Psychiatric Clinic of the New York County Court of General Sessions, 206, 224–27
Psychiatric examinations, 206, 207–8, 213–14, 218–19; 221–22, 306 (n. 99), 306 (n. 107); and sexual psychopath laws, 224–26, 228, 305 (n. 96), 307 (nn. 113–15)

Psychiatrists, 205–8. *See also* Mental hygiene movement; Psychiatric examinations

Psychological development, 7, 8, 91, 148; inattention to, 20; and teenage girls, 114–15, 133–34, 180–81; and effects of sex crime, 147–48, 178, 232

Psychology: new concern with, 147–48, 178; and effects of testifying in court, 157–58. *See also* Child psychology

Psychosexual development: stages of, 3, 15, 20, 149–50, 158, 180–81; concept of, 6, 7, 141, 177, 232, 233, 236; and homosexuality, 150, 158, 181–82, 199–200, 213, 216–17; and African Americans, 151, 213–14; disruption of, 151–54, 158, 181–82, 199–200, 216–17, 285–86 (nn. 59, 64); parents and, 152, 153, 215–16; in sex crime laws, 162–63, 288 (n. 9); working-class response to, 165, 177. *See also* Sex offenders: as sexually immature

Puberty, 4, 21, 141; romantic concept of, 20–21; age of, 22; and age of consent, 89, 91; and marriage, 104–5; and European immigrants, 122–23; and concept of adolescence, 133–34; and child sexuality, 149, 150, 236; and African Americans, 150

Pubescent boys. *See* Teenage boys

Pubescent girls. *See* Teenage girls

Puerto Ricans, 164, 184, 185, 193, 234; as defendants, 180, 183; and concept of ruin, 187–88, 189–90; and adolescence, 188; numbers of, 251 (n. 10), 293 (n. 2), 295 (n. 31)

Purity reform, 76, 87–89, 91, 92

Rape: in New York law, 32, 39, 90–91, 125, 182–83, 219, 257 (n. 77); jurors' understanding of, 32, 33, 89; as physical violence, 33, 42, 89; as assault by an unknown man, 33; and race, 34; degrees of, 39, 90–91, 125, 182–83; press accounts of, 40–41; marriage as response to, 102–3, 110; working-class understanding of, 125–26, 166–67, 183; and age, 169, 178; and molestation, 178. *See also* Adult victims; Age of consent; Child rape; Corroboration requirement; Statutory rape

Richmond, Winifred, 181–82, 293 (n. 7)

Roche, Josephine, 100, 101

Rousseau, Jean-Jacques, 17–18; and puberty, 21

Ruin, concept of, 97–98, 99, 101, 118, 124, 156–57, 166; African Americans and, 99–100, 103, 185, 187, 190–91; and use of force, 102–3, 189; teenage girls' belief in, 103; Irish and, 103; Italians and, 103, 104, 109; judges' belief in, 111, 113, 189; declining influence of, 183, 187, 197, 202, 232; Puerto Ricans and, 187–88, 189–90

Runaways, 77, 100, 117, 118, 179, 184, 185, 192, 200

Second-degree rape. *See* Statutory rape

Seduction, 132, 216; crime of, 33–34, 96, 239, 258 (n. 89), 269 (n. 17)

Sentences: for child rape, 54, 177; for sodomy, 70, 177, 199, 268 (n. 55), 298 (n. 83); for abduction, 86–87; for statutory rape, 131, 132, 268 (n. 55), 295 (n. 40), 298 (n. 83); for carnal abuse, 177

Sex crime. *See* Abduction; Carnal abuse; Child rape; Incest; Rape; Seduction; Sexual violence; Sodomy; Statutory rape

Sex crime panic: sensational crimes and, 139–40, 144–45; press coverage of, 140–41, 145, 155, 171; public expressions of, 142, 164–65; emphasis on child victims in, 142, 211–12, 222, 282 (n. 15); official responses to, 142–44, 146, 156–58, 207, 218–22, 283 (n. 30); and boys as victims, 146–48, 212–13; and childhood innocence,

66–67, 199–202; outcomes of prosecutions for, 69–71, 174–75, 199, 201, 202, 241–42, 244–45, 298 (n. 83); as sign of abnormality, 143; in relation to carnal abuse, 168–69; admissions by offenders to, 175; and drunkenness, 175; as part of sexual psychopath laws, 219; and women offenders, 265 (n. 7)

Statutory rape, 5, 90–135, 179–99; in New York law, 90–91, 120, 182–83, 193–94; and working-class legal culture, 96, 180, 183; cases in which consent cannot be determined, 117–18, 119–21; and consensual acts, 118, 122, 192–93, 196–97; and coerced acts, 118, 121–22, 124–25, 197, 277 (n. 16); age as basis of prosecutions for, 119, 193–94; and passivity of victims, 120–22, 192–93, 194; victims' testimony in court, 122–25; men's admissions to acts of, 125–27, 175, 179, 180, 185–86, 193–94, 278 (n. 28), 297 (n. 73); outcomes of prosecutions for, 128–32, 180, 197, 198–99, 241–42, 244–45, 279 (nn. 31, 39), 297 (n. 73), 298 (n. 83); excluded from sex crime panic, 143, 144, 180–81, 195; and age difference, 182, 197–98, 297 (n. 73); limited enforcement of, 183, 194–97; pregnancy as basis for prosecutions of, 185–88, 194, 198; and paternity proceedings, 186–88, 198, 294 (n. 23); and love, 191–93, 202; and mistake of age as defense, 193–94. See also Age of consent

Strain, Frances Bruce, 181, 183, 293 (n. 6)

Syrians, 166, 174

Teenage boys: in sodomy cases, 66–67, 69–71, 199–202, 227; as defendants in statutory rape cases, 181–82, 197–98; defined as youthful offenders,

182, 198, 293–94 (n. 12). See also Adolescence

Teenage girls, 8, 54–55, 69–71, 74–75, 199, 243; and dependence, 77; in press accounts, 78–79; appearance of, 82, 91, 122–23, 128; and shame, 83; as different from prepubescent girls, 90–91, 123–25, 130, 131, 132, 180–81; marriage of, 92, 98, 101–3, 104, 191, 192; in workforce, 100, 104; character of, 129–30, 131–32, 201; behavior in World War II, 182; in love, 192–93. See also Abduction; Adolescence; Statutory Rape; Working class: understanding of teenage girls

Thom, Douglas, 152

Towne, Arthur, 111, 112, 114

Train, Arthur, 119

Trial briefs, 43–44; for cases of child rape, 44–46, 53; for cases of sodomy, 62, 64, 66–67; for cases of abduction, 79–80; for cases of statutory rape, 119–22, 124, 195; for cases of carnal abuse, 169–71, 291 (n. 39)

True, Ruth, 99, 100, 101, 129

Venereal disease, 43, 131, 264 (n. 72); as corroboration in child rape cases, 51–53

Virginity, 43, 97, 99, 102, 103, 123–24, 147, 166, 183, 187–88, 197, 200

Ware, Caroline, 103

West Indians, 126. See also African Americans: attitude toward West Indians

White, William Alanson, 149–50, 150

White slave trade, 133

Whyte, William, 103

Working class: and criminal courts, 3, 4, 275 (n. 14); and modern culture, 3, 5, 8, 234–35, 289–90 (n. 23); use of law by, 5, 28, 96, 105–8, 183, 184–88, 190, 234–35; impact on prosecutions,

6, 92, 198, 235; attitude toward New York Society for the Prevention of Cruelty to Children, 28, 166; and magistrates' courts, 29, 76–77, 256 (n. 62); reactions to child rape, 40–42, 155, 164–65; attitude toward physicians, 43, 105–6, 166, 265 (n. 17); reactions to sodomy, 60, 265 (n. 17); understanding of age, 86, 92, 104, 134–35, 198, 234; understanding of teenage girls, 98, 101–2, 126, 183; and violence against women, 102–3; understanding of rape, 125–26, 166–67, 183; and psychosexual development, 165, 183; willingness to challenge law, 193. *See also* Legal culture: of working class